SO-ACE-827

THE DECLINE
OF ARISTOCRACY
IN THE POLITICS
OF NEW YORK

1801-1840

harper ✦ torchbooks

*A reference-list of Harper Torchbooks, classified
by subjects, is printed at the end of this volume.*

AMERICAN PERSPECTIVES

EDITED BY BERNARD WISHY AND
WILLIAM E. LEUCHTENBURG

Ray Stannard Baker: FOLLOWING THE COLOR LINE: *American Negro Citizenship in the Progressive Era*, edited by Dewey W. Grantham, Jr. TB/3053

George Bancroft: *THE ORIGIN OF THE AMERICAN REVOLUTION, from "The History of the United States," edited by Edmund S. Morgan.

Hyman Berman (ed.): *THE RISE OF AMERICAN LABOR: *A Reader*.

Randolph S. Bourne: WAR AND THE INTELLECTUALS: *Collected Essays, 1915-1919*, edited by Carl Resek. TB/3043

Louis D. Brandeis: *OTHER PEOPLE'S MONEY, edited by Richard M. Abrams.

Edmund Burke: *EDMUND BURKE AND THE AMERICAN REVOLUTION, edited by Elliott Robert Barkan.

Dixon Ryan Fox: THE DECLINE OF ARISTOCRACY IN THE POLITICS OF NEW YORK, edited by Robert V. Remini. TB/3064

Charlotte Perkins Gilman: *WOMEN AND ECONOMICS: *A Study of the Economic Relation Between Men and Women as a Factor in Social Evolution*, edited by Carl N. Degler.

Alexander Hamilton: THE REPORTS OF ALEXANDER HAMILTON, edited by Jacob E. Cooke. TB/3060

Daniel R. Hundley: SOCIAL RELATIONS IN OUR SOUTHERN STATES, edited by William R. Taylor. TB/3058

Robert Hunter: *POVERTY, edited by Peter d'A. Jones

Helen Hunt Jackson: A CENTURY OF DISHONOR: *The Early Crusade for Indian Reform*, edited by Andrew F. Rolle. TB/3063

Thomas Jefferson: NOTES ON THE STATE OF VIRGINIA, edited by Thomas P. Abernethy. TB/3052

O. G. Libby: *THE GEOGRAPHICAL DISTRIBUTION OF THE VOTE OF THE THIRTEEN STATES ON THE FEDERAL CONSTITUTION: 1787-1788, edited by Lee Benson.

Abraham Lincoln *and* Stephen A. Douglas: *THE LINCOLN-DOUGLAS DEBATES, edited by William H. Freehling.

William G. McLoughlin (ed.): *THE AMERICAN EVANGELICALS: *A Reader*.

Alfred T. Mahan: *AMERICA'S ROLE IN WORLD AFFAIRS: *Collected Essays*, edited by Ernest R. May.

S. Walter Poulshock *and* Robert A. Skotheim, (eds.): *THE BUSINESSMAN AND MODERN AMERICA: *A Reader*.

Walter Rauschenbusch: CHRISTIANITY AND THE SOCIAL CRISIS, edited by Robert D. Cross. TB/3059

Whitelaw Reid: *AFTER THE WAR, edited by C. Vann Woodward.

James Ford Rhodes: *THE COMING OF THE CIVIL WAR (Vol. I); THE CIVIL WAR (Vol. II): an abridgment of "The History of the United States from the Compromise of 1850," edited by Grady McWhiney.

Jacob Riis: *THE MAKING OF AN AMERICAN, edited by Roy Lubove.

Charles Howard Shinn: MINING CAMPS: *A Study in American Frontier Government*, edited by Rodman Paul. TB/3062

Ida M. Tarbell: *THE HISTORY OF THE STANDARD OIL COMPANY: *Selections*, edited by David M. Chalmers.

George B. Tindall (ed.): *A POPULIST READER.

Walter E. Weyl: THE NEW DEMOCRACY: *An Essay on Certain Political and Economic Tendencies in the United States*, edited by Charles B. Forcey. TB/3042

* in preparation

DIXON RYAN FOX

THE DECLINE
OF ARISTOCRACY
IN THE POLITICS
OF NEW YORK
1801-1840

EDITED BY

Robert V. Remini

HARPER TORCHBOOKS
The University Library
Harper & Row, Publishers
New York, Evanston and London

To

My Wife

MARIAN OSGOOD FOX

Inspiring Comrade

THE DECLINE OF ARISTOCRACY IN
THE POLITICS OF NEW YORK

Introduction, Notes, and the Fox Revisions
copyright © 1965 by Robert V. Remini

Printed in the United States of America.

This book was originally published in 1919
by Columbia University Press and is here
reprinted by arrangement.

First HARPER TORCHBOOK edition published 1965
by Harper & Row, Publishers, Incorporated,
49 East 33rd Street,
New York, N.Y. 10016.

TABLE OF CONTENTS

CHAPTER I

THE FEW, THE RICH, AND THE WELL BORN

CHAPTER II

THE COUNTRY-SIDE

CHAPTER III

RULERS DEPOSED

CHAPTER IV
NEW METHODS AND A VICTORY

CHAPTER V
LANDHOLDERS' PRINCIPLES

CHAPTER VI
MR. MADISON'S WAR

CHAPTER VII
CLINTON, DIVIDER OF PARTIES

CHAPTER VIII
PROPERTY OR PEOPLE?

CHAPTER IX

OLD COMRADES AND NEW BANNERS

CHAPTER X

MANUFACTURING BECOMES RESPECTABLE

CHAPTER XI

POLITICAL DISTRACTION

CHAPTER XII

TOM, DICK AND HARRY TAKE A HAND

CHAPTER XIII

TWO VIEWS OF VESTED RIGHTS

ILLUSTRATIONS

The illustrations will be found in a group following page 120.

INTRODUCTION TO THE
TORCHBOOK EDITION

BY ROBERT V. REMINI

Doctoral dissertations can be frightful little monsters. Frequently overblown and badly written, they are monuments to the trivial, the apotheosis of the minuscule. Periodically a lone scholar may come wandering along in search of knowledge and eyestrain and will ask to examine one on microfilm, but after an hour of wrestling with it on a machine that no longer focuses properly he soon tires and returns the dissertation to its proper place in a remote corner of the library. But that is not the whole story, of course. There are many dissertations that illuminate dark areas, that are written with skill and style and respect for the language, that concern themselves with the important and eschew the trivial. At Columbia University some years ago the Faculty of Political Science edited its best dissertations and published them in a series entitled "Studies in History, Economics and Public Law." A cursory glance at the names on this list reveals an extraordinary corps of exceptional scholars, men like Charles Beard, Arthur M. Schlesinger, George L. Beer, Charles E. Merriam, Jr., Guy Stanton Ford, Lynn Thorndike, Preserved Smith, Carlton J. H. Hayes, J. Salwyn Schapiro and Harold U. Faulkner among others. Included on this list is Dixon Ryan Fox. His dissertation, *The Decline of Aristocracy in the Politics of New York,* is now regarded as a minor classic in American history.

Fox's book did more to influence thinking about New

York history during the transitional period from 1801 to 1840 than any book written before or since. It is a uniquely perceptive work in which ideas frequently come flashing off the pages in rapid succession, sometimes so quickly that it is impossible to catch them all on a single reading. Its rich content, impeccable scholarship, unusual mastery of a wide variety of source materials and ease of style, belying its dissertation origins, have earned the book increasing respect not only from historians of the New York scene but from all those interested in American history during the Middle Period.

As long as he could remember, Fox's goals were teaching and writing history, especially western history. Today, the region around the Great Lakes and the Finger Lakes and such cities as Buffalo and Rochester are not very far west, unless you are looking at them from New York City, but in 1801 they were indeed west, and frontier west at that. Although students are quick to notice the obvious influence Charles Beard's emphasis on economic determinism had upon the overall conception of Fox's book, they sometimes miss the more subtle but nonetheless potent influence of Frederick Jackson Turner's frontier thesis upon it. Some of the book's best ideas are variations on the Turner theme, ideas which seek to assess the importance and permanence of aristocracy in shaping the politics of the frontier.

Besides his interest in the west, Fox's earliest affections as an historian were engaged by the history of New York. His enthusiasm for his subject was as contagious as it was intense. He was particularly engrossed in the unique geographic position of the state, located as it was between the New England and Middle Western states and serving as a highway between the two. Carefully he surveyed the movement of Yankees out of their rocky New England abodes into the western stretches of New York, where they mixed with the old Dutch settlers, the Yorkers, and added to the mixture a reliance upon community life that the Dutch had scarcely experienced before. Not that the Yorkers passively accepted everything the Yankees had to offer. Their tough-minded individualism, said Fox, provided a healthy contrast to the Yankee passion for conformity. As long as he lived, Fox cared for and attended the fortunes of these Yankees and Yorkers, finding in their struggles to convert a wilderness into an Empire State themes as spacious, significant and even tragic as any in American history.

Fox's enthusiasm for his subject came naturally; he was a native New Yorker, born in Potsdam on December 7, 1887, to James Sylvester and Julia (Dixon) Fox. Potsdam is a small community located in St. Lawrence County, one of the top tier of counties in the northernmost part of the state just across the Canadian border. The Fox family had migrated to America from Tipperary, Ireland at the time of the "great hunger" in the 1840's when James Fox was about a year or two old. Instead of stopping off in one of the big seaport cities as so many of the Irish were doing, the entire Fox clan headed inland to resume their lives as farmers. For the younger generation farming was scarcely an attractive life, and when James Fox was old enough to work he deserted the farm and became a traveling salesman for a marble and granite company in Vermont. Since he was a man of great charm and wit, he was reasonably successful at his work. Besides, he enjoyed travel and the chance to meet different people. Yet with all his charm he managed to stay single until he was well into middle age. Then he married a young girl in her early twenties, Julia Anna Dixon, a school teacher in Potsdam whose family had migrated from Yorkshire, England. Julia was a Presbyterian; the Foxes staunch Catholics; so the family blamed her for James' abandonment of their religion. Actually she had nothing to do with it. Fox himself had long since given up Catholicism when he joined the Order of Freemasons. Indeed, he was a very active Mason, participating in many Masonic charities and centering much of his social life around the activities and welfare of his lodge.

When Dixon was born the elder Fox was off traveling through New England selling granite and marble. Left to her own devices, Julia named her son after the maternal grandparents, the surname Dixon from her mother and Ryan from her husband's mother. Because the father was away a good deal of the time, his influence on his growing son was slight. But Julia's interest in education, music and art, and her personal commitment to the intellectual life were all absorbed by her son. The two were very close. When "Dick" Fox, after preliminary training in the elementary and high schools, entered the Potsdam Normal School, his mother returned to school with him and both received their certificates of satisfactory completion at the same time.

There were strong historical influences at Potsdam, for scattered around St. Lawrence County were relics of the past that fired the young man's imagination. The most awesome of these were the great estates established over a century earlier by some of the most distinguished Yankee and Yorker families in the state, families such as the Van Rensselaers, the De Peysters, the Schuylers, the Parishes, the Clarksons and others. The more Fox learned about these people and the more he regarded the physical remains of their past glory, the more he was fascinated by their achievements and the distinction they had brought to St. Lawrence. All this did not make Fox an historian, but it laid a burden of emotion on him that would later evince itself in the ways in which he would interpret the history of New York. Several pages in the *Decline* are devoted to these mighty landlords and Fox is especially respectful of them—almost reverential. "So these families came," he wrote, "bringing in a spirit of aristocracy which left its mark . . . upon the county politics. That now they have for the most part disappeared adds a touch of pathos to the story. . . . While others made their way into the wilderness to be rid of every vestige of the feudal system, these came to perpetuate so much of that tradition as could be saved." A friend later noted that if Fox was disposed toward a sympathetic treatment of the members of the New York aristocracy it was not because they were supposedly privileged but because of what he considered their exacting standards of personal conduct, taste and social responsibility.

There was one other important influence at Potsdam: the encouragement of Fox's fascination with history by Edward Flagg, a young history instructor at the Normal School who was a graduate of Yale University. Flagg early recognized Fox's gifts as a prospective historian and helped him to discipline his talent. In later years Fox acknowledged that no other single teacher had had as much responsibility for his becoming an historian.

After graduation from the Normal School in 1907, Fox accepted a position as principal of the district school in Sherman Park (now Thornwood) in Westchester County. When he started the job he was warned by a school board member that the students were a nasty lot and might take it into their heads to toss him out of the building, as they had several times before with other teachers. "If anybody gets thrown out," Fox replied, "it won't be me." So the young hero began his teaching career, and although he stuttered a little the first day on account of nervousness (a sure invitation for defenestration in New York schools) nobody was thrown out, probably because the students reckoned the odds were against them in trifling with this tall, athletic-looking young man whose jaw stuck out just far enough to warn against taking liberties. Meanwhile Fox continued his own education by enrolling at Columbia University where he earned enough credits to receive a B.A. degree in 1911. In his senior year he won prizes in essay writing, public speaking and debate; upon graduation he immediately registered for courses in the Columbia Graduate School.

Just before World War I the Graduate School at Columbia University was staffed with men who were both great scholars and gifted teachers, men in the front ranks of historians, men who were not routinely reciting the interpretations of others but were themselves actively extending historical knowledge. There was Herbert Levi Osgood, trained in the old German system of research which demanded meticulous sifting of all first-hand sources, then their critical assessment and finally their presentation with complete objectivity. A man like Osgood could provide the integrity and discipline that historians must have if they are to approximate truth in reconstructing the past. But the German scientific method can also skewer imagination with a footnote. It can and often does dismiss valuable insights because they lack sufficient documentation, even though they are worth suggesting to other historians as perhaps another way of looking at an historical event. Still, before the historian can recreate the past he should know something about the mechanics and rules of his art, those techniques which have been devised to assist him in avoiding error and in perfecting his craft. Osgood's publications had all the virtues and most of the vices of the German method. His three-volume *The American Colonies in the Seventeenth Century* and the four-volume *The American Colonies in the Eighteenth Century* are devoid of human interest and drama but contain all the minutiae of colonial institutions that anyone could possibly want to know.

Another outstanding scholar on the Columbia staff was William Dunning, whose major subject was the Civil War and Reconstruction; he read his lectures from a carefully-prepared manuscript which was usually on its way to the printer as his next book. Both Osgood and Dunning impressed their students as the very models of dedicated scholars. Both won respect and gratitude from students because of the solid training in historical inquiry they gave in their classes and seminars. Still a third distinguished teacher was James Harvey Robinson, whose course entitled "The History of the Intellectual Class in Western Europe" was aimed at shattering the preconceived ideas of his students and at stimulating them to reconstruct their opinions from the evidence. Robinson was known as the herald of "The New History," a label taken from the presidential address given before the American Historical Association in 1900 by Edward Eggleston. Both Robinson and Eggleston advocated the enlargement of historical studies to include "the totality of human experience," not simply the shuffling back and forth from one country's politics and wars to the next. Eggleston argued for a history that in addition to politics would include social, intellectual and economic events, really anything that helped men grasp the significance of an era or the "true nature of any momentous institution." He demanded a shift from "the drum and trumpet history" to the "history of culture, the real history of men and women."

But perhaps the most distinguished member of the Columbia faculty, despite the reservations of the administration, was Charles Beard who taught political science and whom Fox came to know intimately as teacher and friend. Beard had not yet published his epochal *An Economic Interpretation of the Constitution of the United States,* though in his teaching the importance he placed on economic self-interest in the political and constitutional development of the United

States was clear enough. Like many others Fox understood that Beard was not exclusively an economic determinist, yet he appreciated the validity of Beard's work in providing a "principle of design" for the exposition of American history. Those who disagreed with the Beardian concepts, said Fox, must find other concepts around which to organize their material, because students want "philosophy," that is, to have the material arranged in such a way as to be left with an idea. "In writing general history," declared Fox at a later date, "it may be better to build on a wrong thesis than on none at all."

Fox was profoundly influenced by the Beardian principles, but he was also caught up in the "New History" and became a propagandist for social history. From several of his professors he absorbed the need to use the present as a point of departure in studying the past and to employ the discoveries of related disciplines such as sociology and anthropology to widen his perspectives. Revealing both the Yankee and Yorker within him, Fox admitted the importance of investigating the frontiersman as he chopped his way through the forest and established ideals of self reliance and popular democracy; but he also summoned historians to look beyond the frontiersmen to the men who came afterward with book, scalpel and compass and built a great civilization. It was not economic survival on the new continent alone that mattered, "but the saving and carrying forward of arts and sciences, those refinements and specializations which come from intelligently living together."

Thus, the multiple influences of Beard, Turner, Eggleston, Robinson, Osgood and Dunning can be found in Fox's writings. From Osgood, however, he got more than mere training in the systematic exploitation of source materials. On June 7, 1915, mid-way through his graduate studies, Fox married Osgood's daughter, Marian Stickney Osgood.

By that time he had his master's degree and had already begun to teach undergraduates in Columbia College. Hired in 1912 as a lecturer, he continued teaching at Columbia for the next twenty-two years, winning promotion to instructor in 1913, assistant professor in 1919, associate professor in 1922 and full professor in 1927. His teaching, according to one student, was invariably informative and stimulating, often dramatic and sometimes hilarious. In his classes he tended to emphasize the evolution of American society, working to replace the old "drum and trumpet history" with what he called the new "bum and strumpet history." He was a man of enormous energy and enthusiasm which he transmitted to his classes. He was especially helpful with his graduate students, taking an individual interest in their progress and growth. Among some of his more distinguished progeny were Roy and Jeanette Nichols, Michael Kraus, W. Randall Waterman and John A. Krout.

When Fox began to search for a subject for his dissertation there was no doubt that he would address himself to some phase of New York history, especially the history of upstate New York. He finally settled upon the history of the Erie Canal and spent several months gathering appropriate material. But when he learned that someone else was working on the same subject he quickly abandoned the topic and switched to the whole broad sweep of New York political history from 1801 to 1840. In doing so, he found he could make use of most of the data he had gathered on the canal. He spent better than four years shaping the dissertation, organizing, writing and revising the material under the direction of his mentor, William Dunning.

Entitled *The Decline of Aristocracy in the Politics of New York,* the dissertation was published by the Columbia University Press in 1919, two years after the doctor's degree was formally awarded. In the book Fox set for himself the task of demonstrating how an "aristocracy of birth was changed to one of money," how the old caste lines of New York, so carefully drawn in colonial times, were completely rubbed out. He began by depicting a proud landed gentry, confident in their manner of living; these patricians moved across the state to the very rim of the wilderness where they hoped to perpetuate their way of life. They were conservative in religion and politics but adventuresome in commercial enterprises and in tapping the resources of the state. They belonged to the Federalist party and accepted as inevitable the disparities of rank that separated them from the rest of society. With the end of the eighteenth century, which in point of New York time, according to Fox, came in 1821, they went through a transition, eventually merging with the Clintonian party and finally joining the Whig party. In the process the aristocracy was converted into a business party which accepted political equality as an accomplished fact. "Anything that savored of the feudal system," wrote Fox, "found small support even from the Whigs." True, the aristocracy continued to defend property, but it was property theoretically accessible to all who had the energy to go after it and take it.

The chronicle of the transition of an aristocracy into a business party was not necessarily a "mean and sordid" story, protested Fox, even though that party "had no other steady principle than this: that business should go on." For one thing the transition implicitly conceded the triumph of democratic principles in the politics of the state. For another, if the resources of the country were properly exploited as the business community advocated, it would perhaps bring "comfort and prosperity" to all. Finally, such prosperity meant inevitable power and prestige for the entire nation.

As Fox sketched the route of the transition, he showed

how men were actuated by social and financial interests, and how they accommodated one another in facing the challenges of change. Withal, he revealed how the center of political gravity within New York steadily shifted from the party of landowning aristocrats to the people. Although Fox admitted that earlier historians, such as Jabez D. Hammond and De Alva Alexander, had already covered the ground well, he pointed out that both Hammond and Alexander had woven only an objective narrative of events, while he was after something more important. In explaining the democratization of New York state politics Fox hoped "to throw another ray of light upon the evolution of society in the Empire State."

Here, then, is the major thrust of Fox's book. The *Decline* is one of a small number of pioneering studies that sought through the close examination of an immense catalog of historical data to find some central idea that would lay bare the nature of society, how it worked and how it changed. The treatise is a minor classic in American history because of the striking success with which the author accomplished his task.

To flesh the bare bones of his thesis, Fox did a number of rather remarkable things. Although the book was essentially political in nature, he consulted and introduced into his text an extraordinary range of sources, not simply the manuscript and printed documents of contemporaries, the newspapers, government publications, scholarly articles and secondary works which can be expected in any dissertation, but relevant scientific, religious, economic, literary, genealogical, musical and other materials that frequently alerted him to the most significant facets of New York history. Moreover, he was the first historian to attempt a voting analysis for the state, employing the apparatus of statistics and graphs, showing population changes, divisions by occupation, color and the valuation of property, and offering a workable index to the social and economic determinants of party affiliations.

But more important than Fox's method in spading new information into light were the fresh ideas he introduced into his book. Some are tossed off in brief phrases, some only tentatively offered; but a great many anticipate the whole direction of Jacksonian historiography for the next forty and more years. Although many writers of his own day (and later) were repeating James Madison's contention about how "the most common and durable source" of party division was the unequal distribution of property, Fox amended it with this fascinating thought: "Parties were continued more from memory and habit than from calculated differences of interest." Recent historians have become more and more impressed with habit and memory as determinants of party membership and increasingly less persuaded about the significance of issues and personalities or the unequal distribution of property.

Fox's perceptiveness was demonstrated in still other ways. He noticed, for example, that in developing a special competence for party organization, far beyond the accomplishments of other states, New York altered its history to form many unique political configurations, which still are not fully comprehended by scholars. He understood, too, the urban character of some aspects of Jacksonianism; that local bankers supported the President in his war with the Second Bank of the United States; that the Anti-masons propounded many liberal measures; that both major parties were committed to property ideals, appealed to the masses for support, enacted political reforms, yet halted before the extreme demands of democracy. "The men of wealth," he wrote, "well realized, now liberty and equality had shown their power, that in enthusiastic profession of fraternity lay their only course of safety. Property rights were secure only when it was realized that in America property was honestly accessible to talent, however humble in its early circumstances." The remarkable fact about the *Decline,* as one of his students later commented, was that it showed how much and how far he saw as a young scholar.

Still, the book is not without fault. Fox's heavy reliance on economic determinism was too rigid to do full justice to party growth and development. In later years he indicated some adjustments: "Because of rivalries between English and Dutch, Presbyterian and Anglican, merchants and farmers, and others," he declared, "party spirit early appeared in New York and persisted, in changing manifestations. Yet the party lines were not closely drawn between the rich and poor. So assured were the aristocrats of their social place and so various their backgrounds that they did not move together as one interest; families faced each other as Capulets and Montagues." Another criticism of the book concerns his treatment of suffrage reform; the chapter entitled "Property or People?" has been rightly faulted as excessively severe and limiting in its characterization of the franchise debate.

Fox has also been disputed on his thesis of continuity from Federalist to Clintonian to Whig. Critics have challenged his interpretation by pointing out that the "High Minded" Federalists moved into the ranks of the Democratic party; they have also offered evidence of the disenchantment with Clintonianism by some of the most aristocratic and Federalist families. However, a reexamination of the sources, especially manuscript sources, tends to substantiate Fox's argument. The continuity thesis certainly has its limitations, but it will never be disproved by the aberration of the "High Minded," for this was restricted to a very small group of approximately fifty men whose influence on the main body of Federalists was so slight that even Jabez Hammond noted that they carried "few of the rank and file with them. . . ." Furthermore, their aberration proved temporary; many later deserted the Democrats and rejoined their old Federalist friends within the Whig party.

Another exception cited against the continuity thesis is the evidence that Jeffersonian emigrants from New England who settled in the western counties of New York voted regularly against the Democratic party. But what sources are available again support Fox, or at least indicate a possible economic motivation for this change of loyalties. The Democratic party in New York was ruled by the Albany Regency, a group of singularly astute politicians led by Martin Van Buren. Many of these men, including Van Buren's son John, were directors and stockholders of the Mechanics and Farmers Bank in Albany. This bank exercised enormous control over western growth and expansion, so much so that John Van Buren frankly admitted to his father that banking operations in the west owed their very existence to the Mechanics and Farmers Bank. Since economic decisions emanating from Albany were frequently anti-speculative and conservative it is not surprising that the frustration experienced by westerners found expression in a vote against the Democratic party.

Fox has also been criticized for his method of determining the economic class character of the city wards. His explanations for the exceptions to his conclusions, especially as they relate to Negroes, have been tagged untenable and based on flimsy evidence. In addition, his statistical data has been declared insufficient because it rests principally upon census returns. It has been asserted that "impressionistic" evidence must be added (a suggestion that would cause Osgood and other "scientific" historians to collapse in a dead faint) if the large size and heterogeneity of the New York wards are to be properly understood. Without attempting to settle the argument or deny the need for more sophisticated analysis, one may admit that Fox's conclusions are not final answers, but neither are they without merit. And Fox himself would have been the first to invite refinements of his novel methods of political analysis.

Over the years, therefore, the *Decline* has taken several well-aimed brickbats. No doubt it will be subjected to even further criticism as more is learned about such things as voting behavior, racial and religious influences on party allegiances, and regional determinants in the creation of political issues. This is as it should be; still, historians have a long way to go before they begin to exploit all the remarkable insights into men and events contained in this pioneer study. Fox's book has held up well because he researched widely and intelligently and thoroughly, and because he offered an interesting and provocative interpretation. It is not the only concept to explain social and political evolution in New York, but it is one that continues to be useful and suggestive. Those who wish to demolish his study must match his scholarship. It is ironic that Fox, who in his own day preached the use of new tools and methods, should be attacked today not so much by the traditionalists, who still grind their way through the mountain of manuscripts, but by the scholars who now employ the latest psychological, sociological and "impressionistic" techniques.

The publication of Fox's book elicited a number of favorable reviews. None was overly extravagant, for it is not the kind of book that prompts an extravagant response on first reading. Indeed, the *Decline* is very deceptive in that it is much more complex than one suspects on examining it the first time. Although well-written, and in several parts written with distinction, it lacked the brilliant literary style and wit that typified so much of Fox's later output. Yet, through the years, the book won and held the esteem of professional historians and, for all practical purposes, fixed most of the fundamental ideas and assumptions concerning New York's growth and change during the first half of the nineteenth century. In the literature of the Jacksonian age it remains a book of the first importance.

The same year Fox submitted his dissertation and earned his doctor's degree he joined the New York State Historical Association. Twelve years later he was elected its president, the first such to be chosen from the ranks of professional historians. When he joined the Association he found it little more than a congenial group of lint-picking antiquarians holding strawberry festivals in springtime. By goodwill, tact and persistence he converted it into one of the most professional of its kind in the country. He succeeded in blending the enthusiasm of the layman with the skill of the scholar. He was the joint editor of the Association's quarterly, known later as *New York History,* since its first appearance in 1919. In his campaign to introduce trained personnel into all phases of the state's historical research, he was instrumental in engaging the young but superbly talented Julian P. Boyd as director of Headquarters House in Ticonderoga, and later such other distinguished historians as Edward P. Alexander and Clifford Lord. Fox also helped to plan and carry to completion a ten-volume *History of the State of New York,* published from 1933 to 1937 under the general editorship of the state historian, Alexander C. Flick.

Meanwhile, he added to his own publications. After the *Decline,* he did a commercial outline history and atlas, and upon the death of his father-in-law assisted in the preparation of the four-volume *History of American Colonies in the Eighteenth Century* for publication, writing the last chapter himself. A few years later he brought out a brief

sketch of *Herbert Levi Osgood* (1923). Then followed a
biography of *Caleb Heathcote* (1926) in which the most interesting material concerns social and economic conditions of
Westchester County during the colonial period. But his
best books were *Ideas in Motion* (1935), a collection of
four essays analyzing aspects of intellectual history, and
Yankees and Yorkers (1940), a work of mature scholarship which began as a series of lectures delivered at New
York University.

Much of this output underscored Fox's special interest in
social history. From this and several addresses he gave
on the subject before the American Historical Association
he won recognition as a leader in the field. For some, of
course, social history was and is simply a mass of unrelated
facts. What does not fit into political or economic or in-
stitutional history is tossed into social history, the junkyard
of the historian. For Fox, however, the subject was always
an exciting challenge to cull from a vast array of facts the
unifying themes that slice to the meaning of social evolution.
Because of his leadership in social history he was invited in
1922 to share responsibility with Arthur M. Schlesinger for
editing a multi-volume *History of American Life* that would
emphasize social developments. Carl Becker was also
brought in as consulting editor. Both Schlesinger and Fox
agreed to write individual volumes and it was hoped the
series could be completed in three years; instead it took
twenty-one years. There were many problems in finding authors who could conform to the fundamental purpose of the
series, and some manuscripts, when submitted, required extensive editing. Fox carried a heavy share of this editing
burden until his appointment in 1934 as president of Union
College, one of the oldest schools in the state, located at
Schenectady. His time was then so taken up by other duties
that in the preparation of his own book, *The Completion of*

Independence, 1790–1830 (1944), he was compelled to rely on the able assistance of one of his former students, John A. Krout, who properly shared the authorship of the book upon publication.

Fox was president of Union College for ten years—the years of the Long Depression and World War II. During that time he established the Mohawk Drama Festival, the first cooperative enterprise between an American college and the professional stage; he almost doubled the college's productive capital and nearly tripled library appropriations. What he might have done at the conclusion of the war when colleges were entering a new era of expansion and growth can only be surmised, for he died quite suddenly at the age of fifty-seven. While conferring with officials of the General Electric Company about its plans for supporting the college's special summer session for post-graduate instruction in physics he was seized with a heart attack. He was taken to Ellins Hospital where he died shortly thereafter on January 30, 1945.

Dixon Ryan Fox was a man of extraordinary versatility and accomplishment. He exuded enthusiasm in all the things he did and had a marvelous capacity to excite similar enthusiasms in others. Moreover, he was a man of unfailing kindness and generosity who, on the one hand, could get many people to work together for the completion of a herculean task of scholarship, and then, on the other, very quietly turn out his own individual contributions to history. It is not surprising he could do this, for in him was fused much of what was best of the Yankee and Yorker.

A NOTE ABOUT THE TORCHBOOK EDITION

This edition of *The Decline of Aristocracy in the Politics of New York* is an exact reproduction of the original published by the Columbia University Press in 1919. My footnotes to the text are numbered by letters in order to avoid confusion with the author's original footnotes. Sometime after publication Fox indicated in his own copy of the book certain revisions he wanted to make in Chapter VIII, "Property or People?" In editing this Torchbook edition I saw no need to alter the text as originally published because all of Fox's subsequent corrections were attempts to compress material and improve style. Nevertheless, readers may wish to judge the value and extent of the corrections for themselves, so the revisions are printed below. For permission to publish these changes as well as for much of the biographical information on Fox used in the Introduction, I am most grateful to Mrs. Marian Osgood Fox.

R.V.R.

THE FOX REVISIONS

Page 239. In the margin, at the end of the first paragraph, a horizontal line is drawn under which is written "No footnotes."

Page 240, line 1: The word "the" before "Federalist" is deleted.

Page 240, lines 24–26. These lines are rewritten to read as follows: "few feet distant, now the moderate spokesman of the few 'high-minded' Federalists, who disliking Clinton even cooperated with the Democrats. On the left side of the house, in an aisle" etc.

Page 241, lines 12–13: These lines are rewritten to read: "score of men, 'commissioned,' as George Bancroft said in his *Van Buren,* 'to impede the onward movement" etc.

Page 242, line 5: The word "most" is deleted.

Page 242, lines 15–16: These lines are rewritten to read: "brilliant, penetrating mind and ready wit were famous; and beside Van Ness," etc.

Page 243, line 1: The words "of Albany" are inserted after "Van Vechten."

Page 243, line 3: The entire sentence beginning with the words, "What has been said" is deleted.

Page 243, lines 10–16: Everything is deleted between the words "The former" on line 10 and "had served as an official" on line 16. The sentence now reads, "The former had served as an official" etc.

Page 243, line 18: The words "like Gideon Granger" are deleted.

Page 244, line 5: Lower case for "Council of Revision."

Page 244, line 16 to the bottom of the page, excluding the footnotes: These lines are deleted.

Page 245, lines 1–3: These lines are deleted, and the text picks up with the words, "Some, like the president, would hide" etc.

Page 245, lines 8–10: The entire sentence beginning with the words, "Others of a franker mind" is deleted.

Page 246, line 10: Lower case for "Council of Appointment."

Page 247, line 7: The final sentence of footnote 2 on this

page, beginning with the words "Election of judges," is inserted at the end of the first paragraph.

Page 247, lines 9–12: The entire sentence, beginning with the words "As a majority party" is deleted.

Page 248: The two blocked quotations are deleted. The entire page now reads as follows: "enterprise be not wrecked upon excess, came forward with a compromise calling for a two year term, which was accepted by a scant majority.[1] P. R. Livingston, however, was still determined that the executive be curbed whenever possible. Still following Mr. Jefferson, he had it laid down in the constitution that the governor should address the legislature only by a written message—'the speech,' said he, was 'a relic of monarchy, founded in the love of pomp and splendour and show.'[2] The conservatives believed that those who held property were the able, and that government by the able was preferable to government by the mass. Elisha Williams argued that those in whose hands sovereignty was lodged were trustees for the rest."[3]

Page 249: The entire page is deleted.

Page 250, lines 1–12: These lines are deleted.

Page 251, line 8: The word "Nathan" is substituted for the word "Mr."

Page 251: The first sentence of the blocked quotation is deleted.

Page 251: The final two lines on the page are rewritten to read: "Although the holding specified was left unchanged, there was one element of novelty, the introduction of an equity qualification for those who had not completed purchase and those who held large property or large leasehold."

Page 252: The entire page is deleted.

Page 253, lines 1–9: These lines are deleted.

Page 253, line 18: The words "John Duer" is inserted after the word "delegate."

Page 253, line 21: The words "with an unmistakeable accent of sincerity" are inserted between the words "as" and "he."

Page 253, line 24: The words "and so sincere" are deleted.

Page 256, line 26: The word "large" is inserted before the word "accumulation."

Page 257, lines 14–17: The entire sentence beginning with the words "Their habits" is deleted.

Page 257, lines 20–22: The entire sentence beginning with the words "Knowledge or intelligence" is deleted.

Page 258, lines 2–8: The entire blocked quotation is deleted beginning with the words "I appeal to this convention."

Page 258, lines 10–11: The phrase within the parenthesis is deleted.

Page 259, lines 15–18: The entire sentence beginning with the words "No, sir;" is deleted.

Page 260, lines 4–7: The remainder of the quotation beginning with the word "Penury" is deleted.

Page 261, line 6: The word "Federalist" is changed to the plural possessive.

Page 261, lines 15–21: These lines are deleted.

Page 262, lines 18–22: The entire quotation beginning with the words "That gentleman," is deleted.

Page 264, line 3: After the sentence ending with the word "one." the following sentence is inserted: "When the Federalists, led by Peter A. Jay, sought to extend the same new privileges to Negroes as to whites their opponents laid aside their democratic theory and voted no. The old property qualifications were retained for this small fraction of the voters until outlawed by the Fifteenth Amendment to the Federal Constitution in 1870."

Page 264, line 13: Lower case for "Council of Revision."

Page 264, lines 14–15: The entire sentence beginning with the words "Early in the discussion" is deleted.

Page 265, line 6 to the bottom of the page, excluding footnotes: These lines are deleted.

Page 266, line 1: The words "usual majority" are deleted.

Page 268: In the margin of the page is written: "The achievement of the Workingmen's parties after 1828, by which free schools were introduced, as well as protection of debtors from imprisonment and of mechanics against loss of wages and other consequences of the democratic constitutional reforms, must await discussion in another chapter." There is no indication where this sentence is to be inserted.

AUTHOR'S FOREWORD

At the opening of the nineteenth century democracy was new; men were still described as gentlemen and simple-men, in America as well as in the monarchies across the sea. Disparities of rank were still sustained by those of property, but in a country such as ours, where the touch of energy could turn resources into wealth, prescriptive rights could not long remain unchallenged. In no colony had the lines of old caste been more clearly drawn than in New York; in no state were they more completely rubbed away. How an aristocracy of birth was changed to one of money and was often ousted from control, how Federalists became Clintonians and Clintonians turned into Whigs, is to be the theme of the following pages.

The history of New York state has been well told. Few contemporary narratives have been more full and fair than that contained within Judge Hammond's[a] volumes published in the 'forties. Nor could the general reader want a more complete and readable account than that of Col. Alexander,[b] published some ten years ago. These historians, however, in the manner of the older school, have dealt objectively with events and personalities, without giving much attention to the social and economic causes which went far to make them what they were. The present writer, with a narrower theme, has essayed to penetrate beneath the laws and party platforms in hope of explanations. It is a story he believes

[a] Jabez D. Hammond (1778-1855), a Congressman, state senator of New York, judge of Otsego County and historian whose *The History of Political Parties in the State of New York* (2 vols., 1842) is still the best political history of the state from 1789 to 1840.

[b] De Alva S. Alexander (1845-1925), a Congressman and author of *Political History of the State of New York* (3 vols., 1906, 1909) and a supplementary volume entitled *Four Famous New Yorkers* (1923).

to be of interest, however haltingly related, tracing as it does the fortunes of a class, accustomed by training and tradition to the conduct of affairs, but forced to yield before what seemed to them the great disaster of democracy; it deals with their unpalatable compromises and slow liberalization, and the final welding of a business party appropriate to the conditions of America. It is hoped that thus it may throw another ray of light upon the evolution of society in the Empire State.

To Professor William A. Dunning of Columbia University, the author is under special obligation for the keen but kindly criticism which he has brought to bear upon this study, and for his sacrifice of many hours to the tedious task of reading proof. Professor Herbert L. Osgood has patiently reviewed the manuscript and made valuable suggestions. The author desires also to acknowledge the co-operation of Mr. Victor Hugo Paltsits, Keeper of the Manuscripts of the New York Public Library, of Robert H. Kelby, Librarian of the New York Historical Society, of Dr. Austin B. Keep, and of Professors Charles A. Beard, Carlton J. H. Hayes, David S. Muzzey and Robert Livingston Schuyler, of whose counsel he has frequently availed himself. Notwithstanding this generous aid, he is aware that many imperfections still remain.

Dixon Ryan Fox.

Columbia University, *May, 1917.*

CHAPTER I

THE FEW, THE RICH, AND THE WELL BORN

"WE are all Republicans, we are all Federalists"—the word of peace was spoken by the bland philosopher of Monticello, as he took the chair of state in the spring of 1801. But as it issued from the presses of the great towns to the north, it was not a soothing word; it carried no assurance to the merchants and ship-masters; to them it heralded a peace, not of reconciliation, but of surrender that was bitter in its hopelessness. They had scarce need to read through Jefferson's inaugural to know that agriculture was to be a chief concern of his administration and that commerce would gain attention only as its handmaid.[1] To these Federalists the removal of the seat of government to the Potomac was but the outward sign that the nation's center of gravity had been shifted toward the south, leaving them in their remoteness a benumbing sense that henceforth their portion was to be neglect. The new leader had declared that great cities were but sores on the body politic,[2] and he had indicated to his friends that were he to indulge his own desire, he would wish these states "to practice neither commerce nor navigation, but to stand with respect to Europe precisely on the footing of China."[3]

[1] J. D. Richardson, *Messages and Papers of the Presidents* (Washington, 1899), vol. i, pp. 322-323.

[2] J. P. Foley, *The Jeffersonian Cyclopedia* (N. Y., 1900), pp. 141-142.

[3] Jefferson to Count Van Hogendorp, Paris, 1785, Jefferson's *Writings* (Ford edition), vol. iv, p. 104.

1

Ship-yards and counting-houses were no longer likely objects of the nation's patronage; in the vanity of ignorance, it seemed, wealth and enterprise in trade were fallen into disrepute.

But the troubles that seemed imminent were still more deeply based. The government which Federalists had nursed to robust promise, had, by this sad caprice of fate, been handed over to the ungentle stewardship of its notorious foes. It might now be reasonably expected that the official theory of the United States would be that of the Kentucky resolutions,[a] whose author was exalted to the highest place. This was the man who had complained of using force to curb the Whiskey Insurrection,[1, b] and had said of Shays's[c] exploits in western Massachusetts: "God forbid that we should ever be twenty years without such a rebellion."[2] Here was a chief magistrate whose loud simplicity seemed calculated to neglect all canons of decorum. What was to become of decency and order under such a man? Had the *Federalist* been written all in vain? Were those achievements so dearly wrought by Washington and Hamilton to be tumbled into an ungrateful memory and this nation fall without a protest, simply that a full experiment be given to this fatal doctrine of democracy?

When the word was brought to Hamilton, in the spring of 1800, that the legislature of New York would be "Anti-Federal" and thus the vote of this great state make inevitable the choice of Jefferson,[3] he wrote to Governor Jay

---

[1] Jefferson to James Madison, May 1793, *Writings* (Ford), vol. vi, p. 261, and December 1794, *ibid.*, p. 518; to James Monroe, May 1795, *ibid.*, vol. vii, p. 16.

[2] Jefferson to W. S. Smith, 1787, *ibid.*, vol. iv, p. 467.

[3] The presidential electors in New York were chosen by the two houses of the legislature until after the election of 1824-1825; see J. D. Hammond, *History of Political Parties in the State of New York* (Albany, 1842 *et seq.*), vol. ii, p. 154 *et seq.*

[a] The Kentucky and Virginia Resolutions (1798), written respectively by Thomas Jefferson and James Madison, argued the doctrine of states' rights to protest the Alien and Sedition Acts passed during John Adams' administration.

[b] Whiskey Rebellion(1794), an uprising of Pennsylvania farmers result-

that the "scruples of delicacy and propriety . . . ought not to hinder the taking of a legal and constitutional step to prevent an atheist in religion and a fanatic in politics, from getting possession of the helm of state," [1] and advised the governor forthwith to call a special session of the old Federalist legislature to pass a law which, by redistricting the state, would probably insure a Federalist triumph for New York and thereby for the nation. General Schuyler[a] had likewise urged this trick and assured the governor that

your friends will justify it as the only way to save a nation from more disasters, which it may and probably will experience from the mis-rule of a Man who has given such strong evidence that he was opposed to the salutary Measures of those who have been heretofore at the helm, and who is in fact pervaded with the mad French philosophy.[2]

There were others who joined in this desperate advice,[3] but Jay's good sense withstood more firmly the behests of anger and disgust; he refused thus to conspire to defeat the people's will and rejected this proposal for "party purposes, which I think it would not become me to adopt." [4] That such an expedient could have been seriously talked of by the responsible leaders of the party, shows how critical they thought the juncture in our national affairs. Even Jay looked forward to a dismal fate for this people, whom

[1] Hamilton to Jay, May 7, 1800, *The Works of Alexander Hamilton* (Lodge edition, N. Y., 1886), vol. viii, p. 549.

[2] Philip Schuyler to Jay, May 7, 1800, *Correspondence and Public Papers of John Jay* (Johnston edition, N. Y., 1893), vol. iv, p. 273. General Schuyler feared that Jefferson would embroil the United States in a war with Great Britain.

[3] Schuyler mentions John Marshall as one, *ibid., loc. cit.*

[4] *Jay Correspondence*, vol. iv, p. 272. Lodge's note in Hamilton's *Writings*, vol. vii, p. 551, and D. S. Alexander, *A Political History of the State of New York* (N. Y., 1906-1909), vol. i, p. 92. Both quote this passage inaccurately.

ing from Alexander Hamilton's excise tax which collapsed after troops were called out by President George Washington.

[c] Daniel Shays led a farmers revolt in Massachusetts (1786-1787) to protest high taxes and the foreclosure of mortgages. The rebellion was put down by troops commanded by General Benjamin Lincoln, and Shays was later pardoned by Governor John Hancock.

he saw "permitting their happiness to be put in jeopardy by the worst passions, inflamed and directed by the most reprehensible means." Whether all the ills that threatened could be prevented no man could prophesy, but it was certainly a most unhappy fact that the Federalists themselves did not act together to ward them off. "If the sound and leading friends of their country," he wrote, "could concur in opinion as to men and measures, their efforts would probably be successful, but unfortunately there is too little unanimity in many points, and the want of it exposes us to the hazard of many evils." [1]

The new legislature, meeting in November, justified the Federalists' fears. An electoral ticket had been fashioned which drew support from every faction that had formed among Republicans,[2] and they acted as a whole, while agreeing in their caucus with like unanimity to support George Clinton as their candidate for governor.[3] The Federalists placed in nomination the Patroon, Stephen Van Rensselaer, the social leader of the state,[4] a dignified and knightly figure, and a public servant of honorable reputation.[5] The state campaign of April, 1801, was vigorously fought, but the Federalists could make no headway against the spirit of the times; it was destined that John Jay was to be remembered as the last governor of his party

[1] Jay to Theophilus Parsons, July 1, 1800, *Jay Correspondence*, vol. iv, p. 274.

[2] J. D. Hammond, *Political History*, vol. i, pp. 135-137. Though ordinarily the legislature met in January, it was called in "presidential years" for November.

[3] Jeremiah Van Rensselaer, the candidate for lieutenant-governor, was probably the only man of his name to be found in the Anti-Federal, or as it was now called, Republican party.

[4] D. D. Barnard, *Discourse on Stephen Van Rensselaer* (pamphlet, Albany, 1839).

[5] *N. Y. Civil List*, 1889, p. 742. He was then serving as lieutenant-governor.

[a] Philip J. Schuyler (1733-1804), a wealthy New Yorker, Revolutionary War general, Federalist and U.S. Senator whose daughter, Elizabeth, married Alexander Hamilton.

in New York. After an earnest effort to save appointments for his partisans,[1] he laid down forever the cares and dignities of office. There were no hymns of hope as the distinguished leaders in New York gathered at the banquet board to sound his praises; it was a sad farewell, not alone to the beloved governor, but likewise to the exercise of power and control by their "party of the talents," and as they believed, to the prosperity which such care insured.[2]

Now in 1801, as later, one hears in their pronouncements a constant minor undertone of deep discouragement; the structure of society seemed suddenly turned upside down, with what result no one could foretell.

In New York the rights & the property of the city and state are subject to the vice and folly and poverty of the society [wrote Fisher Ames[a] to Rufus King, in London]. We are now in the Roland & Condorcet[b] act of our Comedy—Whether we go on to the Danton and Robespierre[c] acts depends on time

[1] This controversy was with the majority of the Council of Appointment, which under the Constitution of 1777, consisted of one senator from each of the four great districts of the state, chosen by the assembly and under the presidency of the governor. This officer by the prescription was to appoint all officers, who were not elected, "with the advice and consent of said council" (Article xxiii). The majority in the winter of 1801 were Republicans, and claimed that any member had a concurrent right of nomination with the governor, a contention which Jay would not allow. The deadlock which resulted from this opposition was the principal cause of the Convention of 1801, which in a constructive amendment to the constitution supported the opinion of the majority of the Council. See H. L. McBain, "DeWitt Clinton and the Origin of the Spoils System in New York" (Columbia University Studies in History, Economics and Public Law, vol. xxviii, no. 1), and Charles Z. Lincoln, *The Constitutional History of New York* (Rochester, 1906), vol. i, pp. 56, 178, 191, 531, 600-602, 610-611.

[2] Robert Troup to Rufus King, May 27, 1801, *The Life and Correspondence of Rufus King* (Charles R. King, editor, N. Y., 1894-1900), vol. iii, p. 458. Inasmuch as letters in this work, as well as in the *Jay Correspondence*, are arranged in chronological order, this source will be frequently cited by date only.

[a] Fisher Ames (1758-1808), a leading Massachusetts Federalist and staunch supporter of Alexander Hamilton.

[b] Jean Marie Roland de la Platière (1734-1793) and Marie Jean Antine Nicolas Caritat, Marquis de Condorcet (1743-1794), two moderate

and accident and not on the discernment energy or force of the Feds.[1]

Just as six years before, the Federalists had cleansed the government of most of those who stood with Clinton, so now, by revolution, the Federalists found themselves proscribed.[2] "In this state," wrote Robert Troup, "all power and all the offices are also engrossed by the Democrats."[3] Seriously to contemplate democracy as a kind of government was absurd, wrote Gouverneur Morris in 1801, "for I hold that it is no government at all, but, in fact, the death or dissolution of other systems, or the passage from one kind of government to another."[4] Soon, it might well be, as Hamilton predicted, we should have a despotism, "for a courtier and a demagogue differ only in forms, which, like clothes, are put on and off as suits the occasion."[5]

In the speech and correspondence of the Federalists there recurs the prediction of the final failure of the American experiment, to end in no one knew what form of government. They seemed sorrowfully certain of their destiny to outlive the nation they had labored earnestly to build. "Old Gates used to tell me in 1776," wrote Judge Peters to John Jay, "that if the bantling Independence lived one year, it would last to the age of Methusaleh. Yet we have lived to see it in its dotage, with all the maladies and imbecilities of

[1] Fisher Ames to Rufus King, May 27, 1801, *King Correspondence*.

[2] H. L. McBain, *op. cit.*, successfully combats the claim advanced by Schouler, Henry Adams and others, that the spoils system was invented in 1801 by De Witt Clinton and his Council of Appointment, pointing out that the practice was inherited from the Jay administration.

[3] R. Troup to King, April 9, 1802, *King Correspondence*.

[4] Anne C. Morris, *The Diary and Letters of Gouverneur Morris* (N. Y., 1888), vol. ii, p. 469.

[5] *Ibid.*, p. 475. "Democracy is the first step toward despotism," said the *New York Spectator*, March 5, 1804.

revolutionaries in the French Revolution. After the Jacobins came to power Condorcet was arrested and died in prison, while Roland committed suicide after he learned his wife had been guillotined.

[c] Georges Jacques Danton (1759-1794) and Maximilien Marie Isidore Robespierre (1758-1794), two extremist leaders of the French Revolution.

extreme old age." ¹ Society itself was showing symptoms of decay; the unnatural genius of equality was sapping the foundations of all that had been built in the knowledge and the virtue of the past.² Such influences were admitted through a reckless zeal for novelty which brought on all the troubles. " Among the evils, which periodically flourish amongst mankind," remarked an essayist, " is a spirit of innovation, which has lately gained strength in our borders, and now counteracts the best tendency of regular habits." ³ Jay and King might counsel firm resistance to this innovation,⁴ but it seemed sadly clear to many honest Federalists that " Reason, common sense, talents and virtue, cannot stand before democracy. Like a resistless flood, it sweeps all away; and it has, probably, not yet spent its force." ⁵ The leading editorial of the *New York Commercial Advertiser,* on New Year's Day of 1801, concluded:

We have no grounds to felicitate ourselves on advancing a single step in the theory or practice of government within two thousand years. The opinion that we have advanced, is derived from our pride, founded on our ignorance—an opinion that is a burlesk on an education in pretended science, and our vanity.⁶

As one reads these jeremiads of pessimism, no doubt of their sincerity intrudes to break their force. Here was a

¹ Judge Peters to Jay, July 9, 1808, *Jay Correspondence.*

² Rufus King to Noah Webster, June 30, 1807, *King Correspondence.*

³ *N. Y. Spectator,* April 21, 1806, " Speculations of Decius," published serially.

⁴ Jay to Richard Hatfield, November 8, 1800, *Jay Correspondence,* and Rufus King to Christopher Gore, March 21, 1815, *King Correspondence.*

⁵ " Candidus " in *N. Y. Spectator,* January 18, 1804.

⁶ See also the Rev. Samuel Osgood, *New York in the Nineteenth Century,* a discourse before the New York Historical Society (N. Y., 1867), pp. 14-15.

company of gentlemen accustomed to the power and direction of the government, suddenly reduced to private station and the consciousness of unimportance; but they obviously spoke from larger motives than those of personal resentment. They believed themselves the spokesmen of a class as indisputably fit to rule a state as those guardians to whom Plato entrusted his Republic. One turns with interest to inquire who made up this class thus brought down by the leveling wave of 1801.

For the most part in New York, since the adoption of the state constitution in 1777, the Federalist party had controlled the state,[1] and the Federalist party had been itself controlled from New York city.[2] Here lived the brilliant leader, Alexander Hamilton, who not only had done most to formulate the party's principles and to set forth its political philosophy, but had been its foremost champion on the public platform, its chief exponent in administration and the most effective organizer of its victories. In 1801 he had been for several years in private life and, by untiring exertion, had built up a practice at the bar which brought in a yearly income of some fifteen thousand dollars,[3] yet he was still regarded as the chief directing mind of the party he had founded. The "lullabies" of the new President were but added irritation to his drooping spirit. " Perhaps no man in the United States has sacrificed or done more for the present Constitution than myself, and contrary to all my anticipation of its fate, as you know

[1] J. D. Hammond, *Political History*, vol. i, p. 162.

[2] O. G. Libby, " The Geographical Distribution of the Vote of the Thirteen States on the Federal Constitution" (Wisconsin Studies in History, Economics and Political Science, vol. i, Madison, 1897), p. 18; C. A. Beard, *An Economic Interpretation of the Constitution* (N. Y., 1913), p. 268 *et seq.*, and H. L. McBain, *DeWitt Clinton and the Spoils System*, p. 105.

[3] H. C. Lodge, *Alexander Hamilton*, Boston, 1882, pp. 234-235; D. S. Alexander, *Political History of the State of New York*, vol. i, p. 132.

from the very beginning, I am still laboring to prop the frail and worthless fabric." [1]

Next in dignity among these New York Federalists was Governor Jay, now retiring to the country home that he had built at Bedford, studying the science of the soil from Columella to Sir John Sinclair and busying himself with new breeds of stock and new varieties of melons.[2] Yet his absence from the forum seemed almost to enhance the value of his counsel and he was to be frequently consulted as a grand old man acquainted with the purposes of the founders of the government, and a stalwart foe to all that savored of democracy. " It is not a new remark," he wrote to Canon Wilberforce, " that those who own the country are the most fit persons to participate in the government of it. This remark, with certain restrictions and exceptions, has force in it; and applies both to the elected and to the elector, though with most force to the former." [3] Jay seemed to Federalists a very proper governor; the only vice for which he had been seriously criticized by his opponents, that of prodigality, was in their theory of politics almost a virtue.[4]

Scarcely less important in the early days of the new government was Rufus King. In 1801 he was still minister to England, but long surviving other leaders, he was to become the foremost of his party in the state and in the

[1] Hamilton to G. Morris, February 27, 1802, *Works* (Lodge), vol. viii, p. 591; and to C. C. Pinckney, December 29, 1802, *ibid.*, p. 606.

[2] Jay to Judge Peters, July 24, 1809, and March 14, 1815, *Jay Correspondence*; Jay to Sir John Sinclair, December 16, 1800 and August 8, 1816, *ibid.*; Robert Bolton, *History of the County of Westchester* (N. Y., 1848), vol. ii, pp. 88-91; J. G. Wilson, *Memorial History of the City of New York* (N. Y., 1893), vol. iii, p. 156.

[3] Jay to Judge Peters, July 24, 1809, and to William Wilberforce, October 25, 1810, *Jay Correspondence*.

[4] Alexander Hamilton, *Address to the Electors*, pamphlet, (N. Y., 1801), pp. 19-20.

nation, throughout the first quarter of the century. Four times elected to the Senate of the United States,[1] he represented not alone the great state of New York, but likewise the old caste of gentlemen. A man of wealth and family,[2] the " high model of courtly refinement," appearing always to the last in the small-clothes and silk stockings of the days of Washington, he had in manner a formal courtesy, and something of hauteur and pride, the bearing of a true aristocrat.[3] As to other Federalists of the older school, so to him the ideal statesman was the leader of measures and not the leader of men, administering a government large in power, respected among nations and liberally benevolent in purpose.[4] With Hamilton devoted to the law and money-making, and Jay in deep retirement, the call went forth to King, in London, to hasten home to lead the party in New York, a leadership which, once assumed, remained long undisputed.[5] Like Hamilton and Jay, even after death he lived on in his sons, to aid in leading later parties in New York, the Whig and the Republican.[6]

[1] *N. Y. Civil List*, 1882, p. 446.

[2] He was, among other things, interested in government securities, as is evidenced in the letter to his broker Nicholas Low, June 15, 1802. *Life and Correspondence of Rufus King*, vol. iv, p. 140. See also *ibid.*, vol. i, p. 132; and C. A. Beard, *Economic Interpretation of the Constitution* (N. Y., 1913), pp. 118-120.

[3] See the description by T. H. Benton, in his *Thirty Years View* (N. Y., 1886), pp. 57-58, and *King Correspondence*, quoting from *Faux's Travels*, vol. vi, p. 670 *et seq.*

[4] William Sullivan, *Public Men of the Revolution* (Philadelphia, 1847), p. 59. For personal description, see in *Delaplaine's Repository* (Philadelphia, 1815 *et seq.*), the article by William Coleman (Coleman to King, February 5, 1817, *King Correspondence*), and in *Homes of American Statesmen* (N. Y., 1859), the sketch of King Park by Charles King.

[5] Robert Troup to King, May 6, 1802, *King Correspondence*.

[6] Article on John A. King in *Appleton's Cyclopedia of American Biography*; James A. Hamilton, *Reminiscences* (N. Y., 1869), p. 314, and *N. Y. Tribune*, November 6, 1846.

The last member of this famous four was Gouverneur Morris, who likewise had been distinguished in the effort to establish and to carry out the principles of an aristocratic government, somewhat moderated and toned down to fit conditions in America. It requires no rehearsal here to call to mind the theories of this bluff and testy squire. In his opinion " there never was, and never will be a civilized Society without an Aristocracy," [1] and aristocracy found no more admired exemplar than Morris in his generous service for the public good. In 1801 he was to serve two years more as senator in Washington,[2] then was to give his energies as propagandist for the internal improvement of the state. As public orator and adviser of the party, he was to continue in importance for fifteen years until his death.

These statesmen—Hamilton, Jay, King and Morris, were the models after which the younger generation of Federalists might seek to pattern their social and political careers; but such lordly gentlemen could not be counted on in New York city to do the hum-drum arduous work of ward meetings and inspection at the polls. Turning from the great apostles of Federalism to take note of lesser leaders, we do not, however, reach outside the same exclusive and aristocratic class.

The bar of New York city that argued cases in the old court house on Broad Street at the turning of the century numbered scarcely a hundred.[3] It was a small company, indeed, compared with the tens of thousands that crowd the enormous hives that now weigh down those almost

[1] Max Farrand, *Records of the Federal Convention* (New Haven, 1911), vol. i, p. 545.

[2] *N. Y. Civil List*, 1882, p. 446.

[3] C. H. Hunt, *Life of Edward Livingston* (N. Y., 1863), p. 48; T. E. V. Smith, *The City of New York in the Year of Washington's Inauguration* (N. Y., 1889), p. 61; and C. H. Truax, *History of the Bench and Bar of New York* (N. Y., 1897), vol. i, p. 103.

priceless acres; but within it there were men of gifts and
power, some black-letter lawyers skilled in the confusing
mazes of the common law and some who grasped the larger
principles of polity and rose to high distinction in the field
of jurisprudence. Of all these, the leaders, excepting the
greater Livingstons, who were often absent from the city,
and the erratic Aaron Burr, were of the Federalist party,
and, indeed, not a few had evidenced their conservative
regard for the old king's law by remaining king's men
throughout the War of Independence. Many Tories in their
anxiety that no experiment should interrupt George Clinton's
policy of easy tolerance, had in 'eighty-seven and 'eighty-
eight taken ground against the national constitution; but
when their Anti-Federalist associates shouted applause of
Robespierre, " degenerated into democrats " and, for a
season, lost the ascendancy in the state, the old Tories came
to the conclusion that no good could come from such a
party and quietly came over to the safer company of Mr.
Jay. Such was the course that brought to the Federalist
ranks the Samuel Joneses, father and son, both distinguished
jurists.[1]

One who at first was burdened with the record of a loyalist was Richard Harison,[2] the son of a Tory councillor who

[1]W. A. Duer, *Reminiscences of an Old New Yorker* (N. Y. 1867),
p. 23. This interesting book is made up of a series of letters signed
" Peregrine Mindful," first printed in the *New York American Mail*
during the summer of 1847. The elder Mr. Jones was soon appointed
comptroller of the state by Governor Jay when that office was created
(*N. Y. Civil List*, 1882, p. 160). The son served three terms in the
assembly as a Federalist (*ibid.*, pp. 300-301) after several unsuccessful
attempts at election (*N. Y. Commercial Advertiser*, April 21, 1806).
He was in 1826 appointed chancellor, in which office, with his fairness
and his learning he ably carried on the traditions established by James
Kent. J. D. Hammond, *Political History*, vol. ii, p. 213.

[2] E. B. O'Callaghan, " Biographical Sketch of Francis Harison," *N. Y.
Genealogical* and *Biographical Record*, vol. ix, pp. 49-51. This article
notices the descendants of the subject; *N. Y. Civil List*, 1881, p. 240.

had fled to England; but he had regained the public
favor by his kindness and urbanity, spiced just frequently
enough with dashes of sharp wit. When Washington appointed him a federal district attorney, there had been
some who questioned the propriety of calling to official
station one who, however sound in law and scholarship,
had given comfort to the enemy. But the appointment was
defended on the very ground that his Toryism had been so
notorious. It was thought necessary that, if all of this
class were to be won to the support of the new government,
the Federalist party must evince a liberality which might
equal that of Governor Clinton, who, with the coming of the
peace in 1783, had foreborne to execute those drastic laws
which would have banished Loyalists to Nova Scotia.[1] But
Harison was well fitted in many other ways to contribute
to the prestige of the party, and celebrated no less for his
piety and public spirit than for his strong and constant
loyalty to the principles of Federalism, he was often called
upon to make the statement of the party faith in public
meeting.[2]

The eloquent Josiah Ogden Hoffman, who long survived
the others of this company, adding the wisdom of a rich
experience to the councils of the Whigs three decades later,
had also in the War of Independence "lived within the
lines," as the phrase described those loyal to King George.[3]
Although a lawyer of remarkable astuteness, like others of
this Federalist gentry, he was a man of fashion, and, while
deciding cases as recorder of the city, was likewise a court
of last resort in the quiddities of minuets and precedence at

[1] W. A. Duer, *op. cit.*, p. 25.

[2] Morgan Dix, *The Parish of Trinity Church in the City of New
York* (N. Y., 1898-1906), vol. iii, p. 431; *Memorial of St. Mark's
Church in the Bowery* (N. Y., 1899); *N. Y. Evening Post,* March
26, 1807.

[3] Robert Troup to Rufus King, April 4, 1800, *King Correspondence.*

table.[1]   No less adroit than energetic, and always vehement
and voluble, this young beau had early won the lead of the
state assembly and served as Jay's attorney-general until the
hecatomb of office-holders in 1801.[2]   The partner of Hoffman in the practice of the law was a somewhat graver
person, Cadwallader D. Colden, whom the Federalist
Council of Appointment had selected for the state's attorney
for the counties neighboring New York.[3]   He also came
of stock distinguished for its loyalty to the king, for he was
the grandson of that lieutenant governor who, when thrown
into the Ulster jail, desired to be remembered as one who
had opposed "independency with all his might, and wished
to the Lord that his name might be entered on record as
opposed to that matter and be handed down to the latest
posterity." [4]   With the firmness of this venerable grandsire
he had inherited certain of his scientific sympathies which
led him later to the cause of Clinton; but he ranged himself
no less with others of the bar, to carry on the conservative
tradition of the old official class.[5]

Not all the Federalist lawyers were of Tory families.
Colonel Robert Troup, the close associate of the great leaders,[6] is a fair example of those cautious patriots who went

[1] M. A. Hamm, *Famous Families of New York* (N. Y., 1902), vol.
i, pp. 177-178.

[2] J. D. Hammond, *Political History*, vol. i, pp. 80-81.

[3] *N. Y. Civil List*, 1889, p. 506.

[4] A. M. Keys, *Cadwallader Colden* (N. Y., 1906), pp. 358-369; Lorenzo
Sabine, *Biographical Sketches of the Loyalists of the American Revolution With an Historical Essay* (Boston, 1864), vol. i, pp. 328-330; A. C.
Flick, *Loyalism in New York During the American Revolution* (N. Y.,
1901), pp. 19, 212.

[5] See his many letters in the DeWitt Clinton Mss, 1810 *et seq.*; A. C.
Flick, *op. cit.* He was so fair a man, however, that he sometimes won
the support of Tammany Hall.

[6] Jay to Hamilton, August 30, 1798, *Jay Correspondence*; Troup to
Rufus King, *King Correspondence*, vol. iv, pp. 27, 102, 120, 135, etc.;
L. Sabine, *Loyalists*, vol. i, p. 367.

the middle course with Hamilton. He was, like almost all his friends, a zealous churchman,[1] a gentleman in tastes and manners, and a conservative in politics, with small enthusiasm for the spirit of republican institutions.[2] Though called to service by the Federal government as the first district judge in New York state[3] he soon forsook the ermine for the fat fees of the bar, and later settled into a still more lucrative activity as agent for the Pulteney estate in the Seneca region.[4] There he lived for many years, rich and respected, and, though not in public station, an important influence for Federalism in the West.[5] He served his clients not only in the office at Geneva, but perhaps with more effect in the lobbies of the legislature. Here he spent a good part of his time, and, thoroughly acquainted with the customs of the capital, a master of the friendly hint and suave suggestion, he shrewdly helped or hindered legislation that might bear upon his special interest.[6] He was not the last distinguished lawyer thus to spend a winter month in Albany.

Colonel Richard Varick, who had been recorder and then mayor for a dozen years, until swept out in the overturning, was another leading Federalist in his profession.[7] Austere

---

[1] Troup to Bishop Hobart, May 23, 1827, Hobart Correspondence in Morgan Dix, *Trinity Church*, vol. iv, p. 44.

[2] In his letter to King, June 6, 1802, *King Correspondence*, he speaks of "those who do not admire (and I confess myself among the number) the republican system."

[3] He had given valuable help in the propaganda for the Constitution, as a member of the Federal committee of correspondence, J. D. Hammond, *Political History*, vol. i, p. 39.

[4] W. A. Duer, *Reminiscences*, p. 26.

[5] For example his name headed the nomination for presidential electors in 1808, *N. Y. Assembly Journal*, 1808.

[6] Troup to Rufus King, March 12, 1807, etc., *King Correspondence*.

[7] *N. Y. Civil List*, 1882, p. 415.

and lofty in his manner,[1] his tall figure striking in its closely fitting broadcloth breeches, silver-buttoned coat and spotless stock,[2] renowned no less for his philanthropies [3] than for the entertainments in the ball-room of his house on Broadway,[4] he sustained the dignity of the old Federalist directorate and added to the prestige of his class.

The erudite, sententious Egbert Benson [5] was one whose early Federalism had brought about his choice as delegate, with Hamilton, to the conference at Annapolis in 1786.[6] He now saw the long-awaited judgeship on the Federal bench snatched away by Jefferson's refusal to confirm his predecessor's midnight appointees.[7] Benson served his party in the state in many offices and, in the trying days of 1813, was to stand with those in Congress who poured out indigna-

[1] C. H. Hunt, *Life of Edward Livingston*, p. 51.

[2] His portrait by Henry Inman may be seen at No. 6 Bible House, New York City, in the rooms of the American Bible Society, of which he was a founder and supporter.

[3] W. A. Duer, *Reminiscences*, p. 29; J. S. Schuyler, *Institution of the Society of the Cincinnati . . . in New York City* (N. Y., 1886), p. 533.

[4] *Longworth's American Almanac, New York Register, etc.* (N. Y., 1800), p. 362; Walter Barrett (John A. Scoville) *The Old Merchants of New York City* (N. Y., 1863), vol. i, p. 215. This quaint, gossipy miscellany was printed originally, in part, in the columns of the *New York Leader* about the beginning of the Civil War. The papers were collected and republished with additions in book form in 1863 and several subsequent editions (see foreword to vol. II, edition of 1885). Other chapters were added, published and republished until the standard edition of five volumes was issued in 1885. It is an invaluable work of reference, though, naturally, in its comments upon hundreds of old merchants it is not entirely free from inaccuracies.

[5] C. H. Hunt, *Life of Edward Livingston*, p. 52.

[6] See his account of this mission given in an address before the New York Historical Society of which he was the first president, quoted *in extenso* by A. B. Street, *The Council of Revision of the State of New York* (Albany, 1859), pp. 183-184, note.

[7] Troup to Rufus King, April 9, 1802, *King Correspondence*.

tion and contempt upon " Mr. Madison's war." [1] He, too, was a convinced aristocrat who believed that government could best be carried on by the wealth and talent of society for the benefit of the rest.

Besides these leaders full of public honors, there were many barristers whose standing in the law and in society made appropriate their membership in such a party—John Wells, a man whose eloquence and wit enlivened party meetings, and whose learning qualified him as the editor of the *Federalist Papers*, when those essays were prepared for publication; [2] Nathaniel Pendleton, who, after he had stood with Hamilton on the fatal morning of the duel with Burr, rose to prominence in the legislature and on the bench; [3] and John Lawrence, who served as district judge, and as congressman and senator in Washington. [4] And there were younger men who formed opinion under such tuition; Robert Bogardus, for example, still important in the party when forty years had passed, [5] and the Ogdens, David B., the favorite nephew of Gouverneur Morris, and whom the historian Hammond, generally so temperate in praise, recalled as the " gigantic-minded," [6] and his cousin David A.,

[1] J. S. Jenkins, *History of Political Parties in New York State* (Auburn, 1846), pp. 27, 35, 51 *et seq.* This book is largely a summary of Hammond's *Political History* with some additions.

[2] *Memorial of the Life and Character of John Wells* (N. Y., 1874) ; J. D. Hammond, *Political History*, vol. ii, pp. 135-137. David Hosack in his *Memoir of DeWitt Clinton* (N. Y., 1829) says Hamilton, Wells, Emmett and Clinton were the four most accomplished speakers the state had produced, p. 41.

[3] Appleton, vol. iv, p. 729.

[4] *N. Y. Civil List*, 1889, pp. 598, 603, 628.

[5] General Bogardus was grand marshal at the obsequies of President Harrison in 1841.

[6] Morris, *Diary and Letters*, vol. i,, pp. 549 *et seq.*; J. D. Hammond, *Political History*, vol. ii, p. 480. Were it not too tedious, of course, the roll could reach much further.

whom we shall trace far to the north. Of those who practiced at the bar of the metropolis in the first years of the nineteenth century, small though their number was, the chief part of the talent, which commanded large well-paying patronage, was exerted in the Federalist cause.

Although the actual administration of this party, as well as the public business, was for the most part then, as well as now, left to the skill of the distinguished lawyers, the weight of its support was largely borne by wealthy merchants; we have it on the best authority that the great majority of those extensively engaged in trade a hundred years ago were numbered on its rolls.[1] As one glances over the array of names upon a party ticket, for example that of 1806, and pauses to refresh the somewhat faded memory of these old-time worthies, he soon perceives a certain balance in the interests of the bar and of business.[2] Of the two men named for Congress, one was Nicholas Fish, the banker,[3] and the other, John B. Coles, a flour merchant with large ventures over-seas, who had as alderman for six years represented the wealth and aristocracy of the old first ward.[4] As candidates for the assembly one finds lawyers like Judge Benson, William Henderson and J. O. Hoffman, but their order was not left exclusively to represent the party; there are the names of Selah Strong, who had been alderman for the third ward, and dispensed advice upon the law along with bales and barrels of more material commodities at his Front Street warehouse,[5] Wynant Van

---

[1] Barrett, *Old Merchants*, vol. i, p. 81.

[2] See in *N. Y. Commercial Advertiser*, April 21, 1806.

[3] Barrett, vol. iii, pp. 138-139.

[4] *Ibid.*, vol. ii, pp. 41-45, 68-71, 321; W. G. Davis, " New York in 1801 " in *Views of Early New York* (N. Y., 1904); L. H. Weeks, *Prominent Families of New York* (N. Y., 1898), p. 35. The candidates for the state senate were not residents of New York city.

[5] Barrett, vol. i, pp. 365, 366.

Zandt, another influential merchant who had sat among the city fathers,[1] and John Townsend, an ironmonger with branch stores in Albany.[2] The chairman of the meeting which had made the nominations was John B. Dash, important in the hardware trade,[3] and the secretary, Robert Cheeseborough, was likewise eminent in business.[4]

It was the custom of the time that a ticket so brought forth in public meeting should be recommended to the voters by a long address subscribed by gentlemen of standing in the party. Cornelius Ray, whose name begins the list in 1806, was, perhaps the foremost financier of New York state; for the president of the local branch of the Bank of the United States, and likewise for a term of many years, of the chamber of commerce in the city, was a person of commanding influence.[5] Such a dignitary might well be selected as a proper representative of Federalism, and he was often called upon to serve as chairman at the party meetings.[6] Next comes the name of General Matthew Clarkson, who for almost an entire generation was the president of the Bank of New York, a friendly rival institution, whose principal directors for the most part, like those who served with Ray, were in political agreement with their chief.[7] Clarkson was a man of consequence within the circle of Hamilton and King and Morris, while

---

[1] Barrett, vol. v, p. 243.

[2] *Ibid.*, vol. ii, p. 135.

[3] *Ibid.*, vol. i, pp. 181-183.

[4] *Ibid.*, vol. i, pp. 331, 441.

[5] *Ibid.*, vol. v, p. 40; *Longworth's American Almanac, New York Register, etc.*, 1807, p. 63; 1810, p. 62; 1811, p. 11 *et seq.*

[6] *N. Y. Commercial Advertiser*, April 25, 1806; April 1807, *Albany Gazette*, April 4, 1808, *N. Y. Evening Post*, April 28, 1809, April 16, 1813, *etc.*

[7] See ms. notes on a petition for a St. Lawrence-Champlain Canal, Flagg Mss. (Miscellaneous papers) N. Y. Public Library; *Appleton's Cyclopedia of American Biography*, vol. i, supplement, p. 797; Barrett, vol. i, pp. 270-274; vol. v, p. 40.

his generosity in time and money had made him by a wider world admired and beloved as an edifying example of the fine solicitude which the rich might sometimes exercise in the interest of the poor.[1] Closely following is Isaac Sebring, whose extensive shipping business, as we shall see, did not exhaust the ingenuity and enterprise he loved to bring to bear upon his problems as a party manager.[2] Next is John B. Murray, whose captains trading in the Orient brought back their cargoes of rare and staple teas to increase his fortune. Like others of his station, in the 'thirties he will still be found engaged against the might and strategy of Tammany as alderman for the fifteenth ward, the northern stronghold of his party.[3] Fifth on the list is Archibald Gracie, whose ventures touched in every harbor of the world,[4] a proper member of a company that enrolled such names as Sherred, Minturn, Hone, Le Roy, to pick almost at random, all famous in the annals of the city's trade.[5]

But if those whose business was to fit out ships and barter goods at auction, had found expression of their ideas in the policies of Hamilton, the same was still more true of those who won their fortunes in the skilful management of that less tangible, symbolic wealth of paper, of dividends and mortgage bonds, and those uncertain rights and values so ineptly named securities. Among the presidents of banks, there were not only Ray and Clarkson and Nicholas Fish, twice named for lieutenant governor and several times for

[1] Morris, *Diary and Letters*, vol. ii, p. 458; W. W. Spooner, *Historic Families of America* (N. Y., 1908), vol. iii, pp. 282-284; *The Clarksons of New York* (N. Y., 1875) ; Barrett, vol. i, p. 296.

[2] Barrett, vol. iv, pp. 18-20; and *infra*, ch. iv.

[3] *Ibid.*, vol. i, p. 292; vol. ii, p. 107; vol. v, pp. 190-191.

[4] *Ibid.*, dedication to vol. ii, p. 5.

[5] *Ibid.*, vol. iii, p. 65; vol. iv, pp. 151, 242; vol. iv, pp. 240-244; vol. ii, pp. 160-162.

the assembly,[1] but Henry Remsen, Oliver Wolcott, Varick and Verplanck, who were ranked as party leaders at the beginning of the century.[2] Likewise in this list of 1806 are names of brokers like Nicholas Low[3] and presidents of insurance companies like Gabriel Furman and Elisha Tibbits (who were now and then put up for members of the legislature), Charles McEvers, Frederic DePeyster and William W. Woolsey.[4] It is evident that the wealthy merchants of New York were strongly Federalist. For example, if one foregathered with them in the Tontine Coffee House, which served as the city stock exchange as well as tavern,[5] he would have found in 1801 that four of five trustees of that important institution were members of the party, and even this small minority of one was to be swept away at the next election which brought in a unanimous board.[6] Or if one visited the more ambitious and elaborate merchants' exchange built in later years, he would have seen

[1] Barrett, vol. iii, p. 229; J. D. Hammond, *Political History*, vol. i, p. 294.

[2] See mss. note on petition for St. Lawrence-Champlain Canal, *supra*; Barrett, vol. ii, pp. 10-13; vol. v, 254-255. Gulian Verplanck was the father of Johnston Verplanck and the uncle of Gulian C. Verplanck, both of whom will figure in these pages.

[3] *King Correspondence*, vol. v, p. 40.

[4] Ms. note, *supra*; *N. Y. Commercial Advertiser*, April 21, 1806; Barrett, vol. i, p. 383; vol. ii, p. 266; L. H. Weeks, *Prominent Families of New York*, p. 220.

[5] John Lambert, *Travels Through Canada and the United States of America in the Years 1806, 1807, 1808* (London, 1815), vol. ii, pp. 55 et seq. "An English traveller, who visited New York in 1794, writes that: The Tontine Tavern and Coffee House is a large brick building; you ascend six or eight steps under a portico, into a large public room which is the Stock Exchange of New York, where all bargains are made. Here are two books kept, as at Lloyds of every ship's arrival and clearing out." It remained the stock exchange for many years, W. H. Bayles, *Old Taverns of New York* (N. Y., 1915), pp. 360-361.

[6] Abram Wakeman, *History and Reminiscences of Lower Wall Street and Vicinity* (N. Y., 1914), pp. 55-63.

enshrined within the place of honor in the great rotunda, the statue of Alexander Hamilton.[1]   In such resorts as these the Sage of Monticello was not mentioned with respect. There was still a merchants' party just as there had been before the Revolutionary War.[2]   These men of business did not think themselves discharged from public duty when they had set their names to an address.   As one fingers over the old directories the names appear again as aldermen; Philip Brasher, Samuel M. Hopkins, Peter Mesier, Nicholas Fish, John Slidell and others are recorded as the representatives of the first four wards, in the opening decades of the nineteenth century.[3]

In 1801 the city had over-reached the mark of sixty thousand and stretched northward from the Battery somewhat beyond a mile to the partly wooded hills that sloped back from the Collect or Fresh-water Pond.[4]   The picturesque old names of Out-Ward, Dock-Ward and Montgomerie's had passed into memory and the wards, now simply numbered, were seven in all, reckoning from the south.[5]   There was no Hadrian's Wall that ran through Reade Street from the Hudson to the Park and through Chatham and Catharine to East River, to set the pale of civilization, but the assessor's figures and electoral returns could furnish evidence that somewhere near those streets

[1] W. A. Pelletreau, *Early New York Houses* (N. Y., 1901), p. 22.

[2] C. L. Becker, *History of Political Parties in the Province of New York, 1760-1776* (Madison, 1909), p. 116.

[3] J. F. Jones, *New York Mercantile and General Directory* (N. Y., 1805) ; Elliott & Crissey, *New York Directory*, 1811; D. Longworth, *American Almanac, New York Register and City Directory*, 1801, 1802, 1803, 1805, 1807, 1808.

[4] *A New and Accurate Map of the City of New York in the State of New York in North America*, N. Y., *1797* (New York Public Library). Cf. *Plan of the City of New York*, 1791, in D. T. Valentine's *Manual of the Corporation of the City of New York* (N. Y., 1851), for scale.

[5] J. F. Jones, *op. cit.*, pp. 111-113, for boundaries.

there was a barrier, no less present because it was invisible, which, speaking with the standards of this world, marked off the " better " from the " worse." [1]   And within this favored southern half itself, as one walked toward the Battery, there steadily increased and multiplied all those signs of affluence that flowed from business.   Likewise one remarked the aspect of refinement and prestige which that affluence in part maintained, until with the stately houses by the side of Bowling Green one reached the very sacred inner court of New York gentility.[2]   These mansions with their pilasters and porticos were known as " Quality Row," [3] and in their simple grace made a pleasant background for the fashionable promenade flanked by the greensward and the flower-beds of this old park.[4]

But the aristocratic quarter of the town included other streets near by, extended up Broadway and to the Pearl Street region, north and east.[5]   It is interesting to observe

[1] *Cf.* wards in D. Longworth's *Actual Map and Comparative Plans Showing 88 Years' Growth of the City of New York* (N. Y., 1817), and in L. A. Risse, *New York in 1800* (N. Y., 1900).

[2] Spencer Trask, *Bowling Green* (N. Y., 1898), pp. 41-46; W. A. Duer, *New York as It Was, During the Latter Part of the Last Century,* an address before the St. Nicholas Society, (N. Y., 1849), pp. 11-12, *notes.*

[3] See drawings in Emmett Collection (N. Y. Public Library), and W. A. Pelletreau, *Early New York Houses*, p. 217.

[4] J. M. Mathews, *Recollections of Persons and Events* (selections from his journal, N. Y., 1865), p. 26; Washington Irving and others, *Salmagundi Papers*, no. xii, Saturday, June 27, 1807; A. C. Dayton, *Last Days of Knickerbocker Life* (N. Y., 1897), ch. ii.

[5] " The aristocratic quarter for residences at this period [the opening of the century] was Whitehall, Beaver, Broad, Water, and Pearl Streets, and the lower part of Broadway.   Cherry, Roosevelt, Oak, Madison, Oliver, Harman (East Broadway) and Market Streets were occupied by many people of position and fortune."   C. H. Haswell, *Reminiscences of an Octogenarian, 1816-1860* (N. Y., 1896), pp. 13-14, 21-25; Stephen Jenkins, *The Greatest Street in the World, The Story of Old Broadway, etc.* (N. Y., 1911), p. 43; List of Houses and Lots, valued at £1000

that this was the section which with monotonous fidelity returned its Federalist members to the board of aldermen and the legislature of the state,[1] until about the middle of the 'forties when it became "the test of gentility to live above Bleecker." [2] The fourth ward was less wealthy than its neighbors to the south and east, and became less regular, though even this was still to be relied upon in any party crisis; but with the growth of the city another ward came to take its place. Even before 1800 the gentry about the Green, those few of them who had their carriages,[3] had occasionally driven out to visit country friends who lived more spaciously among their groves and orchards, their gardens and cow pastures, in the open reaches of the farmland.[4] These suburban residences, some of them of great cost and dignity,[5] grew in number and filled in the meadows toward the Hudson, each new resident content with fewer acres. In 1805, when some readjustments were in process in districting the upper sections of the city, a new ward was created, the ninth, which took in the remainder to the north.[6] This region also for the next quarter of a century though not populous, was fairly constant in the balance against the

and over in 1799, J. G. Wilson, *Memorial History of the City of New York*, vol. iii, pp. 150-152; J. F. Mines, *A Tour Around New York, and My Summer Acre, Being the Recreations of Mr. Felix Oldboy* (N. Y., 1893), pp. 124-127.

[1] For example, *N. Y. Evening Post*, November 18, 1801, April 30, 1802, April 28, 1803; *N. Y. Spectator*, April 29, 1804, etc.

[2] W. A. Pelletreau, *Early New York Houses*, p. 78.

[3] *Appleton's Cyclopedia of National Biography*, article Herman LeRoy.

[4] Charles King, *Progress of the City of New York During the Last Fifty Years* (N. Y., 1852), pp. 6-8.

[5] List of Houses and Lots, etc. Wilson, *loc. cit.*; William L. Stone (Jr.), *History of New York City* (N. Y., 1872), p. 319.

[6] *Cf.* Map of city in 1804, D. T. Valentine's *Manual*, 1849, with J. F. Jones, *Directory*, etc., 1805, p. 116.

democrats who made their homes in the less lovely purlieus of " the Swamp." [1] From this rehearsal it is plainly to be seen that those districts, where wealth and social standing made their citizens anxious to encourage commerce upon the one hand and to conserve the old traditions of a ruling class upon the other, were, as should reasonably have been expected, found upon the side of Jay and Morris and Van Rensselaer.

Another source of power in supporting the tradition of strong government was the Episcopal Church, whose clergy in the trying days before the war had met the cry for armed rebellion with the stern and certain doctrine that God had stablished states and commanded the obedience of peoples to authority.[2] The sentiment and preaching of the

[1] In 1806 the Fourth Ward is missing from the Federalist column; in 1809 the Ninth Ward is added to it, *N. Y. Spectator*, May 6, 1807, November 23, 1809, May 1, 1812, etc. The following table from the *Census of the Electors and Total Population of the City and County of New York*, pamphlet (N. Y., 1807), p. 5, giving the ratio of the two may serve, under qualified suffrage, as an index of the intensity of wealth:

Wards	Inhabitants	Electors
1st	7,954	1,086
2nd	7,551	1,042
3rd	7,709	1,118
4th	9,236	1,331
5th	12,739	1,901
6th	9,861	1,421
7th	19,487	3,140
8th	6,067	1,023
9th	2,926	339

The small number of electors in the Federalist ninth ward were owners of considerable property; it usually returned the smallest Federalist majority, see *N. Y. Herald*, May 2, 1810.

[2] Dr. Myles Cooper, *The American Querist* (N. Y., 1774), queries 90-100; A. C. Flick, *Loyalism in New York During the Revolution*, p. 9, note; and the pamphlets of Bishop Samuel Seabury and the Reverend T. B. Chandler.

church had been deeply loyal, and it was not surprising that when news reached New York that the fateful step of separation had been taken, Trinity parish had been torn with bitter strife, and that many, if not most, of its influential members had taken ship for Nova Scotia when the British troops departed from the city,[1] or stayed behind in a precarious hope of toleration at the hands of the new government. If republics, according to the ancient proverb, were ungrateful, perhaps (and the outcome justified the trust) they might not be vindictive. The Whig Episcopalians to whom fell the conduct of the parish, and in consequence, perhaps a controlling influence in the church of New York state, had differed from the rest of the communion as to the right of independence, but they were little less opposed to any deep and sudden change in the powers of the state. It was an article of faith that the mandates of the civil power should be obeyed, without the church assuming responsibility for their righteousness. A republic it might be, but subjects should be taught obedience and support to those whom Providence had called to government. Years had not stayed the force of Hooker's stern injunction:

Sometimes it pleaseth God himself by special appointment to choose out and nominate such as to whom dominion shall be given, which thing he did often in the commonwealth of Israel. They who in this sort receive power have it immediately from God, by mere divine right; they by human, on whom the same is bestowed according to men's discretion, when they are left free by God to make choice of their own governor. By which of these means soever it happen that kings or governors be advanced unto their states, we must acknowledge

[1] M. Dix, *Trinity Church*, vol. i, ch. xxiii, and vol. ii, ch. i; Flick, *op. cit.*, p. 36 (an obviously exaggerated statement); and *United Empire Loyalist Convention* (Toronto, 1884), p. 110.

both their lawful choice to be approved of God, and themselves to be God's lieutenants, and confess their power His.[1]

Robert Troup, one of the committee that brought the parish through the war, could understand the soundness of such teaching. The more he saw of the progress of Jacobinism in his state, he wrote to King long after, the more he realized the need of setting up a college for the training of the clergy of his church, and it was this impulse that urged his interest and support in the founding of the institution at Geneva.[2]

It was not surprising that the clergy beheld with apprehension the ominous rise of Jefferson; for not only had he beaten down the power of the establishment in Virginia,[3] but of late there had grown up a cult of deism around this bold profaner of the sacred word, who applied the gauge of human reason to the inspired history of Genesis and criticized the accounts of the creation and the deluge.[4] It is possible that like their Calvinist neighbors to the eastward they deemed this rather liberal Unitarian little better than an atheist. In their consciences they no doubt shared the awful anger of the Congregational ministers who from their pulpits thundered wrath upon "the Jereboam who drave Israel from following the Lord, and made them sin a great sin;"[5] yet they never acquired the political influence claimed and exercised by these leaders of New England.

[1] Richard Hooker, *Of the Laws of Ecclesiastical Polity* (1665), bk. viii, ch. ii, verse 5; (N. Y., 1845), vol. ii, p. 228.

[2] R. Troup to R. King, June 1, 1807, *King Correspondence*.

[3] Thomas Jefferson, *Works* (Ford edition), vol. i, p. 52, and *Notes on Religion*, *ibid.*, vol. ii, p. 95.

[4] Jefferson to Charles Thomson, 1786, *ibid.*, vol. iv, p. 338, and *Notes on Virginia*, *ibid.*, vol. iii, p. 116-118.

[5] Henry Adams, *History of the United States* (N. Y., 1889), vol. i, p. 80; H. S. Randall, *The Life of Thomas Jefferson* (N. Y., 1858), vol. ii, pp. 648-652.

With Episcopalians Mr. Jefferson might be wrong in his opinions but he was President; with the eastern clergy he might be President but he was a vicious and a pestilent man. Massachusetts had been founded as an ecclesiastical experiment. It was a place where those who worshipped rightly might worship undisturbed, but the clergy with their knowledge of the Scriptures were expected to make clear the ways and means by which this might be accomplished. John Calvin himself had declared that the function of the state was merely to produce conditions under which the ministers might work out the ideal commonwealth of the elect, and thus they were regarded to be oracles above the civil law.[1] The absolute authority of these early days of sainthood had dropped away somewhat, but still the ministers were expected, now and then, to give suggestions to the state, and in the crisis precipitated by the change of 1801 they made a stubborn fight to preserve their influence.

With the Episcopal divines the case was different. The Erastian tradition of their church deterred them from too active meddling in affairs of state, and though personally favorable to Federalism, as no doubt their order was, they put forth no pamphlet fulminations against the lawful government and undertook no prominent rôle in party contests. The contrast in theory was sharp; in New England the clergy were responsible for the state, the New York Episcopalians responsible to it; while the battle raged between the former and the arch-blasphemer at Washington, the latter confined their active work in politics to the ballot on election day. Yet, as we shall see in the city and elsewhere in the state, the Episcopal Church was a quiet stronghold of the "decency-and-order" party, and a parish vestry might easily adjourn from talking about tithes and charities, to have its

[1] *Institutes of Christian Theology* (edition of 1539), bk. i, chs. vii, viii; bk. iv, chs. viii, ix, x.

members meet again in some neighboring long-room as a Federalist caucus.

The influence of Columbia College in this respect must not be neglected. To its foundation half a century before, Trinity parish had contributed a tract of land with the understanding that the president of the new institution was ever afterward to be a member of the Episcopal communion,[1]—a provision which was incorporated in the college charter and ever afterwards observed. Under Dr. Cooper[a] and his fellow teachers, the college had taught loyalty to the king, and after it assumed the name Columbia it was far from the extreme in its preaching of new doctrines. Liberty it certainly expounded, but its fraternity savored of benevolence, and equality was not commended. The trustees, among whom Federalism was almost unanimous, kept an anxious eye upon the teaching; when a president was sought, Alexander Hamilton, in some inquiries, made it clear "that his politics must be of the right sort." [2] Of the four great Federalist leaders of the state three were its sons, and the fourth, Rufus King, a trustee for eighteen years.[3] After speaking of such men as these and Robert Troup and Egbert Benson, an early historian of the college goes on to say: "The foremost lawyers at the bar, and jurists on the bench of our State and city, and in the United States courts, have been among the alumni of Columbia; such as— to select a few names not before enumerated: Harison, Jones, Ogden, Hoffman, Wells, Robinson, Lawrence," [4]

[1] J. H. Van Amringe and others, *History of Columbia College* (N. Y., 1904), pp. 84, 97; M. Dix, *Trinity Church*, vol. i, p. 280; and the interesting letter of Dr. J. M. Mason to Rufus King, February 10, 1810, *King Correspondence*.

[2] Hamilton to James A. Bayard, August 6, 1800, *Hamilton's Writings* (Lodge), vol. viii, pp. 559-560.

[3] W. A. Jones, "The First Century of Columbia College," *Knickerbocker Magazine*, February, 1863.   [4] *Ibid.*

[a] Dr. Myles Cooper (1737?-1785), second president of King's College, now Columbia University, and an active loyalist who was forced to flee to England during the American Revolution.

which, with the exception of Beverly Robinson, who, as a Tory, was obliged to change his residence to Nova Scotia,[1] almost calls the roll of the important Federalists practicing at law in New York city. This tradition was to be continued under the presidencies of two leading Federalists and Whigs, William A. Duer and Charles King; it long remained a " family college" for old New Yorkers who cherished the memory of Hamilton, Morris and Jay.

[1] E. Ryerson, *The Loyalists of America and Their Times* (Toronto, 1880), vol. ii, pp. 197-198.

CHAPTER II

POLITICS AND PREJUDICE THROUGHOUT THE COUNTRYSIDE

ALTHOUGH Federalism had flourished chiefly in the city of New York, there were other sections of the state, where, as in those which centered in Albany and Hudson, it was the ruling philosophy of politics. The influence of old families like the Schuylers and Van Rensselaers, reinforced by the economic power of the wealthy merchants who moved across from Massachusetts and Connecticut, persisted in unquestioned strength long after the prestige of the aristocracy in the metropolis had been challenged and reduced.[1] Albany had recently been made the permanent capital of the state,[2] and though it boasted then but five thousand people, it was destined partly through this dignity to add an extra thousand every year for many decades.[3] In 1801, however, it was a third or fourth rate town, as a captious chronicler declared, penned in upon its hills by endless thickets of pine, and "indeed Dutch, in all its moods and tenses; thoroughly and inveterately Dutch."[4] The old fam-

[1] *Cf.* O. G. Libby, *The Geographical Distribution of the Vote of the Thirteen States on the Federal Constitution*, p. 18, for the vote in 1788.

[2] In 1797; A. J. Parker (editor), *Landmarks of Albany County* (Syracuse, 1897), p. 301.

[3] See table in Joel Munsell's notes to G. A. Worth, *Random Recollections of Albany*, 1800-1808, p. 20. These interesting reminiscences were first published in Albany, 1849, soon followed by a second edition in 1850 entitled *Random Recollections, etc. With Some Additional Matter*, the large appendix being recollections of Hudson. In 1866 Munsell published the work referring to Albany with copious notes, in large and small paper editions.

[4] *Ibid.*, pp. 20, 27.

31

ilies gained their income largely from their spacious holdings granted in the years gone by, and, in their leisure, they were not averse to taking part in the political contests of the day.[1] The venerable General Philip Schuyler, of whose services to Federalism we shall speak again, was soon to make over to his heirs his home and his six thousand acres.[2] Shattered by the shock of the tragic death of one son-in-law, the admired Hamilton, he sank into a decrepitude that found a speedy end in death, leaving the leadership of the Dutch aristocracy to another daughter's husband, Stephen Van Rensselaer, called by universal courtesy, the Patroon.[3]

This new leader in society and politics was, at the beginning of the nineteenth century, the richest man in New York state,[5] and the largest landlord in the country, with his scores of square miles parceled out on leasehold tenure, yielding a large income from the rents and quarter-sales.[6] He had been elected to the first assembly summoned under the new Federal Constitution, two years later had been pro-

---

[1] *Random Recollections of Albany*, pp. 42-49.

[2] C. Reynolds, *Albany Chronicle* (Albany, 1906), p. 396; O. Tilghman, *Memoir of Lt. Col. Tench Tilghman* (Albany, 1876), p. 23.

[3] B. J. Lossing, *The Life and Times of Philip Schuyler* (N. Y., 1860), vol. ii, pp. 474-475; Bayard Tuckerman, *Life of General Philip Schuyler* (N. Y., 1904), pp. 269-271. Schuyler died November 18, 1804. Since lordships, manors, etc., were abolished by the legislature of the new government just before Stephen Van Rensselaer became of age, he could not with accuracy be called the sixth lord of the manor or the eighth patroon. Although local custom gave the title of patroon to others like the Knickerbockers and the Van der Heydens, when used alone it was always understood to refer to Van Rensselaer. See G. W. Schuyler, *Colonial New York* (N. Y., 1885), vol. i, pp. 227-231; John Woodworth, *Reminiscences of Troy from its Settlement in 1790 to 1807* (Albany, 1860; published first in pamphlet form in 1853), pp. 90-93; and A. J. Weise, *Troy's One Hundred Years* (Troy, 1891), p. 23.

[4] Henry Adams, *History of the United States*, vol. i, p. 27.

[5] E. P. Cheyney, *The Anti-Rent Agitation in the State of New York* (Philadelphia, 1887).

moted to a quadrennial term in the senate of the state, and had then served six years as lieutenant-governor. In the spring of 1801 the Federalist party had rallied with genuine enthusiasm to make him governor, but to no avail. The influence he wielded in the party both before and after this first disappointment was, as we shall see, not unconnected with his power as landlord, but his reputation as a man was such as to draw the homage of men's hearts. Even in relations with his tenantry he was generous to a fault;[1] courteous and affable in manner, with an habitual expression of kindness and good will in language and in countenance that seemed never to forsake him,[2] he seemed the blameless model of the old nobility that would have pleased Lord Chesterfield[a] or Mr. Lecky.[b] For he added to these personal attractions, a sound judgment and a character that marked him within the Dutch church and without as one of highest standards of morality.[3] He was a gallant champion to whom the partisans of the rule of aristocracy could point with comfortable pride.

Beside him in the leadership of the old Dutch families stood Abraham Van Vechten, descended from a lesser landed squire.[4] He was a fine "specimen of a class he loved to represent. If he was somewhat heavy in appearance

---

[1] G. W. Schuyler, *op. cit.*, vol. i, pp. 227-231; S. W. Rosendale, " Closing Phases of the Manorial System in Albany," *Proceedings of the New York State Historical Association*, vol. viii, p. 243. It was his leniency which produced the long accounts whose claims in enforcement brought on the Anti-Rent troubles after his death in 1839, see Cheyney, *op. cit.*

[2] J. M. Mathews, *Recollections of Persons and Events*, p. 69.

[3] *Ibid.*, p. 70.

[4] L. H. Weeks, *Prominent Families of New York*, p. 592. He was not graduated from King's College as erroneously stated in A. J. Parker, *Landmarks of Albany County*, part i, pp. 147-148, and G. R. Howell and J. Tenney, *History of the County of Albany* (N. Y., 1886), p. 133; cf. *Catalogue of Officers and Graduates of Columbia University* (N. Y., 1912).

[a] Philip Dormer Stanhope, 4th Earl of Chesterfield (1694-1773), an English statesman, orator and writer, best known as the author of a series of letters to his son designed to instruct the young man in his education.

[b] William Edward Hartpole Lecky (1838-1903), English historian

and slow in his movements, he had all the staid solidity and strength which marked the Hollanders in their best days, and he never appeared either in public or private without commanding universal respect." [1]   He refused an appointment to the bench tendered to him, while yet young in practice, by Governor Jay, but during the first two decades of the century he spent a part of nearly every year in the senate or the assembly, finding joy in fighting for his Federalist principles.[2]   It was in accord with the conservatism of his well-to-do constituents that by argument and vote in the convention of 1821, he gave all his support to the dictum of Chancellor Kent, "that to the beneficence and liberality of those who have property, we owe all the embellishments and the comforts and the blessings of life." [3]   Logical in reasoning and eloquent in speech, famous for his faith in old theories of government by men of wealth and social standing, no less than for his mordant sarcasm in attacks upon the new, he held an independent course quite to the last and scoffed at the intrigues by which his party sought to play with factions of the enemy.[4]   Supported by such strong lieutenants as Johan Jost Dietz,[5] Dirck Ten Broeck,[6] Hermanus Bleecker,[7] and Colonel James Van Schoon-

[1] J. M. Mathews, *op. cit.*, p. 71.

[2] Howell and Tenney, *op. cit.*, p. 133; Munsell's notes to G. A. Worth, *Random Recollections*, pp. 61-63; *N. Y. Civil List*, 1889, pp. 374-377, 420-424.

[3] J. D. Hammond, *Political History*, vol. ii, pp. 21, 30.

[4] D. S. Alexander, *Political History of the State of New York*, vol. i, pp. 168-169; J. S. Jenkins, *Political Parties*, p. 199. See especially his speeches after the Van Ness charge, January 26, 1820, as reported in the *Albany Daily Register*.

[5] *N. Y. Civil List*, 1889, pp. 416-422, J. S. Jenkins, *op. cit.*, p. 59.

[6] *Civil List*, pp. 415-418, and Jenkins, p. 64.

[7] *Civil List*, pp. 424-425, and Bleecker to Rufus King, February 16, 1816, *King Correspondence*.

whose *History of England in the Eighteenth Century* (8 vols., 1878-1890) is a classic in its field but which reflects the author's distrust of democratic reforms.

hoven,[1] he showed how the Dutch aristocracy could join hands with the merchants in New York to oppose the party of the artisan and little farmer.[2] Through Albany, Rensselaer and Columbia counties, the wealthier of the old stock were Federalist in politics.

The Dutch, however, were not left in undisputed sway within these upper river counties. In 1790 in Albany there were not more than five New England families,[3] but in the following decade the westward movement set in from Massachusetts and Connecticut, and "the detested word *improvement* was on every lip," for the New Englanders brought in an enterprising, innovating spirit and set about buying and selling to such purpose that many merchants made their fortunes. These men, for the most part, reared in Federalism near the sea-coast, attached themselves again to the party now under Van Rensselaer and Van Vechten.[4] Yet this alliance was not made without some swallowing of old resentments, as the easterners brought with them an ancient jealousy of all things Dutch.

Throughout their home-land thirty years before, there had broadly spread a conviction that the Dutch New Yorkers who laid claim to the Hampshire grants beyond the proper bounds of Lake Champlain were something less than honest, and old prejudices had been renewed and deepened in the last days of the colonies; it was this feeling which had, in part, brought on the bickerings of the Revolutionary officers and the undeserved disgrace of

---

[1] *Civil List*, pp. 367, 373-375, 412, 413, and Jenkins, p. 84.

[2] Compare the list of 220 signers of a Federalist petition in the *Albany Gazette*, April 18, 1808, with a similar list of Republicans in the *Albany Argus*, April 9, 1813. The Yates family were an exception to the rule.

[3] Munsell's notes to Worth, *Random Recollections*, p. 33.

[4] Worth, pp. 42-44.

General Schuyler.[1]   The antagonism had survived and often-times the feeling was expressed with hearty emphasis.   A politician recently arrived in the Mohawk valley, was asked how starting with a Yankee one could make a Dutchman. "Break his jaw and knock his brains out," was the quick rejoinder; and when asked how a Dutchman could be made a Yankee, he retorted with as little hesitation, "Can't do it, sir; ain't stock enough." [2]   There were some of these New England Federalists who were induced with difficulty, if at all, to concur in the nominations of the Patroon,[3] but as the leaders grew in consciousness of common interest, these differences were composed, so that the party was finally pitted in full strength against the party of the mechanics, already recognized as such, at the beginning of the century, and led by Benjamin Knower.[4]   However this adjustment was accomplished, Albany and Rensselaer have, from that day to this, been ranged in opposition to the forces led by the sachems and the chiefs of Tammany Hall.

In the region about Troy much the same conditions pre-vailed.   When New York was still New Netherland, certain

[1] B. J. Lossing, *Life and Times of Philip Schuyler*, vol. i, pp. 198-203; vol. ii, chs. xvi and xvii; Bayard Tuckerman, *Life of General Philip Schuyler*, pp. 223 et seq.; G. W. Schuyler, *Correspondence and Remarks upon Bancroft's History of the Northern Campaign of 1777, and the Character of General Philip Schuyler* (N. Y., 1867), p. 25.

[2] M. M. Bagg, *The Pioneers of Utica* (Utica, 1877), p. 64.

[3] "There is a knot of Jacobins at Albany among the federalists, formed of New England people (of which our friend Lovel is I be-lieve one) as opposed to the Dutchman, who have been able to prevent the nomination of the patroon for a member of assembly, to which he had consented merely because he thought it might bring out more gov-ernor votes at the Election. It was this factious view that nominated Southwick as a federal Senator." Wm. Coleman to Rufus King, April 16, 1816, *King Correspondence*.   The name "Jacobins" here seems merely an abusive epithet.

[4] G. A. Worth, *Random Recollections*, pp. 50-52.

pioneers with the consent of the Van Rensselaers had purchased lands from the Mohegan Indians, eastward from the town of Beverwyck, now Albany.[1] The country lying somewhat off the lines of travel was but slowly settled, until, near the beginning of the eighteenth century, much of it fell into the possession of two notable Dutch families, the Van der Heydens and the Knickerbockers, who, though simply landlords, and, indeed, at one time holding only under lease, were commonly styled patroons.[2] With their large holdings, like their neighbors across the Hudson, these landed families gave their support to the conservative party. In 1801 young Herman Knickerbocker, then in his early twenties, was coming into prominence and, being "possessed of wealth and great personal influence, he was soon chosen to fill important offices." He was elected to Congress and then to the legislature where, hailed by all as the Prince of Schaghticoke, like Van Rensselaer and Van Vechten he represented the old caste. "Bred from his childhood to association with some of the most distinguished Men of an Age remarkable for its high-toned Courtesy, and to the Controul of a large family of Slaves, his Manners acquired the blending of Suavity with Dignity peculiar to those accustomed to early Intercourse with the World, and the early Habit of Command." It is not surprising that

---

[1] A. J. Weise, *History of the City of Troy* (Troy, 1876), pp. 8-11.

[2] Derick Van der Heyden purchased in 1707, *ibid.*, p. 14, and Johannis Knickerbocker in 1709; John Woodworth, *Reminiscences of Troy from its Settlement in 1790 to 1807*, p. 91, note. The name was originally spelled Knickerbacker, but Washington Irving's orthography made up in popular acceptance what it lacked in historical accuracy and is not now to be gainsaid. The second edition of Woodworth's *Reminiscences* (here cited) contains the valuable notes of Joel Munsell and others. Judge Woodworth was competent to write of political life, having held a variety of offices from loan commissioner in 1792 to justice of the supreme court of the state; see A. B. Street, *Council of Revision of the State of New York*, pp. 196-198.

such men from their land offices and family seats exerted influence for Federalism.[1]

As in Albany, however, the Dutch aristocracy were obliged, with better or worse grace, to welcome immigrants who came across the Berkshires. As soon as the settlement of Van der Heyden's Ferry grew into a village and in 1789 took the name of Troy, homeseekers of the better class, largely from the middle parts of Massachusetts, made their appearance, building shops and bringing in commercial habits that transformed it into a thriving town.[2] The more important of these newcomers were Federalists in politics, and their success in merchandising confirmed their old allegiance to the party of the creditor; all or nearly all the larger merchants of Troy and Lansingburgh, near by, were of this party. George Tibbits, who came in from Rhode Island and who became the wealthiest among this class, was for a quarter of a century the political leader of the county, relying always on the strong support of his fellow men of business.[3] In 1801, then, the power had been wholly in their hands for more than a decade, and though overwhelmed at the next election, they soon regained control with fair continuance, and with the help of the farmers who traded with them, gave the Rensselaer region a rather firmly fixed political character.

To this, however, there was set no county boundary. In

[1] Woodworth, p. 85 (notes), pp. 91-93; A. J. Weise, *op. cit.*, p. 16, ch. ii, and *Troy's One Hundred Years*, pp. 21-26. For more detailed description of the ancient splendor of the Knickerbockers, see W. B. Van Alstyne, " The Knickerbocker Family," in *N. Y. Genealogical and Biographical Record*, vols. xxxix and xl; *Knickerbocker Magazine*, vol. i, p. 1 *et seq.*, and vol. xl, p. 1 *et seq.*; and particularly General E. C. Viele, " The Knickerbockers of New York Two Centuries Ago," *Harpers' New Monthly Magazine*, vol. liv (1876-1877), pp. 33-43.

[2] L. K. Mathews, *The Expansion of New England* (Boston, 1909), p. 153; A. J. Weise, *Troy's One Hundred Years*, p. 29.

[3] Woodworth, *op. cit.*, pp. 36-40, 42.

Washington County, to the north, the Federalists likewise
acquired an ascendancy almost unvarying. General John
Williams, the friend of Philip Schuyler, was the largest
landholder the county ever knew,[1] and was (perhaps because
of this) the leading Federalist.[2] Owing to the influence of
such men as Williams and the Duers of Fort Miller, and
to the numerous settlements of old Scotch stock, who had
held to England throughout the Revolutionary War and
whose sympathies could not be enlisted to support the
French enthusiasms of Jefferson, as well as to the New
Englanders who made their homes in Kingsbury and Salem,
the region east of Lake George and the Upper Hudson was
started on its path of straight and constant regularity in
opposition to the Democratic party.[3] Federalism became a
kind of fixed religion; nearly half a century after the
" Revolution of 1800," when party politics in New York
had undergone strange, bewildering mutations, Washington
was still referred to as an old " Federal county." [4]

Probably no settlement was made in New York state
with higher hope of a great commercial future, than was
Hudson. When in 1774 the Congress met in Philadelphia
and drew up an agreement to cut off trade with England,
a measure which soon provoked retaliation, the whalers of
Nantucket saw their business slide from bad to worse, until
war and the appearance of the British frigates brought on
complete annihilation. With the restoration of peace, when
hope revived, some of them decided to seek out a new port
far enough removed from main roads of travel to be safe

---

[1] *The Salem Book* (Salem, N. Y., 1896), pp. 77-78; *History and
Biography of Washington County and the Town of Queensbury*
(Richmond, Indiana), 1894, pp. 393-400.

[2] C. H. Hunt, *Life of Edward Livingston*, p. 69; *N. Y. Commercial
Advertiser*, March 18, 1816.

[3] *History and Biography of Washington County*, pp. 41, 44, 80.

[4] *N. Y. Tribune*, November 14, 1846.

from visitation by the enemy's fleet, if ever war broke out
again. Acting on this resolution, certain brothers Jenkins
prospected along the Hudson River and finally picked out
Claverack Landing as blessed with harborage for ships of
any likely depth and surrounded by a country rich and
fertile. A company was formed to conduct this enterprise
and was joined, among others, by several Quakers from
Providence, Newport and Martha's Vineyard, it being provided by the specifications of agreement that all must be
whalers or merchants of good standing.[1]

Here was a community which naturally gave support to
the business party in their domestic policy and in their
overtures toward England in the interest of commercial
friendship. It had cast a heavy vote for the new Federal
Constitution,[2] and had applauded all the measures for
strengthening the navy and establishing the nation's credit in
the ports across the water, so that the election of Mr. Jefferson seemed to its merchants, in the words of one of them,
the wealthy Reuben Folger, " a signal to the nation to heave
to, under bare poles." [3] Columbia County, of which Hudson
was the small metropolis, though yielding later, now and
then, to the blandishments of its distinguished son, Van
Buren, was long known as a Federalist stronghold, the object of whole-souled affection or of fear, according to one's
sympathies, in the days when the party was controlled by
the "Columbia Junto." Of these men who played such
prominent parts in the triumphs and vicissitudes of Federalism, it is necessary to speak in some detail.

[1] A. R. Bradley, *History of the City of Hudson* (Hudson, 1908),
chs. iii, iv, and viii; Franklin Ellis, *History of Columbia County*
(Philadelphia, 1878), pp. 152-165; L. K. Mathews, *The Expansion of
New England*, p. 155; S. B. Miller, *Historical Sketches of Hudson*
(Hudson, 1862), p. 6-8.

[2] O. G. Libby, *Geographical Distribution of the Vote, etc.*, p. 18.

[3] G. A. Worth, *Random Recollections of Albany (and Hudson)*, p. 53.

Oliver Wendell Holmes, moved by his incorrigible curiosity, once inquired of Gulian C. Verplanck who was the most remarkable person he had ever met.

Now it must be remembered [writes the essayist] that this was a man, who had lived in a city that calls itself the metropolis, one who had been a member of the State and National Legislatures, who had come in contact with men of letters and men of business, with politicians and members of all professions, during a long and distinguished public career. I paused for his answer with no little curiosity. Would it be one of the great ex-Presidents whose names were known to all the world? Would it be the silver tongued orator of Kentucky or the " Godlike " champion of the Constitution, or our New England Jupiter Capitolinus? who would it be? " Take it altogether," he answered, very deliberately, " I should say Colonel Elisha Williams was the most notable personage I have ever met with." [1]

The man to whose memory such tribute could be paid came to Hudson as a young attorney in 1800.[2] Unlettered, saving what professional knowledge he had gathered in the courts and in his rather superficial preparation for the arguments of particular cases, he had certain native talents that marked him out as a leader.[3] In a young community physical attractiveness is no doubt of far more importance than in those larger and, by social experience, more sophisticated; Williams, as his portrait shows, was a man distinguished in appearance, tall and broad of chest, his forehead, nose and chin, such as pass with physiognomists

[1] O. W. Holmes, *The Poet at the Breakfast Table* (Riverside edition, Boston, 1891), pp. 330-331. Dr. Holmes was at fault in giving Williams a military title.

[2] Wm. Raymond, *Biographical Sketches of the Distinguished Men of Columbia County* (Albany, 1851), p. 1.

[3] J. A. Hamilton, *Reminiscences*, p. 41.

as evidences of great strength of character.[1] "He was indeed the most God-like form I ever beheld," records one witness; "it seems as if the Creator, in the formation of his body and mind, designed to make a magnificent display of skill and workmanship."[2] "His was a majesty of person and of mien," declares another.[3] Chancellor Kent long remembered "his commanding eye and dignified and attractive person."[4] It was easy to think good of such a man. Then, too, his was a generation in which the spread of literary education had not kept pace with the interest in public questions,[5] and in such a time a gift of eloquence was of first importance. Testimony to his vivid fancy, ready wit, his easy, pleasant grace, and melodious voice, vibrant now and then with what admirers were wont to call a "soul-subduing pathos," comes to us from divers sources.[6] Thomas Addis Emmett, whose experience in Ireland had been broad, declared him to be the greatest advocate he had ever met.[7] In such a man lapses in historical learning and occasional puerilities in political philosophy might be forgiven.[8]

It is difficult to associate with Williams any great move-

[1] See portrait in S. W. Williams, *The Genealogy and History of the Family of Williams in America, More Particularly the Descendants of Robert Williams of Roxbury* (Greenfield, Mass.), 1847, p. 131.

[2] Wm. Raymond, *op. cit.*

[3] *N. Y. Commercial Advertiser*, June 30, 1833.

[4] Quoted in S. W. Williams, *op. cit.*, p. 132.

[5] For illustration of the illiteracy then prevalent, one may examine the legal advertisements of the newspapers of the day, noticing how many are signed by mark.

[6] J. A. Hamilton, *Reminiscences,* p. 41; P. F. Miller, *A Group of Great Lawyers of Columbia County* (based on his father's recollections), (N. Y., 1904), pp. 118-125; Wm. L. Stone (Sr.) speaks of his inimitable grace of manner, quoted in S. W. Williams, p. 143.

[7] Franklin Ellis, *History of Columbia County*, p. 84.

[8] J. A. Hamilton, *loc. cit.*

ment or reform; he was, in contrast to a leader such as
Rufus King, a manager of men and not a man of measures.
Yet his contemporaries, captivated by his sparkling wit and
genial grace, or at times reduced to a submissive awe by his
corroding sarcasm, believed that had he but decided to go
himself to Washington, instead of finding satisfaction in
nominating others to this mission, "he might have ranked
with Adams, Webster, Clay, Calhoun and other illustrious
Americans, for he possessed talents at least equal to any
man in the nation." [1]　But the more impartial witness soon
observes that these talents were not suited to that theatre
upon which beats a fiercer light.　As we shall see, he was as
effective when near to the state legislature as when sitting
in it, for he and his colleagues of this Columbia Junto
brought more things to pass by friendships and occult suggestions within the corridors of Albany, than by the driving
force of argument.　He wrote little and invented little; such
effective service as he undoubtedly accomplished did not
make for lasting fame; a generation later his name meant
nothing to so well informed a man as Dr. Holmes.[2]

Most of what has here been said of Elisha Williams
might be said as well of William W. Van Ness, except that
possibly he possessed more matter if not less art.　"Thank
God!" exclaimed his friendly rival at the bar, when Van
Ness was elevated to the bench, "I have no longer an opponent to beat me by asking the foreman of the jury for a
chew of tobacco." [3]　Those who knew him pronounced him
blessed with every gift which might bring popularity and

---

[1] Wm. Raymond, *op. cit.*, pp. 4-5.

[2] *Cf.* S. W. Williams, *op. cit.*, p. 135; testimony of Stone and Mc-
Kinstry, *ibid.*, pp. 137-145, and of Chancellor Kent, p. 132; Elizabeth
Cady Stanton, *Eighty Years and More* (London, 1898), p. 7.

[3] F. Ellis, *History of Columbia County*, p. 90; D. Hosack, *Memoir
of De Witt Clinton* (N. Y., 1829), pp. 449-450.

power,[1] and though very young when he came to Hudson to begin his practice, just in time to take a part in the campaign against Jefferson,[2] he was soon recognized to be a man of talent. He was at the age of thirty-one appointed to be a judge of the supreme court by a Council controlled by members of his party, and was soon accepted as the "leading spirit of the political clique which guided the Federal party in the middle and western districts of New York."[3] He was associated with Alexander Hamilton in the famous Croswell trial of 1804 and became, in some degree, his successor as the brilliant party leader of the conservatives within the state. Yet here, too, it was a leadership due to personality; the charm of his urbanity, the fine sallies and imagery of his most ordinary conversation, endeared him to men's hearts. He, too, wrote little and can be judged only through the eulogies of his admirers and the arraignments of his enemies.[4]

The third member of this famous junto was Jacob R. Van Rensselaer, probably inferior to his associates, and yet recalled by one who knew his region well as the cleverest of his race and name.[5] He was somewhat older than Williams and Van Ness, but not less active in the arduous work of party politics, riding far and wide to check up votes, and spending many days and nights in Albany in an unofficial way.[6] He was elected to the assembly for nine terms, once serving as speaker, and for a year was attorney

---

[1] J. D. Hammond, *Political History*, vol. i, p. 217.

[2] P. F. Miller, *A Group of Great Lawyers*, p. 139.

[3] J. A. Hamilton, *Reminiscences*, p. 42.

[4] *N. Y. Statesman,* Proceedings of Columbia County Bar, and D. D. Barnard, quoted by Wm. Raymond, *op. cit.*, pp. 21-31.

[5] G. A. Worth, *Random Recollections of Albany* (and Hudson), p. 52.

[6] N. E. Whitford, *History of the Canal System of the State of New York*, N. Y. Assembly Documents, 1906, vol. v, pp. 62-63.

general,[1] yet he made few speches and, though his letters show him to have been a cultivated man, he wrote no pamphlets or newspaper essays, by which his political philosophy may be judged. He was accounted a very popular man, an able parliamentarian, and " a bold, active and zealous politician." [2]

Thus personal attractiveness may account in a large degree for the importance of the junto, but there was not lacking a solid base of economic sympathy with Federalism. Williams was widely noted as appreciating the emoluments of his profession and gave much time to speculation, chiefly in wild lands. It was his custom to follow closely all the sales of land for unpaid taxes, to buy and hold until the price advanced, and then sell to the settler,[3] thus founding, for example, the community of Waterloo in Seneca County. By this practice he earned from his opponents the epithet of "harpy," but earned as well a fortune of between two and three hundred thousand dollars, then regarded a great sum of money.[4] Van Rensselaer, though belonging to the younger branch of that great family,[5] held title to a substantial section of the town of Claverack, but his business

---

[1] *N. Y. Civil List*, 1889, p. 177.

[2] P. F. Miller, *op. cit.*, pp. 114-117; F. Ellis, *op. cit.*, p. 91; see also D. Hosack, *De Witt Clinton*, pp. 434-435. A fourth name sometimes associated with the three treated above is that of Thomas P. Grosvenor, Williams' brother-in-law, who came to practice law in Hudson in 1803, and, with great size and voice, and a simple style of statement, was an able and tireless opponent in Congress of the policies of 1812; see *Baltimore Federal Republican*, quoted by Wm. Raymond, *op. cit.*, pp. 39-41, Miller, pp. 144-145. For a sample of his invective see his oration at Hudson, July 4, 1806, in New York Public Library.

[3] Wm. L. Stone (Sr.), " Narrative of a Journey in 1829" in *Publications of Buffalo Hist. Soc.*, vol. xiv, p. 258.

[4] *N. Y. American*, March 6, 10, May 12, 1819. Wm. Raymond, p. 1.

[5] *Appleton's Cyclopedia of American Biography*, article Van Rensselaer.

was not confined to rents and mortgages. For example,
in 1817 he made an offer to the state to build the Grand
Canal from the Hudson to Lake Erie on a contract calling
for $10,000,000, though inasmuch as arrangements were
undertaken by which the canal was actually constructed for
$7,602,000, his offer was not deemed acceptable.[1] Van
Ness had no such passion for acquiring wealth as had
Elisha Williams,[2] but it was, as we shall see, his participation as a promoter and a beneficiary, along with Williams,
Van Rensselaer and Grosvenor, in a Federalist banking
scheme, that brought about the political downfall of them
all. Though more intimately associated with the lawyers
of the country towns, they had sufficient taste for speculation to understand the wants and prejudices of their fellow
partisans in the markets and exchanges of the city. This
sympathy enabled them to lead the party in the state.

There remains one other town along the river where
Federalism had a following for many years, Poughkeepsie,
which like Hudson was hopefully developed as a whaling
port.[3] James Emott, a member of an old Anglican and
Tory family, and later one of the richest men of Dutchess
County,[4] was the party leader. His fortune was not
yet ascendant in the county, nor did he taste the
fruits of triumph until the reaction due to the embargo in 1808, when, as we shall see, his election to the

[1] J. R. Van Rensselaer to De Witt Clinton, March 11, 1817, De Witt
Clinton Mss., and E. R. Johnson in *Cyclopedia of American Government*, vol. i, p. 675.

[2] See remarks of Williams on Van Ness, Wm. Raymond, p. 30.

[3] P. H. Smith, *General History of Duchess* [*sic*] *County* (Pawling,
N. Y., 1877), p. 365; Edmund Platt, *The Eagle's History of Poughkeepsie*
(Poughkeepsie, 1905), p. 96. Mr. Platt's book may be considered one
of the best local histories in New York state.

[4] P. H. Smith, p. 129; E. Platt, pp. 90, 115, 135; Appleton, vol. ii,
p. 352. He was resident for a time in Albany.

Eleventh Congress brought a leader to the House hailed as foremost of the opponents of the War of 1812.[1] In managing the party in Poughkeepsie, he had the constant and enthusiastic aid of Thomas Jefferson Oakley, who, having been christened before the author of the Declaration of Independence became a party leader, now did what he could to live down so embarrassing a name.[2]

As the story of the Federalist party is unfolded, the Dutchess County leaders will appear in company with Barent Gardenier, who lived across the river in old Ulster County and joined with Emott in the attack on "Mr. Madison's war."[3] Gardenier had no easy task after Ulster changed to Jefferson in 1804. and for a season was obliged to yield the honors to his astute antagonist, Lucas Elmendorff, whom Van Buren was said to claim as his preceptor in the art of politics.[4] In this county, no less than in the neighboring Delaware and Dutchess, was felt the influence in politics of the great landlords, especially the Livingstons, whose fortunes were for many years combined with those of Jefferson.[5]

The country south of Ulster, that, lay along the river toward New York was, to the Federalist eye, quite hopeless.

[1] Platt, pp. 91-92 quoting *Poughkeepsie Journal*; *N. Y. Civil List,* 1882, p. 450.

[2] Platt, p. 83.

[3] J. J. Levinson in *History of Ulster County* (A. T. Clearwater, editor), Kingston, 1907, p. 484.

[4] N. B. Sylvester, *History of Ulster County* (Philadelphia, 1880), pp. 102, 103; W. Barrett, *Old Merchants of New York*, vol. iv, pp. 63-64; A. T. Clearwater, *History of Ulster County*, p. 484.

[5]*History of Delaware County,* W. W. Munsell, publisher (N. Y., 1880), ch. viii; Jay Gould, *History of Delaware County and Border Wars of New York, Containing a Sketch of the Early Settlements in the County and a History of the Late Anti-Rent Difficulties in Delaware with Other Historical and Miscellaneous Matter Never Before Published* (Roxbury, N. Y.), 1856, chs. xi-xiii.

Here at the beginning of the century were men of many sorts. The great holdings had, most of them, been broken into modest farms — the *bouweries* of the Dutch and the scattered lands tilled by the descendants of the Palatines, whom, more than a century before, Louis XIV had harried out of western Germany, and the well-disposed (and thrifty) government of England planted in this region to gather naval stores.[1] And here and there were little farmsteads of those who had moved across from Westchester or come in from the uplands of Connecticut. Such people had not been impressed with Hamilton's commercial policies, in nation and in state, and cherished no transplanted sentiment in favor of the Adams family. Even Newburgh which might, like Poughkeepsie, have put some trust in the party of the trader, had, interestingly enough, fallen under the influence of some free-thinking foreigners, with their Society of the Druids and their paper, *The Rights of Man,* and had become a citadel of infidelity. Here the seed of Jeffersonian democracy fell upon a fertile soil.[2]

The "Great West" of 1801 began not far from Albany, and it was known for many years as largely Democratic, or,

[1] Many of these, as is well known, had tired of their labor for an alien state and migrated first to set up for themselves in the fertile Mohawk region, where their presence is remembered through such names as Palatine Bridge and German Flats, and then moved again to the still more inviting valleys of Pennsylvania; see S. H. Cobb, *The Story of the Palatines* (N. Y., 1897).

[2] E. M. Ruttenber and L. H. Clarke, *History of Orange County* (Philadelphia, 1881), pp. 127, 245, 250-251, 254-255. The works of Thomas Paine and Matthew Tyndall enjoyed a surprising vogue in the Newburgh district, while the Congregational Church, the sign and substance of New Englandism, never gained a foothold, *ibid.*, pp. 269-270. In the time of the embargo Orange County was overwhelmingly Republican, *ibid.*, 73-74. When the doubtful Col. Burr could not be elected to the legislature or the Constitutional Convention of 1801 from New York city, Orange County was selected as a constituency which would elect anyone who bore the name Republican. J. D. Hammond, *Political History,* pp. 136, 141.

to use the official name, Republican. The ruthless march
of General Sullivan against the Iroquois, and the treaties
which the vanquished chiefs had subsequently signed, had
opened up the country to the Genesee, and during the last
decade of the eighteenth century, a growing number of
white men, many of them from the hills just west of the
Connecticut, had penetrated far into this wood-land. Much
has been written of the frontiersman; often in times past
he has been pictured as a Cooperesque, romantic hero,
something more than common stock, with his flashing eye
and supple, graceful form; perhaps it is as well that this
figment of the fancy with its impossible heroics, has been
laid aside as the dead material of literary archaeology.
Sometimes he appears as turbulent and lawless, finding
better fellowship with wolves and foxes than with decent
people in the settled region, or again he is described as a man
of faith and courage, carrying the torch of civilization,
building his academies and churches, the best manhood that
the east had to contribute. Of these latter pictures both
must be accounted accurate, though of two separate divisions in the westward march. Following the first and giving
way before the last, Timothy Dwight in his extensive travels
detected an intervening group, steadier in habit than the
outcast trapper, clearing land and building their rude cabins,
though for want of capital, quite as often losing them again
to meet the heavy mortgages.[1] Finally there came from
the east thrifty, energetic immigrants moving frequently
in large companies of neighbors or religious congregations.
New England was, as every student knows, as far from a
democracy as was Scotland, which it so much resembled,
and among these last newcomers there were many families

---

[1] Timothy Dwight, *Travels in New England and New York* (New
Haven, 1821), vol. ii, p. 459 *et seq.*; L. K. Mathews, *Expansion of New
England*, p. 148.

from that precious fraction of society that by tradition ruled those commonwealths.[1] This third element in the expansion of New England was largely Federalist in politics, and one may find pure democracy somewhat frowned down in such communities as Troy, Utica and Canandaigua, where it settled.[2]

The stories of the soldiers who had fought against St. Leger and Burgoyne, had, as retold in Connecticut, attracted favorable attention to the Mohawk Valley. Judge Hugh White's company of settlers who founded Whitestown in the following decade, were the pioneers of such civilization in the old west of New York,[3] though they were soon joined by similar communities who settled Kirkland, Utica and Rome. Here in Oneida County at the beginning of the century there flourished a group of towns having the air and aspect of New England. Yet there were other elements, for one leading citizen was a Van Rensselaer ("the elegance and profuseness of his domestic courtesies" were matters of town pride), and the other was Colonel Benjamin Walker, who had come from London to New York before the war, during which he had become an aid to Washington, and had taken up his home in Utica as land agent for the Earl of Bath. He was, as might be expected, a stout Episcopalian and a Federalist, and had been elected in 1800 for a term in Congress.[4] The enterprise of Utica soon expressed itself in manufacturing, so that by the War

[1] H. L. Osgood, *The American Colonies in the Seventeenth Century* (N. Y., 1904), part ii, ch. i.

[2] L. K. Mathews, *op. cit.*, p. 150 (map).

[3] Pomroy Jones, *Annals and Recollections of Oneida County* (Rome, N. Y.), 1851, pp. 786, 790; James Macauley, *The Natural, Statistical, and Civil History of New York* (Albany, 1829), vol. iii, pp. 420, 425.

[4] M. M. Bagg, *The Pioneers of Utica; Being a Sketch of Its Inhabitants and Its Institutions, with the Civil History of the Place, From the Earliest Settlement to the Year 1825—The Era of the Opening of the Erie Canal,* (Utica, 1877), pp. 68-69, 116.

of 1812 industry was well begun.[1] It was fitting that one who invested in these enterprises a fortune gained from speculation in land values, Thomas R. Gold, was to be for many years a tower of strength in the party of the state.[2] Almost as influential was Judge Morris S. Miller, who was soon to move to Utica from his land agency for Nicholas Low in Lowville. By marriage to a daughter of the Bleeckers (who somewhat resented this intrusive Yankee) he acquired a quarter of a million dollars, and, fastidious in dress, eloquent in speech, and unfailing in support to the Episcopal Church, he soon engaged the favorable attention of a Federalist town, and was sent to serve in Congress.[3]

But Judge Jonas Platt was the county's foremost party leader. When in 1809 he carried the western district which throughout its ample mileage was thought to be reliably Republican, it demonstrated two unquestionable facts: That Judge Platt was the strongest candidate his party could present the following year for governor, and also that more settlements of the Whitestown type were being founded in the west.[4] Certainly in the first years of the century that type of settlement was rare, the conspicuous exceptions being Canandaigua and Geneva,[5] which were still the outposts of the new civilization. The country was yet new in its society; Buffalo was scarcely founded (though even here a bitter contest had begun)[6]. Rochester was yet an unnamed wilder-

---

[1] M. M. Bagg, "The Earliest Factories of Oneida," in *Transactions of the Oneida Historical Society*, 1881, p. 114.

[2] P. Jones, *Annals*, p. 795; M. M. Bagg, *Pioneers*, p. 199; *N. Y. Journal*, April 7, 1810.

[3] M. M. Bagg, *Pioneers*, pp. 236-237; M. S. Miller to John Jay, May 11, 1809, *Jay Correspondence*.

[4] P. Jones, *Annals*, p. 791.

[5] G. S. Conover, *History of Geneva* (Geneva, 1879), p. 34.

[6] Crisfield Johnson, *Centennial History of Erie County* (Buffalo, 1876), pp. 106-108, 116, 117.

ness,[1] and of modern Syracuse there was then but the
meagre hamlet of Bogardus Corners, straggling out beside
the salt wells of the Onondaga Marshes.[2] Of those who
lived along the jagged, changing line of ultimate settlement,
many must have shocked good Dr. Dwight, and no doubt
earned the epithet given them by one impatient witness, a
" heathenish and dissolute crew."[3] They had no traditions
which could be opposed to the doctrine of equality.

An old historian of Oneida, Judge Pomroy Jones, sum-
marizes thus the early politics of his own section and the
country to the north:

After the formation of the county in 1798, it was found to
contain a Federal majority. Subsequent to the organization
of St. Lawrence County in 1802, the Democratic party for the
next two or three years was in the ascendent. In 1805 the
Counties of Jefferson and Lewis were taken from Oneida,
which left it with a Federal majority of twelve to fifteen hundred. This was a powerful majority, when it is recalled that
scarcely one-half of the citizens were voters, as the old Constitution of the State contained that most aristocratic and odious
provision requiring a freehold qualification of $250 to entitle
the citizen to the privilege of the elective franchise.[4]

St. Lawrence County, whose loss the Oneida Federalists
no doubt bewailed, was settled almost entirely by companies
who came across Vermont and Lake Champlain, bringing
with them a respectful memory of old New England and the

[1] J. M. Parker, *The Opening of the Genesee Country, Publications
of the Rochester Historical Society*, 1892, vol. i, pp. 59-66.

[2] C. E. Smith, *Pioneer Times in the Onondaga Country* (Syracuse,
1904), pp. 223, 229-230.

[3] G. H. McMaster, *History of the Settlement of Steuben County*
(Bath, 1853), pp. 25-31, 78, 89. Much of the land of the so-called
Holland Patent was opened for settlement only after 1800, Arad
Thomas, *Pioneer History of Orleans County* (Albion, 1871), pp. 23-25.

[4] P. Jones, *Annals and Recollections of Oneida County*, pp. 54-55.

principles of the Adams family.[1] They had able leaders
of their own, like Roswell Hopkins, who had been a Federalist judge in Vermont,[2] besides those who had come
northward from New York to lead in politics as well as sell
them land.[3] It remained, like the counties to the east,
largely Federalist for many years.[4] Jefferson and Lewis
Counties, named, it will be noticed, for two distinguished
Republicans, and little mourned when severed from Federalist Oneida, had been settled in a considerable part by
foreigners, including Germans, Swiss and Irish, as well as
a group of Frenchmen who came later, led by the famous
LeRay de Chaumont, the treasurer of Napoleon.[5] Since
most of these people had taken leave of Europe to escape
oppression, they were naturally inclined in this new land of
liberty to take their stand, as soon as they were qualified,
against those who had supported the Alien Laws of 'ninety-
eight.

In this age of printed paper, when books and periodicals
have come from luxuries to be a commonplace of life, when
travel is within the compass of the leanest purse, when
education is not only offered freely but is forced upon the
citizen, it is not easy to imagine how gross and glaring were
the inequalities among mankind a century ago. Without
the common school, government by all the people might
seem to sober sense a reckless and a dangerous experiment
(though it might be well observed that popular government
is what has brought the common school). The doctrine of

---

[1] L. K. Mathews, *Expansion of New England*, pp. 160-61.

[2] F. B. Hough, *History of St. Lawrence and Franklin Counties*
(Albany, 1852), p. 595; *N. Y. Civil List*, 1889, pp. 422-424.

[3] See *infra*, ch. v.

[4] *N. Y. Spectator*, May 16, 1809, May 13, 1812, May 12, 1813, May 10,
1815, May 15, 1815, *etc.*

[5] F. B. Hough, *History of Lewis County* (Albany, 1860), pp. 70-73,
75, 107, 119.

democracy had but recently been preached, and men were intensely partisan upon the question of its merits; it seemed then a bold innovation and, to those to whom a change might mean a loss, a dubious one indeed. But the democrats who had shouted their huzzas at the phrase, "All men are created equal," had been mightily impressed with the new doctrine. They were determined to wrong nobody, but to gain their just share of a birthright which the aristocrats, in defiance of all the axiomatic principles of the rights of man, selfishly withheld.

The contest in which these lines were sharply drawn was made more bitter by reflection from across the sea. For once opinion on domestic and on foreign policy so merged as to make division perfectly complete. The enthusiasts for the equality of man, which contemplated, by the way, ample protection for the debtor, were ardent partisans of revolutionary France where all their theories seemed justified by accomplished facts. The wealth of Federalist merchants, on the other hand, could be continued and increased only when the way was easy to and through the English ports, where by tradition of two centuries they found their customers. They reasonably desired the triumph of the mistress of the seas, and a cordial understanding with the British admiralty as to the customs duties and the rules of trade. But to be a partisan of England meant to be a partisan of Burke; no one should tamper with the old safe ways by which wealth was preponderantly represented for its own protection, and the government so properly conducted by learned men of leisure should by no fatuous philosophy be given over to them that drive oxen and whose talk is of bullocks, nor to the carpenters and workmasters. To some, at least, not all occupations were of equal honor.[1]

---

[1] *Cf.* Edmund Burke, "Reflections on the French Revolution," *Works* (Boston, 1884), vol. iii, pp. 296-298.

This disparity of views, so easily infused with deep emotion, was the basis of a bitter party strife, that had certain elements of a war of classes.

Whether one were a Federalist or a Democrat was not merely a question of election day, but a matter of concern throughout the year, a consideration that entered into the commonest business of life. There were permanent political clubs that met in frequent conclave in their favorite taverns;[1] and sometimes in small communities where accommodations were somewhat limited, the contrast was significant. A citizen of Hudson described the quarters of the village Democratic Club as in the lower regions of a dingy general store; there, " round a red hot stove in an atmosphere blue with smoke, seated on old pine benches and wooden bottomed chairs, with the dust and cobwebs of twenty years undisturbed on the shelves, met the great Anti-Federal fathers of the city." But " the Federal Club, of which Elisha Williams, one of the most influential men in the State was the acknowledged leader, always met in the best furnished room of one of the public houses."[2] Each party was a social as well as a political organization, and each maintained a well-trained instrumental band drawn from its membership.[3] Prejudice struck very deep in Utica; as the gentry of the town, mostly well-to-do and several of them college graduates, gathered in the home of Colonel William Williams to sip Madeira furnished by that hospitable publisher,[4] they liked to chant a ballad written by a member of the group, beginning:

[1] W. H. Bayles, *Old Taverns of New York*, p. xvi.

[2] G. A. Worth, *Random Recollections of Albany (and Hudson)*, pp. 48, 51.

[3] A. R. Bradley, *History of the City of Hudson*, pp. 71-72.

[4] The mss. diary of William Williams is now in the possession of Miss Nellie Williams, Utica, N. Y.

> " The rabble all in council met
> To plan a democratic fête."

It was not considered " elegant " to be a Democrat in Utica.

But sometimes the feeling went much further. There were certain banks in New York and Albany where a follower of Jefferson could not be accommodated.[2] When in Trenton Falls a woolen factory was begun in 1812, when good cloth could fetch ten dollars a yard, it was expressly stated that no Democrat would be permitted to buy stock.[3] In Rhinebeck, Dominie Romeyn refused to give the name of Thomas Jefferson to an infant presented at the font. The dominie was a follower of John Adams, and the helpless parents had to stand by while their son was christened John.[4] In the country districts life was, in its isolation, somewhat primitive. There were few of those diversions which to-day enrich existence, and emotional energies seeking for expression might easily be confused with political conviction, to make well-marked and lasting feuds. Especially was this true in a generation trained to religious dogmatism and sharp categories of wrong and right. Judge Woodworth who, in the first years of the nineteenth century, had seen boycotts and frequent violence grow out of party hatred in the town of Troy, wrote gratefully long after of the improvement he had witnessed. When friends complained that conditions in the early 'fifties were not all they should be, the pious man repeated the counsel of Solomon: " Say not then, what is the Cause that former Days were better than these? For thou dost not inquire wisely concerning this." [5]

[1] M. M. Bagg, *Pioneers*, p. 159.

[2] J. D. Hammond, *Political History*, vol. i, pp. 325, 332.

[3] J. F. Seymour, *Centennial Address Delivered at Trenton, N. Y.* (Utica, 1877), p. 28.

[4] H. M. Morse, *Historic Old Rhinebeck* (Rhinebeck, 1908), pp. 240-243.

[5] John Woodworth, *Reminiscences of Troy, 1790-1807*, p. 44.

CHAPTER III

Rulers Deposed

It was once observed of Aaron Burr that his sole claim to virtue lay in the fact that he himself had never claimed it.[1] The frankness of this gifted man as to his rules of private conduct, no doubt retained the loyalty of friends who had been won by his engaging manners, yet the historian cannot but wish that he had left behind some serious defence of his political career, that a better case might be made out in his behalf than seems warranted by the evidence of deeds. In want of any such, the judgment of his motives must be formed on inference, and complete agreement here may scarcely be expected. That in 1801 he intrigued for the presidency, when by an accidental tie he seemed to have as many votes as Jefferson, is to be gathered only from a train of circumstances. He held mysterious conferences with Federalists, arrangements were concluded by his followers with that party's congressmen from doubtful states, his chief lieutenant was allowed to spread a false report as to opinion in New York, while he himself assumed a shifting and equivocal position and took no steps to check the movements which he must have known were managed in his name; this ill-timed reticence may have thwarted his ambition. When the choice of the electors of the country was properly expressed by Congress and Jefferson declared elected, Aaron Burr took up his humbler duties with his party's confidence in his integrity hopelessly impaired.[2] It

[1] W. A. Duer, *Reminiscences of an Old New Yorker*, p. 24.

[2] James Parton, *The Life and Times of Aaron Burr* (Boston, 1876), ch. xvi; and the excellent account in J. D. Hammond, *History of Political Parties in New York State*, vol. i, pp. 139-143.

was known that certain New York Federalists, like Judge Cooper and David A. Ogden, had been his active agents in the contest at the capital;[1] when, early in the following year, he was put prominently forward at a Federalist banquet, to the surprise of his enemies and the consternation of his friends,[2] it was obvious that his Republicanism might well be called in question.

In the state campaign in 1801 the followers of Clinton, Livingston and Burr stood united,[3] but the new government had scarcely been inaugurated when the proscription of the Burrites, along with the Federalists, was begun. The new Council of Appointment, directed by DeWitt Clinton, the ambitious nephew of the governor, and Ambrose Spencer, recently apostatized from Federalism, left few offices in the hands of those who had served the late administration, and consistently refused appointments to all followers of Burr.[4] A pamphlet warfare was begun, not surpassed in all the annals of American campaigns. A certain John Wood, who had written a *History of the Administration of John Adams* in the Republican interest, particularly of Burr, was now requested by his patron to suppress the most offensive passages, for the purpose, it

[1] "Aristides," *An Examination of the Various Charges Exhibited Against Aaron Burr*, etc., pp. 56-57 (see *infra*).

[2] A full account of this episode is given by J. P. Van Ness in a letter to his brother W. P. Van Ness, April 2, 1802, Van Ness Mss., N. Y. Public Library.

[3] A broadside (N. Y. Public Library) "To the Independent Electors of the State of New York," 1801, is signed, among others, by John Swartwout and Oliver Phelps, who became Burrites; Elisha Jenkins and Adam Comstock, who became Clintonians; and Ebenezer Purdy and Erastus Root, who became Lewisites. Burr, had, of course, been very active in the campaign, Hamilton to J. A. Bayard, February 22, 1801, Hamilton's *Works*, (Lodge edition), vol. viii, pp. 589-590.

[4] J. D. Hammond, *op. cit.*, vol. i, pp. 170-184; Henry Adams, *History of the United States*, vol. i, pp. 288-289.

was charged, of making easier Burr's approach to the New England Federalists. This charge was published early in 1802 in *A Narrative of the Suppression by Colonel Burr of the History, etc.,* by a Citizen of New York, who turned out to be James Cheetham, the editor of a paper lately started in the cause of Clinton. Wood and others replied defending Burr, while the author of "the Narrative" returned not only an *Antidote to John Wood's Poison,* but likewise a full *View of the Political Conduct of Aaron Burr, Esquire,* purporting to trace (not always with nice accuracy) his partisan irregularities during the past twelve years. Wood published a rejoinder, but Burr's cause found an abler champion in William P. Van Ness, whose arraignment signed "Aristides" was marked by ferocity no less than by finesse. It has been declared unrivalled since the days of Junius, and it circulated more widely through the country than any earlier pamphlet except *Common Sense.*[1] That these editors and pamphleteers looked upon

[1] J. D. Hammond, *op. cit.,* vol. i, p. 189; see also the analysis and criticism of the pamphlet by D. S. Alexander, *A Political History of the State of New York,* and *New York Spectator,* January 11, 1804. This contest, of course, belongs only incidentally to the present narrative and the contents of these brochures, however illustrative of the political writing of the time, cannot here be summarized. The order of appearance of the principal items is as follows: "A Citizen of New York" (James Cheetham) *A Narrative of the Suppression by Colonel Burr of the History of the Administration of John Adams* (N. Y., 1802); "A Yeoman," *Strictures upon the Narrative of the Suppression by Col. Burr of Wood's History, etc.* (N. Y., 1802); *A View of the Political Conduct of Aaron Burr, Esq., by the Author of the "Narrative"* (N. Y., 1802); John Wood, *A Correct Statement of the Various Sources from which the History of the Administration of John Adams was Compiled and the Motives for its Suppression by Col. Burr; with Some Observations on a Narrative by a Citizen of New York* (N. Y., 1802); "Warren" (Cheetham) *An Antidote to John Wood's Poison* (N. Y., 1802); John Wood, *A Full Exposition of the Clintonian Faction* (Newark, 1802); James Cheetham, *Nine Letters on the Subject of Aaron Burr's Political Defection* (N. Y., 1803); "Aristides" (W. P.

their controversy as something graver than a war of rhetoric, was evidenced by two duels fought among them, and by other challenges which were with difficulty satisfied outside the code. The Republican party in New York was cloven squarely into two unequal parts—the Jeffersonians, now in complete control, and the followers of Aaron Burr.

The "little band," as Cheetham called his enemies, contained some politicians of good reputation, who found much to admire in the undoubted talent of the Vice-President; but with them were associated, by common acceptation, "nearly all the needy and desperate adventurers in the community," [2] augmented, one by one, by those who failed of offices at the hand of the discriminating Clinton Council of Appointment.[3] By most of the distinguished leaders of the Federalist party Burr was despised and spurned. Hamilton, in 1800, had called him "as true a Cataline as ever met in midnight conclave;" [4] Morris, as Senator in Washington, had "greatly disapproved and openly disapproved of the attempt to choose Mr. Burr;" [5] Robert Troup had scored him as a sneak.[6] They had exulted at beholding the breach he made among their enemies, until they saw how dangerous was the fascination of this outcast Democrat when turned toward their own following.

Van Ness), *An Examination of the Various Charges Exhibited Against Aaron Burr, Esq., Vice-President of the United States; and A Development of the Characters and Views of his Political Opponents* (Philadelphia, 1803); James Cheetham, *A Reply to Aristides* (N. Y., 1804).

[1] Clinton's Letters to Henry Post, *Harper's Magazine*, vol. l, p. 565, and Alexander, *op. cit.*, p. 128.

[2] Theodore Sedgwick to Rufus King, August 24, 1802, *Life and Correspondence of Rufus King*.

[3] Cheetham's *View*, p. 94.

[4] To James A. Bayard, August 6, 1800, *Works* (Lodge), vol. viii, p. 562.

[5] A. C. Morris, *Diary and Letters of Gouverneur Morris*, vol. ii, p. 404.

[6] To R. King, April 24, 1802, *King Correspondence*.

Federalism itself seemed dead; to call it from the tomb would need a sorcerer. It is not surprising that in their extremity the great mass of Federalists were giving ear to such a man as Aaron Burr. In spite of Hamilton and others an understanding was effected. "The long anticipated coalition between a few pretended Republicans and the Federalists," wrote Cheetham in the spring of 1802, " appears at length to be formed."[1] The old leaders might seek to brand this as a falsehood, and recite sarcastic requiems over the Vice-President as a " gone man," but Hamilton admitted that, " unluckily we are not as neutral to the quarrel as we ought to be."[2] Yet nothing more could rightly be expected, for, sulking in defeat, these leaders had failed to keep their party firm in doctrine. In many districts now no candidates were named for Congress or the legislature;[3] and it was not surprising that lieutenants and subalterns would bring in that mean, enfeebling policy of offering themselves as makeweight between the factions of the enemy. Nothing could more strikingly illustrate their consciousness of bankruptcy; such wretched huckstering soon cost them the respect of everyone, not leaving out themselves.[4]

In 1804 the Federalist leaders determined on a rally. Rufus King, who had recently returned from England, was a man on whom as candidate for governor they might unite with full enthusiasm. He was besought by letters and addresses, including those from old associates in Massachu-

---

[1] *N. Y. American Citizen*, May 3, 1802.

[2] To R. King, June 3, 1802, *King Correspondence*: and Troup to King, June 6, and December 12, 1802, *ibid.*

[3] *N. Y. Evening Post*, April 27, 1802.

[4] When in 1803 the Federalists in New York City were cheered into putting up some candidates for the assembly, the Burrites rallied ostentatiously to their support, *N. Y. Evening Post*, April 26, 1803, and *American Citizen*, April 28, 1803.

setts; but in these last he soon detected that a Federalist governor of New York would be expected to take part in a conspiracy, already hatched and well developed in New England, for a secession of the northern group of states. To such proceedings he would give no countenance and, though personal ambition might thus have been well served, concluded to content himself with the barren honor of the nomination for Vice-President.[1] In this disappointment to the party Burr saw his opportunity. Full of sounding promises, he had himself put up for governor. Overtures were made to him by the most desperate of the intriguers, who found him ready for co-operation.[2] Some substantial county leaders of the Republicans also, such as Peter B. Porter of Ontario, John Van Ness Yates of Albany, Senator James Burt of Orange and others, came out strongly in his favor.[3]

The Livingstons and Clintons, who still could be considered Jeffersonians (for the Virginia interest was always joined against the most powerful Democrat in New York state), hearing that George Clinton now sought the vice-presidency as a kind of respectable retirement, nominated as their candidate for governor, Chancellor John Lansing, who had been prominent in public life since colonial days. However, when he subsequently found that if successful he would be expected to be but a passive instrument in the hand of DeWitt Clinton, this gentleman refused to be continued as a nominee, although his reasons were kept secret for three years. After some deliberation and balancing of

[1] T. Sedgwick to Hamilton, and Hamilton to King, Hamilton's *Works* (J. C. Hamilton edition), vol. vi, p. 553; King to Hamilton, February 24, and March 1, 1804, *King Correspondence*; H. C. Lodge, *Life of George Cabot* (Boston, 1878), p. 447.

[2] Henry Adams, *Documents Relating to New England Federalism* (Boston, 1877), p. 354.

[3] J. D. Hammond, *op. cit.*, vol. i, p. 203.

names, there was selected as a substitute, Chief Justice
Morgan Lewis, the brother-in-law of Chancellor Livingston,
a man whose three score years and amiable and easy-going
temper seemed to promise pliability. Of one thing Hamilton was certain, that no honorable man could vote for
Aaron Burr. In a meeting of his partisans convened in
Albany, he had advised them, in case they could themselves
put up no candidate, to give support to Lansing, upon whose
honesty at least they might rely.[1] When the chancellor
was no longer to be had, he tried again to induce Rufus
King to stand.[2] His efforts were in vain, he then advised his
friends to vote for Lewis, although the prospect of success
under such a leadership seemed far less bright.[3]

The campaign was one of the most hotly fought the state
has ever seen. How many Republicans Burr could pull
away from Clinton and how many Federalists from Hamilton, was the question to be answered. Some papers of the
latter party, like the *New York Commercial Advertiser,*
had been willing to support Lansing as one who stood superior to his associates, though they still would have
preferred a nomination of their own;[4] but when his name
was exchanged for that of Morgan Lewis, who was looked
upon as a mere place-man of the Livingstons, they slowly
drew away. First there was some criticism of the manner
of his nomination, for it had been by legislative caucus, a
mode not yet familiar. The next month they were speaking
of Burr's strength in the west; and two weeks later were

[1] *N. Y. Morning Chronicle*, February 17, 1804.

[2] Hamilton to King, February 24, 1804, Hamilton's *Works* (J. C.
Hamilton), vol. vi, p. 559.

[3] J. D. Hammond, *op. cit.*, vol. i, p. 209.

[4] *N. Y. Spectator*, February 25, 1804; "The Livingstons are at all
events to be excluded ... The family has seen its day, and has served
its purposes," *ibid.*, January 18, 1804, see also in this issue their reasons
why a Federalist ticket would have been preferable.

among his strong supporters.[1]   The greatest single influence in producing this opinion was a broadside signed " Plain Truth," which appeared early in March.   When newspapers were scarce and costly, the broadside was of great importance as an instrument of propaganda.   A handbill, circulated from a corner store or pasted to a tree or fence post at a cross-roads, was sure to reach an audience which party orators could seldom gather; important politicians driving out among constituents did not disdain to stack the dodgers carefully beneath their gig-seats to parcel out among the faithful.

The author of "Plain Truth" declared that "we already see the extent of power and of influence possessed by families who monopolize most of the valuable and influential situations in the state; who are sufficiently numerous and sufficiently eager to officer the whole of them."   He enumerated in two columns fourteen such places held by members of the Clinton family with $53,500 paid as salaries, and twelve held by the " Noble Family of Livingston " worth $33,950.[2]   This species of attack was nothing new; " Lord Livingston's " rapacity had been a theme of scribblers even before the war.[3]   Ever since the chancellor, disappointed at being overlooked by Washington in apportioning the major offices of state, had, in 1791, called in his numerous kin and renounced the Federalist party, the obloquy of the apostate had been settled on this house.[4]   The

---

[1] *N. Y. Spectator*, March 10, 24, 1804.

[2] This broadside is in the collection of the N. Y. Public Library. These figures were corrected in a subsequent edition to read $49,750 and $33,950.

[3] A. M. Keys, *Cadwallader Colden*, p. 362.

[4] It was a " House of Republican Nobility of which one of the younglings had been heard to say, with true democratic humility, that to be born with their family name is a fortune to any man." *N. Y. Evening Post*, February 26, 1802.

Clintons, though without the prestige of their high-born colleagues, had won political success and married wisely, until to be a cousin of DeWitt was thought to be a passport to high station. The Federalist papers had long inveighed against these two ambitious families and their greed for salaries;[1] men of that party had themselves been so berated as aristocrats, they seized upon this opportunity to turn the epithet upon their foes. The figures of " Plain Truth," then, gave the theme of the campaign.

Colonel Burr was introduced by his supporters as one whose chief claim to the public confidence lay in the fact that he was unencumbered by connections.[2] He was a

single man, like Mr. Jefferson, having no family, should he be chosen Governor, to provide for out of the public Treasury, or to distract his executive attention from the calm, undisturbed contemplation of public utility, and who by the late sale of his property, for the honest payment of his debts, is become now free from all pecuniary embarrassments, with a comfortable residuary independency.[3]

Surely such an introduction would fall strangely on a modern ear. Against Morgan Lewis the Burrites brought up not only his membership in a " numerous and pride-bloated family," but also his caucus nomination. The public seemed yet to consider party politics, with its inevitable discipline, as something vicious in the state.

Our representatives were sent [complained another handbill] not to make our governors, but to make our laws; and with

[1] For example, *N. Y. Evening Post*, April 15, May 1, 1802; April 28, 1803.

[2] See broadside, "To All Independent Electors" (N. Y. Public Library).

[3] Broadside, "Pretentions upon which Colonel Burr merits the free suffrage of his Fellow-Citizens," and "Jefferson & Burr against the Clinton & Livingston Combination." Of course Jefferson was, in fact, a widower with married daughters.

blushes have many of them confessed, that they were drilled
like soldiers, and compelled to sign the nomination, under pain
of being denounced and calumniated in the newspapers and
incurring in every shape the persecution of DeWitt Clinton.[1]

That Lewis once had been a Federalist, abandoning a de-
clining party and attaching himself to the strongest, was
further cause to hate him.[2] " Toby Tickler's " campaign
paper *The Corrector* threshed the charges over day by day.

This shower of bills was returned in kind by the Lewisites.
" Plain Truth's" statistics were branded as a fabric woven
half of lies. " A Republican and no Burrite" declared the
total of the " family " salaries cited would not foot to more
than $35,000, which he claimed was less than was received
from the state treasury by the nearest minions, or the " little
band," of Colonel Burr himself. The writer then attempted
an elaborate rebuttal to the estimates of his opponents,
maintaining, certainly with want of candor or of information, that the appointive office of the mayor of New York
(remunerated, as it was, by every kind of fee) was worth
scarcely a third of the stated $15,000.[3] " Republican
Economy," declared that all freeholders jealous of the
public trust should refuse support to Colonel Burr, as he
was in truth the candidate of the spendthrift Federalist
party. Other broadsides then rehearsed, with gross par-
ticularity, Burr's miserable amours (that is, a number of
them), naming streets and houses.[4] All that had been said

---

[1] Broadsides, "An Elector," " To All Independent Electors."

[2] Broadside, " Republicans Attend."

[3] *Cf. N. Y. Spectator*, February 11, 1804; J. D. Hammond, *op. cit.*,
vol. i, pp. 180, 263, 291; Robert Troup to Rufus King, January 12, 1810,
King Correspondence. One broadside went further, declaring that the
Burrites, among them, got $59,000, and as to the mayoralty "the pre-
decessor of the present mayor lost money by the office, and Mr.
Clinton may not have a cent"; from " Republican Measure " (*loc. cit.*)

[4] Broadside, " The Following Hand-bill " (*loc. cit.*)

against " the Cataline " by Federalists in 1801 was now reprinted in great glee by their opponents. Men that he had cheated, and men that he had bullied when he served as colonel in the war, were induced to write their wretched statements, to be scattered broadcast through the state. On the other hand, the Burrites claimed that office-holders were generally laid under contribution to provide a fund for bribery, and were warned that, in case of victory for Burr, they would all, as Judge Spencer had bluntly said, be obliged to go to work.[1] Clintonian broadsides printed lists of disappointed office seekers who now joined the " little band." [2] Clinton sent his agents through the state who discovered a trick that afterward became more common: " In the Southern Counties it is rumored that the Western Counties are favorable to their candidate. In the western parts the same falsehood is related of the Southern. The middle is informed of his ascendancy in the Eastern and the Eastern is told of his prodigious force in the Middle." [3]

Such was the character of a campaign which many thought would lead to bloodshed;[4] a quarrel of men for profit, in which apparently no word was spoken as to measures or the larger concerns of public policy. Its sordid details make unpleasant reading, and yet may no doubt be studied with instruction by those who cry decadence in our modern day, and grieve because our politics has lapsed from pristine purity. In the decade of which this year was near the middle, the civic honor of New York fell to a bottom not passed between the times of those two models of corruption, Lord Cornbury and Grand Sachem Tweed. In

[1] J. D. Hammond, *op. cit.*, vol. i, p. 177.

[2] See, for example, a list of forty-one in " To Genuine Republicans " (N. Y. Public Library).

[3] DeWitt Clinton Mss., Letterbook I, March 14, 1804 *et seq.*

[4] *N. Y. Spectator*, January 25, 1804.

this adversity King, Jay and Morris spoke unheeded, while weaker partisans forsook their leaders to run after a god strange indeed.

The Clintons and Livingstons were victorious by a vote of nearly three to two. A comparison of the returns with those for senators in 1803, discloses that for every Republican who cast his vote for Burr, a Federalist, convinced by Hamilton, supported Lewis.[1] Burr was now a man without a party. He had been taken by the Federalists only as a war-chief, as the towns of Italy had taken Braccio and Sforza, to fight their battles for them. In such arrangements victory alone may be a ground of permanence; and Burr had lost. Before the final canvass the relations between Burr and his Federalist following were becoming strained, and after it the feeling grew into an open quarrel.[2] Burr himself well knew that although Hamilton had not been often in the public prints, his had been the hand that had withheld sufficient Federalists to compass the defeat. Before the campaign had been fairly started he had written to his daughter, Theodosia, that Hamilton would favor anybody " who could have a chance against A. B." [3] Apparently this strange and reckless egotist now thought the world too small a place for two such rivals; the duel that he provoked, with its tragic end, is too well known to be recorded here. But if the enlightened leadership of Hamilton was taken from the Federalists, so likewise was the baleful influence of

[1] D. S. Alexander, *Political History*, vol. i, p. 138.

[2] F. A. Bloodgood to John Tayler, March 26, 1804, Tayler Mss. (N. Y. Public Library) ; "Already do the Burrites & the Federalists begin to quarrel among themselves. The former charge the latter with deception, & they retaliate with saying that the Burr party are a 'Little Band' indeed." Maturin Livingston to Charles D. Cooper, April 30, 1804, Cooper Mss. (N. Y. Public Library).

[3] To Theodosia Burr Alston, February 16, 1804, M. L. Davis, *Memoir of Burr* (N. Y., 1837), vol. ii, p. 277.

Burr, who in the scorn of a whole generation soon became a man without a country.

It was characteristic of the Federalist leaders that their next united effort should be in the interest of a bank. In 1803 a number of gentlemen belonging chiefly to that party had, as a private company, begun a banking business in the city of New York. The legislature, believing that such enterprises should not be carried on without a charter, at their next session had passed a restraining act on private banking, though excepting the Merchant's Bank, as this was called, until the spring of 1805.[1] Now the Clintons (which is to say DeWitt) had acquired control of the Manhattan Company, a bank in New York city, and their spokesmen in the legislature soon gave notice that no charter would be granted to a rival if their opposition could prevent it. The able agents of the Merchant's Bank, however, by liberal use of money, as a subsequent investigation clearly showed, succeeded in their project, and it was a matter of no small interest to the state that Governor Morgan Lewis forsook his old Clintonian associates to express his full approval of the charter. No exception could be taken to the arguments upon which he defended his opinion, but to Mayor Clinton and his brother-in-law, Judge Ambrose Spencer, all argument was frivolous; the Livingstons had revolted, the coalition was at an end, henceforth these " two lordly families " were to be as Capulet and Montague. To allow the leader to be with his following in person, DeWitt Clinton was made senator from the southern district.[2] The Livingstons were declared schismatic and were denominated Lewisites

[1] *Cf.* broadsides, "Anthropos" and " Wm. I. Vredenburgh to his Constituents" (N. Y. Public Library) ; *N. Y. Spectator*, April 17, 1805; J. D. Hammond, *op. cit.*, vol. i, pp. 332 *et seq.*

[2] See broadside, "Address to the Republicans of the State of New York, April 23, 1805" (N. Y. P. L.), giving the resolutions of a public meeting of Clintonians in New York city, Theodorus Bailey, chairman.

or Quids. For years the state would see-saw back and forth, at each turn dumping out the office-holders of the faction which could not hold the Council of Appointment.[1]

The Federalists at first looked on with impartial exultation at the troubles of their opponents. " Our State concerns continue to be an object of contest with the Demagogues of the day," wrote Robert Troup. " Demagogues Clinton & Co. by the superiority of the manoeuvres, have carried a council of appointment against the wishes and efforts of Demagogues Lewis & Co." [2]   In different sections, notably in New York city, Federalist groups appeared with apparently the health and vigor of old times, and called to mind their former glory:

Who rescued the nation from the imbecility and anarchy of the old confederation? Who proposed and advocated the constitution of the United States? Who carried that constitution into operation, and by whose efforts was the country raised in a few years, from a state of disorder and bankruptcy, to a proud eminence of dignity and prosperity? [3]

Yet shrewd spectators doubted their ability to cope with Clinton by themselves. " The feds. appear sanguine here," wrote John Swartwout to his fellow Burrite, William P. Van Ness, " but I think have not the stamina of exertion in them. Their strongest men have held back, Rufus King for instance. This I think evinces that the leaders do not believe in success." [4]   The Burrites had themselves been sadly split. In December 1805, some of their leaders effected a bargain of peace with the Clintonians, but in

[1] *E. g.* the office of secretary of state between 1793 and 1813, as recorded in the *N. Y. Civil List*, 1881, p. 157.

[2] To Rufus King, February 3, 1806, *King Correspondence*.

[3] Address in the *N. Y. Commercial Advertiser*, April 19, 1806.

[4] J[ohn] S[wartout] to W. P. Van Ness, April 18, 1806, Van Ness Mss.

February, four days after this was publicly announced, many who could not stomach such a feast of union met with New York city Lewisites in Martling's Long Room, to pledge undying hatred to Clinton and his men. These "Martling Men," soon finding their direction in the sachems of the Tammany Society, seldom faltered in their fight until their foe had passed beyond this life.[1] When war was thus openly declared between Clintonians and Lewisites, Swartwout's prophecy was proved correct. The Federalists under William W. Van Ness (the brilliant cousin of "Aristides"), despite all pleas for strict neutrality,[2] began to give support to poor Governor Lewis, whose endowments were not those of a self-reliant leader and who already had sought their counsel in private conferences.[3] All this, the Clintonians declared, did not surprise them; they had seen "men having a great interest in the community" gravitating toward the Livingstons, and it was to be expected that the Livingstons would turn toward the Federalists.[4]

More and more the Federalists were convinced that their

[1] J. D. Hammond, *Political History*, vol. i, *passim*. The Burrites who negotiated with Clinton soon found that he recognized no obligation on his part, and came to hope that the Federalists would try a contest independently, thinking that they might detach the governor from his family shackles, and, with their better art and energy, become themselves the leaders against Clinton.

[2] "Another Federalist" in *N. Y. Spectator*, March 1, 1806, and "Fabricius," *ibid.*, May 3, 1806.

[3] "Judge Benson will tell you the precious confessions which Lewis is constantly making when alone with federalists. I have listened until my contempt for the governor has been lost in my pity for the man." Robert Troup to Rufus King, February 11, 1806, *King Correspondence*.

[4] See broadside "To the Republicans of the State of New York" April 3, 1806 (N. Y. P. L.) signed by DeWitt Clinton, Adam Comstock, John Tayler, Nicholas Staats, Jedediah Peck and 55 other members of assembly.

policy of opportunism must be continued. Colonel Robert Troup, a well-informed observer at the capital in the early days of 1807, came to this conclusion:

As to the situation of the Federalists, although it is better than it was, yet it is by no means such as to enable us to elect a Governor from our own party. For the present we must be content to rest our hopes of a future Federal State administration on the fall of the Democratic party by the weight of its own vices and divisions. To let the former take their natural course and to give root and vigor to the latter seem to be the melancholy course which genuine patriotism presents.[1]

Too much must not be expected of the governor. Excommunicated from the Democratic fold, he must realize that what support he might receive from Federalists would not come from any personal respect, but in the hope that he might be a useful means to bring again the reign of Federalism. Although they might set hope on being granted a supreme court judge, let them look for little more from the Lewisite Council which would soon be chosen, since

Federal appointments would stamp the Governor's administration with so strong a character of Federalism, as to shake the confidence, and endanger the support of his democratic friends. It is said that the union in the 5th ward at the last election in New York, and the subsequent voting of the alderman and assistant alderman of that ward with the Federalists, has much injured the Governor's cause in the country.

Troup thus suggested that King warn his too high-tempered friends that they ought to bear inevitable disappointment with proper fortitude. This view Van Vechten and others of the calmer leaders were well known to share.[2] On the

[1] Troup to King, January 6, 1807, *King Correspondence.*
[2] *Ibid.*

other hand some aspirants were restless, like Peter Jay Munro, who " squinted at the Mayoralty of New York." [1]

The Council went to Lewis, the Federalists, as prophesied, supporting all his candidates, thus making possible success.[2] In equally avoiding the Clintonians and the Federalists, the Council's choice was limited, and many of the appointments gave good ground for ridicule. One member of the Council, John Nicholas, lately from Virginia, was for a straight-forward open course, choosing always that supporter of the administration who might seem best qualified; but, observes Judge Hammond, the historian, " it was impossible for him to understand the sinuosities of New York politics." [3] Some Federalists in disappointment were for breaking off entirely with Lewis, though Troup, on his part, was as much disgusted with some who had demeaned themselves in office-seeking.[4] Judge Van Ness, who in his war on Clinton through the eastern counties, now and then grew impatient because not all the Federalists would discover genuine enthusiasm for the cause of Lewis, admitted that " If we lose the election it is because the temper and views of our party have been entirely misunderstood and wantonly sported with by the Council." [5]

By the middle of March 1807, there was begun a movement to throw off their connection with the Lewisites and

[1] Troup to King, January 26, 1807, *King Correspondence.*

[2] *Ibid.,* January 27, 1807.

[3] J. D. Hammond, *Political History,* vol. i, p. 245.

[4] Troup to King, February 17, 1807, *King Correspondence.* Lewis' reappointment of his son-in-law, Maturin Livingston, who was unpopular among the better lawyers, as recorder of New York city, and Dr. Thomas Tillotson, his brother-in-law, as secretary of state, provoked much opposition.

[5] W. W. Van Ness to Sol. Van Rensselaer, March 18, 1807, Mrs. C. V. R. Bonney, *A Legacy of Historical Gleanings* (Albany, 1875), vol. i, pp. 158-159.

give all attention to the party candidates for the legislature. "Let the Federal Republicans once more rouse from their slumbers," it was urged.[1] A pamphlet soon was circulated as *Hamilton's Advice; or an enquiry into the propriety and consistency of Gov. Lewis' being supported by the Federalists, while they oppose the election of all his friends;*[2] but the party papers answered, that the author "ought to weigh well the consequence of putting forth any opinions, which, so far as they may have any effect, may divide, distract, and of course, weaken the Federal party in this crisis." Individuals might decide their courses as they liked, but he who would detach others from the body of the party, would so far scatter and diffuse its energies.[3] Support to Lewisites was justified upon high grounds of patriotism.

Are the duties of the Federalists [inquired an editor] confined to the welfare of the party? Are our professions of regard for the general good, false and elusive? . . . On the contrary are we not bound in duty to ourselves and to the public, to give our votes in favor of the party or the man, who, in our view would do the least mischief to the state.[4]

"To give our votes to neither," it was later said, "was to permit the stronger of the two to succeed, and was equivalent in its consequences to our giving him our direct and effective support."[5] Their consciences thus quieted, they proceeded very gingerly to give their aid to Lewis against Daniel D. Tompkins, who was thought to be a figure-head for Clinton. In what would now be called the keynote speech, Richard Harison refrained from mentioning the

---

[1] *N. Y. Spectator*, March 18, 1807.

[2] N. Y. 1807, cited in *N. Y. Evening Post*, March 22, 1807.

[3] *N. Y. Evening Post*, March 22, 23; *N. Y. Commercial Advertiser*, March 23; *N. Y. Spectator*, March 24.

[4] Zachariah Lewis in the *N. Y. Spectator*, March 28, 1807.

[5] *N. Y. Evening Post*, March 26, 1807.

governor by name, but in a hesitating and half-hearted way suggested that of their enemies one part was better than the other.[1] During April Federalists in Albany acted ostensibly as individuals in joining Lewisites against the other faction, as for instance, in the rescue of the charter of Columbia College from destruction by the Clinton men. But the combination wore the aspect of something shameful and clandestine; the Lewisites were pledged to the support of Federalists in the west, but the arrangement was hinted at in whispers as if those who knew were all conspirators.[2] It was in a brief resurgence of their self-respect that the Federalists named Rufus King to head their ticket for the assembly. As soon as the name of this distinguished statesman was presented to the public, the columns of the Clinton press were solidly drawn up against him; but to understand their principal attacks one must consider an issue which came to play no little part in New York state, the alien vote and its antagonism to the Federalists.

England's long misgovernment of Ireland has been of consequence to many nations in driving Irishmen across the seas; but to none more than to our own, and here to no state more than to New York. These immigrants who could so easily adapt themselves to novel circumstances, did not need the mutual support of great embarkations and close settlements; they came in steadily, family by family, scattering here and there, though many stayed within the city, so that in the last days of the colony Irish names were becoming common.[3] With the setting up of the new nation

---

[1] *N. Y. Evening Post*, March 26, 1807.

[2] Troup to King, April 7, 1807, *King Correspondence*.

[3] " Irish Colonists in New York," *Proceedings of the New York State Historical Association*, vol. vii, pp. 94-123. The roster of provincial troops of New York in the French and Indian War shows a number of pages where a fifth are Irish names, see *Collections of the New York Historical Society*, 1891.

it seemed clear that many more would come, and in the apprehension that political rights so dearly bought might be too cheaply shared with aliens, the Tammany Society, as early as May 12th, 1791, refused its offices to the "adopted citizens." [1]   The troubles of 'ninety-eight sent more exiles to America, some of them, like Thomas Addis Emmett and William James MacNevin, gentlemen of finest culture, whose tastes, perhaps, would have allied them with the aristocracy, but whose revolutionary training as United Irishmen directed all their sympathies toward the policies of individualism.   It was not surprising that they should enter with enthusiasm into the war on " Anglomen and monocrats " like Adams and the other sponsors for the Alien Laws.   By the party of their choice, not only in the city but throughout the towns and villages of the state, they were welcomed as efficient leaders. [2]

Such men as these became supporters of DeWitt Clinton, himself of Irish blood and through his life a friend of Ireland. [3]   In later years an Irish citizen of New York city in an address recalled that

while a Senator of the United States you stood foremost in preparing and carrying into law the existing mode of naturalization . . .   When many of us fled from despotism, and sought refuge in this emancipated land, the spirit of intolerance pursued us across the Atlantic and spared no effort to embitter our existence, and prolong our sorrows ; . . . you rebuked with

[1] Gustavus Myers, *History of Tammany Hall* (N. Y., 1901), pp. 36-37.

[2] *Cf.* M. M. Bagg, *The Pioneers of Utica*, pp. 137-142, 376-379, on John C. and Nicholas Devereux and John Devlin.

[3] In 1789 we find him reading, before a literary society, a paper called "A Dream of Ireland" (DeWitt Clinton, Mss. Miscellaneous Papers). In 1822 he wrote a series of letters which he signed " Hibernicus " (*Letters on The Natural History and Internal Resources of the State of New York*, N. Y., 1822).   There are among his papers many addresses from groups of Irishmen.

effect that churlish and savage jealousy, from which professed republicans are not always exempt . . . Even here, a qualification oath was required from members of the Legislature, which could not be consistently taken by members of the Catholic faith! On this as on every other occasion, reason and justice found you their able and successful advocate.

The recipient of this praise admitted in reply that he had not been " insensible to those natural predilections, which every man must entertain for the country of his ancestors."

The Irish voters became the center of lively partisan controversy. Charges passed from side to side. It was claimed that when the naturalization law was changed, Clinton's friends assembled a society to school the immigrants in party politics to swell his following.[2] On the other hand Clintonians accused the Federalists of cautioning their inspectors at the polls to refuse the suffrage to twenty-six new voters unless they bought their stamped certificates—which would cost five dollars—and then purchasing for sequestration all available stamps.[3] Certainly the Irishmen proved no disappointment to their teachers in New York city and elsewhere in the state, their loyalty to Clinton was so acceptably expressed.[4]

The jealousy of strangers is nothing new in human

[1] DeWitt Clinton Mss., March 16, 1816.

[2] John Wood, *A Full Exposition of the Clintonian Faction*, p. 20; "Aristides," p. 17.

[3] *N. Y. American Citizen*, May 1, 1802. To meet this subterfuge, the court records themselves were brought to the polls, see John Wood (*loc. cit.*) ; " It is needless for me to mention the ridiculous and irregular proceeding of Wortman, in running to the poll with the books of the Mayor's Court under his arm, and with a troop of ragged aliens at his heel, when stamp certificates could not be procured."

[4] The Irish and other immigrant voters turned the election from the Federalists to Clinton's man, for example, in Saratoga County; John Taylor of Charlton, Saratoga County, to John Tayler of Albany, April 9, 1803, Tayler Mss.

history, and here the feeling of antipathy for those whose ways were different was intensified by the glaring inferiorities in the standards of living among the newcomers.   Not only were they different in race, religion, and political tradition, but uncouth, uncleanly, ignorant, unskilled, and frequently immoral.[1]   Besides all this the prejudice against the Catholics, that had expressed itself in the Lord George Gordon riots in England, was widespread in America as well.[2]   On Christmas, 1806, near St. Peter's Church in Barclay Street, mobs of nativists and Irishmen set upon each other with such savage force that much blood was spilt, one man was stabbed to death, and many houses would have been sacked had not Mayor DeWitt Clinton arrived at the height of the tumult.[3]   Here surely was sufficient ground for animosities in politics, and an occasion was soon forthcoming for their expression.

When in 1807 Rufus King was induced to head the Federalist ticket for the assembly in the city of New York, his name was scarcely printed in the party papers, when Thomas Addis Emmett in the columns of the *Citizen* began a virulent attack upon him, as one whom he and every other Irishman had just cause to hate.[4]   It seems that in 1798 when King was minister of the United States in England he heard that the British government contemplated banishing the Irish state prisoners to America.   He straightway protested on the principle that the United States should not be considered as a Botany Bay for those whom England stamped

---

[1] L. D. Scisco, *Political Nativism in New York State* (N. Y., 1901), p. 18.

[2] J. G. Shea, *History of the Catholic Church in the United States* (N. Y., 1888), vol. ii, p. 158.

[3] *American Register*, vol. i, p. 14, cited by L. D. Scisco.   On Clinton's hold on the foreigners, see his Letterbook, February 13, 1808, DeWitt Clinton Mss.

[4] *N. Y. American Citizen*, April 9, 1807.

as undesirable.[1] Emmett now charged that King was so confirmed a royalist that he desired no more real republicans admitted to America, and branded him before the state as the acknowledged foe of liberty. When Coleman[a] of the *Evening Post* adduced a set of documents to prove that Emmett's conduct while in Ireland had merited severest punishment, the accused replied that these papers must have been supplied by King, and that in such a source of information no confidence could well be placed.[2] Other " state prisoners " in New York expressed their hatred of the Federalists,[3] and the cry against their ticket was taken up by the Hibernian Provident Society, which had recently been incorporated for social and charitable purposes, and which entered the campaign with a regulation that any member who should vote for certain candidates should be expelled, thus forfeiting his claims upon the common funds.[4] Of all this the Federalists expressed a deep abhorrence; James Kent and others talked of having Emmett disbarred,[5] and resolutions were unanimously passed in party meetings, " that the prompt interference of the honorable Rufus King, late minister of the United States at the court of Great Britain, and the timely remonstrance made by him . . . were wise and prudent. a decisive evidence of his patriotism and fidelity to his public trust." [6]

The challenge of the Irish received a formal answer. On April 18, 1807, the Federalist *Commercial Advertiser* came

---

[1] See *King Correspondence*, vol. ii, appendix iv, pp. 635-648, for King's account of this note.

[2] *Ibid.*, vol. v, p. 15 *et seq.*   [3] *Ibid.*, p. 24.

[4] *Report of the Trials of Jenkins vs. Van Rensselaer*, pamphlet (Albany, 1808), p. 15.

[5] R. Troup to R. King, April 11, 1807, *King Correspondence*.

[6] *Jenkins vs. Van Rensselaer*, pp. 15-16.

[a] William Coleman (1766-1829), editor of the New York *Evening Post*, a newspaper that began as a Federalist organ but eventually moved to the Democratic side and supported Andrew Jackson in the presidential election of 1828.

forth with columns headed with the "American Ticket." The name was taken up with great enthusiasm; it announced that nativism was accepted as the leading issue and it was used as the party designation for several years.[1] " I observe that your ticket in New York is called the American ticket," wrote Colonel Troup to King. " Would not this be a favorable occasion for our party to assume a popular and significant name, free from the hobgoblins attached by many to Federalism? This is a subject worthy of consideration."[2] By the Republicans the name was generally scorned. " The present American Ticket," declared a broadside, " was once the Federal ticket, next the Federal Republican ticket. One hitch more and it will be right—the Tory ticket—then with great propriety they might put a King on it."[3] But the menace of the immigrant was not underrated by King's followers. " The naturalization bill in New York," wrote Troup again, " I fear will defeat our assembly ticket."[4] The Federalists might address the Tompkins men with their " Warning to the Gallico-Hibernico-Tom-Clintonians,"[5] but they could not win upon so lean an issue.[6] James Cheetham, refugee from England, and the vehement Em-

---

[1] *Albany Gazette*, April 18, 1808; *N. Y. Spectator*, April 30, 1808; *N. Y. Commercial Advertiser*, April 28, 1809.

[2] Troup to King, Albany, April 11, 1807, *King Correspondence*.

[3] T. E. V. Smith, *Political Parties and their Places of Meeting in New York City*, pamphlet (N. Y., 1893), an amplification of an address before the N. Y. Historical Society.

[4] Troup to King, April 24, 1807. He referred to easier mode of naturalization revived under Jefferson.

[5] *N. Y. Spectator*, April 29, 1807.

[6] Irish immigration from about 1808 to 1816 was much reduced because of the dangers of travel due to the Napoleonic and American wars; see for these years, Stephen Byrne, *Irish Emigration* (N. Y., 1873), and W. J. Bromwell, *History of Immigration to the United States* (N. Y., 1855), p. 14.

mett, to whom he loaned his columns, were not the only leaders in abuse. Citizen Genêt, who as George Clinton's son-in-law now lived in Greenbush,[1] assailed King not only as an English sympathizer, but as downright dishonest in the administration of a will,[2] and others raked up charges equally absurd. "Should I congratulate or condole with you on the loss of your election?" wrote Charles Jared Ingersoll[a] when the report of King's defeat reached Pennsylvania. "I imagine if it was not the wish of others, it could not be your own to be put up and pelted at by Irishmen and Frenchmen."[3]

Although New York city and the Federalist counties gave majorities to Lewis, the Clinton ticket was successful. All that the Federalists had to show for their strange alliance was the place of William W. Van Ness in the supreme court,[4] which the Lewisites had granted before the election. They bore no testimony for their principles, they came forward with no program, they seemed in truth but pitiful Epigoni of the old party of the masters. Such was the sad condition of the Federalist party in America. Disheartened by defeat, and well realizing that their doctrine of strong, paternal government would not again be easily accepted by the voters at the polls, they dimmed their lamps, that once had burned so brightly, in hope to steal in unobserved within the shadow of some faction more reputable with the scorned, but now all powerful, "average men" who held the gates. In Massachusetts they were following the same ignoble, paltering course of surreptitious

---

[1] G. A. Worth, *Random Recollections of Albany* (Albany, 1865), p. 70.

[2] This was the famous case of Staats Long Morris' widow, *N. Y. American Citizen*, April 27, 1807.

[3] To Rufus King, May 14, 1807, *King Correspondence*.

[4] J. D. Hammond, *Political History*, vol. i, pp. 240-247.

[a] Charles Jared Ingersoll (1782-1862), an historian and Congressman who was influential in the annexation of Texas. He was an ardent nationalist and protectionist.

coalition;[1] in Pennsylvania the case was worse.[2] Such procedure was but little less destructive of what prestige the party had retained, than the policy of rule-or-ruin which the easterners had tried in 1804 and would attempt again.

By such men as John Jay these tendencies were deplored. When the news reached Bedford he wrote to an old friend:

As to the election, it is not clear to me what will be its precise effect in relation to the Federalists. If as a *party* they judged it to be expedient to favor Mr. Lewis, I think they should as a *party* have openly and decidedly declared and resolved that they would support him. The language of the Federal leaders to the party seems to amount to this, *viz.*; On this occasion you may leave your standard; you may go home, and every man is at liberty to do what may be right in his own eyes, but we nevertheless intimate to you, as an opinion to which we *incline*, but do not explicitly adopt, that it may be better for us to have Mr. Lewis than Mr. Tompkins for our Governor. I do not like measures of this kind. I fear that they tend to disorganize and sever us, and that they do not manifest that degree of resolution, self-respect and dignity which our motives, objects and situation demand. Had the party resolved to support Mr. Lewis, I certainly should have voted for him. As a mere individual, judging what was proper for me to do, I declined voting for either of the candidates.[3]

The disgrace of this intrigue weighed heavily upon the older men, but to the young disaster had a tonic value. The

[1] Christopher Gore to King, December 25, 1807, *King Correspondence*.

[2] The Federalists never captured the state of Pennsylvania, see W. M. Cornell, *History of Pennsylvania* (Philadelphia, 1876), p. 469.

[3] To Peter Van Schaack, May 4, 1807, *Jay Correspondence* (Johnston's edition). This letter shows how much in error was Hammond's information that after his retirement, Jay never read the papers. *Cf. Political History*, vol. i, p. 155.

very shame to which the party of their fathers had descended, stirred in them a resolution to forget those things that were behind, and throwing off all secret and despised connections win triumph, if they could—at least, regain their self-respect. Their problem was how to adapt their methods to the spirit of the times. We may turn, then, with no little interest, to study how they tried to draw supporters to their cause.

CHAPTER IV

New Methods and a Victory

WHAT has been called the "Democratic Revolution" produced small difference in the outward aspect of our institutions, but in forwarding some tendencies and curbing others it registered a fundamental change in our political philosophy. It was not a judgment in the rivalry of favorite fads; the forces matched were not suddenly discovered, but had been developed in the conflict between the old tradition and the new environment, which makes the slow and painful metamorphosis we know as progress. Inertia in history does not have to be accounted for; it is an axiom in sociology no less than physics that things must stay till they are moved, and mankind would have given no surprised attention if the idea of aristocracy, that the few are born to rule the many, hallowed by centuries of custom in the "old country," had been transplanted to the new.[1] Indeed, one reads but scantily among the records of the colonies who is not impressed with how much of this idea was carried over to America. There were accepted barriers between gentlemen and simple-men, between those who wore their periwigs and silks and those who dressed in homespun. Such was the normal system of society; since under it the social peace had been preserved, it seemed entitled to continuance, at least so thought the comfortable classes. The Federalists like all conservatives seemed justified by time.

But there were factors in the making of America that

[1] *Cf.* Leon Fraser, *English Opinion of the American Constitution and Government* (N. Y., 1915).

84

were bound to modify this system. The settlers of this country had come across the sea to found new homes where they might have a larger opportunity for unhampered worship or well rewarded work. The essence of separatism and ambition is self-reliance, which, since with few exceptions they came of their own will, was common to them all. The free land of America had made them self-dependent and made control imposed upon them seem against all natural right. For a variety of causes they had determined to be free from England, justifying their boldness upon the doctrine of the equal dignity of men. But the Declaration of Independence, as has often been remarked, was written as a campaign document; equality was postulated only as a basis for the claim of liberty, a philosophy which the conservatives were willing to endorse when intended only for the export trade. It was some twenty years before they were embarrassed by this memory. But philosophies insist on being universally applied. The American success sent out a stimulus that was received in France, tremendously increased and then sent back again across the sea. What Jefferson had written when George the Third brushed aside the guards of liberty, seemed suitable to quote when Hamilton and Fisher Ames made their great affirmations of the privileges of property. Democracy was becoming a national ideal. The Federalists with their business program failed to recognize this fact, or, if they did perceive it, they would not stoop to mingle with the common folk, scorning arts by which they might have thrived. In this they were more nice than wise; the last decade had made that clear, at least to younger members of the party.

The old system of following policies irrespective of popular opinion was gone forever, wrote J. Q. Adams to Rufus King in 1802:[1] " it never can and never will be re-

---

[1] J. Q. Adams to King, October 8, 1802, *King Correspondence.*

vived. The experiment, such as it was, has failed, and to attempt its restoration would be as absurd as to undertake the resurrection of a carcass seven years in its grave." Noah Webster writing from Connecticut took the same position.

There is one particular in which, I think, the leading gentlemen of the Washington School have uniformly erred. They have attempted to resist the force of current opinion, instead of falling into the current with a view to direct it. . . . Between the unbending firmness of a H————n, [and] the obsequiousness of a J————n, there is a way to preserve the confidence of the populace, without a sacrifice of integrity.[1]

One reason why the people had rebuked the Federalist leaders was founded on the impression that they were leading toward a monarchy. Many of the opposition papers ceased to use the name Federalist in their editorials, and preferred to talk of the " Aristocrats," [2] whereas their own name Republican seemed to invoke the loyalty of all those who believed in the existing form of government. Something must be done to set the people right.

The change of rulers [declared a writer in the *New York Spectator*, in 1804] which this state and the United States have experienced, may be ascribed more to names and to the charm of words, than to any conduct or measure of the federal administration. It is probable that nothing has tended so much to alienate the affections of the people from the federal administration as the malicious insinuation, that the federalists are friends to monarchical government . . . These Machiavellian politicians by the same magic have annexed a peculiar

[1] Noah Webster to King, July 6, 1807, *King Correspondence*.

[2] *Poughkeepsie Journal* in *N. Y. Evening Post*, November 24, 1801; *N. Y. American Citizen*, May 1, 1802, *etc.*

property to the name republicanism. . . . It now stands thus, republicans can do no wrong.[1]

A shrewd reform was already under way, for two years before, certain papers had rechristened the party with a reassuring title; Federalists were gone, they said, and Federal Republicans had come to take their place.[2] In the botany of politics a rose may change its perfume with its name. Now the Federalists took counsel as to the designation of their enemies.

Jacobin [they thought, was] too offensive to obtain currency as a universal name, and excepting to the leaders of the party, unjust; the appellation of republican is claimed in common by both parties, and therefore is not the least discriminative; whereas *democrat* being the name taken by themselves and liable to no objection on our part, is that which alone should be used in writing of our political opponents.[3]

Most Federalist editors accepted this advice, though the change offended certain stalwarts of the old régime.[4]

The Jeffersonians in New York city had early learned the use of various social aids to partisan fidelity. Societies were formed where mutual encouragement might circulate with pots of ale, and plots be laid against the enemy. But since this enemy controlled the government, those plots were said to smack of treason. Washington had issued his warning against such secret clubs, and Hamilton, "the

[1] *N. Y. Spectator*, March 31, 1804.

[2] *N. Y. Evening Post*, April 19, 21, 1802.   [3] *Ibid.*, May 3, 1803.

[4] Speaking in 1816, Judge Benson referred to "my own party, the Federal party, by their primitive perfect name without the subsequently invented addition of Republican. Is it not in the Constitution itself, that those who formed it were Republicans? Suppose, yes — then 'the expression of it wholly inoperative.' Suppose, no— will calling themselves so make them so?" *Memoir, read before the Historical Society, etc.*, pamphlet (N. Y., 1817), p. 51.

servile copyist of Mr. Pitt (so wrote Thomas Jefferson) thought he, too, must have his alarms, his insurrection," and had joined his chief in condemnation.[1]   But the Columbian Order, or as it was more generally known, the Tammany Society, soon stripped of Federalist members, survived to menace Federalism in New York. This famous order had been founded, it was professed, for charitable and social purposes, and now that it assumed a more ambitious rôle it by no means forgot its earlier functions; for under any government approaching a democracy, bounties to the poor and entertainments are well mixed with party politics.   The Federalists in 1800 saw with confessed dismay the effectiveness of their opponents' methods, and Hamilton himself, who through the late campaign had berated Tammany and all its sons, now quietly proposed the flattery of imitation.   Writing to James A. Bayard in 1802, he set forth a plan of a " Christian Constitutional Society," shrewdly propagandist even in its title, which should have its branches in all cities to promote true patriotism.   The party must become the patron of the poor; one proposition was to " institute in such places—1st, societies for the relief of immigrants; 2nd, academies, each with one professor, for instructing the different classes of mechanics in the principles of mechanics and the elements of chemistry.   The cities have been employed by the Jacobins to give an impulse to the country." [2]   Apparently this well-laid scheme was not put into practice, but the suggestion was not lost.

Jefferson's embargo, in 1807, so stiffened the resistance of the business interests that the Federalist party in New York, as elsewhere, shook off its lethargy of hopelessness and entered into the contest for control.   No expedient

[1] Jefferson to Monroe, May 1, 1795 (Ford edition), vol. vii, p. 16.

[2] Hamilton to Bayard, April 1802, Hamilton's *Works* (Lodge) vol. viii, pp. 598-599.

which had brought success to their opponents might be left untried. They had observed by what devices the Tammany Society had drawn support from classes who had no ear for studied argument. They had seen this organization in its menacing vitality spread to other cities and register new victories. Such methods seemed adapted to a democracy: taste could not be considered, the Federalists resolved to adopt them before it was too late. In the spring of 1808, Isaac Sebring,[1] a prosperous merchant of the city, with the aid of Gulian C. Verplanck and Richard Varick, conceived a project by which he thought this might be accomplished. If the Federalists had no leader who could rival Jefferson in winning the great mass of men, at least they had the name of Washington, whose potency grew with the years, and to turn this asset into current value, on July 12th, a society was formed to keep fresh his memory and carry out his principles. For its foundation, it is not at all unlikely, Mr. Sebring forwarded the money; Colonel Varick gave the prestige of his patronage; and Verplanck, then but twenty-two years old, supplied the ardor and enthusiasm of youth. Whatever were the sources of its early strength, the Washington Benevolent Society was immediately successful. The new society, like that of Tammany, held its meetings in secret and engaged to promote good fellowship among its members and to relieve those who were in want. It was particularly hospitable to old soldiers of the Revolution, but

[1] Sebring was born in Dutchess County, but moved to New York before the Revolution. He had enlisted in the army as a quarter-master and fought in some campaigns about the city. He had become wealthy and prominent in the Federalist party in the city, sitting as alderman for the first ward (see *supra*, ch. i) and frequently as chairman of public party meetings (*e. g. N. Y. Commercial Advertiser*, February 27, 1809). He later lost his fortune and was glad to be appointed to a clerkship in the Custom House under Samuel Swartwout; W. Barrett, *Old Merchants of New York*, vol. iv, pp. 18-20; J. A. Roberts, *New York in the Revolution* (N. Y. 1898), p. 135.

through its charm of mystery and picturesqueness it appealed to men of high and low degree; no workman was too humble to be welcomed to its ranks to march for Federalist principles. Its pose was of impartial patriotism—a harmless affectation, since no one was deceived.

The society held its first public celebration on February 22nd, 1809, marching to the Zion Church to hear a discourse by Samuel M. Hopkins; and such support had been accorded to the enterprise that, in the evening of that day, more than a thousand sat down to supper in five taverns, the president and his honorary staff appearing several times at each, that no one might feel slighted.[1] The plan was soon adopted in other cities and villages of the state. Everywhere appeared the little manual called *Washington's Legacy,* which contained his portrait, his Farewell Address (not leaving out his solemn warning against secret political clubs!), and sometimes a "Chronological Sketch of the Life of the Author of the Foregoing Address." [2] Often, too, the constitutions of the nation and the state were printed,[3] and a blank certificate of membership to be filled in by the local officers. The statement of the constitution of the society is not uniform, but that of the town of Galway, in Saratoga County, may serve as an example.[4] Besides commemorating Washington, " It is to promote harmony and unity of sentiment among the members; to endeavor to collect and diffuse correct information on matters respecting

[1] *N. Y. Commercial Advertiser,* February 23, 1809.

[2] See edition for Essex County (N. J.) Washington Benevolent Society, 1812 (N. Y. P. L.)

[3] For example, edition for Augusta, N. Y. (Albany, 1816). Sometimes the society served a town, sometimes a county, and sometimes both together. See Private Journal of DeWitt Clinton, p. 86, in W. W. Campbell, *Life and Writings of DeWitt Clinton* (N. Y., 1849).

[4] *Constitution of the Washington Benevolent Society of Galway, in the County of Saratoga* (Albany, 1812).

our state and national affairs, as a means of inculcating sound political principles . . . and a constant watchfulness against the intrigues of men to whatever political party they belong." An indirect attack was made on Jeffersonians when it required that, "No person that is an atheist, a deist, a profane swearer, a drunkard, or doth not respect the Christian Sabbath, shall be received as a member of this society." Benevolences from the common chest were to be granted to poor members, but to guard against abuse it was provided that not more than two dollars a month should be given to an applicant without a general vote. Largely for this purpose each member paid a dollar as initiation fee and fifty cents a year as dues.

The society spread far beyond the boundaries of the state.[1] It followed Tammany to Rhode Island,[2] and was taken up in Connecticut, Massachusetts, New Hampshire, and especially Vermont, while Pennsylvania and New Jersey each had their local organizations, that in Philadelphia enduring until after 1820.[3] It had "runners" who spent their time in organizing branches, and developing such fraternity and loyalty among the members that Republican conventions roundly condemned the society as dangerous to

[1] *Cf.* Harlan H. Ballard, "A Forgotten Fraternity" in *Collections of the Berkshire Historical and Scientific Society*, vol. iii, no. 4 (1913), pp. 279-298; and E. F. Hanaburgh, "News for Bibliophiles" in *The Nation*, October 30, 1913.

[2] W. A. Robinson, *Jeffersonian Democracy in New England* (New Haven, 1916), p. 89, citing M. W. Jernegan, *The Tammany Societies of Rhode Island*.

[3] T. E. V. Smith, *Political Parties, etc.* The New York Public Library has the best collection of "Washington's Legacies" orations, poems, etc. known to the author; other collections are to be found in the N. Y. Historical Society Library, the Boston Athenaeum (see Catalogue, part v, p. 3264) and the American Antiquarian Society Library. In the last named is a satire called *The First Book of the Washington Benevolents, etc.* Many items are scattered among town libraries.

the nation, because of secrecy and friendship for Great Britain.[1]

It was the element of secrecy that most perturbed the Madisonians; no guess was too extravagant as to what took place behind locked doors and curtained windows. In New England after 1812, when recruiting officers were baffled by mysterious counsel to the young, the Republicans cried out in wrath against the "Washington Benevolents." Desertions and escapes were charged to their cabals; and when some candidate for Congress or the legislature whose outlook had been hopeful was overwhelmingly defeated by a Federalist at the polls, outraged partisans of Madison averred that the records of this pestilent society, if they were once forthcoming, would lay bare a scandalous conspiracy. Fantastic fabrications were made to pass as the awful oaths required of its members, and committees were appointed to watch closely for some overt act on which to base a charge of treason. The Federalists, of course, exulted at the furor their society created, each new outcry proving its effectiveness.[2]

Yet their secrets were innocent enough. Several years ago, by accident, there was discovered in Berkshire County, Massachusetts, an ancient volume of ledger-like appearance, which, after pasted clippings had been steamed away, disclosed in fair round writing the ritual of the Washington Benevolent Society.[3] There was provided for their monthly meetings a punctilious ceremonial requiring ten officers, and, to insure a uniformity in the conduct of their business, regular reports were forwarded to the parent society in New York. The neophyte was solemnly assured that

[1] *Vermont Republican*, January 12, 1810 and February 10, 1812, quoted by Robinson, *loc. cit.*

[2] H. H. Ballard, *loc. cit.*, pp. 279, 290.

[3] *Ibid.*, pp. 285-287; this discovery was made by Mr. Ballard.

during the administration of Thomas Jefferson " our right
has been impaired, our constitution disregarded, and dis-
sensions and distress have prevailed among our citizens."
As he was examined for the last induction, he was asked
as to his country, "Are you willing to use your exertion to
preserve it against the inroads of despotism, monarchy,
aristocracy, and democracy?"[1]

It was customary for the society on Washington's Birth-
day and the Fourth of July to listen to patriotic oratory,
more or less frankly Federalist in flavor; the great departed
chieftain was commemorated as summing up the civic
virtues. He it was, said Samuel M. Hopkins, making the
first of these addresses in February, 1809,—he it was, who
prevented us from rushing into the abyss of French fraternity. What had been the fate of most republics in the
world? " Where were Switzerland, Genoa, Venice and
Holland? Where had been America but for Washington?"[2] One year later, Peter A. Jay, speaking when
America had felt the pinch of Napoleon's Continental
System, thought it timely to berate the French and the ideas
of revolution so dear to Jeffersonians.

Washington [he said] was not to be fascinated by the syren
song of equality . . . and uninfected with the absurd and pernicious sophisms of these modern days, he never apostasized

[1] It is likely that in devising this ritual, the authors had taken some
suggestion from the Society of the Cincinnati, then entirely Federalist
in sympathy (see toasts as given in *N. Y. Evening Post*, August 14,
1811) and of whose New York chapter, Col. Varick was the president
when he co-operated in the foundation of the Washington Benevolent
Society; see John Schuyler, *The Society of the Cincinnati in New
York* (N. Y. 1886), p. 333. There was usually an oration at the monthly
meeting, see Abimelech Coody (G. C. Verplanck) *Letter to Dr. Samuel
L. Mitchill, M. D., etc.* (N. Y., 1811), p. 11.

[2] S. M. Hopkins, *An Oration delivered before the Washington Benevolent Society, in the City of New York, at Zion Church, on the Twenty-
second of February, 1809* (N. Y., 1809), in N. Y. Hist. Soc. Collections.

[*sic*] from the belief of his fathers and thought it was no matter of importance either to individuals or to the public, whether there were one God or twenty.[1]

But many orators were not content with these indirect attacks. Gulian C. Verplanck, the society's young secretary, had the previous July delivered an oration wherein he first recalled the prosperous days of Federalism. But at length the wisdom of the nation slept;

so completely were the people drugged with the opiates of flattery and fair profession, that they lay in stupid lethargy, and saw their navy dismantled and their commerce left to the mercy of every petty pirate. They saw without indignation, the temples of justice broke open and the judiciary, the foremost bulwark of our liberties, thrown down and trampled under foot. Unmoved, they beheld a system of executive corcuption and unconstitutional influence sprouting forth from the head of the administration, spreading through every department of the state, and enveloping the representative majesty of our nation in its broad and poisonous shade.

Madison, now come to power, if not himself destructive, was the patron of the admirers of French licentiousness.[2] Josiah Quincy, who somewhat later addressed the Boston branch, inquired of " Our rulers—who are they, and what is true of them? Mr. Madison is President; Mr. Monroe, Secretary of State; Mr. Gallatin, Secretary of the Treasury; Mr. Armstrong, Secretary of War. Every man of them

---

[1] P. A. Jay, *An Oration delivered before the Washington Benevolent Society in the City of New York* (N. Y., 1810), in N. Y. Pub. Library.

[2] G. C. Verplanck, *An Oration delivered July 4th, 1809, in the North Dutch Church, before the Washington Benevolent Society* (N. Y., 1809), in Columbia University Library; a somewhat inaccurate quotation is to be found in C. P. Daly, Biographical Sketch in *Proceedings of the Century Association in Honor of the Memory of Gulian C. Verplanck* (N. Y., 1870).

in Washington's day the enemy of his policy." [1] Such was
the style of oratory addressed to this society in its various
branches throughout its dozen years of life; most famous
Federalists were glad to speak before it, from Gouverneur
Morris, who gave the counsel of the passing generation, to
Daniel Webster, who vouchsafed the promise of the new. [2]

The Tammany Society had a home in Martling's Tavern,
which the Federalists were wont to call contemptuously
"the Pigpen." Sebring and his colleagues in the enterprise
boldly set about to shame their rivals by building a great
hall, to be maintained exclusively for party purposes. At
the evening meeting, February 22, 1809, it was decided to
sell 8000 shares of stock at ten dollars each. During the
spring a plot was purchased on the corner of Reade Street
and Broadway, and on the Fourth of July, the society proceeded, with much pomp and pride, to lay the corner stone
of Washington Hall, probably the first edifice in America
so built for party purposes. [3] The stone was set in place by
the president, Isaac Sebring, with all formality. "Built by
the friends of Washington," he said, "may it never be
polluted by the enemies of that illustrious and revered
statesman." [4] This solemn cermony then completed, the

---

[1] Quincy's speech is reprinted in full in the *New York Spectator*,
May 12-15, 1813.

[2] G. Morris, *An Oration delivered July 5th, 1813 before the Washington Benevolent Society in the City of New York* (N. Y., 1813),
in N. Y. P. L.; see also in same library addresses by Noah Webster,
Isaac C. Bates, etc. and by Sedgwick in *N. Y. Evening Post*, July 5,
1811; *The Writings and Speeches of Daniel Webster* (Boston, 1903),
vol. xv, p. 583. In the New York Society Library there is *An Oration
delivered at Washington Hall, February 22, 1814 before the Washington Benevolent Society of the City of New York, in commemoration
of the nativity of George Washington*, by H. W. Warner. *Cf.* Ode
read with this, *N. Y. Commercial Advertiser*, February 23, 1814.

[3] Tammany Hall was not begun until the following year.

[4] *N. Y. Commercial Advertiser*, July 5, 1809. The inscription was

company marched to the North Dutch Church where an ode was sung, and the oration we have mentioned was pronounced by Gulian C. Verplanck.

The imposing building with high pediment and decorated cornice was hailed as a monument to Federalist enterprise; but although some well-to-do members like Philip Hone, bought twenty-five shares or more,[1] only about half the necessary funds to pay for its erection were subscribed. Sebring was obliged to borrow heavily, and, in 1817, the hall was sold as a hotel, though still considered as the headquarters of the party, and the stopping place for most New England Federalists passing to and from the nation's capital.[2]   But what was done by the " Benevolents " in New York city was orthodox for all the chapters, and soon other Washington Halls were built as temples for the faithful. Such were those in Albany and Troy, in Stockbridge, Massachusetts,[3] and the more commodious structure put up in Third Street, Philadelphia.[4]

The pageantry of the society was likewise soon reduced

---

as follows: " This Corner Stone of Washington Hall was laid July 4th, 1809, being the 33rd Anniversary of the Independence of the United States of America by the Washington Benevolent Society, Instituted 12th July, A. D. MDCCCVIII."

[1] *Diary of Philip Hone* (edited by Bayard Tuckerman, N. Y., 1889), vol. ii, p. 247.

[2] The last public celebration of the society in New York City was held in 1817, although meetings are spoken of as late as 1820, T. E. V. Smith, *op. cit.*, p. 11 *et seq.*   The hotel was renovated in 1827 and burned in 1844. See also W. Barrett, *Old Merchants of New York*, vol. iv, pp. 18-19.

[3] H. H. Ballard, *op. cit.*, pp. 282, 290; Mrs. C. V. R. Bonney, *Legacy of Historical Gleanings*, vol. i, p. 281. Even the negroes had their "Washington Benevolent Association of Africa," see *Analectic Magazine*, vol. xiii (1819), p. 279.

[4] B. J. Lossing, *Cyclopedia of United States History* (N. Y., 1881), vol. ii, p. 1478.

to code, following the New York precedent. The members always marched in thirteen grand divisions, each preceded by a banner with the name and, possibly, the " counterfeit presentment " of a hero of the Revolution, the choice not left to chance but specified in order—Hancock, McDougall, Putnam, on to Hamilton, the last. The chief standard of the line was always that of Washington, richly fringed and mounted, and generally escorted by the war-worn veterans of the Revolution.[1] The cultus of the Father of His Country had in one short decade reached to such development that " relics," like his gorget, were sometimes carried in the honorable place of the procession.[2] It was customary for an officer, perhaps the first vice-president, to carry in his hand the sacrosanct Farewell Address, while others bore the Constitution and the Declaration of Independence. There were other flags and pennants commemorating each some glorious event, such as the Christmas victory at Trenton or the surrender of Burgoyne. until with bands and banners, mounted men and carriages, and the thousands four abreast, the eye was surfeited with splendor. The ceremonies of Rogation Week in mediaeval Rome could scarcely have been more nicely ordered. It was the public ritual of nationalism—performed, ironically enough, by the party of the Hartford Convention.[3]

In a letter to his father, Peter A. Jay describes the ceremonies in which he bore a part:

The Celebration of yesterday occasioned much exultation

[1] *N. Y. Commercial Advertiser*, July 3, 5, 7, 1809, July 3, 1811, July 3, 1813; H. H. Ballard, *loc. cit.*

[2] *Massachusetts Historical Society Proceedings*, 1876-1877, pp. 401-404.

[3] The credit for this success should doubtless go to Col. Richard Platt who was the marshal of the society's model celebration on July 4, 1809. It was he who had managed the great " Federal parade " of 1789. *N. Y. Commercial Advertiser*, July 5, 1809 and W. A. Duer, *Reminiscences of an Old New Yorker.*

among the Federalists. The Society walked in procession and amounted to more than two thousand. Many Gentlemen kept aloof, but it was one of the most respectable assemblages of people that I have ever seen. It consisted of substantial Shop keepers and Mechanicks, of Men of the middling Class, and of a considerable Number of old Revolutionary officers and Soldiers. Almost all of them possess Influence and can bring to the poll other votes besides their own.[1]

All this meeting and marching and dining was not without effect in New York city. The recovery of the majority in the common council, which had been lost in 1804, was attributed to the efforts of the society, and it was natural that they should conduct an elaborate illumination.[2] The "Washington Benevolents" and their friends of the Hamilton Society, which met in Hamilton Hall in Cherry Street,[3] let no occasion pass without a parade and a feast with its innumerable toasts.[4] When in 1834 William Sullivan was writing an account of the celebrations of the various branches in 1812, he remarked, "If ever the day shall come when like perils shall overtake the good citizens of the United States, let them remember this example."[5] In this connection, then, it is apposite to note the observation of a pamphleteer in 1840, that the Tippecanoe Clubs of that

[1] P. A. Jay to John Jay, February 23, 1810, *Jay Correspondence.*

[2] I. N. Phelps-Stokes, *Iconography of Manhattan Island,* (N. Y., 1915), vol. i, p. 406, and T. E. V. Smith, *loc. cit.*

[3] *N. Y. Evening Post,* July 3, 1811; W. H. Bayless, *Old Taverns of New York* (N. Y., 1915), pp. 408, 423.

[4] Members of Congress were always specially invited. It is interesting in 1811 in New York to find a mechanic toasting the merchants, and a merchant the mechanics. The sentiments grew bolder at these banquets as the night wore on. For the order of march of the Hamilton Society, see *N. Y. Spectator,* July 6, 1811.

[5] William Sullivan, *Familiar Letters on Public Characters and Public Events, from the Peace of 1783 to the Peace of 1815* (Boston, 1834), p. 348.

year, with all their extravagances, were but lineal descendants of the Washington Benevolent Society.[1]

Such were the new devices by which Young Federalism
sought to make its fellowship attractive. For a season they
enjoyed success,[2] but this was due, in large part, to a
measure of the national government, inevitably so unpopular as to give the opposition a cause of dignity, and,
therefore, once again respectful hearing. Shortly before
Christmas in 1807, a docile Congress passed the President's
embargo bill, and by thus "regulating" commerce made
the first of that long series of convincing demonstrations
that the Jeffersonian party could not serve and could not
understand the economic interests of the north. In New
York, as in New England, the Federalist merchants and
their friends recognized it as a stroke so patently impolitic
that, in the reaction, which was sure to follow hard upon
its execution, they took hope of permanent relief. They
could suffer, almost with enthusiasm, if their plight might
break the patience of the public. Although in the winter
and spring of 1808 the suffering was yet chiefly in anticipation, all realized that here was an issue on which the party
might appeal no less to patriotism than to self-interest.
Essays on the gloomy prospect now filled the columns of
the Federalist prints,[3] sharing space with resolutions and

---

[1] C. G. Greene and B. F. Hallett, *The Identity of the Old Hartford
Convention Federalists with the Modern Whig-Harrison Party Carefully illustrated by Living Specimens, and Dedicated to the Young Men
of the Nation* (*Boston Morning Post*, extra, August, 1840, in Cornell
University Library).

[2] It had scores of branches and tens of thousands of members. Its
decay began with the declaration of peace in 1815. William Cobbett,
in his *Weekly Register*, May 13, 1815, said that this society in the
Federalist states was like the British Literary Fund, "a scheme for
attaching hack writers to the government under the guise of charity."
See S. E. Morison, *Harrison Gray Otis* (Boston, 1913), vol. i, p. 301.

[3] A good example is the series of letters by Rufus King appearing
in the *Evening Post*, see King to T. Pickering, February 5, 1808, *King
Correspondence.*

petitions; and this was by no means confined to New York city. What were "the army and navy of John Adams—the eight per cent loan—stamp act, direct tax, carriage, loaf sugar, and whiskey tax, all the old so-called abominations," to this new monstrosity.[1] Campaign songs appeared which recalled the glorious days a decade since,

> " When federal men did stand at helm,
> We shipped off many a cargo—
> When Wheat and all produce was high,
> 'Cause there was no embargo,—"

the good old days of Tom Truxton and Toby Lear, when America had struck the enemy and not herself.[2]

The New England Federalists saw here an opportunity to discredit the President and his "official candidate," James Madison, whose election had been ordered for the autumn. The Essex Junto of Massachusetts called a convention to discuss the nomination for the impending contest. The " delegates " were self-selected or chosen by small groups of gentlemen in council. In the party methods here Otis and his colleagues did not contemplate a reference to the people; it was, as usual, a movement *for* the people, by the wise and good. To bring about the meeting, which was scheduled for New York, Judge Egbert Benson suggested committees of correspondence, which were formed for states and counties, and engaged in some preliminary discussion. Otis thought the Clintons, feeling slighted in the preference for Madison over George Clinton, then Vice-President, might be supported by the Federalists. But the committees of New York would not endorse a coalition. "We have condescended twice," wrote Abraham Van Vechten, " to tamper with Democratic candidates, and in both instances

[1] *Albany Gazette*, March 17, 1808.
[2] *Ibid*, February 29, 1808.

have been subjected to severe self-reproach . . . Our experimental knowledge of the Clintonian system is a powerful antidote against affording it any facility here." When the Federalists met, from the south as well as north, C. C. Pinckney was selected as the candidate for President and Rufus King for the second office. The New York committee sent out announcements to their correspondents in the different states.[1]

Jefferson's subservience to France was held up to indignation, while England holding out against Napoleon was pictured as the champion of liberty. Even her impressment of the sailors on our ships, which, since the encounter of the " Leopard " and the " Chesapeake " had occasioned bitter protest, was now easily excused.

If England abandon the right, the British sailors would desert. . . . They would engage in our service for less wages than their own (for engage they must, there being no other way for them to gain a livelihood). Our native American sailors, of course, would be thrown out of employ. Which ought we to encourage, foreign sailors or our own? . . . In case of war no reliance could be placed on foreign sailors.[2]

There was widely published through the state a speech of Barent Gardenier, a congressman from Ulster County, who complained of Jefferson's diplomacy as wrapped in secrecy, and for the boldness of his charges was challenged to a duel.[3] The Federalists of New York city announced a

[1] Van Vechten to Otis, S. E. Morison, *Otis*, vol. i, p. 307; Jacob Radcliffe, J. O. Hoffman, C. D. Colden and S. Jones, Jr. (the N. Y. committee) to the Federal Republican Committee of Charleston, S. C., *ibid.*, pp. 314-315; also *ibid.*, p. 304. In spite of the mode of designating delegates, this may be called the first national nominating convention.

[2] See " Peace" in *N. Y. Spectator*, April 13, 1808.

[3] *N. Y. Evening Post* and *Albany Gazette* March 3, 1808. In this duel with G. W. Campbell, Gardenier was severely wounded, see *Albany Gazette,* March 14, 1808; H. von Holst, *The Constitutional and Political History of the United States* (Chicago, 1876), vol. i, pp. 210-211.

motto which might have been developed into the first party platform in America: " No Embargo—No Foreign Influences—No Mystery—Freedom of Debate—Freedom of Suffrage—Freedom of Navigation and Trade—Liberty and Independence." [1] The Republicans realized that now they had a foe no longer to be scorned. [2] When the vote was taken the Federalists had not only their old districts by the upper Hudson and the Mohawk, but a number of new counties, though not including New York city. [3] The ardent efforts of Williams, Van Ness, and J. R. Van Rensselaer gave the party a larger majority in Columbia County than it had ever known before. [4] The party delegation sent to Congress, including James Emott, Barent Gardenier, K. K. Van Rensselaer, Herman Knickerbocker and Robert LeRoy Livingston, was a credit to the state. [5]

Each new law conceived to stiffen and complete the embargo, threw more numbers and more strength into the Federalist opposition. In New York the conditions soon grew intolerable. The port was full of shipping, but the masts stood gaunt and bare of sails through the spring and summer. The wharves and quays were clean of boxes, bales or casks; counting-houses which had been scenes of bustle and activity were now deserted, many vainly advertised for rent. Of all the carts that had rattled through the streets, scarcely one in ten was now offered for employment; while idle clerks com-

---

[1] *N. Y. Evening Post,* quoted in *Albany Gazette,* April 25, 1808.

[2] See DeWitt Clinton to George Clinton, April 3, 1808, DeWitt Clinton Mss.

[3] *Albany Gazette,* May 1-5, 1808.

[4] Martin Van Buren to DeWitt Clinton, April 16 and April 30, 1808, DeWitt Clinton Mss.; W. W. Van Ness to Sol. Van Rensselaer, April 30, 1808, vol. i, p. 484.

[5] *Albany Gazette,* May 5, 1808.

miserated seamen, and merchants gathered in the Tontine Coffee House to frame petitions.[1]

The effects were by no means limited to New York city. At Albany, when no canvas was unfurled upon the river at the melting of the ice in 1808, the carters and the bargemen joined the sailors in their complaint.[2] The farmers about Utica, led by Thomas R. Gold and Jonas Platt, protested that the value of their land depended on the free way for their surplus produce to the European markets. Without this they could not make their payments to land agents. With respect to the Mohawk Valley, they said in a petition to the President, where the foreign sale of potash and flour was the chief source of their ready money, this measure in its rigid execution would "arrest the further progress of those settlements, blast the experiments of the husbandmen, and ruin the flourishing frontier counties of the state."[3] Although the Oneida Federalists three years later gladly put their money into manufacturing, in 1809 they professed to fear its drawing off of labor from its customary pursuits.[4] The same complaint came from the districts further west. When wheat dropped from two dollars to seventy-five cents the bushel, Colonel Troup, in Geneva, as agent for the Pulteneys found difficulty in collecting rents.[5]

[1] John Lambert, *Travels through Canada and the United States of North America in the Years 1806, 1807, 1808* (London, 1814), vol. ii, p. 55 *et seq.*

[2] *Albany Gazette*, March 17, 1808.

[3] *N. Y. Spectator*, September 13, 1808.   [4] M. M. Bagg, *op. cit.*

[5] Troup to King, Albany, March 7, 1808, *King Correspondence*; J. D. Hammond, *Political History*, vol. i, p. 265. For a time it seemed likely that DeWitt Clinton might make common cause with the Federalists on the embargo. Since the beginning of Mr. Jefferson's second term, Clinton had been chafing at the natural preference of Virginia for Madison rather than his uncle, the Vice-President, as party leader. He at first opposed the embargo, and letters came to

Although some Federalists, like Gouverneur Morris, were still pessimistic,[1] most of the leaders, howsoever they might suffer in their private purses, saw here the flood tide of fortune for the party. They affected to consider any laborers who were employed by Republicans as doubtless bullied into voting for embargo policies. It was the sense of a meeting held in New York city

that all electors who shall be deprived of employment, or otherwise persecuted, in consequence of the free exercise of the right of suffrage, are entitled to the protection of the Federal Republicans of this city, and we hereby pledge ourselves to these and the public, that to the utmost of our power we will countenance, encourage, and protect all citizens who may thus be persecuted.[2]

It was in the spirit of the new attempt to make the party popular with the lower classes, that some enthusiasts were anxious to silence for all time the irritating cry of Toryism. To understand this imputation it is necessary to revert to an earlier campaign.

The contest of 1807 had been enlivened by an episode, which recounted may suggest a commentary on the ways of politics a hundred years ago. On April 2, 1807, the *Albany Register,* a Clinton paper, produced an affidavit which read as follows:

Col. Nicholas Staats of the County of Rensselaer, being duly sworn deposeth—that he the said Nicholas was a member of

him which hinted at Federalist support for the venerable George Clinton (see his Mss., September 16, 1808), but he subsequently changed his mind on the commercial policy though he was never reconciled to the Virginia dynasty.

[1] He spoke of doubts as to "whether to make an effort to put good men in power or remain quiet spectators. I am of the latter opinion." *Diary and Letters*, vol. ii, p. 512.

[2] *N. Y. Evening Post*, April 25, 1809.

the House of Assembly for the County of Rensselaer in the session of 1806—that in the month of January of the same year, and on the day before the Assembly proceeded to the choice of the Council of Appointment, he the deponent was waited upon by Solomon Van Rensselaer, adjutant general of the State—that said Van Rensselaer intimated to him, the said Nicholas Staats, that the Governor was his (the said Nicholas') friend; that he, the Governor, had appointed the sheriff of Greene County to gratify him:—That the said Van Rensselaer requested the deponent to call at Mr. Skinner's Coffee-House and see Mr. Van Ness and Mr. Shurtleff, two federal members of the house, who, the said Van Rensselaer assured him wished to converse with him, as this deponent understood, upon the subject of choosing the Council of Appointment . . . That the said Van Rensselaer further pressed the subject of the Council, and intimated unequivocally to the said Nicholas, that if he would vote for the ticket which was to be supported by the Governor's friends, mentioning the name of Mr. Woodworth in particular, as one who would be on the said ticket, that in that case he, the said Nicholas, would be promoted to or made a Brigadier General. . . . [1]

Solomon Van Rensselaer, who was a cousin of the Patroon, apparently aware what useful service could be rendered by a good red herring, declared some four days later that this affidavit had been extracted under pressure by Citizen Genêt, a man who should be given small consideration, inasmuch as he had recently been threatening the United States with an attack by General Bonaparte.[2] Genêt denied this charge,[3] whereupon a Federalist general meeting,

[1] Shurtleff was a member of assembly from Albany County, *N. Y. Assembly Journal*, 1807, p. 3. The proceedings of the trials later conducted in Albany may be found in a pamphlet *Report of the Trials of Jenkins vs. Van Rensselaer* (Albany, 1808, N. Y. State Library). See also *Albany Gazette*, March 14, 1808.

[2] Supplement to the *Albany Republican Crisis*, April 6, 1807.

[3] *Albany Register*, April 13, 1807.

at the capital, expressed its full confidence in Van Rensselaer's word. The Republicans, not so to be discredited, likewise gathered to declare, on motion of Judge Tayler, that they wholly disbelieved that the ex-minister had made the threat.[1] Van Rensselaer, as might have been expected, took this as a passing of the lie. The chairman of the meeting, Judge John Tayler, being too decrepit to be dealt with, he sent the secretary, Elisha Jenkins, a challenge to a duel, to which, to his chagrin, no response was made. Soon seeing Jenkins on the public street, he stole up behind, struck him to the ground insensible, and then walked on without concern. On passing toward the State House square, some angry words were exchanged with old Judge Tayler, who, with the more efficient help of Dr. C. D. Cooper, his son-in-law, and another, set upon Van Rensselaer to such purpose that he was all but killed, and kept in bed for half a year. It was charged that Governor Lewis standing by allowed Van Rensselaer to use his cane.[2]

It was long before the echoes of this brawl had died away. As in 1804 when Burr's following had been called "the sons of sworn king's men,"[3] so now again was raised the stale reproach of Toryism.

Republicans, [admonishes a curious old handbill] see the Reign of Terror revived with all its violence and horror—see young tories attacking old Whigs—because they are Republicans! Judge Tayler, whose head is white with the hoar of years, fought the battles of our independence, and has ever since been a firm and undaunted whig. But what shall we say of Morgan Lewis, the Governor of the State? Behold him, encouraging tumult and violence! Behold him lend his cane to an up-

---

[1] *Jenkins vs. Van Rensselaer*, pp. 13-17.

[2] *Ibid.* At the trials the most eminent counsel in the state appeared. Verdicts were awarded to both sides.

[3] Benj. Howe to John Tayler, September 17, 1804, Tayler Mss.

start Tory; behold him assisting that tory to do violence to Judge Tayler, a revolutionary soldier—a Senator in this State —an old man and an inflexible Republican. Is such a man fit to be the Governor of a free people! Republicans! rise in your might, and put down this infamous composition of Toryism and Apostacy.[1]

This was a generation which was sensitive to such appeals. Men then in middle life remembered Tories as the terror of their childhood. Grizzled " skinners," in recounting sufferings and adventures, still kept bright the fires of hatred in what had been the neutral ground. Citizens of New York city could with bitterness recall their seven years of banishment while Loyalists enjoyed their property within the lines. Cherry Valley and Oriskany were names still hideous with the memory of murder. Broadsides written by Republicans in 1807 which called to mind the horrors of the scalping knife and prison ship did not fail of their effect; it would never do to let the Tory-Federalists regain control.

In 1809, when the Federalists were again the objects of this old hue and cry, some daring spirits urged the cleansing of their party of this stain by the ostracism of all those to whom the charge of Toryism might be applied. But such proposals stirred the indignation of the older leaders. Colonel Troup in Albany, writing to Rufus King, made no secret of his heat.[2]

On the subject of unanimity [he wrote] permit me to remark, that we are alarmed with late reports from New York. We are told that our friends are divided into two parties who have become, or are likely to become, open enemies to each other; the one contending that persons liable to the charge of toryism, from having resided within the British lines, or from

[1] Quoted in T. E. V. Smith, *Political Parties*, etc., p. 9.
[2] Albany, April 4, 1809, *King Correspondence*.

being descended from those who did so reside, ought to be excluded from the ticket about to be formed; and the other contending that the exclusion of such persons would be illiberal, unjust and impolitic. If these reports be well founded it would be highly gratifying to your friends here, if you would be kind enough to employ your weight and influence, and endeavor to heal the division and restore harmony . . . The advocates of exclusion; besides incurring the imputation of illiberality and injustice, stand opposed by a long and uninterrupted course of practice. Soon after we regained possession of New York, we permitted the Tories to enlist under our banners; and they have since manfully fought by our side in every important battle we have had with the democracy; some of them in the character of officers, and others in those of common soldiers. And when monies have been necessary to support our cause, many amongst them never scrupled to pay their quota of the general tax. Moreover we ought not to forget their zealous and useful service in our great contest for the constitution; which I presume was intended to have the effect of putting us on an equal footing with regard to the rights and honors of citizenship. Why therefore should these our good friends be now branded with the odium of " British sensibility " and drummed out of our ranks? My soul revolts at the very idea of a measure so illiberal—so unjust—and indeed so excessively cruel! . . . We often had on our tickets men denominated tories. In this list, I name our worthy friends Mr. Harison, Mr. Cornelius I. Bogert and Mr. Josiah O. Hoffman and to their names we may add those of Mr. John Watts, Mr. John De Lancy and Mr. William Cock with several others. What would the generous heart of our ever to be lamented friend Hamilton induce him to say of this excluding project, if he were capable of participating with us in our present patriotic and noble struggle? But the mere mention of his name calls to my mind and fills my breast with emotion, which prevents my enlarging & compels me to conclude with assuring you of the pure and exalted esteem, with which I am,

My dear sir,

Your humble Servant,

ROBT. TROUP.

It is probable that King's good sense responded to his friend's suggestions; at least there was no further talk of reading out all those who had been Loyalists.

In the following campaign the Republicans revived the charge which proved so useful. In an address issued from a meeting held in Albany, they accounted for the wealth of Federalists on the ground that as Tories in the Revolution, they had saved their property unimpaired while the Whigs impoverished themselves in patriotic sacrifice.

And as property is too universally the basis of influence [they said] these Tories soon took the lead in our affairs; their brethren who had been expelled from our shores returned to take advantage of our maganimous clemency, and to strengthen the party against liberty. Some distinguished apostates from the Whig ranks went over to this party—and by this artful combination the people were deluded . . . These gentlemen were for a government of energy . . . and as the tory principle is that of arbitrary power, it was natural for the friends of that principle to side with ranks of the latter gentlemen.[1]

The election in 1809 in New York gave the Federalists their first victory for a decade.[2] Five senators out of eight, representing the eastern and western districts, were returned, and a majority of the lower house. Especially gratifying was it that the contest had been waged squarely as a single and united party. "It is with peculiar pleasure, I inform you," wrote Morris S. Miller of Utica, to John

[1] *Proceedings of the Republican Meeting of the Citizens of Albany, March 13, 1810* (Albany, 1810). This address was written by Solomon Southwick. The *N. Y. Journal* habitually referred to the "Federalist Tories;" for example, April 7, 21, 1810.

[2] This was in spite of a slight reaction in public sentiment in favor of the national administration, which followed the publication of the so-called Erskine Treaty. King claimed they were published when they were, to influence the New York election. King to C. Gore, April 27, 1809, *King Correspondence*.

Jay, " that in every part of the District the election has been bottomed and conducted on decided Federal principles; in no County has there been any arrangement or concert with either section of the Democratic party." [1]   But the cautious Jay would not suddenly become too sanguine.

How few of the favorable changes which have taken place are imputable to patriotic and correct principles, time and experience only can decide . . . Personal and pecuniary considerations appear to have acquired a more than ordinary degree of influence; many sacrifices of public Good have and will yet have to be made to them.[2]

Although the Federalists, in gaining a majority of the assembly, had won the right to name the much-desired Council of Appointment, the circumstance that there were no members of their party sitting for the middle or southern districts in the senate caused them some embarrassment. The Councillors from these districts, therefore, must be Republicans. But of the two, of which necessity compelled selection, one, to the scandal of his party, when chosen proved amenable to their persuasion and was content to join with the two Federalists to make a majority of the five.[1]

The professions of abhorrence at the system of partisan proscription, which the Federalists had made throughout the decade, had not been taken very seriously, for it was charged with much show of truth that it was Abraham Van Vechten in Jay's administration, and not Clinton, who

[1] May 11, 1809, *Jay Correspondence.*

[2] Jay to M. S. Miller, May 22, 1809, *ibid.*

[3] J. D. Hammond, *Political History*, vol. i, pp. 280-282, for a discussion of the " Robert Williams Council," which this treachery gave to the Federalists. It will be remembered that the Council consisted of the governor, and one senator from each of the four great senatorial districts, these latter chosen by the assembly.

should have the credit or the blame of its invention. It was therefore no great surprise that the new council straightway set out to expel the officers of government, from the well-remunerated mayor of New York to the inspector of staves and heading in the smallest hamlet in the state—in all six thousand more or less. The disposition of the mayoralty elicited a contest. Some men of higher principles among the party, like Van Vechten, proposed a self-denying measure of cutting down the compensation, known to be some fifteen thousand dollars, to a figure more proportionate to the pay of other state officials, and Richard Harison, who was familiar with the city charter, promised to prepare a bill to serve this purpose. Troup, who was first recommended as a candidate, was quite in favor of reduction, but when because of his engagements as land-agent he withdrew his name, the other applicants were not as generous and the matter was soon dropped. Jacob Radcliffe was at last appointed, though the supporters of Colonel Richard Varick and Nathaniel Pendleton well nigh broke up the party in the city.[2] As to other lucrative appointments there was likewise much loud disagreement, and Troup writes that in disgust he had "withdrawn all communion respecting appointments.[3]

[1] *Proceedings of the Republican Meeting of the Citizens of Albany,* p. 8 *et seq.*; *cf.* H. L. McBain, *op. cit.*

[2] Troup to King, January 12 and February 27, 1810, W. W. Van Ness to King, February 8, 1810, *King Correspondence*; also De Witt Clinton Mss., March 17, 1810.

[3] " It is asserted by some who pretend to know, that Williams will not agree to Morris's appointment to the clerkship; and that nothing will be done with this office until after election. From appearances Gardenier now stands a better chance for that office than Morris—Benson is here asserting the claims of his brother to the same office; but I conjecture without any probability of success. Benson says he would not have the office himself if offered to him. He is contending for principle, and this demands his brother's restitution. A more ob-

This patronage was but the first course of a feast which the Federalists hoped might be continued. They determined for the first time in a decade, to name a candidate for governor, and nearly four months before the spring election of 1810, a meeting held in Albany nominated Jonas Platt of Oneida, recently elected to the senate by a large majority. Colonel Nicholas Fish, the banker, was selected for lieutenant governor. It was generally understood that the amiable Tompkins, whose suspected preference for Madison and the Virginians had not as yet cost him the support of Clinton, would stand for re-election, and the campaign was soon under way. The Federalists warned solemnly against the return of Clinton's nepotism, claiming that in the first two years of Tompkins' administration many cousins of the family had been pensioned from the school fund.[1] Republicans, united for the moment as to Clintonians and Martling Men, disdained to talk of favoritism while the Federalist Council carried out its own proscription, and as we have seen, they again trumped up the charge of Toryism to make odious their enemies. Labored essays by the Federalists were produced to demonstrate that this charge was quite unfair,[2] and in their songs they carefully addressed themselves as Whigs, but for all this it was easy for their enemies to charge them with the prejudices of aristocrats. Their candidate who, when in Congress, had supported the Sedition Law[3] had recently proclaimed his poor opinion of democracy:

jectionable doctrine than that of principle could not be broached. To urge it is to make yourself ridiculous—and accordingly the Judge is laughed out." Troup to King, February 27, 1810, *King Correspondence*.

[1] See broadside, " Platt and Liberty, A New Historical Song for the New-York Election, 1819, 22 verses, to be sung slowly to the tune of Yankee Doodle or of Wilkes' Wriggle," Emmett Collection, 11,400; see also *N. Y. Evening Post*, April 12, 1810.

[2] For example, *N. Y. Evening Post*, April 16, 1810.

[3] *Washington Register*, quoted in *N. Y. Journal*, April 24, 1810.

Where two or three are met together for factious purposes [he said ironically] even there is the *Majesty of the People* in the midst of them. To a man of common sense and honesty it is a stumbling block; to a man without ambition it is foolishness . . . Within the limits of the constitution, I may occasionally be willing to be employed, but the office of your *servant* I will never submit to.[1]

" If you want a master, vote for General Platt," responded the Republican newspapers.[2]

The Federalists later claimed that their enemies stirred up class prejudice; they said the voters were assured

that the rich and the poor had separate interests; that the cartmen and the mechanics were held cheap by the merchants; and that the buying and selling part of the community were always opposed, in all things to the laboring part: That, let what would happen, it must be the poor only who would be sufferers: but as to the federalists they were all rich and the natural enemies of republicans.[3]

The imputation of such theories the Republicans did not deny, but rather justified them by appeals to the dignity of laborers. The cartmen and the mechanics were as necessary to their haughty masters, they maintained, as the Tory lordlings were to them.[4] Such exhortation moved the *Evening Post* to say, that in its apprehension democracy and republicanism were not convertible terms. "The tendency of the former is to anarchy and misrule, whilst that of the latter is to produce order, to cultivate natural liberty, protect the rights of citizens, impart to the Government stability, honor and virtue."[5]

[1] Quoted in *Proceedings of Republican Meeting . . . Albany, . . . 1810*, p. 8.
[2] *N. Y. Journal*, April 7, 1810.
[3] *N. Y. Evening Post*, May 3, 1811.
[4] *N. Y. Journal*, April 7, 21, 1810.
[5] *N. Y. Herald*, May 2, 1810.

General Platt had once in the senate called for applause for British magnanimity in the spontaneous disavowal of the attack upon the "Chesapeake," providing thus another text to his opponents. The Federalist traders and their friends, of course, made no secret of their strong aversion to a breach with the "mother country," and their cause was watched with much solicitude by British agents in New York and Washington, yet there were no charges of a treacherous connivance such as those which passed so freely to the east.[1] In the campaign they tried to turn the scale against their enemies by fastening upon them the awkward and absurd name of "French Tories," to counteract the sentiment of gratitude borne toward France as our ally in the Revolution.[2] A campaign song explained:

> "The French, 'tis true, in their own way,
> Look'd steady on: but seem'd shy;
> Until *we* fought; and gain'd the day;
> Then soon became our ally." [3]

The embargo was, of course, still a major issue in party politics, and the merchants and the farmers were advised to vote for "Platt, Commerce, and the Constitution," [4]

---

[1] "In spite, however, of the vehemence of the Senate, Mr. J[ackson] states that Federalism is constantly gaining ground in New York, and that the sentiments of all Classes of People are every day becoming more favorable to H[is] M[ajesty's] Interests." Mr. Jackson (the British agent) to Earl Bathurst, February 16, 1810, in mss. Precis Book kept by "The Most Noble the Marquis Wellesley &c. &c. &c." (in N. Y. P. L.), p. 55. Later the agent saw that there was small chance of electing a Federalist governor or legislature in New York, but said, "if the democratick Party evince no greater Talent or Energy than has been hitherto seen in their measures their Power will be formidable only to their own country." *Ibid.*, p. 78. See also Jackson to the Marquess of Wellesley, *ibid.*, vol. ii, pp. 86 and 162.

[2] *N. Y. Journal*, April 24, 1810.   [3] "Platt and Liberty," *loc. cit.*

[4] *N. Y. Evening Post*, April 16, 1810.

while attempts were made to rally to the standard all ship-
wrights and rope-makers, mariners and smiths.[1] The Republican newspapers would not forget the story of Emmett's
martyrdom, at the hands of Rufus King;[2] but, although the
Federalists again in New York city offered an American
ticket,[3] a serious attempt was made throughout the state to
get some voters from these "imported patriots," as their
song suggests:

> " Come Dutch and Yankees, Irish, Scot
> With intermixed relation;
> From whence we came, it matters not;
> We all make, now, one nation,"[4]

and other groups were especially addressed as, for example,
the Quakers of Columbia County.[5] The Federalists appealed to the glories of twenty years before, and though
they admitted that Adams' presidency was in some ways
regrettable, denied that the party should be generally
charged with that responsibility.[6] Since John Adams had
stood by his son in support of the embargo, his name,
never glorious in New York state, was now mentioned at
best with apology.[7] Indeed their doggerel well sets forth
the opinion of the party as to the presidential record:

[1] *N. Y. Herald*, April 21, 25, 1810.

[2] *N. Y. Journal*, April 21, 1810.

[3] *N. Y. Herald*, April 7, 11, 1810.

[4] " Platt and Liberty."

[5] Elisha Williams and J. R. Van Rensselaer of that county had
worked earnestly to prevent a tax of $10 a head on Quakers for exemp-
tion from military duty, *Hudson Balance*, quoted in *Albany Gazette*,
April 7, 1808. During the campaign of 1810 Van Buren reports his
efforts to capture the Quaker vote for the Republicans, Van Buren to
Clinton, April 19, 1810, DeWitt Clinton Mss.

[6] *N. Y. Evening Post*, April 7, 1810.

[7] J. T. Morse, *John Adams* (Boston, 1896), p. 326.

> " Through eight bright years the *Federal Sun*
> Maintained his glorious station;
> While we were rul'd by *Washington*
> How happy was our nation!
>
> > Yankee Doodle, we were free;
> > Our rights were all protected,
> > Our trade was safe in every sea;
> > At home we were respected.
>
> " Then Adams 'rose and took the helm
> But could not steer so nice, long:
> That Man's not fit to rule a realm
> Who *once* goes right—but *twice* wrong.
>
> > Yankee Doodle; fire and tow;
> > How can that man e'er hit right;
> > Who's sometimes fast—and sometimes slow—
> > Who'll sometimes run—and yet fight?" [1]

But Federalism in New York could not be saved by ballads of poetical disclaimer. The unpopular embargo had been given up for the milder system of non-intercourse; the ancient grudge against Great Britain was now deepened by that government's renunciation of the Erskine treaty; the Republicans, then at a truce among themselves, stretched every nerve to regain their power of appointment. As a result the Federalists lost heavily except in New York City and the Albany and Mohawk districts [2] and the Republicans swept the state.

So closed a decade properly enough, in which humiliaton and defeat had been the portion of the Federalists. Their tradition and their theory of politics had been repudiated by the people of this country, though many of their policies were well continued. Fortunately the party, with its bold projects of construction, did not die with its defeat. It lived on under other names and leaders to supply the

---

[1] " Platt and Liberty."

[2] J. D. Hammond, *Political Parties*, vol. i, pp. 285-287; John T. Irving to W. P. Van Ness, May 3, 1810, Van Ness Mss.

courage of great undertakings, but not until it had responded somewhat to the spirit of America and been liberalized into a forbearance as to government by all the people. That the party in New York had thus persisted in the face of its adversities well shows the impulse of its old enthusiasms. It had ordained the system of our government and by its energy and skill in solving the initial problems of its conduct, had compelled the admiration of the world. Because of this achievement, as with the "grand old party," which two generations later was considered to have saved the fabric from destruction, the cause of Federalism could and did command a loyalty almost romantic in its sentiment. The memory of great personalities like Washington and Hamilton made any slowing down of party zeal seem much like treason. But the reasons for continuance did not all grow out of history. There was a consciousness of common interest among the business classes, who, as we have shown, made up the unchanging core of the Federalist party. In commercial centres like New York these men were bound to act together in defense. against the antagonism of the planters of the south upon the one hand and their allies, the wage-mechanics, on the other. In local contests on the chartering of banks as in the greater issue of the embargo, the party of the merchants and investors had a part to play, but, as we have also seen, this group was held together by other ties than those of business. Comprising as they did a social class, they realized that a weakening of political organization would appear as a surrender of pretensions to consequence and rank, which they were not prepared to yield.

From the morning when John Jay gave up his office of governor, the Federalists of New York state were found in the minority, forming often a scarce moiety of that. Yet in certain sections of the state their dominion was retained.

almost never to be seriously challenged. In Albany and Rensselaer Counties, for example, elective offices were kept within the party. While Van Rensselaer, Williams and Van Ness retained their power in Columbia, no Democrat of whatsoever faction could look forward to advancement by his neighbors. Certain wards in New York city would have voted for a branded thief as soon as for a Jacobin. In other counties in the east the balance was so even that the excitement at elections never slackened. It was natural that in all these regions any talk of giving up the Federalist party would have been greeted with derision. The success these leaders won at home stirred their ambition to keep firm the organization in less fortunate localities, in hope of larger victories. It urged them to intrigues by which some Federalist measures might be smuggled through the legislature, or some small bit of patronage be granted by the five great arbiters at Albany. Throughout the score of years, or more, which marked the slow decline of Federalism, it elected no executive to carry on the policies of Jay; yet party effort seldom flagged, newspapers were founded and sustained, tireless politicians rode through every county from the Hudson to the lakes, pamphleteers wrote reams of argument, and enthusiasts invoked the halting muse of campaign poetry. The secret of this obstinate vitality is found in the constant hope of capturing the Council of Appointment. 1810, 1813 and 1814 were years of nourishment, at other times the prize was tantalizing in its nearness; there was always a prospect of electing a majority of the assembly.

If this appetite for office moved small men to action, the statesmen of the party did not despair of bringing in again the rule of Federalist principles. The juggling tricks of management which had already made the state a by-word, the utter lack, as yet, of any larger constructive program, that had distinguished those who held control, seemed to them too sad afflictions to be long endured. They rested their hopes, as Troup had said, upon the fall of the Democratic party by the weight of its own vices and divisions. How, by the adoption of a Democratic leader, they drew a sharper line between themselves and the Democracy, is to be the theme of another chapter.

CHAPTER VI

LANDHOLDERS' PRINCIPLES

THE hypothesis that economic interest was the inner cause of party struggle in the early days of the republic has taken on the dignity of an "interpretation." [1] Assume a broad antipathy between those whose property was in the soil and those who drew their profit from enterprise in trade and industry, and a surprisingly long array of facts seem dutifully obedient in illustration. From the coming of the peace of 1783 into the first years of the new century, the conflict grew more bitter as these diversities with all their implications, embodied in the personalities of Hamilton and Jefferson, became more clearly realized. Though no one would postulate a reasoned, selfish calculation as the only basis of partisan allegiance, nor refuse to see the many other forces that lift and sway the minds of men, certain it is that underneath the surface passion in the cause of France or England, deeper, perhaps, than the philosophy that formed itself in labored essays in defence of liberty or order, and more stable than the personal affection toward one champion or another battling in the field of politics, was this consciousness of divergent economic interests to be helped or hindered by new laws. But in New York, at least, as we shall see, the lines of party demarcation throughout the first decades of the nineteenth century, seemed to fade somewhat and grow uncertain. For this also there were many causes, but one seeking for a diagnosis of conditions which allowed this softening of an

[1] C. A. Beard, *Economic Interpretation of the Constitution* and *Economic Origins of Jeffersonian Democracy* (N. Y., 1915) ; and " Politics and Education," *Teachers College Record*, vol. xvii, no. 3, pp. 1-12. Professor Beard presents the antithesis as between farmers and bondholders, but the capital of the latter was generally applied as well to other enterprise.

2. THURLOW WEED

1. JOHN JAY

PARTY LEADERS—OLD AND NEW

3. ELISHA WILLIAMS

4. GULIAN C. VERPLANCK

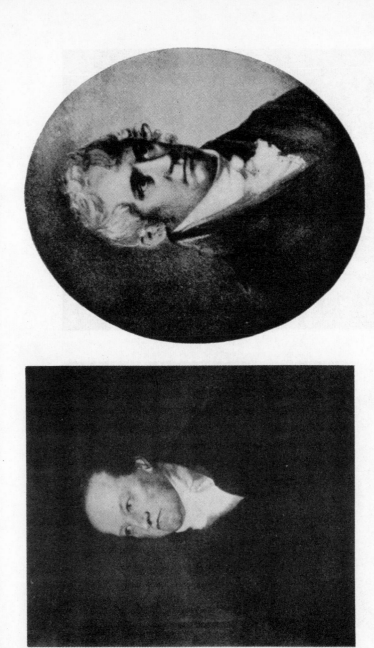

5. DE WITT CLINTON

6. STEPHEN VAN RENSSELAER

7. WILLIAM H. SEWARD

8. JAMES KENT © Charles Barnmore, Publisher New York

animosity but recently so virulent, reasonably turns to an examination of this economic factor, to which so much has recently been traced. Was there in New York the same well marked opposition between the man of lands and the man of bonds and shares of stock as has been noticed in some sections of the country?

A hundred years ago the city of New York, now the doorway of a nation, was a great commercial city in its promise rather than as yet in its achievement.[1] Though the merchants' ships were turning toward the Orient [2] and their wharves were piled with bales from over all the seven seas, the path of the trading schooner did not seem the only way to wealth as it did from Massachusetts.[3] But there were fortunes for hazard in New York, saved from the wreckage of the war and ready for what investment would secure the largest income. One attractive prospect was furnished by the wide and unmarked lands, wild, perhaps, but reported to be fertile, that stretched out to the north and west within the boundary of what was to become the Empire State. The state itself was rich in land, even before it compounded with Connecticut and Massachusetts for their claims and holdings.[4] Those officers like the Morrises,[5] whose war claims were paid by grants of land, saw

[1] *Cf.* E. E. Pratt, *Industrial Causes of Congestion of Population in New York City* (Columbia University Studies in History, Economics and Public Law, vol. xliii, 1911), p. 13.

[2] T. Pitkin, *Statistical View of the United States* (Hartford, 1816), p. 208.

[3] *Ibid.*, see tables of tonnage owned in the different states in 1810, pp. 391-392. New York City was just coming to the lead.

[4] J. H. Hotchkin, *History of Western New York* (N. Y., 1848), pp. 1-10. This work is less useful to our purpose than its title promises, being concerned almost exclusively with the progress of the Presbyterian church.

[5] Richard and Lewis Morris were so granted three thousand acres in what was then Montgomery County. M. A. Hamm, *Famous Families of New York*, vol. ii, p. 34.

in these the bases for a larger business that might be prudently increased by purchase.

The men of wealth in New York city had no settled prejudice against holding real estate; not only were there close connections with the Schuylers and Van Rensselaers, but in most families of the gentry there were large-acred cousins, of whose prosperity there could be no doubt. A description of the great estate at Duanesburgh with forty thousand acres in Albany County,[1] must have stirred the fancy as related in Judge Duane's drawing room in Nassau Street;[2] or that of " Hoffman's Castle " at Red Hook in Dutchess County, owned by relatives of the fashionable Wall Street Hoffmans;[3] or of the princely home at old Fort Miller where reigned the famous Lady Kitty Duer," [4] who now and then came down to bring new splendor to the balls at the Assembly Rooms.[5] The attention of large investors was already fixed upon these lands while they were still dispensed by the colony land office, and the bidding grew far brisker in the early days of statehood. As one glances down the pages of the *Calendar of Land Papers* [6]

---

[1] A. A. Yates, *Schenectady County, Its History* (N. Y., 1902), pp. 410-412; M. A. Hamm, *op. cit.*, vol. i, p. 123. James Duane retired to this estate after his failure in business in 1792. Duanesburgh was included when Schenectady County was formed.

[2] *New York Directory* (1793), p. 44; see Emmett Collection, number 13,246.

[3] F. Hasbrouck, *History of Dutchess County* (Poughkeepsie, 1909), p. 428; J. H. Beers, *Biographical Record of Dutchess County* (Chicago, 1897), p. 571; *N. Y. Genealogical and Biographical Record*, vol. v, p. 117; *New York Directory*, 1800; M. A. Hamm, *op. cit.*, vol. i, pp. 173, 178. The Hoffman holdings in Ulster County also were extensive.

[4] Wm. L. Stone (Jr.), *Washington County* (N. Y., 1901), p. 131.

[5] C. W. Bowen, *History of the Centennial Celebration of the Inauguration of George Washington*, pp. 57-59.

[6] The full title is *Calendar of New York Colonial Mss. indorsed Land Papers, 1643-1803* (Albany, 1864).

one sees many familiar Federalist names, William Bayard, the Bleeckers, C. D. Colden, Duane, James Emott, Nicholas Fish, and many others, who held land by grant or purchase from the state. Alexander Hamilton invested all his surplus earnings in the lands about Oswego [1] which would pay a rich dividend only after years of waiting, so that his tragic death left his widow " land poor," as the phrase went, and a fund had to be subscribed by friends to make sure her comfort.[2] His friend, Cornelius I. Bogert,[3] had large holdings in what is now Hamilton County, while the Roosevelts [4] had purchased largely in what is now Oneida.[5] James Watson, the Federalist United States senator, held over sixty thousand acres, somewhat to the north.[6] The extent of

[1] J. C. Churchill, *Landmarks of Oswego County* (Syracuse, 1895), p. 13.

[2] Gouverneur Morris to Robert Morris, July 14, 1804 (A. C. Morris, *The Diary and Letters of Gouverneur Morris*, vol. ii, p. 459) : " Our friend Hamilton has been suddenly cut off in embarrassments which would have required years of professional industry to set right : a debt of between fifty thousand and sixty thousand dollars, a property which in time may sell for seventy or eighty thousand, but which if brought to the hammer, would not in all probability fetch fifty." Matthew Clarkson to Rufus King, August 20, 1894, *King Correspondence*, vol. iv, p. 404, speaks of the subscription. The following from J. A. Hamilton, *Reminiscences*, p. 78, is interesting: "At a dinner party in New York, shortly after the close of the Revolutionary War, at which were present Messrs. G. Morris, John Jay, Richard Harison, John Delafield, Robert Lenox, Nicholas Low, J. O. Hoffman, and Alexander Hamilton, the question was discussed whether the purchase of wild lands or of lots in the suburbs of the city would be the more profitable. [Some, including Hamilton] invested in lands in the northern counties of the state."

[3] *Land Papers*, p. 923.

[4] *Cf.* C. A. Beard, *Economic Interpretation of the Constitution*, p. 270.

[5] D. E. Wager, *Oneida County* (Boston, 1896), pp. 119-121.

[6] *Documentary History of New York* (Albany, 1850), vol. iii, pp. 647, 653, 654; Jenkins, *Political Parties*, pp. 50, 67, 73, 84. Watson was also candidate for lieutenant-governor in 1801, (A. Hamilton) *Address to the Electors of the State of New York* (pamphlet, N. Y., 1801), p. 3, and for Congress, C. H. Hunt, *Life of Edward Livingston*, p. 74.

speculation in unsettled land that centered in the counting rooms of a Federalist firm like LeRoy, Bayard and Co. seems hardly credible;[1] no considerable section of the state remained unmentioned in their ledgers. The subject of Federalist land holding in New York, indeed, could be properly examined only by a long laborious research.

Let us take for our example a single county, St. Lawrence, almost the farthest and then the least accessible from the city of New York. Here great tracts of land were held by General Knox,[2] John Delafield,[3] Nicholas Low,[4] Josiah Ogden Hoffman,[5] Frederic DePeyster,[6] Philip Brasher,[7] Garrett Van Horne,[8] Stephen Van Rensselaer,[9] Philip Schuyler,[10] David M. Clarkson,[11] and, greatest in the area of his holding, Gouverneur Morris.[12] These were men

---

[1] This was the greatest private commercial enterprise New York ever knew up to the eighteen-thirties, Barret, *Old Merchants of New York* (N. Y., 1862), pp. 31, 46, 160-164, 302-305, *etc.* There are thirteen boxes and more than two thousand unassorted pieces of manuscript, together with twenty-five volumes, dealing with the operations of this company, in the collection of the New York Public Library.

[2] F. B. Hough, *History of St. Lawrence and Franklin Counties*, pp. 241, 246. The section of Dr. Hough's work which deals with early land arrangements is fully documented.

[3] *Ibid.*, pp. 243, 246, 247, *etc.*   [4] *Ibid., loc. cit.*

[5] Gates Curtis, *Memorial of St. Lawrence County* (Syracuse, 1894), p. 84.

[6] J. H. French, *Historical and Statistical Gazetteer of New York State* (Syracuse, 1860), p. 576. The DePeysters were intermarried with the Van Hornes, Clarksons, etc. W. A. Duer, *Reminiscences of An Old New Yorker*, p. 37.

[7] T. Weed, *Autobiography, etc.*, vol. i, pp. 394, 401.

[8] Hough, *op. cit.*, p. 244.

[9] French, *op. cit.*, p. 578. There are towns in St. Lawrence County named Depeyster, Brasher and Rensselaer.

[10] Article in *N. Y. Times*, June 7, 1903.

[11] Hough, p. 244.   [12] French, pp. 577, 580.

of wealth and influence in the Federalist party, but they were as keenly interested in the politics of land as in that of trade or banks or industrial securities. Neither the one nor the other could be neglected by lawmakers at Washington or Albany without grave havoc in the counting books of these investors.

No statesman of New York had been heard with more respect in party councils than Gouverneur Morris. Learned in the lore and technic of governmental science, acquainted with the courts of Europe, generous in service for the public good, possessed of an enormous fortune, he seemed a type of what was best and most respectable in Federalism; and no one more than he was representative of that party's landed interest in New York. The boundaries of his own estate of fifteen hundred acres at Morrisania [1] did not limit his concern in the welfare of real property. He purchased heavily not only in the St. Lawrence region, where the towns of Gouverneur and Morristown now remain as monuments,[2] but also in the western wilderness.[3] With a dauntless zeal to see and know, he made his way time and again by forest trail and bark canoe along the Mohawk Valley and slowly westward to Niagara, or through the woodlands of the north to Montreal.[4] When in January 1816, Congress addressed itself to the problem of a permanent revenue in time of peace,[5] the New England Federalists, in the interest of the shipping class, arrayed themselves against the great plantation owners of the south [6]

[1] *Diary and Letters of Gouverneur Morris*, vol. ii, p. 378; J. A. Hamilton, who settled the estate, gives an account of Morris's property in his *Reminiscences*, pp. 46-47.

[2] French, *loc. cit.* [3] *Diary and Letters*, vol. ii, p. 379.

[4] *Ibid.*, vol. ii, pp. 390, 439, 513, 520, 591, etc.

[5] *Annals of Congress*, 1816-1817, p. 687, etc.

[6] Henry Adams, *History of the United States* (N. Y., 1891), vol. ix, pp. 112-115.

in the contest as to whether land or imports should bear the burden of taxation. The New York Federalists, encumbered by much unproductive land, were by no means at one with their Massachusetts friends. Many, it cannot be doubted, subscribed to the doctrine laid down by Gouverneur Morris in a letter to Rufus King: [1]

I fear we differ in opinion on the subject of taxation . . . Some patriots (*sans terres*, if not *sans culotte*) cry out " Tax land-speculators and oblige them to sell." Take care, gentlemen patriots. If taxing speculators should become fashionable, stocks may perchance be annoyed. . . . Speculators, as such, are not respectable, but they are necessary and in no case more so than in the settlement of wild land. It has been tried to prevent accumulation of large tracts in few hands by confining grants to small tracts, but experience has proved that, until rich men purchase up these small tracts, the country cannot be settled. It is absurd to suppose a person with scarce a second shirt to his back can go two or three hundred miles to look out a farm, have it surveyed, travel back again to the office for a patent, etc., clear the land, cut a road, make a settlement, and build house and barn, and then an owner under a prior grant may come forward and take possession. . . . As things now stand, the conflict of title is generally between men able to stand the shock. [2]

[1] Jared Sparks, *Life and Correspondence of Gouverneur Morris* (Boston, 1832), vol. iii, pp. 343-344. Of course this attitude was by no means new in 1816, as the following from the *N. Y. Spectator*, January 4, 1804, dealing with the action of the New England Federalists and others in the Congress, 1803, makes clear: " We do not here intend to charge the individuals who have conducted the business in this, or in other states, with any intentional mismanagement. But, that the Proprietors of uncultivated lands have, contrary to the spirit and intent of the law, sustained immense losses, no one, at all informed on the subject, can doubt. And it would gratify the feelings of the friends of justice to see a Bill passed in Congress, that would cut up the evil by the roots."

[2] In a letter to Randolph Harrison, May 3, 1816, *Diary and Letters,*

His argument, it seems, was not in vain, for King later changed his mind and cast his vote against so disagreeable a discrimination.[1] If the interpretation of real and personal estate as the basis of our parties be correct, some explanation of the waning vigor of the Federalism of New York may proceed from this uncertainty in so important a political division.

There is another phase of Federalist land holding which must not be neglected. The conquest of the wilderness by pioneers from the old communities along the sea coast has been the stirring theme of much of our historical writing. We have followed with keen interest the great migration from New England with its stalwart men of thrift, of fearless thought and deep religious purpose,[2] and those who threaded through the southern Alleghenies to lay out broad plantations beside the Mississippi.[3] In a smaller and more intimate way there is much of interest in the expansion of the New York gentry, and in how Federalist families came to build their homes in lands cleared from the forest. We have formed some notion of their purchases, sometimes a hundred thousand acres, sometimes more. To convert their holdings into a more manageable wealth they sent promising young friends into the wilderness, as agents, who could bargain with the settlers. Then, full of faith in their great

vol. ii, p. 599, he says: "Observe, I pray you, that in England there is no unproductive land. Even their pleasure grounds yield something in venison and the pasturage of cattle, besides the increase of timber. The British land tax, therefore, falls on a revenue. But not a fifth part of our land yields anything." See also his letter to Moss Kent, March 3, 1816, Sparks, *op. cit.*, vol. iii, p. 350.

[1] R. King to G. Morris, March 15, 1816, *King Correspondence.*

[2] L. K. Mathews, *The Expansion of New England* (Boston, 1909), ch. vii.

[3] *Documentary History of American Industrial Society* (Cleveland, 1909), vol. ii, pp. 219 *et seq.*

enterprise, they advised their law clerks to essay the opportunities of a new country; then, lastly, younger sons themselves set out with wives and families to build stately houses on their great domains. It is a story not without romance, and certainly of great importance in accounting for the spread of Federalist influence throughout the inland counties of the state.[1] This subject, also, in its scope forbids a general treatment within our compass, and for convenience's sake we may turn again to St. Lawrence County to trace this second phase of Federalist connection with the land.

In 1792 Samuel Ogden[2] with Josiah Ogden Hoffman bought an extensive tract of land sloping northward to the shore of the St. Lawrence, and two years later sent a young friend, Nathan Ford, to explore it and conduct its settlement.[3] A man of force, like most of his profession, and a Federalist like John Delancey[4] and John Delafield who had gone before him to this St. Lawrence Valley,[5] he rose to prominence in the politics of the county of which he was the pioneer,[6] as a public official[7] and as a leader of his

[1] Here, in the early days of the republic, the influence of the Federalist party was very small; see O. G. Libby, *Distribution of the Vote of the Thirteen States on the Federal Constitution* (Wisconsin Studies in History, Economic and Political Science, Vol. I), p. 18. It is interesting to compare the party's fate beyond the Alleghenies, see H. C. Hockett "Federalism and the West" in the *Turner Essays* (N. Y., 1910), pp. 113-135.

[2] The Ogdens were a great land-owning family. David A. Ogden purchased about 200,000 acres of the Indian lands in western New York, "The League of the Six Nations," in *New York Civil List*, 1889, p. 212, *et seq.*

[3] F. B. Hough, *op. cit.*, p. 589.

[4] Robert Troup to Rufus King, April 4, 1809, *King Correspondence.*

[5] *Land Papers*, pp. 748-766.   [6] G. Curtis, *op. cit.*, p. 155.

[7] *N. Y. Civil List*, 1889, p. 492.

party.[1] Riding far and wide through this sparsely settled country, the arbiters of rents and payments, often in position to be of service to the settler, the influence of land agents like Judge Ford, or Benjamin Raymond, the agent and surveyor for Clarkson and Van Horne,[2] was considerable indeed. But the land agents were not left unsupported. In the offices of the distinguished lawyers of the city there were other young men of ambition. Louis Hasbrouck, a student under J. O. Hoffman and Cadwallader D. Colden, by the counsel of his patrons and of his friend, Judge Ford, set forth from New York City in 1804 to build a home in far St. Lawrence,[3] wending a slow way with family and slave, wagons and pack-horses. Here, agreeable to his political training, he served as the first clerk of the county, as assemblyman and senator, and was a leader of his party, Federalist, National Republican and Whig.[4] In that same year, encouraged by the progress of his brother Nathan, David Ford, a zealous politician of the Federalist school, came in 1804 to be the pioneer of Morristown.[5] John Fine, a graduate of Columbia in the class of 1809 with Murray Hoffman, Bishop Onderdonk and Dr. Francis, likewise came northward six years later to grow rich in land and

[1] *E. g.* he was the delegate to the Federalist meeting, March 1808, *Albany Gazette*, April 1808, and to the convention that nominated Rufus King for Governor in 1816. Wm. Henderson to R. King, February 20, 1816, *King Correspondence.* Judge Ford's Federalism was so well known that when in the sack of Ogdensburg in the War of 1812, his house escaped pillage, wise-acres drew an inference, see *Albany Argus*, April 9, 1813.

[2] Letter from William Raymond, Esq., to the author. Benjamin Raymond was made " Judge and Justis " by the Federal Council of Appointment of 1813, *Albany Argus*, March 5, 1813.

[3] F. B. Hough, *op. cit.*, p. 594.

[4] In 1802, *Civil List*, 1889, pp. 380, 425, 540; T. Weed. *Autobiography, etc.*, p. 414.

Hough, *op. cit.*, p. 589.

play his part in politics.[1]   Young lawyers like land agents contributed to build a modest aristocracy.[2]

But these were not all.   The gentry who centered in the drawing rooms of those fashionable streets running eastward from Broadway, all had their coats of arms, and history of knights and squires and manor houses with wide-stretching acres in the counties of old England.[3]   To lord it over docile tenantry, and ride at hunt through one's own forest, made up a part of what was most attractive in the family legends of a storied past.   It is not surprising, then, to see some younger sons of these land holders fascinated by the prospect of reproducing in open reaches of the north something of the dignity and spaciousness of the life of the country gentleman they so naturally admired.   David A. Ogden, who had been the partner of Alexander Hamilton in law-practice,[4] gave up his professional connection in 1812 to carry into execution a plan which he had for some years cherished, to remove to the St. Lawrence, and fix his permanent residence on its beautiful shores.   In pursuance of this, he built a fine and substantial dwelling on the island opposite the village of Waddington and commenced its improvement as a farm, which comprises nearly eight hundred acres.   He was at this time in the prime of life and carried with him those tastes for rural employments, which he had imbibed in early life, which with his favorite literary pursuits, were well calculated to

[1] Hough, *op. cit.*, p. 586.   A town was named for him.   For various reasons Judge Fine subsequently became a Democrat.

[2] There is no attempt to prove here that all land agents or that all young lawyers from New York city were Federalists, but many who were of that tradition contributed, in association with the resident proprietors, to bring a political influence alien to the frontier spirit. *Cf.* F. J. Turner, *The Significance of the Frontier in American History* (Madison, 1894), pp. 27-29, where the frontier democracy is discussed.

[3] *N. Y. Genealogical and Biographical Record*, vol. v, pp. 115-118.

[4] In this he was associated with his brother, *Appleton's Cyclopedia of American Biography*, vol. iv, p. 560.

render his residence agreeable, not only to himself, but to those who might associate with him.[1]

But the great stone house surrounded by its grove of maples was renowned not only for its gracious hospitality and atmosphere of an exotic culture; the plans of Federalist politics were often there matured in council. The proprietor represented the county in the assembly two years after he took up his residence, twice was county judge and served a term in Congress,[2] while younger relatives were prominent, Gouverneur Ogden as a Federalist congressman,[3] and William Henry Vining, a nephew of the latter, elected to the assembly in 1821.[4]

The Ogdens in the splendid isolation of their island were not left to be the only county family; other names familiar in Federalist annals were to be transplanted to St. Lawrence. Soon after the close of the War of 1812 came the Clarksons, to improve their holdings by the Racquette River,[5] building noble houses, " Holcroft," " Homestead," " Woodstock," clearing forests into meadows reminiscent of the fields of Yorkshire whence their ancestors had come.[6] Next came

[1] Hough, *op. cit.*, p. 600. See also Ogden-Ford papers, printed, in part, *ibid.*, pp. 372-401.

[2] *Civil List*, 1882, pp. 302, 363, 451. He did not serve as senator, in spite of the misprint of his name for that of Isaac Ogden, the Democrat from Walton, N. Y., in the *N. Y. Senate Journal*, 1816, p. 1. *Cf. Civil List*, 1882, p. 254.

[3] W. W. Van Ness to R. King, January 31, 1816, *King Correspondence.* Gouverneur Ogden also served as Surrogate, *Civil List*, 1882, p. 370.

[4] *Civil List*, 1882, p. 307, and Hough, *op. cit.*, pp. 611-612.

[5] G. Curtis, *St. Lawrence County*, part ii, p. 34; *The Clarksons of New York* (N. Y., 1875, in the New York Genealogical Society Collection).

[6] W. W. Spooner, *Historic Families of America* (N. Y., 1908), vol. iii, pp. 276-286. The Clarksons had begun early in land speculation, an entry in the *Land Papers*, p. 49, recording a title taken by Matthew Clarkson, the immigrant, in 1697.

the son and namesake of Richard Harison, the Tory-Federalist leader in the city of New York,[1] laying out a manor house, with high wall and cobbled court, looking down upon the long rapids of the River Grasse.[2]   Here he too strove to reproduce old England and give the country-side its atmosphere.   I have before me a score of volumes from that portion of the family library which was so laboriously carried with wagon-loads of furnishings to the seat established in this country won so recently from wilderness. *Mill's Husbandry*,[3] impressive in five volumes, and *Patoun's Treatise on Surveying*, these had no doubt been brought from old Berkshire, years before, with Pope and Gibbon; the poems of St. John Honeywood and J. G. Brooks, they had bought as good New Yorkers; and in bound files of agricultural magazines throughout the 'thirties the final phase is represented.   Thus in a library we see the outline of a family history.   Some miles to the south and west a spacious home was built by Henry Van Rensselaer, fourth son of the Patroon,[5] and near Ogdensburg there lived the Parishes, the friends of Gouverneur Morris.[6]   Though

[1] E. B. O'Callaghan, "Biographical Sketch of Francis Harison," *N. Y. Genealogical and Biographical Record*, vol. ix, pp. 49-51; J. S. Jenkins, *History of Political Parties in New York*, p. 33 *et seq.*; Rob't Troup to R. King, April 4, 1809, *King Correspondence*; *N. Y. Civil List*, 1889, pp. 124, 412, 413.

[2] The community that grew around this mansion they named Morley from a relative of the Harison family. J. H. French, *Gazetteer of the State of New York*, p. 575.

[3] London, 1765.

[4] Archibald Patoun, *A Complete Treatise of Practical Navigation ... to which are added the useful theories of Mensuration, Surveying, and Gauging* (London, 1762).

[5] G. Curtis, *St. Lawrence County*, p. 325. He served a term in Congress, 1841-1843, *N. Y. Civil List*, 1889, p. 605.

[6] Morris, *Diary and Letters*, vol. ii, pp. 74, 389, 407, 415, 418, 431, 445, *etc., etc.* The Parishes had come to America on Morris' suggestion.

themselves but indirectly interested in party struggles, they had many a line of influence that ran through the county [1] from their homes—those mansions looking out upon extended parks and prim and formal gardens, fenced in by a long-remembered great brick wall over-grown with roses.[2] Here President Monroe was entertained [3] and distinguished visitors from Washington, New York or Albany always stopped to spend a night or two in a gentleman's establishment of the traditional type.[4] "All had an old baronial air, and one could easily imagine the entire place brought bodily from some foreign country and set down in the midst of this quiet town." [5]

So these families came, bringing in a spirit of aristocracy which left its mark, as we have seen, upon the county politics. That now they have for the most part disappeared adds a touch of pathos to the story. Theirs was a spirit foreign to the custom of the country; while others made their way into the wilderness to be rid of every vestige of the feudal system, these came to perpetuate so much of that tradition as could be saved. But the aloofness of this gentry, so proper to their social theory, could not be comfortably preserved, and, bound by an inflexible endogamous rule, these branches of the families slowly withered and passed into memory, though leaving after them an influence that increased respect for "the few, the rich and the well-born."

But it should not be thought that St. Lawrence County was singular in these respects, or has been unfairly taken as a type. Change the names of Ogdens and their town of

---

[1] Curtis, *op. cit.*, p. 153.   [2] *N. Y. Times*, June 7, 1903.

[3] Curtis, *loc. cit.*

[4] H. G. Spafford, *Gazetteer of the State of New York* (Albany, 1824), p. 404.

[5] Curtis, *op. cit.*, p. 350.

Ogdensburg for the Platts and Plattsburg,[1] or trace the fortunes of the Lows of Lowville, settled by the son of Nicholas Low,[2] or of their neighbor, Moss Kent, brother of the chancellor,[3] or of William Henderson, whose lands lay along the shore of Lake Ontario; [4] turn to the three LeRoys, brothers-in-law of Daniel Webster,[5] who gave their name to a town near the Genesee [6] and the same condition is observed. Instead of Nathan Ford insert the name of Egbert Benson, Jr.,[7] as land agent, or that of Colonel Robert Troup, who at Geneva managed the great Pulteney estate,[8] and who bore a leading part in the Federalism of New

[1] D. M. Hurd, *History of Clinton and Franklin Counties* (Philadelphia, 1882), pp. 149-156, 176. Zephaniah Platt settled here, bringing his family and slaves in 1801. The town had been founded under his direction about twenty years before, see *N. Y. Assembly Journal,* 1792-1793, p. 14.

[2] F. B. Hough, *History of Lewis County*, pp. 135, 137, 142, 163; also DeWitt Clinton to Cornelius Low, November 25, 1820, Clinton Mss. (Letterbook V).

[3] *Ibid.*, p. 163, Jenkins, *Political Parties*, p. 71, and *N. Y. Genealogical and Biographical Record*, vol. iv, p. 85.

[4] Henderson was an important politician in New York having been the party candidate for assembly in 1807 (*N. Y. Spectator*, April 22, 1807) and for Congress in 1808 (*Albany Gazette*, April 25, 1808). He settled in what is now Jefferson County, F. B. Hough, *Lewis County*, p. 82.

[5] G. T. Curtis, *Life of Daniel Webster* (N. Y., 1870), vol. i, p. 345.

[6] F. W. Beers, *Gazetteer and Biographical Record of Genesee County* (Syracuse, 1890), p. 480. Daniel LeRoy was the son-in-law of Nicholas Fish, M. A. Hamm, *Famous Families of New York*, vol. i, p. 139.

[7] He was the nephew of the famous Federalist judge, and became a man of importance in the west, F. W. Beers, *loc. cit.*; letter to DeWitt Clinton, December 30, 1818, Clinton Mss.; to P. G. Childs, February 5, 1822, Childs Mss.; and to John Tayler, March 13, 1815, Tayler Mss.

[8] O. Turner, *History of the Pioneer Settlement of the Phelps and Gorham Purchase* (Rochester, 1851), pp. 279-280.

York,[1] and the story is repeated, varying in details but broadly similar to that we have rehearsed. Sometimes, as with the stock of General Jacob Morris [2] who, like General North of Duanesburgh,[3] had gone inland to improve his family holdings, an offshoot was sent far to the westward to reproduce in a second and a third series, as it were, the landed gentry of New York.[4] The Morrises had increased their grant so that when the General made his slow way up the Susquehanna valley as a herald of civilization, his share amounted to five thousand acres.[5] Setting his slaves [6] to fell the trees and saw them into boards, he built a home in what became the town of Morris, and then turned much of his attention to the politics of that young country. He was the first Otsego County clerk, served three years in the assembly and four years in the senate of the state.[7] In the early days of the new century the county was the scene of bitter struggles at elections.[8] Jedediah Peck, the shrewd itinerant preacher, organized the new democracy, while General Morris and Judge Cooper were the Federalist leaders.[9]

[1] His name headed the Federalist nominations for presidential electors in 1812, *N. Y. Senate Journal*, 1812, p. 23. There were of course some Republican land-holders and land agents, but they were not numerous.

[2] M. A. Hamm, *Famous Families of New York*, vol. ii, p. 34.

[3] *Ibid.*, vol. i, p. 123, and Appleton, *op. cit.*, vol. iv, p. 534.

[4] *History of Dane County, Wisconsin* (Chicago, 1880), p. 1016. W. A. P. Morris, son of General Jacob, went to Madison, Wisconsin, in 1870. His daughter married and went to live in North Dakota.

[5] E. F. Bacon, *Otsego County* (Oneonta, 1902), p. 32.

[6] H. Child, *Gazetteer of Otsego County* (Syracuse, 1872), p. 79, for examples of manumission.

[7] *N. Y. Civil List*, 1889, pp. 373, 374, 414, 539.

[8] See *Political Wars of Otsego County; or the Downfall of Jacobinism*, pamphlet (Cooperstown, 1796).

[9] F. W. Halsey, *The Old New York Frontier* (N. Y., 1901), pp. 365-367.

William Cooper was the mirror of partisan perfection as a Federalist squire.[1]   Coming north soon after the Revolution, he became the master of great estates but vaguely bounded; when the country grew in population he recalled with honest pride that " there were 40,000 souls holding land, directly or indirectly, under me."   In 1800 he set up a claim to having placed the plough upon more acres than any other man in all America.[2]   Having brought his family and a retinue of slaves and other servants, numbering fifteen,[3] he built Otsego Hall, a great rectangular stone house with castellated roof and gothic windows,[4] surrounded by box hedges and wide lawns trimmed precisely by black gardeners, far surpassing any other home in the old west.[5]   This was the citadel of Fedalism and the council-place of party methods for the Otsego country, for not only did Judge Cooper serve nine years as first judge of the county and two terms in Congress,[6] but he rode far and wide in the cause of Jay and later Aaron Burr, always preaching the old and musty

[1] Unlike all others mentioned in this chapter he came from New Jersey rather than New York city and the near-by counties, but he represents the same trend in all particulars.

[2] See quotations from letters in F. W. Halsey, *op. cit.*, pp. 359, 360, *etc.*

[3] S. M. Shaw, *History of Cooperstown* (Cooperstown, 1886) and Halsey, *op. cit.* p. 358.

[4] This was built in 1799, taking the place of the so-called manorhouse which was the original home. Views of its exterior and interior may be seen in the volume of the *Cooperstown Centennial* (Cooperstown, 1908), and Halsey, p. 362, and especially in Mary E. Philips' copiously illustrated *James Fenimore Cooper* (N. Y., 1913). The grounds are now the village park.

[5] S. T. Livermore, *History of Cooperstown* (Albany, 1862), pp. 45-46. The Hall was built on the lines of the Van Rensselaer manorhouse, where Cooper was a frequent visitor, but seems to have surpassed its model, Philips, *op. cit.*, p. 8.

[6] *N. Y. Civil List*, 1881, pp. 359, 446.

doctrine that government had better be left to gentlemen, and that simple folk should vote as they were told.

The influence of this squirearchy was thus socially conservative, looking backward to the Tory models across the sea; and in no particular, perhaps, was its expression more clear and unmistakeable than in its cherishment and patronage of " the Episcopal mode of worship, so friendly to Government, so hostile to Jacobinism." [1] Let us turn again to the Federalist families we have cited as examples. The Parishes, as true English gentlemen, laid out a plot for the churchyard and a little glebe, and were the principal contributors to an edifice and an endowment.[2] The Ogdens, long vestrymen of Trinity, set up a modest church in the hamlet by their island.[3] The Clarksons, who in New York city had likewise worshipped there for generations, erected near their homes another Trinity, now beautified by rich memorials of the family.[4] The Harisons, descended from the comptroller of the mother parish, built another of that name at Morley.[5] The year that young Cornelius Low arrived in Lowville, another Trinity was begun.[6] The LeRoys, far to the westward, endowed their St. Mark's with land and money,[7] while their neighbor, Colonel Troup,

---

[1] Robert Troup to Rufus King, *King Correspondence*, vol. v, p. 37.

[2] Curtis, *St. Lawrence County*, p. 383.

[3] M. Dix, *The Parish of Trinity Church in the City of New York* (N. Y., 1905), vol. iii, p. 30, extracts from the parish minutes wherein aid is promised for its support. The Ogdens were among the founders of the Protestant Episcopal Society for Promoting Religion and Learning in the State of New York, see Appleton, *loc. cit.*

[4] Curtis, *op. cit.*, part ii, p. 34. They also built and patronized churches in near-by towns.

[5] M. Dix, *op. cit.*, vol. iii, p. 429; Curtis, p. 459.

[6] F. B. Hough, *History of Lewis County*, pp. 137, 170. The date is 1818.

[7] F. W. Beers, *Gazetteer and Biographical Record of Genesee County*, pp. 480, 491.

was a steadfast champion of Episcopal tradition and among
the founders of Geneva College (later Hobart) where its
ministers were to be trained.[1]   In Otsego County the two
Federalist leaders were likewise the supporters of the
church.   Judge Cooper was chiefly instrumental in building
up its influence in the town that bears his name and sent his
son, the future novelist, to the old Tory rector of St. Peter's
in Albany for a schooling that no one nearer was thought
fit to give.[2]   General Morris, as a zealous Anglican built a
church in 1801 to make provision for his parish in the town
that bore his name, continuing its leading patron; and his
children at the home, some distance from the village, set
up a memorial chapel.[3]   There is no intention here to prove
the old English church a school of Federalism, yet that cast
of thought which for three hundred years had made a point
of holding " it to be the duty of all men who are professors
of the Gospel to give respectful obedience to the Civil
Authorities, regularly and legitimately constituted "[4] could
not have been hospitable to the doctrines of the Constitution
of 1821.   It is safe to suppose that not many Jacobinical
Democrats were confirmed as Bishop Hobart made his
round of visits.[5]

All the families we have instanced were important in the
party of the state; among the Federalist nominations for
the electors of 1816, for example, are found the names of
Jacob Morris, William North, Matthew Clarkson and

[1] M. Dix, *op. cit.*, vol. iii, p. 197; see also many letters from Troup
to Rufus King on church matters, *King Correspondence.*

[2] S. T. Livermore, *History of Cooperstown*, p. 51; T. R. Lounsbury,
Life of James Fenimore Cooper (Boston, 1882), p. 6; and letter from
the Reverend Ralph Birdsall of Cooperstown, N. Y. to the author.

[3] H. Child, *Gazetteer of Otsego County*, pp. 111-113.

[4] Articles of Religion, XXXVII, *Book of Common Prayer.*

[5] See M. Dix, *op. cit.*, Hobart Correspondence in vols. iii and iv, for
the extent and numbers of these visits.

Gouverneur Ogden.[1] At home this landed " quality " stood as reminiscent Catos praising, in a day of innovation, the older stable English way. Slowly but surely this influence of conservatism was distributed through the counties of the state, contributing somewhat, it cannot be doubted, to check the spirit of democracy,[2] and affording support respectable in character if not great in its extent, to the party that traced its evolution under John Quincy Adams, Henry Clay and William Henry Seward.

A hundred years ago throughout the countryside men were still described as Gentlemen and Yeomen; [3] the social and political prestige of landed property, of the " proud, polished, and powerful aristocracy deep-rooted in the soil," [4] was a familiar fact to be decently acknowledged as a beneficent provision for the welfare of the race. Judge Cooper's son, the famous novelist and the heir of this prestige, in the preface to *The Chainbearer,* his story of the anti-rent disturbance, adverted to the dangers that must follow in the train of any change:

The column of society must have its capital as well as its base. It is only perfect while each part is entire, and dis-

---

[1] *N. Y. Senate Journal,* 1816-1817, p. 16.

[2] Of course their kind of settlement was but partially similar to the Hudson River manors. Lands were sold for profit in fee simple, instead of held in lease with annoying dues. Hence settlement was encouraged, not retarded, by the presence of these proprietors, since they offered opportunities that self-respecting Yankees could embrace without disgrace. *Cf.* F. J. Turner, *The Old West* (Madison, 1909), pp. 195-198, and his authorities, for a discussion of the effect of feudal tenures and the exploitation of the settlers.

[3] See, for example, the certificate of admission to the bar of Dominick I. Blake, the friend of Hamilton (see signatures on Hamilton's will, Hamilton, *Works,* Lodge edition, vol. viii, p. 634), preserved in the Emmett Collection in the New York Public Library, Document 11310; a deed, *ibid.,* Document 11337, and numerous deeds in the Schuyler Mss., Land papers.

[4] Theodore Roosevelt, *Gouverneur Morris* (Boston, 1891), p. 14.

charges its proper duty.   In New York the great landholders
long have, and do still, in a social sense, occupy the place of this
capital.   On the supposition that this capital is broken, and
hurled to the ground, of what material will be the capital that
must be pushed into its place!   We know of none half so likely
to succeed, as the country extortioner and the country usurer!
We would caution those who now raise the cry of feudality and
aristocracy, to have a care of what they are about.   In lieu of
King Log, they may be devoured by King Stork.[1]

But the influence extolled, and often properly enough, as
so kindly and paternal, might not be exerted with the finest
scruple and could be bent to purposes sinister indeed.   As to
how these great Federalist landlords could play an ugly part
in politics if so disposed, no better example could be found
than in the case of Judge William Cooper.

In 1792 an Anti-Federalist legislature saw fit to notice
some of his irregularities, in the conduct of late elections in
his county, with a resolution for impeachment.[2]   Scores of
addresses and petitions were received, and the major portion
of the time of the assembly for a weary month exhausted in
the examination of the witnesses.   Although no sufficient
evidence was found to warrant his removal as an official,
enough was learned to leave no doubt as to what might be
accomplished by a great landlord with tenants in arrears.
One testified that the judge " had been round to the people
and told them that they owed him, and that unless they
voted for Mr. Jay, he would ruin them."   " Judge Cooper
then said to me," testified another, " ' what, then, young
man, you will not vote as I would have you—you are a

---

[1] J. Fenimore Cooper, *The Chainbearer* (N. Y., 1846), pp. viii-ix.

[2] *N. Y. Assembly Journal*, 1792-1793, pp. 140, 141, 145, 146, 149-152,
155, 156, 170, 184, 186, 204, 206, 240, 244-246 (citations are given in
full as the *Journal* is not indexed).   The Federalists by a virtually
solid vote did what they could to prevent the inquiry, but without avail,
ibid., p. 150.

fool, young man, for you cannot know how to vote as well
as I can direct you, for I am in public office.' " He was a
testy and choleric gentleman easily wrought into passion,
and his debtors, knowing that he took his politics as a serious business, were constrained to form opinions on his
model. It was thougnt that seven hundred votes were
brought into the Federalist column by this squire's well-
supported threats.[1]

Of course not every landlord took these high-handed
means. In the campaign for the election of governor in
1801, some over-zealous friends of the Patroon, who led
the forces of the Federalists, gave out that those of the
tenantry of Rensselaerswyck who owed for rent, of which
there were probably thousands, would be prosecuted if they
failed to cast their ballots for the manor-lord. Credulity
was nothing strained by this report, but Stephen Van
Rensselaer won wide praise for generosity by publishing
assurance that no such proscription was intended. "After
such a noble and magnanimous declaration," wrote Judge
Hammond, who was much impressed, " I am not at all
surprised that in the county of Albany the patroon received
two thousand one hundred and thirty-eight votes, while
Gov. Clinton received but seven hundred and fifty-five." [2]

[1] *N. Y. Assembly Journal*, 1792-1793, pp. 186-187, 189, 191, 193. Judge
Cooper's partisan activities were not estopped by this publicity. We
later hear complaints of his having gerrymandered Otsego County.
J. D. Hammond to Martin Van Buren, January 23, 1816, Van Buren Mss.

[2] J. D. Hammond, *Political History*, vol. i, pp. 161-162. In the campaign of 1813 when Van Rennselaer ran for governor, a letter was
raked out of some private file, which had been written twenty years
before during the campaign of 1793. The Federal *N. Y. Commercial
Advertiser*, April 23, 1813, quoted the *Albany Register* as follows:
" It purported to offer to such of his tenants as were his ' real friends,'
the remission of his ' quarter sale ' privilege or right; and will anyone deny that he had not the right of doing what he pleased with his
property? And will anyone have the hardihood to censure a landlord
for a measure calculated to ameliorate and improve the condition, and
promote the happiness of his tenants? "

At any rate, whether from admiration, fear or gratitude, the tenants of the Van Rensselaers had uniformly been accustomed to select the proprietor, some member of the family, or some designated friend, to represent them in the legislature,[1] and for more than half of the first forty years of the republic a Van Rensselaer sat in Congress as the member for the district of the upper Hudson.[2]   Such was this family influence that in 1821 Judge Van Ness could write to General Solomon Van Rensselaer:

I saw the Chancellor [James Kent] yesterday and had a long talk with him on the subject of the Convention.   I am authorized in saying that if you think proper to nominate him as one of your candidates, he will not decline.   We all here think he ought to be in the convention and I hope you will send him if you can.[3]

The influence of the land-holders, however, did not operate alone in the fear or loyalty of tenants.   Limitations on the suffrage in America, as but a hasty view makes clear,[4] have been removed with much delay and hesitation;

[1] D. D. Barnard, *Discourse on the Life and Services of Stephen Van Rensselaer, with an Historical Sketch of the Manor of Rensselaerwyck*, pamphlet (Albany, 1839), p. 68. Mr. Barnard speaks especially of the colonial period, but the practice was continued. The *N. Y. Civil List*, 1889, p. 742, has nearly a column of the names of offices held by the Van Rensselaers.

[2] "It is mentioned as illustrating the influence formerly exercised by the Dutch landed proprietors that during the first forty years following the organization of the federal government under the Constitution (from 1789 to 1829) the district embracing Albany was represented for *twenty-two* years by gentlemen bearing the name of Van Rensselaer and connected with the family of the Patroon, that is to say Jeremiah Van Rensselaer, two years, Kilian K., ten years; Solomon and Stephen ten years in the aggregate." Mrs. C. V. R. Bonney, *A Legacy of Historical Gleanings*, vol. i, p. 393.

[3] W. W. Van Ness to Gen. Solomon Van Rensselaer, May 16, 1821; Mrs. Bonney, *op. cit.*, vol. i, p. 367.

[4] C. A. Beard, *American Politics and Government* (N. Y., 1912), pp. 8-11.

that the holding of real property was indispensable in making a wise citizen was generally believed throughout our thirteen colonies.[1] When the suggestion of equality of rights that followed from the Declaration of Independence expressed itself in new demands for the extension of the suffrage, the conservatives, the Federalists, made firm remonstrance. Gouverneur Morris speaking in the convention of 1787 warned his colleagues that any innovation here was fraught with peril. " Give the votes to the people who have no property," said he, " and they will sell them to the rich who will be able to buy them." [2] Apparently as long as suffrage was restricted to the holders of the land, virtue would retain her throne; this was an article of faith with those who took their stand against democracy. " It is impossible," said Chancellor Kent, long after,[3] " that any people can lose their liberties by internal fraud or violence, so long as the country is parcelled out among freeholders of moderate possessions, and those freeholders have a sure and efficient control in the affairs of government." No one

[1] A. E. McKinley, *The Suffrage Franchise in the Thirteen English Colonies in America* (U. of Penn., Philadelphia, 1905), *passim*; see pp. 208-226 for the discussion of the franchise in colonial New York. " In New York City in the elections of 1735, 1761, and 1769, the actual voters numbered about eight per cent of the population." This was a much larger proportion than in many other colonies, p. 487. That in the country districts of New York must have been considerably smaller, as the Constitution of 1777 allowed the franchise to all of the " freemen " of New York city and Albany (Article VII) among whom there were mechanics and others without real property while all landless men outside these cities were excluded.

[2] Max Farrand (editor), *The Records of the Federal Convention,* vol. i, p. 545. Several other times he advocated a freehold qualification for the vote for congressmen, *ibid.*, vol. ii, pp. 201, 202, 207, 209. See also J. Allen Smith, *The Spirit of American Government* (N. Y., 1907), p. 37.

[3] Carter, Stone and Gould, *Reports of the Proceedings and Debates of the Convention of 1821* (Albany, 1821), p. 220.

may doubt that both these gentlemen and many others of their party, spoke from the conviction of their hearts; no doubt they felt that universal suffrage would be the fertile cause of all electoral chicanery; yet when the chancellor delivered his memorable defence of the old qualification, experience had shown that this alone had not provided against human weakness. Landholders in New York state while this qualification was in force,[1] were no more severely upright than their prototypes across the sea.

The student of the elective franchise as it developed in England is familiar with the practice known as " fagot holdings," whereby the wealthy politician, possessed of many acres in his county, was wont to cut them into strips, more or less exactly equal to the qualifications of a voter, and then carefully assign them to his landless neighbors, to make them legal and indubitable freemen for the three or four days of election only. Such practices, of ancient origin. became the subject of considerable legislation as late as 1832.[2] The example of these squires had not been lost.

[1] The Constitution of 1777 provided that the senators, governor and lieutenant-governor were to be chosen indirectly by freeholders "possessed of freeholds of the value of one hundred pounds, over and above all debts charged thereon," F. N. Thorpe, Federal and State Constitutions (59th Congress, House Document, No. 357, Washington, 1909), vol. v, pp. 2630, 2632, (Articles X and XVII). To vote for member of assembly, and hence for congressman, one "shall have been a freeholder, possessing a freehold of the value of twenty pounds, within the said county, or have rented a tenement of the yearly value of forty shillings," and been rated and actually paid taxes to the state, Article VII, *ibid.*, p. 2630. The pounds referred to are in the American estimation, not English, and hence the sums are to be understood as two hundred and fifty dollars and fifty dollars respectively. see C. Z. Lincoln, *Constitutional History of New York State*, vol. i. p. 640.

[2] *E. g.* Act 7 & 8 Wm. III, c. 25; 10 Anne, c. 23; 2 & 3 Wm. IV, c. 45 s. 20. The abuse has been defined as " conveyance not intended to give any real interest, made for the purpose of a particular election. and

Martin Van Buren has left a reputation for a matchless erudition in the devious ways of party management. In his younger days he served out a novitiate as a local leader of Clintonians,[1] later his implacable foes, with a success that marked no ordinary promise. In his native county of Columbia, however, he found one practice in which his Federalist rivals, land owners as they were, could easily excel. His summary sent to his chief after the election of 1810 is worthy of quotation:[2]

I have once more with shame to inform you that this county has given 527 majority for Platt & about the same for assembly & Congress—all the made voters voted for assembly & Congress—if you will look at the Voters between this year & last you will find that there have been rising of 600 votes made in the County of which our friends made about one-third—in Chatham our friend Dorr after he had made about a Dozzen got one of the *Judas Breed* into his Camp who gave up his Deed to the Federalists—this broke us up there—in Claverack our friends made more than they did—in this city they made more than us—& in the lower town where we had no body to make or to be made they played the very devil with us—in the single town of Gallatin Robert LeRoy Livingston[3] this

with an understanding that the property should be reconveyed where the transaction had served its turn." W. R. Anson, *The Law and Custom of the Constitution*, Fourth edition (Oxford, 1909), vol. i, pp. 106, 127. The Act of 1832, 2 & 3 Wm. IV, c. 45, required that property cited in qualification should have been held a year.

[1] That is from 1807 to 1813; E. M. Shepard, *Martin Van Buren* (Boston, 1888), pp. 45-59.

[2] Martin Van Buren to DeWitt Clinton, April 28, 1810, Clinton Mss. If President Van Buren kept a copy of this letter it may not be surprising that he did not include it among the papers he desired to be preserved, *cf. Calendar of Van Buren Manuscripts* (Washington, 1910).

[3] The Livingstons, of course, as a family had left the Federalists in 1790. "It is, however, to be remarked, that some of the Livingstons who resided in Columbia County, did not change with the chancellor, but continued their adherence to the federal party," J. D.

morning admitted to me that he had made 190 — Elisha Williams [1] was there during the whole election to fill up the Deeds—So that upon the whole we have reason to felicitate ourselves it is no worse. . . . [Here follows a sentence difficult to decipher claiming, apparently, that the Fedalists had sent in eight hundred deeds] . . . I am sorry for Columbia but have done all I could—King George has issued too many pattents for us. If some friends had laid off their scruples earlier we would have reduced their majority to about 250 which is all they are honestly entitled to.

King George having " issued too many pattents " to the aristocracy, the Federalists could make two fagot voters where their humbler rivals could make one. Republican solicitude at their success—for the practice was probably well known in more counties than this one [2]—was no doubt a motive in carrying through a law at the next session of the legislature, entitled " An Act to prevent Frauds and Per-juries at Elections," etc.[3] To discourage this kind of manufacture it specified that anyone offering to vote for governor, lieutenant-governor or senator, who fell under the suspicion of the inspector at the polls, must swear that he was

possessed of a freehold in my own right, (or in the right of my wife, as the case may be) of the value of two hundred and fifty dollars, within the state, over and above all debts charged thereon, and that I have not become such freeholder fraudu-

---

Hammond, *Political History*, vol. i, p. 107. Robert LeRoy Livingston was one of these, *Albany Gazette*, May 2, 1808; he served as congressman from 1809 to 1813, see *N. Y. Civil List*, 1889, p. 603.

[1] See *supra*, ch. ii.

[2] For two examples of how the Republicans had themselves used this device in the campaign of 1801, see Barrett. *Old Merchants of New York*, vol. i, p. 281, and E. Vale Blake, *The History of the Tammany Society* (N. Y., 1901), pp. 50-51.

[3] *Laws of the State of New York*, Thirty-fourth Session (1811), p. 287.

lently, for the purpose of giving my vote at this election, nor upon any trust or understanding, express or implied, to reconvey such free-hold during or after election . . . and further, that I will true answers make to any interrogatories which shall be put to me by inspectors of election, touching the situation and boundaries of such freehold, from whom and by what conveyance I derive title to the same.

But it was in the voting for the members of assembly (and by that same test for Congress), where the property qualification was much lower, that most trouble was expected. Here the provision was still more exacting; the voter must take oath that " I am and have been for six months next and immediately preceding the election, a freeholder, and am possessed . . . of the value of fifty dollars." It was thought unlikely that any landholder would give up six months' rental that the Federalist vote of his district might be enlarged.

For it was the Federalists who feared the operation of the law; theirs they recognized to be the loss if voters were no longer to be "made." When the proposition came before the senate, Judge Platt, aware how hopeless would be any opposition to the bill against the immovable Republican majority, catching at what straws he could, moved a proviso " that it should not take effect until after the next election." [1] Possibly in this way one year, at least, might be salvaged. But the majority must have smiled at such a hope; the proviso was supported by eight senators, of whom all but one were Federalists.[2] When the act was passed the seven who stood fast against it were Hall, Hopkins, Paris, Phelps, Platt. Stearns and Williams, all men of the old party who had been elected in the great revolt of 1808

[1] *N. Y. Senate Journal*, 1811, p. 163.

[2] *Ibid.*, p. 164. This minority constituted nearly one-third of the members present.

and 1809.[1] In the assembly there was a similar alignment.[2] The landholding Federalists had done what they
could to save a useful practice, but the *Zeitgeist* had gone
on.[3]

The Federalists as landlords found their largest common
interest in the projects for the inland waterways which
would enhance the value of their property throughout the
state. Intelligent observers had early seen great possibilities. Washington had written in the first year after the
Revolution:

I then traversed the country to the head of the eastern
branch of the Susquehanna, and viewed the Lake Otsego, and
the portage between that lake and the Mohawk River at Cana-
joharie. Prompted by these actual observations, I could not
help taking a more contemplative and extensive view of the
vast inland navigation of the United States . . . [and] the
goodness of that Providence, which has dealt her favors to
us with so profuse a hand. Would to God we may have
wisdom enough to improve them.[4]

[1] J. S. Jenkins, *History of Political Parties in New York State*, pp.
126, 131-133. Robert Williams had been chosen as a Republican, but
after his election as a member of the Council of Appointment he had
uniformly acted with the Federalists, thus giving them a majority, and
was henceforth called an apostate by his former party, *Jenkins*, pp.
121, 133. Williams, unlike the others, had been elected in 1807. For
party affiliations see also the *N. Y. Senate Journal*, 1811, p. 196.

[2] *N. Y. Assembly Journal*, 1811, pp. 315, 360.

[3] It is probable that the practice did not entirely disappear, until
the extension of the suffrage in 1821. "Tammany [in 1820] charged
that in the construction of the Erie Canal, land had been cut up in
slips to make additional voters for Clinton and cited the county of
Genessee [sic], which, though polling but 750 freehold votes in 1815,
gave nearly 5,000 votes in this election." Gustavus Myers, *The History
of Tammany Hall*, p. 66, note; Myers cites no authority for this
statement.

[4] G. Washington to the Chevallier de Chastellux, 12 October, 1783,
Works (Ford edition), vol. x, p. 325. See also his letter of the same
date to Lafayette, *loc. cit.* Elkanah Watson, who claimed to be the

But for the statesmen or the capitalists who had witnessed only the first steps in our national development, nothing was harder than to take a " contemplative and extensive view " of the improvement of other people's land at the general cost to taxpayers. Perhaps even the Father of his Country found this enthusiasm easier when he recalled his property between the ranges of the Alleghenies.[1] Though a liberal interpretation of constitutions, state and national, was needful to the policy of internal improvement by appropriation from the public chest, Federalists, as such, were not of necessity committed to these schemes. It was not until New England saw her destiny in manufactures, and recognized the need of quicker transportation for the bales of raw and finished goods carried back and forth to pay her dividends, not until the presidential speeches of John Quincy Adams, that the old Federalists of Boston voted for canals and turnpikes in the regions far beyond the fall line. In 1817, in Congress, when Calhoun's persuasive prophecies almost carried through the principle in its most liberal application, the Federalists from Massachustts voted no.[2] Cyrus King, the brother of the senator from New York, voiced their protest in a short and simple phrase: " The post roads of New England are now good . . . If they are not so elsewhere let those concerned make them so." [3] And throughout the first and second decades of the century this was the attitude, in general, of the coastal cities toward the clamorous frontier.[4]

originator of the plan of a long western canal, says it was a conversation with Washington which tended to "kindle a flame in his mind" and start his explorations, E. Watson, *History of Canals in New York State* (Albany, 1820), p. 9.

[1] See his Will, *Works* (Ford edition), vol. xiv, p. 283, and A. B. Hulbert, *Washington and the West* (N. Y., 1905).

[2] *Annals of Congress*, 1817-1818, pp. 230, 398, 922, 1062. [3] *Ibid.*, p. 914.

[4] Professor F. J. Turner has prepared maps (not yet published) showing how the favorable vote on such propositions steadily increases westward from the coast.

On the other hand the Federalists of New York city and the Hudson River counties seemed more anxious for the progress of appropriations at Albany or Washington than were the followers of Jefferson, a fact of no small interest in accounting for their later coalition with the Clinton forces. They too engaged their fortunes on the sea, but not exclusively; unlike their fellow partisans of Boston they had lands to settle and develop. It was Gouverneur Morris in the tent of General Schuyler, one evening in the long campaign of Saratoga, who pictured the not distant day when connection would be made between the Hudson and those "great western seas." [1]   Philip Schuyler, shrewd, enterprising, public-spirited, was not a man to lose this vision; he became the Father of Canals in New York state,[2] though to Morris goes the credit for the project of the Grand Canal itself.   While on his visit to England in 1761 Schuyler had seen the great canals that Brindley had but lately finished, and had been impressed with what such a work might mean connecting the Hudson near his home with Lake Champlain.[3]   Learning of Elkanah Watson's plan of a canal between Lake Ontario and the Mohawk, in 1791,[4] he be-

[1] Jared Sparks, *Life etc. of Gouverneur Morris*, vol. i, pp. 495-504.

[2] In the New York Public Library there are preserved nearly a thousand pieces of his manuscript papers dealing with canals.   General Schuyler's importance as a landholder needs hardly to be mentioned. There are preserved eleven boxes of his land papers, beside several volumes and many extra items.   See also J. C. Hamilton to A. C. Flagg, July 26, 1826, Flagg Mss. (Misc. Papers).

[3] B. J. Lossing, *The Life and Times of Major General Philip Schuyler*, vol. i, pp. 40, 180; vol. ii, pp. 464-471.   On his return he prevailed upon the governor Sir Henry Moore "to look into the matter of rendering the Mohawk River navigable by the construction of such canals as might be necessary to overcome the rapids at the Little Falls and elsewhere."   H. W. Hill, "Waterways and Canals in New York State," *Buffalo Historical Society Collections*, vol. xii, p. 37.

[4] See E. Watson, *op. cit.*

came the chief patron of internal improvements in New York. His efforts in the legislature produced " An act for establishing and opening lock navigation within the State," [1] and he organized two companies to build canals to Ontario and Champlain, presiding over both.[2]

Capital to sustain such large enterprises would naturally be sought within the " party of merchants and commercial men," [3] but these might well have been as skeptical as the merchants in New England, had it not been for the landed interests of themselves, their relatives and friends. Certainly these moneyed men of New York City did not hesitate. A partial list recording eighteen holders of the stock of these two companies is preserved with General Schuyler's papers.[4] Besides the Holland bankers [5] we find mostly names of Federalist landholders, or their close associates. Robert Troup and Richard Harison lead with ten shares each. LeRoy

---

[1] *Laws of 1792*, ch. xl; see also David Hosack, *Memoir of DeWitt Clinton* (N. Y., 1829), Appendix S. The bill was managed in the assembly by John Williams, a Federalist from Washington County. See Elkanah Watson, *History of Canals in New York State* and "Warren" (James Cheetham) *An Antidote to John Wood's Poison*, pamphlet, (N. Y., 1802), p. 47, and C. H. Hunt, *Life of Edward Livingston* (N. Y., 1863), p. 69.

[2] The Western Inland Lock Navigation Company and the Northern Inland Lock Navigation Company. The stockholders seem to have been almost identical, see Schuyler Mss., " Canals " box 1. Schuyler proposed the route actually followed by the Champlain Canal, H. W. Hill, *op. cit.*, p. 131. The report of 1792 of the "Committee to Explore the Western Waters...for...Inland Navigation," is reprinted in the *Documentary History of New York* (Albany, 1850), vol. iii, pp. 659-670.

[3] Levi Beardsley, *Reminiscences* (N. Y., 1852), pp. 118-119.

[4] " List of Stockholders in the Western Inland Lock Navigation Company who have made payment agreeable to the requisition of the board of the 11th of April, 1793; " the same for the Northern Company shows but two variations in names. Schuyler Mss. " Canal Papers."

[5] Of these there were four firms mentioned, naturally interested in the western lands by reason of the Holland Purchase. See *Journal of the Assembly of N. Y.*, 1792-1793, p. 22.

and Bayard,[1] and Rufus King[2] come next with five. Then John Lawrence, King's successor in the Senate, who was among the most extensive landlords,[3] and Gilbert Aspinwall,[4] the wealthy merchant whose relatives held land.[5] Other names, like those of William Inman who owned a hundred thousand acres in the north[6] and Frederick Scriba whose vast holdings stretched along the shores of Lake Ontario,[7] piece out the list; and as one turns over the voluminous correspondence, many Federalists of the same kind are mentioned as stockholders—General Abraham Ten Broeck,[8] Jonas Platt.[9] Colonel J. Van Schoonhoven,[10] Goldsborough Banyar (John Jay's son-in-law),[11] and

[1] They later donated 2,500 acres for the Erie Canal, and Robert Troup for Sir William Pulteney made also a large grant, S. H. Sweet, "Documentary Sketch of New York Canals," in Annual Report of the State Engineer, N. Y. Assembly Documents, 1863, vol. i, p. 99.

[2] King became quite active, dispensing much of the company's money and planning with the engineers, see Schuyler to Wm. Weston, February 11, 1793, and R. King to Schuyler, February 17, 1793. Schuyler Mss.

[3] Land Papers, pp. 503, 506, 551, 569, 658, 668, 796, etc., etc.

[4] A. A. Aspinwall, The Aspinwall Genealogy (Rutland, 1901 [?]), p. 72.

[5] Land Papers, p. 689.

[6] Documentary History of New York, vol. iii, p. 647.

[7] J. C. Churchill, History of Oswego County, see account of the town of Scriba, etc.

[8] To Schuyler, June 11, 1793; Schuyler Mss. He was the Federal candidate for mayor of Albany in 1790, J. D. Hammond, Political History, vol. i, p. 48.

[9] To Major de Zeug, May 21, 1793, Schuyler Mss.

[10] B. Bleecker to Schuyler, May 17, 1793. Schuyler Mss.; J. A. Roberts, New York in the Revolution (Albany, 1898), p. 120; Jenkins, Political Parties, pp. 63, 84, 130, etc.

[11] B. Bleecker to Schuyler, January 1, 1793, Schuyler Mss.; W. W. Spooner, Historic Families of America, vol. iii, pp. 152, 163. For the lands held by Banyar, see Land Papers, pp. 731, 736, 970, 1017, etc. He later turned Republican.

Dominick Lynch, the founder of Rome,[1] most of them large proprietors of land.

In the movement for the Grand Canal the initial step was taken by Gouverneur Morris.[2] In 1803 his plan recounted to scientists and engineers produced a deep impression,[3] and began an enterprise which was later aided by the Clintons. That he held great tracts along the Genesee, and sought to interest others in their purchase, must have been a factor in his propaganda.[4] His name came first among the original canal commissioners of 1810,[5] of whose report he was the author,[6] and it was Morris who with Clinton went to Washington in a vain attempt to get a federal grant.[7] But there were other leading Federalists who made common cause with him and Schuyler. Thomas R. Gold [8] had brought in the resolution

[1] To Schuyler, July 24, 1792, Schuyler Mss.; Walter Barrett, *Old Merchants of New York*, vol. i, p. 171. *Diary of Philip Hone*, vol. i, pp. 5, 18, 35, etc. Samuel Jones was also a stockholder, Jones to Schuyler, July 14, 1792.

[2] His enthusiastic letter to John Parish, December 20, 1800, is quoted in part by D. Hosack, *Memoir of DeWitt Clinton*, p. 252, *et seq.*

[3] By 1803 he was also projecting a shorter canal " from the head of the Onondaga River and carried on the level as far east as it will go, and, if possible, into the Mohawk River; then, in a direct course as circumstances will permit to Hudson's River, making locks as the descent may require." *Diary and Letters*, vol. ii, p. 390. Clinton himself in a letter in his papers (no date) gives Morris credit for originating the scheme, Hosack, p. 301, and A. B. Hulburt, *Historic Highways* (Cleveland, 1904), vol. xiv, ch. ii.

[4] F. W. Halsey, *The Old New York Frontier*, p. 370, and Sparks, *Life etc. of Gouverneur Morris* (To Jefferson, February 26, 1791, and December 21, 1792), vol. ii, pp. 121, 249.

[5] *N. Y. Civil List*, 1889, p. 224.

[6] H. W. Hill, " Waterways and Canals," pp. 72-73.

[7] Morris, *Diary and Letters*, vol. ii, p. 535.

[8] See Robert Troup to Rufus King, April 11, 1807, *King Correspondence*; F. A. Bloodgood to John Tayler, April 5, 1804, Tayler Mss.; and *supra*, ch. ii.

of 1808 looking toward a full survey[1] and Jonas Platt revived the subject in the senate during his campaign as candidate for governor in 1810,[2] while the Patroon and Abraham Van Vechten carried through the measure in the assembly.[3] Of the first canal commissioners four out of eight were Federalists and three Clintonians.[4] Apparently the interest in such improvement, connected as it was at first with land values, had become a settled party policy.

When the war was over, at a great New York mass meeting that sought again to forward the canal scheme, William Bayard, the great Federalist proprietor, was the chairman.[5] J. R. Van Rensselaer, the party leader from Columbia County, was the most active lobbyist at Albany[6] for the canal, and sought the contract for its construction at $10,000,000.[7] Robert Troup was the most effective propagandist in the west,[8] and Cadwallader D. Colden formed opinion in its favor in New York city, where support was sadly needed.[9] In the assembly Judge Pendleton

---

[1] *N. Y. Assembly Journal*, 1808, p. 297.

[2] *N. Y. Senate Journal*, 1810, p. 99. "Be assured Sir, it will ever be to me a subject of just pride, as well as the most pleasing reflections, that I had the honor of coöperating with You in initiating and promoting our great system of internal navigation." Jones Platt to DeWitt Clinton, Oct. 4, 1823. See also Thomas Eddy to Clinton, Oct. 4, 1823, DeWitt Clinton Mss.

[3] N. E. Whitford, *History of the Canal System of the State of New York*, N. Y. Assembly Documents, 1906, vol. v, pp. 62-63.

[4] Gouverneur Morris, Stephen Van Rensselaer, DeWitt Clinton, Simeon DeWitt, William North, Thomas Eddy and Peter B. Porter. Only the last came to be known as a Tammany man, and he, in the 'thirties, became a Whig. See Follett Papers.

[5] See petition in *New York Canal Laws*, vol. ii, p. 122.

[6] N. E. Whitford, *op. cit.*, p. 81.

[7] J. R. Van Rensselaer to DeWitt Clinton, March 11, 1817, Clinton Mss.

[8] Hosack, *op. cit.*, p. 423; also see letters to DeWitt Clinton, Feb. 25, Dec. 3, 5, 9, and Jan. 13, 1819, Clinton Mss.

[9] *Encyclopedia Britannica*, 11th edition, under Colden.

(who had been Hamilton's second in the duel with Aaron Burr), William A. Duer, Abraham Van Vechten, T. J. Oakley, James Emott and especially Elisha Williams were leaders in support of the measure, while Lucas Elmendorf and P. R. Livingston, two of the foremost Democrats, led the opposition.[1] In the senate George Tibbits[2] was its champion, and it was he who devised the plan adopted by the state to pay for the canal.[3] When the vote of 1816 was recorded, said a broadside issued to the voters of the west, it was observed that but two Federalists had voted against the project, which received a treatment so unkind from their opponents. " The Federalists as a body have adhered closely to our interests." [4] In 1817 no member of the party in the senate voted nay. No eleventh-hour repentance of the

[1] N. E. Whitford, *op. cit.*, pp. 83, 93, 94.

[2] A Federalist from Rensselaer, see Jenkins, *Political Parties*, p. 171.

[3] D. C. Sowers, *Financial History of New York State* (N. Y., 1914), p. 62.

[4] *The Grand Canal Defeated by a Democratic Senate* (in the collection of the New York Public Library). " The first step towards its destruction was a motion by Mr. Van Buren to strike out a large portion of the Bill which the House had passed—and the second was to form a new one, which leaves the business in a worse condition than if it had never been taken up.

" Will the electors support men who are thus regardless of their most important interests? It appears that but 2 federal senators voted in favor of Mr. Van Buren's motion to strike out the bill from the Assembly. The federalists as a body have adhered closely to our interests. To the permanent interests of the Western District especially, while the Senators from this part of the state have generally voted against them. Let us turn our attention to a different set of men." Van Buren later came to the support of a measure which proved so popular, and made a speech in its favor at the following session. He even for a time considered internal improvements at national expense, see C. E. Dudley to Van Buren, Dec. 23, 1821 and J. C. Hamilton to Van Buren, Dec. 21, 1826, Van Buren Mss.

[5] *N. Y. Senate Journal*, 1816-1817, *cf.* votes on presidential electors and on the bill, pp. 16, 356. The bill when passed was nearly vetoed

Tammany leaders could erase this memory.[1] So the Federalists, whose interest in canals had followed their concern in lands, won the gratitude of the western section, which, in contrast to its former practice,[2] became a stronghold of the opposition to the Democratic party.

When other canals were projected it was to be expected that land-owning Federalists would be active in support. It was natural that Nicholas Low [3] and Henry Remsen (once John Jay's private secretary) [4] should desire their great properties improved, when the Black River Canal was proposed in Clinton's administration, and that many wealthy members of the party in the city of New York should ask for the connection between Lake Champlain and the St. Lawrence, which the governor had so warmly advocated.[5] In 1824 a petition was presented in the interest

in the Council of Revision. The story of how Chancellor Kent flouted the advice of Vice President Tompkins, in voting for the bill, is to be found in William Kent, *Memoirs of Chancellor Kent* (Boston, 1898), pp. 168-170.

[1] The Tammany party " ridiculing as a ruinous and visionary project, the efforts which have been made for connecting our Atlantic seaboard with our great inland seas,—and when driven from their hold, by the torrent of public opinion, affecting to be all at once the great patrons of the undertaking, and seizing into their own hands its officers and its patronage." Broadside, *Address to the Electors of Oneida and Oswego* (signed Bill Smith, chairman, 20th March 1821) in the New York Public Library; C. G. Haines to De Witt Clinton, Sept. 10, 1819, Clinton Mss., and letters in 1821, Childs Mss.

[2] See *supra*, ch. iii.

[3] Levi Beardsley, *Reminiscences*, p. 285.

[4] Henry Remsen had purchased heavily in the lower Adirondack region, see *Land Papers*, pp. 651, 671, 725, 731, 743, 748, etc., D. E. Wager, *History of Oneida County*, p. 119, and M. A. Hamm, *Famous Families of New York*, vol. ii, p. 78.

[5] C. Z. Lincoln, *Messages from the Governors* (Albany, 1909), vol. iii, pp. 68, 69. See also *N. Y. Canal Laws*, vol. ii, p. 228, and H. W. Hill, *op. cit.*, p. 146.

of this latter enterprise by certain citizens of the city.[1] Among its less than two score names there are those of many Federalists that can thus be easily explained. Richard Harison,[2] Herman LeRoy,[3] Daniel McCormick,[4] Thomas Morris,[5] Garret Van Horne,[6] Hezekiah B. Pierpont,[7] R. M. Lawrence,[8] Matthew, Thomas S. and Levinus Clarkson,[9] Philip Brasher,[10] Frederick Depeyster,[11] LeRoy, Bayard and Co.,[12] Charles McEvers,[13] Elisha Tibbits,[14] Henry Remsen and Nicholas Low. There were others who though not owning land in this vicinity were glad to give approval to the principle; for example Nicholas Fish,[15] who at one time owned nearly fifty thousand acres in Broome County and much more beside, and Cornelius Ray,[16] a proprietor of several square miles in Chenango. This list may help explain how it was that Federalists began a policy of large expenditure for such improvement in New York.

[1] A copy is preserved among the Miscellaneous Papers of the Flagg Mss.

[2] See *supra*, ch. i.

[3] His family held land in St. Lawrence County, see G. Curtis, *St. Lawrence County*, part ii, p. 34.

[4] *Land Papers, e. g.*, p. 1008.

[5] *Ibid.*, p. 658.

[6] Curtis, *op. cit.*, p. 462.

[7] F. B. Hough, *St. Lawrence and Franklin Counties*, pp. 713-714.

[8] A relative of Senator John Lawrence.

[9] Curtis, part ii, p. 34.

[10] Thurlow Weed, *Autobiography, etc.*, vol. i, pp. 394, 401.

[11] J. H. French, *Gazetteer of New York*, p. 576; W. A. Duer, *Reminiscences*, p. 37.

[12] *Hough, op. cit.*, p. 429.

[13] Associated with LeRoy, Bayard and Co.

[14] He and his family held land in this section, see J. H. French, *Gazetteer*, p. 578 and *Land Papers*, p. 921.

[15] *Land Papers*, pp. 737, 810.

[16] *Ibid.*, pp. 714, 720.

In this brief survey we have sought to trace the influence and counter-influence of the frontier and Federalism in New York state. We have seen the venture of these old New Yorkers in the wild lands of the west and north, vast and princely in extent, and have heard their protest when that section of their party that saw hope alone in trade and manufactures, sought to fix the burden of taxation upon the land. We have followed friends and younger members of the families to new homes close beside the wilderness itself, and seen the strange distinction of plebeian and patrician in these far outposts of civilized society. We have seen them socially conservative—in manners, in religion and in the theory of politics—but bold in planning for industrial enterprise; and heard them preaching the gospel of a generous development of the imperial resources of the state, which sounded to the ears of the mechanic and his party in the city, as vague, star-misty stuff.[1] This interest in canals and waterways became a mighty factor in the fortunes of their party after it took on the names, Clintonian and Whig.

The enthusiasm of the Federalists in New York city and the Hudson Counties, for these artificial waterways, was not based wholly on their landed interest. Calculating business men, who foresaw the independence of this country in manufacturing, realized how such connection would contribute in transportation to and from the fields and markets.[2] They understood the arguments that issued from the western counties,[3] by reason of " the simpathy of

---

[1] *National Advocate*, June 10, 17, 24, 25, 27, July 10, August 4, 19, Sept. 6, 17, 1817; *N. Y. Assembly Journal*, 1818, p. 120.

[2] Philip Hone is a good example of such Federalists; he was heavily interested in the Delaware and Hudson Canal, see letters to A. C. Flagg, January 9, 1827 and October 17, 1828, Flagg Mss. Miscellaneous Papers, and DeWitt Clinton to Philip Hone, October 6, 1826, Clinton Mss. (Letterbook VIII).

[3] It was certainly not surprising that the west should desire an improvement that raised the price of wheat fifty per cent before it was completed, D. C. Sowers, *Financial History of New York State*, p. 60.

mercantile pursuits and the friendship bred by dependence." [1]
Yet at first, we have seen, it was probably their natural concern in the prices of the land they had for sale, that fastened
their attention on these projects for development. We find
five senators who represented New York state in Washington, the last three party candidates for governor, two score
of leaders in the state, and their respectable supporters,
foremost in the prosecution of canal construction. All were
wealthy Federalists, and all, or nearly all, possessed of
lands enormous in extent. It seems an inference not un-
warranted, without uncharitably charging them with want
of public spirit (since the common good was forwarded at
once with theirs), that there was some connection in these
facts.

The importance of this Federalist paternity for the canal
schemes brought to final triumph by Clinton, transcends
that of a mere episode. By reason of the issue often joined
with Tammany on one side and their opponents on the
other, there grew up in the western counties a doctrine that
no good thing could come from counsels of the Democrats.
Because the party of Schuyler, Morris and Van Rensselaer
had served their interest far more faithfully than those who
listened to the sachems in New York, they developed a habit
of constant opposition to the latter's candidates. A decade
or so later, when the Whigs took up the party struggle, in
a manner more in keeping with the spirit of the time, but
still imbued with Federalist traditions; these counties each
November, quite regardless of gains and losses in the other
sections of the state, voted their support with perfect
regularity. Acting on the " friendship bred by dependence,"
the Whig leaders made it a cardinal point of faith, that
the state should be internally improved though, as the
Democrats maintained, it might entail a debt of forty
millions. [2]

[1] T. N. Butler to DeWitt Clinton, March 12, 1809, Clinton Mss.

[2] F. W. Seward, *William H. Seward* (N. Y., 1891), vol. i, pp. 503-504.

CHAPTER VI

Mr. Madison's War

GULIAN C. VERPLANCK was a disappointment to the older
Federalist leaders. No one of the rising generation had
shown brighter promise than this young founder of the
Washington Benevolent Society; his eloquence and energy,
it had been supposed, were permanently dedicated to that
party's cause. Hence it was with some concern that, in
January, 1811, they read through a pamphlet signed by one
"Abimelech Coody, Ladies' Shoemaker," known to be
Verplanck.[1] For here, against all usage, the ardent politicians of both sides were held up to an impartial ridicule
in their raw-head-and-bloody-bones recitals of French spies,
Old Tories and the Prison Ships. The pamphlet set forth
that the simple shoemaker had won ten thousand dollars in a
lottery and sought counsel as to how he might invest his
" funs." A Federalist schoolmaster warned him solemnly
against the Manhattan Bank; its president, he knew, was in
the pay of Bonaparte. He had it recently from Dr. Dwight
and Oliver Wolcott that a French spy had tried to stab
good Colonel Fish for fear if he became lieutenant-governor
he might remove the bank's French clerks. The school-

[1] This is now a rare pamphlet. The full title is as follows: *Letter
to the Hon. Samuel L. Mitchill, M. D., Representative in Congress
from the City of New York; Professor of Natural His. &c. on the
Danger of Putting Money into the U. States and Manhattan Banks,
with Sundry Novel Speculations on Insurance Stock, Domestic Manufactures and the Best Mode of Vesting a Capital, " So as to Make Both
Ends Meet."* The author has used the copy in the Library of the New
York Society, endorsed as presented by " C. Clims, Gent. 22nd January 1811."

master advised him to put his money in the " Branch Bank " under Mr. Ray, but he was soon stopped by a Democratic friend who told him that the Bank of the United States was about to be blown up, as was proper since the cashier was a nephew of the Lord Mayor of London. He was prepared to risk his fortune in a ropewalk, when he heard the building had been burned by British agents. New York insurance stocks he understood were but the playthings of the French. In his extremity he thought of going into politics and possibly become a " congress-man, for Mr. Baron Gaudenier says that's the best trade going."

This ridicule of the idea of a French party and this impertinent jibe at Barent Gardenier were resented by the Federalist papers.

Mr. Coody calls himself a Federalist, [wrote William Coleman in the *Evening Post*] because he votes on the Federalist side, and sometimes, I believe, contributes alms to the Federalist purse, but if honest Abimelech would go over to the other party at once, his open apostasy would be of more service to us than either his vote or his money, and for this plain reason, because he now has some little influence among certain Federalists, and he exerts it only to do mischief.[1]

The independence of Verplanck was all the more astonishing when one called to mind his Tory-Federalist ancestry,[2] yet a trace of heresy might have been discovered in his oration of July 4th, 1809, when he had said that the protection of their rights could always be confided to the common people.[3] Perhaps it was the influence of Edward Livingston, with whom he studied for two years, that was

[1] *N. Y. Herald*, April 6, 1811.

[2] W. C. Bryant, *A Discourse on the Life and Writings of Gulian Crommelin Verplanck*, delivered before the New York Historical Society (N. Y., 1870), pp. 5-14.

[3] *Supra*, ch. iv.

responsible for these developments;[1] he was evidently out of patience with the stiff-necked Hamiltonians, and his democratic tendencies were soon to be dramatically revealed.

On the morning of the sixth of August, 1811, Trinity Church was crowded to the doors with relatives and friends of the seniors of Columbia College, who were that day to receive their degrees. Upon the temporary platform set up before the chancel were seated the professors, the president, and the doughty provost, Dr. John M. Mason, on whom, in fact, devolved the conduct of the college.[2] One by one the young men, in balanced and sententious periods, delivered their orations on the glories of the arts or the message of the past, possibly without producing deep impression, until there came the speech of John B. Stevenson. He had been assigned to be respondent in a brief discussion as to the right of representatives to disregard instructions and, being a Republican in politics, it had been suspected that his zeal might outrun decorum. Acting under an old by-law of the trustees. certain of the faculty, which was almost wholly Federalist in sympathy, had examined the draft of his oration, and suggested a more temperate statement. They would not have their students, they declared, " pronounce any sentiments which might injure themselves or dishonor the institution." [3]

[1] A correspondence was kept up between Verplanck and Livingston after the latter went to Louisiana, see Verplanck Mss. in possession of W. E. Verplanck, Fishkill, N. Y., also Biographical Address of Chief Justice Daly in *Proceedings of the Century Association in Honor of the Memory of Gulian Verplanck* (N. Y., 1870), pp. 24-25.

[2] J. H. M. Knox, " John M. Mason, S. T. D," in *Columbia University Quarterly*, vol. iii, pp. 26-34. Dr. Mason preached the funeral sermon on the death of Hamilton (Morris, *Diary and Letters*, vol. ii, p. 352) and was first designated as the biographer of that statesman (*King Correspondence*, vol. vi, p. 165).

[3] Statement of the Faculty of Columbia College, *N. Y. Spectator*,

But on Commencement Day, young Stevenson, to the consternation of the reverend gentlemen behind him, spoke right on without regard to any of their emendations. As he closed he was quietly advised by one of the professors that his degree could not be granted on that day. However when the parchments were distributed, egged on by certain friends, he came forward, but to meet refusal. Hugh Maxwell, a relative by marriage,[1] leaped to the platform to voice a loud objection, and " a species of riot commenced, with hissing clapping, and noisy exultation." [2] Verplanck now ran forward with some others, demanding of the provost an explanation of his course with Stevenson. The reasons were not satisfactory, and he harangued the now excited audience, moving that the thanks of the meeting be given Mr. Maxwell for his spirited defense of an injured man. The motion was lost in uproar. An Irishman proposed three hearty groans for Dr. Mason; young Republicans threw up their hats and were for hustling out the officers. Colonel Varick crying " Order," was insulted; Oliver Wolcott was silenced; Mr. Dunscombe, their colleague in the board of trustees, declared that the degree would not be conferred, if he answered with his life—an announcement greeted with a general laugh. No valedictory was delivered; the president pronounced no benediction, but hastened from the church. Party indignation now flamed

July 10, 1811; the account in the text is based chiefly upon the evidence presented at the subsequent trial for riot, and reprinted in a pamphlet (now marked "very rare") called: *The Trial of Gulian C. Verplanck, Hugh Maxwell, and others for a Riot in Trinity Church at the Commencement of Columbia College in August, 1811* (N. Y., 1821). I have also used the newspapers of the day.

[1] G. A. Morrison, Jr., *History of St. Andrew's Society of the State of New York* (N. Y., 1906), p. 104.

[2] Statement of the Faculty.

high, and Verplanck and Maxwell with some others were soon haled before the mayor's court for riot.[1]

The mayor was DeWitt Clinton, who seems fully to have realized the political importance of the trial. He had been narrowly elected lieutenant-governor in the spring,—the incumbent, General Broome, had died—though the Republicans of his own district had voted chiefly for Marinus Willet, as the Martling candidate, or even for Colonel Fish, the Federalist.[2] The spirit of the Clinton papers sagged, and it was known that his enemies within the party would spare no pains to put him out of power.[3] His ill-disguised contempt for Madison and the national administration had lost him popularity, yet in this opposition it seemed quite possible that he might win the confidence of his old foes the Federalists; at least the time seemed opportune for an attempt.

When the trial for riot came, the witnesses were duly questioned, and Dr. Mason, smarting in his wounded pride, rolled out his invective against the Jacobins; then the mayor's time had come. In his denunciation he far outdid the Federalist champions: the learned counsel for defence had wasted time when they declared the matter was a mere affray or rout; their authorities were bad. " We have no hesitation in declaring that the disturbance which took place

[1] The friends of Mr. Stevenson (who later became famous as a physician) on seeing the Statement of the Faculty published an elaborate reply in the *N. Y. Commercial Advertiser*, August 12. The trial, after a speedy indictment by the grand jury, was held on August 17 before what was officially known as the Court of Sessions, see C. P. Daly, *op. cit.*, and E. Vale Blake, *The History of the Tammany Society*, pp. 50-51.

[2] *N. Y. Herald*, April 3, 6, 13; *N. Y. Columbian*, April 19; *N. Y. Spectator*, May 18, 1811. The Constitution of 1777 allowed this plurality of offices.

[3] " O " to Clinton, March 14, 1811, DeW. Clinton Mss., and J. H. Douglass to W. P. Van Ness, Feb. 15, 1811, VanNess Mss.

on the occasion alluded to, is the most disgraceful, the most unprecedented, the most unjustifiable, and the most outrageous, that ever came within the knowledge of this court." Toward Verplanck, "shaping himself with all the self created importance of a second Daniel," he was especially severe. Readers of the Federalist papers the next morning learned that the mayor "after a very conciliatory but impressive address (which we think should be laid before the public)," had been content to fine Verplanck and Maxwell two hundred dollars each.[1] The tirade from the bench had a wide political effect. "You have," a friend assured him, "become extremely popular with the Federalists for your charge and sentence on the rioters at the late commencement."[2] But he had as well, as we shall see, won the undying hatred of Gulian C. Verplanck.

Few men were more informed as to the doings of the Federalists than were the British agents in America. In September 1811, Mr. Foster wrote to the Marquess of Wellesley that no candidate for president was generally talked of; in November he reported certain rumors of strange coalitions; before Christmas he had learned that DeWitt Clinton was to be proposed. The new ratio of representation in the Congress made New York the most important state and much might be risked to gain it.[3] The "detestation of mobocracy," which had so marked his censure of the rioters, had favorably impressed the party to the east, and they were willing to support the mayor of New York, expecting as reward appointment to some foreign embassy or financial

[1] *N. Y. Commercial Advertiser*, Aug. 18, 1811. There were five others also tried, convicted and fined.

[2] Ambrose Spencer to Clinton, Sept. 23, 1811, DeW. Clinton Mss.

[3] Mr. (afterward Sir) A. J. Foster to Marquess of Wellesley, Sept. 17, Nov. 29, Dec. 21, 1811, Precis Mss. Books (N. Y. P. L.), vol. ii.

favors from the government.[1] The *rapprochement* in New York state daily grew more manifest as the winter wore away.

Certain Federalists had made application for a charter for a bank. It soon became a party question; Governor Tompkins opposed it with all the power of his office, resorting to the extreme expedient of proroguing the legislature lest the bill become a law. In the spring campaign of 1812 it was the universal theme of conversation from the taverns to the senate chamber. Meetings for and against the Bank of America were held throughout the state.[2] Republicans accused its agents of buying a majority by unstinted bribes. Yet in all this DeWitt Clinton showed surprising unconcern, even though the fortunes of his own Manhattan Company were to be affected; while his party clamored loud against the Federalists and their project, he refused to make opinion on this question any test of regularity. His brother-in-law, Judge Ambrose Spencer, who had been his closest coadjutor, now shook off connection with one who had such nice respect for the feelings of the Federalists. John Armstrong, soon to be appointed to the cabinet, and Judge Tayler, both old Clintonians, likewise refused their countenance. "The body-guard of Clinton was tainted with the odor of the bank." Although the legislature had a strong Clintonian majority, it was with difficulty that a

[1] Wm. Sullivan, *Familiar Letters on Public Characters* (Boston, 1834), p. 349. "Some of the leading Feds," wrote Christopher Gore in Massachusetts, "are sanguine that by associating with Democracy, they may obtain an immense Bank, and amass princely fortunes," to King, Feb. 17, also Feb. 7, 1812.

[2] *Albany Republican*, April 18, 22, 29, May 6, 13, 27, 1812. For an interesting bank proposal on the part of the Republicans, see letter from Samuel Osgood, Feb. 22, 1812, Osgood Mss. (N. Y. Historical Society).

caucus was induced to nominate the leader for the presidency.[1]

On the nineteenth of June war with Great Britain was proclaimed. The Federalists declared their worst fears realized; the French democrat, Thomas Jefferson, and his imbecile successor had in their mismanagement made disgrace and bankruptcy inevitable. Peace must be restored as soon as might be; as to the presidency, which must be decided in the autumn, any change would be for the better.[2] Clinton's agents were in Washington and in New England, peace men with the Federalists, and with Republicans complaining of the need for more vigor and efficiency in the conduct of the war, all things to all men, careless as to means so long as Clinton's fortunes were advanced.[3] The Federalists of the most extreme temper, like the Essex Junto which had so harassed John Adams, were ready, as with Burr, for any dark conspiracy. But in New York the party was divided. Gouverneur Morris, now convinced that the Union must sooner or later be divided on the queston of the "negro votes," thought it desirable to support his friend of the canal board, so as to assert the independence of the north.[4] J. O. Hoffman, who had conducted

---

[1] J. D. Hammond, *History of Political Parties in the State of New York*, vol. i, pp. 305-310, 312-315; J. S. Jenkins, *Lives of the Governors of the State of New York*, pp. 257, 260; D. D. Barnard, *A Discourse on...Ambrose Spencer*, Albany, pp. 84-89; Ambrose Spencer, *Defense*, etc., Albany, 1843 (N. Y. State Library); *King Correspondence*, vol. v, p. 265 *et seq.*

[2] Wm. Sullivan, *Familiar Letters*, p. 349.

[3] *King Correspondence*, vol. v, p. 265 *et seq.* This series has been used by D. S. Alexander, *Political History of the State of New York*, vol. i, pp. 202-206.

[4] Morris to B. R. Morgan, Aug. 20, 1812, J. Sparks, *Life and Writings of Gouverneur Morris*, vol. iii, pp. 273-274; also Morris, *Diary and Letters*, vol. ii, pp. 542-543. The reference here is to the "three fifths" compromise in the Federal Constitution.

some private negotiations, pledged the city delegation to
the mayor. Emott, D. B. Ogden, Jones and several congressmen conferred, hesitating somewhat (for they knew
the mayor well), but finally agreeing to support their
Massachusetts colleagues in the cause of Clinton. The candidate spared no promises, referring to himself as an
American Federalist, when occasion suited. At the same
time some Republicans came to his support under the impression that he would carry on the war much more
effectively than Madison.[1]

The Federalists themselves were active in the cause of
peace. Rufus King, Gouverneur Morris, General Clarkson,
Colonel Varick and Richard Harison drew up a set of resolutions for a meeting to be held in Washington Hall. Other
meetings were conducted through the southern counties with
large attendance. On the last day of July, Dr. Mason of
Columbia came to King with a proposal from the mayor.
He was, the agent said, prepared in all ways to resist the
influence of the south, and desired, if it were possible, to
have a conference with the Federalist leaders that New
York might be united in the cause. King went to Morrisania to report the plan to Morris, Jay and Clarkson.
King himself was loath to hold an interview with Clinton,
but consented to be present provided that nothing more
than the welding of a peace party be made a subject of the
conversation. Dr. Mason was apprised and the conference
arranged. On the appointed day, again at Morris' home,
the little company was gathered. The resolutions for the
coming meeting in New York were read to Clinton, and
he observed, writes King,

that he supposed that he did not differ from us in opinions

[1] J. D. Hammond, *op. cit.*, vol. i, pp. 353, 449-450. See Hoffman's letter
to H. G. Otis, July 17, 1812 as printed in S. E. Morison, *Harrison
Gray Otis*, vol. i, pp. 316-317.

respecting the public affairs and that he entirely approved of the Resolutions that had been read to him. But as his friends, comprehending a great majority of the Republican Party in the State, were divided in their opinion respecting the war—prejudices against England leading some of them to approve the war,—Time was necessary to bring them to one opinion . . . [and] that for these Reasons the proposed Peace meeting in the City should be deferred for four or five weeks.[1]

The candidate desired no untimely publication of his various professions.

Rufus King opposed this dubious connection; when Clinton said that if elected President, he would administer the government upon the principles of Hamilton, King, for one, was not impressed.[2] Talking to his friends he made certain observations which illustrate his good sense.

I observed to them [he writes] that I looked upon Mr. Clinton as upon every Leader of a Faction; that so long as he went on according to their views and bias, so long he wd. lead them, but as soon as he opposed their views, and more certainly as soon as he united with the rival Faction for any purpose, he would be deserted by his own.

With Spencer, Tompkins, Armstrong and Tayler all against him, it was doubtful if he could bring over much Republican support, yet unless he could bring numbers he was not worth accepting. It was of less importance, said King, that the party gain a transitory power than that their reputation and integrity should be preserved unblemished. Coalition with a foe they had so long reviled would tarnish all concerned. Clinton and his partisans would publish such reports of the arrangement as might suit their purposes, and when the mischief had been done, the Federalists

[1] *King Correspondence, loc. cit.*

[2] J. A. Hamilton, *Reminiscences*, p. 44.

might be obliged to answer with ill-credited denials.[1]
After the conference King went to town, saw Harison, Egbert Benson, Peter Radcliffe and some others, and
the peace meeting was arranged for the following week.
" Gentlemen of the very first standing in society " were
there; Colonel Fish was chairman, and the resolutions,
which suggested a convention of the friends of peace, presented by John Wells and D. B. Ogden, were passed with
great enthusiasm.[2]

Shortly after the declaration of war, William Sullivan,
the president of the Boston branch of the Washington
Benevolent Society, was at Saratoga Springs to take the
waters. While walking in the groves one day with some
New England friends, a project was conceived of calling
a convention of Federalists to meet in New York city in
the early autumn, and the gentlemen went home to prepare
opinion and arrange the delegations of their respective
states.[3] Agreeable to this plan more than seventy representatives gathered on the fifteenth of September as a party
convention, though keeping the close privacy of a caucus.[4]
King was in attendance; lest since his own name had been

[1] *King Correspondence*, vol. v, pp. 270-271.

[2] *N. Y. Evening Post*, August 18, 1812. One resolution was "that
representatives be chosen in the several counties, discreet men, friends
of peace. These representatives can correspond or confer with others,
and coöperate with the friends of peace in our sister States in devising
and procuring such constitutional measures as may secure our independence and preserve our Union, both of which are endangered by the
present war." See H. C. Lodge, *Life and Letters of George Cabot*
(Boston, 1875), p. 523.

[3] Wm. Sullivan, *Familiar Letters*, pp. 350-351.

[4] *N. Y. Evening Post*, Sept. 19, 1812. The convention like that of
1808 was organized by irregularly chosen committees of correspondence.
The New York committee was Jacob Radcliffe, C. S. Riggs, J. O.
Hoffman, D. B. Ogden and John Wells; S. E. Morison, *Otis*, vol. i,
pp. 308-309, note.

mentioned for President his absence might be misconstrued. He stated his desire that a true Federalist be nominated, even though it meant defeat. Mr. Madison could not ruin the country in four years, and at the expiration of that period, the country, tired of mis-rule, would bring the Federalists to power with as much support as Jefferson's in 1800. Against Clinton, he is said to have pronounced a most impassioned invective, becoming " so excited during his address that his knees trembled under him." The meeting dragged on for three days and was about to be dispersed with no agreement, when Harrison Gray Otis, rising in behalf of Clinton and speaking at first with hesitation, hat in hand, delivered an appeal so eloquent in summing up the troubles of the country and the crying need for change, that his candidate, though not formally endorsed, was generally accepted.[1]

The controversy grew bitter in the press and on the platform, for Clinton's enemies were not tender of his sensibilities. His apostasy was scornfully proclaimed and his opinions on the war set up in vitiating parallel.[2] " Washington " and " Hamilton " addressed the country to his prejudice, and King was quoted as desiring no aid from treachery.[3] When the legislature was convened on the second of November to choose presidential electors, three tickets were presented, the Martling Men or Madisonians, the followers

---

[1] Sullivan, p. 350, says he was regularly nominated, but it appears from evidence adduced by S. E. Morison in his *Otis*, vol. i, pp. 310-311, that the resolutions were ambiguous, and that the nomination of Clinton was not understood by a number of members. John Jay was mentioned as a candidate, but it was objected that, superannuated and unpopular, he " could no more be president than Seneca could Emperor." S. Dexter to H. G. Otis, Sept. 12, 1812, Morison, *Otis*, vol. i, p. 319.

[2] *E. g.* pamphlet, *The Coalition*, N. Y., 1812 (N. Y. P. L.).

[3] *Washington to the People of the United States* (Boston, 1812), p. 28, and *Hamilton to the People of the United States* (N. Y., 1812), pamphlets in the N. Y. P. L.

of Clinton, and those Federalists who had taken King's advice to stand alone. The spring election had retained a small Federalist majority in the lower house,[1] but since they voted in joint session with the Democratic senate, their cause was hopeless as a party. Enough, then, cast their ballots with the Clinton men to give him the vote of the state, though many stalwarts voted for their old associates.[2] In the total electoral vote of the country, however, Madison defeated him, though by no great majority; all his balancing and shifting had been useless.

Meanwhile attention in the state had been fastened on the conduct of the war, which might mean an invasion into the region by the lakes and the St. Lawrence. The President had scarcely called upon the governor for the quota of New York, when it was announced that Stephen Van Rensselaer, the Patroon, had been called to lead the troops. No little comment was aroused. It was generally understood that this distinguished Federalist was to be his party's candidate for governor at the election in the spring. Why had Tompkins picked him out for this responsibility? It is true he had been adjutant general of the state, but this had been an office more of dignity than practical importance; he was no military man.[3] Was he tendered this position as a compliment, in hope of winning Federalist support to the war policy? Some were ungenerous enough to think that Tompkins did not dislike to put his rival in a place of danger. Considering the difficulties of the service a failure seemed inevitable and the General's eulogists have not neglected to suggest that Tompkins was quite willing

[1] *N. Y. Spectator*, May 6, and *N. Y. Commercial Advertiser*, May 25, give the returns by counties.

[2] *N. Y. Senate Journal*, 1812-1813, p. 8; J. S. Jenkins, *Lives of the Governors*, p. 265.

[3] Mrs. C. V. R. Bonney, *A Legacy of Historical Gleanings*, vol. i, pp. 195, 260.

that that failure should be fixed upon the Federalists.[1] Acceptance or refusal would alike entail disgrace, the Democrats were watching for a sign of cowardice. Whether or not these charges were well founded, the event gave them some color; Van Rensselaer sought to lead his men across the Niagara River to gain the field at Queenstown; as state troops for defence they would not follow into Canada; the detachment which obeyed commands was cut to pieces; the failure was complete.[2] The Patroon had suffered all that Tompkins could have wished.

The Federalist majority in the lower house, as has been pointed out, was not enough to carry a joint session; hence when his party nominated Rufus King for the Senate of the United States, many thought it but a courtesy. He was a "Federalist of the old school," as those were called who would not join with Clinton,[3] and consequently he could not hope for much support from the old adherents of the latter. It was, then, a matter of no small surprise to those outside the arcana of the leaders that the vote was found to give him the election. Certain evidence has been preserved that connects the result with a bargain made by the agents of the Bank of America the year before,[4] but surely few more happy consequences have proceeded from so wrong a cause; it was the restoration of a statesman to the councils of a nation. He went to the Senate with the prestige of some "democratical assistance," announced the maxim that to

[1] D. D. Barnard, *Discourses on Stephen Van Rensselaer* (Albany, 1839), p. 27; J. W. Redway, "General Van Rensselaer and the Niagara Frontier," *Proceedings of the New York State Historical Society*, vol. viii, (Albany, 1909), p. 20; *N. Y. Spectator*, Nov. 11, 1812.

[2] See the excellent account of the battle, with reports and correspondence, in Mrs. Bonney's *Legacy*, vol. i, pp. 256-298.

[3] J. D. Hammond, *op. cit.*, vol. i, pp. 349-350.

[4] *Ibid.*, p. 344. Hammond claims to have direct knowledge of this bargain but exonerates King from any connection with it.

end the war, however unjust and deplorable it was, was now to fight it to a decent finish—and by this stand became an oracle with the Democracy.[1]

Whatever may have been the Federalist power in joint session, their control of the assembly gave them the Council of Appointment. As three years before, the spoils of victory were portioned out among the party, but a special interest was shown in the question of the mayor of New York. Mr. Clinton had discharged his duties with much energy and spared no pains to put the city in a posture of defense, yet he was still in name a member of the opposition.[2] If he were named for reappointment it would offend the Federalists of the old school; if he were refused, those Federalists who had recommended him to other states for the highest office of the nation would be stultified. General Platt, then sitting on the Council, had been among the latter group, and, though knowing it would be offensive in some quarters, proposed the mayor for renomination. Peter Radcliffe, another member, claimed the office for his brother Jacob who had served in 1810; Radcliffe was passed by for Clinton and, as we shall see, became embittered toward his party.[3] But the clemency accorded Mr. Clinton was not extended to his friends in office; the time had not arrived for a general party coalition.

The acceptance of this Federalist patronage by the mayor himself seemed a final insult to Judge Spencer and the Madisonian or Martling faction. They nominated Governor Tompkins for re-election and for lieutenant-governor, they ignored Clinton, the incumbent,[4] for Judge

[1] King to Gore, Feb. 14, 1813, *King Correspondence*; see also *ibid.*, vol. v, pp. 292, 310, and John Lovett to Col. Sol. Van Rensselaer, June 22, 1813, Mrs. Bonney's *Legacy*, vol. i, p. 301.

[2] David Hosack, *Memoir of DeWitt Clinton*, p. 52.

[3] Wm. Henderson to King, Feb. 21, 1813; Hammond, vol. i, pp. 346-350.

[4] It will be remembered that he held both this office and that of mayor.

Tayler. The Republican party was now definitely broken; Clintonians soon published an address declaring that they would not support the Tompkins ticket, and inveighing against Virginia domination and its agents in New York, they charged that the bounty of the general government " has been lavished on the most unworthy objects; the most uniform, decided, influential, virtuous and able men of the republican party have been proscribed; George Clinton, the father of his country—yes, George Clinton, was publicly denounced at a meeting of these Martling Men." [1] Never again would Clinton bring together the Democracy; his paper the *Albany Register* was abandoned by the Madisonians and the *Argus* set up in its stead.[2]

With the opposition so divided the Federalists were sanguine of success. The Patroon, as had been expected, was proposed for governor. There had been some opposition to his name because he had ordered state troops to cross at Queenstown. Some wanted his kinsman Colonel Solomon Van Rensselaer, who had won the laurels of a hero on that fatal day, but he would not stand against the leader of his family.[3] General Van Rensselaer was an amiable man, a friend to both " schools " of the party, and with a record for honesty and service that made his name attractive.[4]

[1] *Address to the Republican Citizens of the State of New York* (Albany, 1813), also noticed in the *Albany Argus*, April 30. The address was supposed to have been written by Clinton. It was signed by him, Pierre Van Cortlandt, Simeon DeWitt, Archibald McIntyre and thirty-seven others. George Clinton had recently died.

[2] " I am highly pleased that the *Albany Argus* is established at the seat of our Govt as it is of Greatest importance that such a paper should be established at Albany to buck the Albany Register and to prevent the Republicans being misled by such a Vile paper as the federals formerly called it but now they say it is the best in the State." Caleb Hyde to C. D. Cooper, Feb. 7, 1813, Cooper Mss. (N. Y. P. L.).

[3] Wm. Henderson to King, Feb. 21, 1813.

[4] S. Van Rensselaer to King, Feb. 12, 1813, George Huntington of Oneida was named for lieutenant-governor.

The nominations were presented in the party papers as of the " Friends of Peace, Liberty and Commerce," [1] but there was some difficulty in explaining the candidate's position on the war. Some said he had opposed it, but there was his record at the crossing of the Niagara. Federalists maintained he had not volunteered, but had responded to the governor's commands; they were answered that as a free man, he had gone without compulsion.[2] The Federalists said that Tompkins had neglected Colonel Solomon Van Rensselaer when he lay wounded in the hospital at Buffalo —was this the soldier's friend? [3] The governor's prorogation of the legislature on the question of the bank was now recalled against him, and it was charged that he was controlled by Virginia and the west.[4] The Federalist arguments again won a majority of the assembly, but Van Rensselaer could not overcome the popularity of Tompkins. " The Farmer's Boy " was chosen for another term.[5]

When John C. Calhoun and his young colleagues forced the peaceful Madison to attempt the conquering of Canada, the concurrent majorities in all of the co-states were not deemed indispensable. It was professedly a war for the freedom of the seas, to which the shipping states seemed obstinately indifferent. " Free Trade and Sailors' Rights " was a cry that rallied to the government's support every class throughout the country—save the traders and sailors. New England merchants and ship-captains preferred to run their risks to the closing of all commerce on a point of

[1] *N. Y. Commercial Advertiser*, April 7.

[2] *Albany Argus*, April 9, 16.

[3] *Albany Gazette*, April 10, 1813, and Mrs. Bonney's *Legacy*, vol. i, pp. 282, 292, 293.

[4] *N. Y. Commercial Advertiser*, April 26, 28, 1813.

[5] *N. Y. Spectator*, May 5, 15; *N. Y. Commercial Advertiser*, May 8; and *Albany Argus*, May 7, 1813. The southern, middle and western senatorial districts went Republican, Hammond, vol. i, p. 358.

dignity, and when defeated by the planters and frontiersmen, they resorted to " a larger patriotism " that sought to
stultify the government. In their exasperating course they
were not followed by New York.

Even the Federalists along the Hudson and the Mohawk,
though resentful of Virginia domination, were less resolute
in their defiance than their blue-light brethren to the east.
Seafaring men, who so keenly felt the restrictions of the
war, did not comprise so large a fraction of their population.
They had no caste of clergymen to preach the holiness of
hating southerners. Class prejudice was not so perfectly
coincident with partisan division, for the Livingstons and
their like could scarcely be included with the mob. But
above all the circumstance that New York was in constant
danger of invasion from the north (while New England
for reasons military no less than moral was immune),
made overt opposition to the government less popular in
that state. Of course, there were some extremists who in
their denunciation could vie with Otis, Strong and Quincy.
Gouverneur Morris drew up a paper of some nineteen fools-
cap pages arraigning Jefferson and Madison in outrageous
terms, and forwarded it to Albany in hope of having it
adopted as a legislative report.[1] In the first year of the
war he urged his nephew, D. B. Ogden, to " get the ear of
a committee of the whole House and draw in its own
hideousness a picture of our administration " and then
broach a scheme for a convention with delegates from all
the counties in the state to decide whether they should join
New England in *any* necessary measure. Ogden was much
too sensible to follow this advice, but Morris made no secret
of his strong convictions; to him secession seemed inevitable
and the sooner it was done, the better for all concerned.[2] On

---

[1] Wm. Henderson to King, *King Correspondence*, vol. v, p. 296.

[2] Morris, *Diary and Letters*, vol. ii, p. 562. He called the Hartford
Convention a tame affair, J. Sparks, *Life and Writings of Gouverneur
Morris*, vol. iii, p. 326.

the other hand, some Federalists boldly broke with the majority of their party, heartily supported Madison and Tompkins in their conduct of the war, were applauded as great patriots by the Republicans, and were elected to the legislature by Republican votes.[1] The majority of Federalists in New York were between the two extremes.

Most leaders deplored the war and sharply criticized the administration, though one does not find the tendency toward treason that marked the utterance of their Massachusetts friends. The answer of the assembly to the governor's speech in November, 1812, drafted by Elisha Williams, J. O. Hoffman, and Daniel Cady of Montgomery County,[2] expressed their sentiment in language courteous but firm. They understood the dangers of the state, the exposed frontier, in parts quite unprotected, and the enemy's flotillas on the lakes. They appreciated the embarrassments of the governor, yet still they would rebuke him for too great a preference for the northern garrisons while New York city lay the prey of any British fleet. What glory might not rest upon the American cause, if the prudent naval policy of Washington and Adams had been carried on by their successors! The few redeeming honors of the year had been achieved by ships they had provided. "The burthen of this war has fallen on this state," they said, "and in proportion to our evident exposure ought to be our means of resistance." Yet they would not sanction any order of the forces of the state beyond its boundaries. They described the war as "sudden and unexpected," and, though opposed in this by the Republicans in debate, having the majority they made the phrase a part of the address.[3]

---

[1] Hammond, vol. i, p. 376. [2] *N. Y. Spectator*, Nov. 11, 1812.

[3] *N. Y. Assembly Journal*, 1812-1813, pp. 30-32; *N. Y. Commercial Advertiser*, Nov. 9, 1812.

As the months wore on in discouragement they became more clamorous for peace. In their answer to the governor the following year, when again they held the power in the assembly, they took a higher tone. The government of the United States, they complained, did not desire peace; the delegation sent to Europe at the Czar's suggestion was but a ruse to raise the credit of the nation in the money market. Yet what money could be borrowed would be used to hasten ruin to the country. As to schemes of taxes in the state to support the general government, which Tompkins had outlined in his speech, they would not endorse them. New York needed her resources to protect herself; let no money leave the state. That the war had been a failure was no surprise to them, when they considered the shameful unpreparedness, which had been an article of faith with Democrats, and the character of the men who had been chosen as commanders.

"It is much to be regretted," they remarked, "that as the general government selected their own time to commence this war, they had not, if they believed the war necessary, first provided a respectable and efficient force with which to carry it on." There should have been no lust of conquest and no expeditionary forces, but as Americans, they were mortified to hear the governor exult "that our troops have shown prowess in defending our country eighteen months after the commencement of a war which the American people were told was to put the Canadas in our possession six months from the time it was declared." One draft of the address praised the magnanimity of England in suggesting peace "at a moment when the British nation, after a struggle of near twenty years, has succeeded by the aid of her allies, and the God of armies, in saving the world from universal domination and stands upon a high eminence among the nations of the earth." But not many thought such encomiums appropriate, and this sentence was struck out.[1] Such sentiments were aired in public meetings, and the party papers set themselves no limits in their abuse of Madison and apology for England. Like all minorities they claimed an unrestricted liberty of speech.[2] In tolerating all these calumnies the government exhibited a self-restraint in harmony with the creed of 1801, although had they followed Federalist precedent and passed sedition laws, they might have added civil conflict to their troubles.

Of the navy (the old favorite of the Federalists) and the brilliant achievements of its commanders, the assembly wanted " words to express their admiration. Inhabitants of a great commercial state, the people of New York must rejoice to hear your Excellency speaking in terms of approbation of that species of national force which alone can be effectual to maintain and defend our rights upon the ocean." [3] Scarcely had the legislature met when Charles King, the Senator's second son, then twenty-five years old, brought in a set of resolutions: " That though we cannot approve the disastrous and destructive war in which we are engaged, the House of Assembly of the people of the State of New York feel great satisfaction in expressing their admiration of the conduct of Com. Perry," of Burroughs, Lawrence and Allen and the other heroes who had lost their lives at sea; and " That, in the opinion of this house, the conduct of our naval commanders and seamen during this ruinous war, ought to satisfy every reflecting mind that our commercial rights are to be defended and

---

[1] *N. Y. Assembly Journal*, 1814, pp. 68-74, 98-104.

[2] See A. Van Vechten's speech and Sedgwick's resolutions at a meeting in Albany, *N. Y. Evening Post*, Sept. 14, 1812. In the first years of the war they held a number of such meetings to insist upon the right of free speech. But since the government did nothing to curb their utterance, the meetings were discontinued as superfluous.

[3] *N. Y. Assembly Journal*, 1814, *loc. cit.*

maintained by a navy, and not by embargoes and commercial restrictions."

The Republicans had no objection to hurrahing for the navy, but they could not pass unchallenged the epithets which King and his supporters fastened on the war at large. William Ross declared them to be most impolitic in the effect which they would have upon the enemy, and others of his party claimed that to call the cause unjust affixed the guilt of murderers upon the fighters whether on the sea or on the land. To damn the war and praise the warriors seemed to them a curious confusion. But the Federalists would not subtract a word. They had called the war destructive and disastrous only, said D. B. Ogden, though he, before God and his country, would have voted for the resolutions had they said unjust as well. It was an iniquitous war, "commenced, as he believed, for the purpose of humbling the importance of the northern states." John B. Coles would praise the navy while he expressed his detestation of the war. Samuel Jones declared that seamen had no right to voice their own opinions, theirs but to obey commands; this spirit he would cordially applaud. William A. Duer maintained that they alone had rescued our flag from disgrace. Others acclaimed the honorable course of Perry who, like many other naval officers, was known to be at heart against the war.[1] A few days after the resolutions were passed the Federalists of New York city, three hundred and fifty of them with Richard Varick at their head, gave a banquet in Washington Hall to Commodore Chauncey. There was manifested great enthusiasm for the "guardians of our commerce," but no word was said in honor of the army.[2]

[1] *N. Y. Assembly Journal*, 1814, pp. 17-18, 23-24, 26-29; *N. Y. Spectator*, Feb. 9, 1814.

[2] *N. Y. Commercial Advertiser*, Feb. 5, 1814. At the meeting of the

The Federalists let pass no opportunity to rail against Napoleon. When in 1814 Holland was emancipated, the Dutchmen of the party were called to a meeting in Albany by the Patroon, Van Vechten, J. R. Van Rensselaer and Hermanus Bleecker. Great satisfaction was proclaimed at seeing curbed this arch-disturber who had so well illustrated the inevitable tendency from demagogue to despot.[1] When the emperor was sent to Elba the leaders of the party, Jay and King, with John B. Coles and General Clarkson, met at Mr. Gracie's and planned a solemn celebration. An assembly was convened and after a prayer of thanksgiving by Dr. Mason, Gouverneur Morris pronounced an " oration of triumph to celebrate the downfall of Bonaparte and the restoration of the Bourbons," while King presided at a public dinner in the evening.[2] But soon these gentlemen had more serious concerns than toasting Louis XVIII of France.

Washington Benevolent Society in New York city, Feb. 22, 1814, the navy was toasted, but not the army; and in the ode recited before the society on July 4 of that year, this distinction was again observed, *ibid.*, Feb. 23, and July 5, 1814. Like opinions were expressed by the New York Federalists in the Thirteenth Congress. Two-thirds of the thirty members of the delegation in the lower house were of that party, Moss Kent, Morris S. Miller, T. P. Grosvenor, Samuel M. Hopkins, and others, all known from their aged colleague as " Judge Benson's Boys." Thomas J. Oakley was especially effective. " He is prompt, luminous and pointed," said a member. " In the most shrewd and cunning manner he assails the President, yet in such cautious phraseology, that no old Foxes can check him." Another declared that if the Federalists in Congress had accepted his exclusive leadership the administration would have been prostrated. See John Lovett to Joseph Alexander, June 17, 1813, in Mrs. Bonney's *Legacy*, vol. i, pp. 299-300, and Hammond, vol. i, pp. 357, 428. A volume of their speeches, which were circulated as pamphlets, is now in the Cornell University Library.

[1] *N. Y. Commercial Advertiser*, Feb. 17, 1814.

[2] *Oration delivered June 29, 1814 in Celebration of the Recent Deliverance of Europe from the Yoke of Military Despotism* (pamphlet, 23 pp. in N. Y. P. L.) ; *Jay Correspondence*, vol. iv, pp. 374-375; Morris, *Diary and Letters*, vol. ii, p. 565.

In the summer of 1814 General Ross, after routing the militia at the " Bladensburg races," marched on to Washington, burned the capitol and plundered the President's house. The sea-coast towns were set in a flurry. What Admiral Cockburn had done in Chesapeake Bay he might do again in the Delaware or in the Hudson. The city of New York was carefully made ready by Clinton, who remained as its efficient mayor until removed by the Madisonian Council the next winter; and Federalists, confronted with the prospect of bombardment, joined hands with the Republicans. No longer did they content themselves with giving money for relief of sufferers along the lakes.[1] The rolls of " The New York Hussars " contained such names as Robert Troup, Nicholas Low, John A. King, Robert Ray, Herman Le Roy, Cornelius Schermerhorn and I. V. Coles. Charles King became a captain in the state militia, James G. King, his younger brother, became an aid to General Stevens, J. R. Van Rensselaer raised a troop of soldiers to march down from Columbia County.[2] When some complained because the banks suspended payment, Rufus King addressed a meeting stating " that in such a time of peril and danger as the presént it was the duty of all well disposed citizens to join in the defense of each other and the country;" the banks had been driven to this last expedient and should be supported. " The enemy is at our doors," he said, " and it is now useless to enquire how he came there; he must be driven away and every man join hand and heart, and place shoulder to shoulder to meet him." [3]

The enemy did not molest the city of New York, but the

[1] See letter from Clinton, Feb. 21, 1814, DeW. Clinton Mss., and *N. Y. Assembly Journal*, 1814, p. 3.

[2] *King Correspondence*, vol. v, pp. 426-427, note.

[3] *N. Y. Evening Post*, Sept. 2, 1814.

spirit of resistance which the rumor had developed did not easily die down; many Federalists who had joined the militia for home defense, remained in arms to fight in other quarters, and others cheered their new decision. " Things being what they are," wrote John Jay, " I think we cannot be too united in a determination to defend our country, nor be too vigilant in watching and resolutely examining the conduct of the administration in all its departments." [1] King in Congress led the Federalists to vote supplies and money to the troops, and pledged his private credit to the governor of New York state if he should need it to complete his budget.[2]   Though at first a sharp opponent of the war, he now bent all his energies to bring it to a close by stiff resistance to the foe.

This spirit was not shared by all the party.   Morris wrote long and earnest letters of remonstrance.

How often, in the name of God, how often will you agree to be cheated?   What are you to gain by giving Mr. Madison Men and Money? . . . I feel myself bound in Duty and Honor to declare that anything like a Pledge by Federalists to carry on this wicked War, strikes me like a Dagger to my Heart.[3]

Many looked with hope to the Hartford Convention[a] which was meeting in the autumn.   Even King, feeling great confidence in the character and patriotism of the members of that body, rejoiced that New England was to speak in words that would be heard.   Madison, he said, had been ignorant of the true opinion of that section, depending, as had George the Third, upon reports of sycophantic ap-

---

[1] *Jay Correspondence*, vol. iv, p. 379.

[2] *King Correspondence*, vol. v, pp. 410-411, 422-424; *N. Y. Evening Post*, Jan. 13, 1815.

[3] Morris to King, Oct. 18, 1814, *King Correspondence*.

[a] The Hartford Convention (1814) was called to review the grievances of New England occasioned by the administrations of Thomas Jefferson and James Madison and the War of 1812. Its recommendations were nullified by news of the Treaty of Ghent ending the war and Andrew Jackson's victory over the British at New Orleans.

pointees.[1] But Morris hoped for more than a mere protest.
There was, he thanked God, some sense in Massachusetts,
and should the rest of New England join her, all might be
well. What was needed was " An Union of the commercial
States to take Care of themselves, leaving the War, its expense and its Debt to those choice Spirits so ready to declare
and so eager to carry it on." [2] As for the old Union, he
considered it dead since the repeal of the Judiciary Act in
1801.[3] Judge Benson also hoped that the Hartford body
would take a " federal course." Yet the majority of Federalists had been stoutly opposed to any scheme of secession.

Resolved, unanimously [ran the record of a public meeting in
the spring of 1813] that the friends of Peace, Liberty and
Commerce, are also the friends of the union of these States;
and that although they believe it was never the intention of the
union, that the rights of any one part should be sacrificed to
the prejudices, interests, or corrupt purposes of another, yet
they consider a dissolution of the union as an event which can
only be contemplated with horror.[4]

After a year and a half when it was proposed by Van
Vechten, Tibbits, J. R. Van Rensselaer, William A. Duer
and others that a convention from the counties be held to
consider a participation with the easterners, there was little
or no response.[5] One thing is very evident, as Judge Hammond says, that the Federalists of New York as a party
never sanctioned the proposals of the Hartford Convention.[6]

The Federalists, who had capitalized discontent to such

[1] *King Correspondence* (memorandum), vol. v, pp. 444-446.
[2] Morris to King, Oct. 18, No. 1, 1814.
[3] S. Van Rensselaer to King, Oct. 25, 1814.
[4] *N. Y. Spectator*, April 28, 1813.
[5] *N. Y. Evening Post*, Sept. 28, 1814.
[6] *Political History*, vol. i, p. 388.

good purpose, refused, naturally enough, to be comforted by peace. By party politicians the prosperity of the nation while ruled by their opponents is dreaded as an affliction; old hardships must not fade from memory. " The storm is passed by," said they. " As peace men we rejoice at it; but humbly hope that our countrymen, with a due sense of the calamities they have escaped, will remember the guilty authors of their sufferings and dangers." Who could forget the miserable failure of the conquest of the Canadas, the threats of conscription, the deceits and tricks by which boys under age had been inveigled from their homes to join the army, or the oppression of an administration which had laid such taxes to pay usurious premiums. Lands and houses, carriages and harnesses, furniture, leather, paper, hats, tobacco—what had escaped the assessor's lists? [1] Such memories as these, so potent in minds of moneyed men, built up the Federalists' strength in the spring campaign of 1815, so that as the votes were counted for the members of assembly, it was clear that the Republican majority would be slight indeed. Only the almost solid west had made even such a margin possible, and the death or illness of some members from that section, made it likely, as the body was convened in January, that the Federalists would gain control of the Council of Appointment. [2]

How this was circumvented is too notorious in the history of the state to need complete recounting here. [3] The vote for speaker was carried by the Republicans by a majority of one, but the Federalists straightway charged that this one should be thrown out. The clerk of Ontario County had

---

[1] *N. Y. Commercial Advertiser*, April 21, 24, 1815.

[2] *Ibid.*, April 26, *et seq.*; *N. Y. Columbian*, Jan. 4, 1816; Wm. Henderson to King, Jan. 19, W. W. VanNess to King, Jan. 31, and T. Dwight, Feb. 10, 1816.

[3] See Hammond, vol. i, pp. 413-418.

" most corruptly and flagitiously " given his certificate to Peter Allen rather than to Henry Fellows, the Federalist opponent, because the ballots for the latter, though more numerous, had some of them borne his first name in abbreviation rather than in full. No one questioned the intention of the electors of Ontario, yet by repeated votes in which Allen's was decisive, it was determined to proceed to choose the council of appointment before the house considered Fellows' petition for instatement. A Democratic council, therefore, was selected, and then Fellows was admitted. It took a hardy partisan to say a word for such a naked fraud, and Federalists hoped for more profit from popular disgust, than could have come from capture of the council. An assembly, and a governor as well, might now be gained at the spring election of 1816.

Judge William W. Van Ness had promised the year before, with some reluctance, to resign the certain honors and emoluments of his position, and risk the contest as a candidate.[1] But now that the Council of Appointment had been lost, his resignation would elevate a Democrat to the supreme bench, and by that office to the Council of Revision;[2] hence another candidate for governor would be preferred. About a hundred politicians of the party were convened at Albany in no little agitation. A committee waited on the judge but he was firm in his refusal, and the body was with difficulty kept from adjourning without any nomination. A resolution was passed that the choice of the

[1] "I am urged to consent to a measure which will ruin one if it succeeds, and I am told the party will be ruined if I don't consent. I take it for granted I shall be compelled to yield contrary to my wishes—my feelings—my interests—and my judgment." W. W. Van Ness to Sol. Van Rensselaer, Oct. 17, 1815, Mrs. Bonney's *Legacy*, vol. i, pp. 325-326.

[2] This council under the Constitution of 1777, composed of the governor, the chancellor and the judges of the supreme court, held the veto power, see A. B. Street, *The Council of Revision*.

majority would be the choice of all, but none of the many names could gain support of a majority, although James Emott missed by only one. Once more adjournment was considered, or, what would be worse, a nomination of the judge with certainty of declination, when some one presented the name of Rufus King.

" It was impossible to describe the enthusiasm with which this nomination was received, when it was strongly urged to the Convention that under present circumstances we had every reason to hope that Mr. King would not decline." [1] Eight letters from gentlemen of wealth and station were that very night dispatched to the senator in Washington. " Your Acceptance of the Nomination," said one signed by five friends and leaders, " is essential to preserve the Harmony and Unity of the federal party in the State." [2] Without the magic of his name the convention would have broken up, wrote General Jacob Morris. Chancellor Kent saw in his action the success or ruin of the conservative element in the state. The Patroon urged him to deliberate, at least, before he came to a decision; if favorable, he would electioneer for him with all his zeal and influence. T. J. Oakley assured him that the leaders asked this favor only from the deepest sense of duty to the party. Theodore Dwight declared that if New York could not be redeemed Federalism in the United States was doomed. It was known that Clinton would be named, if King's refusal made it possible for Clintonians to count on Federalist support. It was charged by Democrats, indeed, that the Federalists had known that King would not accept and had announced him as a candidate merely to cover their design of later

[1] Wm. A. Duer to Wm. Henderson, Feb. 16, and J. R. Van Rensselaer to King, Feb. 16, 1816.

[2] Signed by H. Bleecker, Peter A. Jay, J. G. Lansing, Jno. Duer, and J. R. Van Rensselaer.

joining hands with Clinton. If the senator declined, sufficient of the party, it was feared, (for there were now more real Clinton men among the Federalists than among their opponents) would fulfill the prophecy of the Democrats.

King was not the only leader of unblemished reputation, but the others of that kind had not the force to win. On the other hand, as to the stronger men, scandals of the Bank of America charter were not forgotten and even Van Ness had been unpleasantly mentioned.

There is such a cloud over the character of several gentlemen, who may be considered the leaders of the party of this State [wrote D. B. Ogden to King] that I have long feared that the most respectable men of the community would withdraw in disgust from taking any interest in our politics, or any part in our elections . . . Your election would be a new era in Federal politics and men of high character and honor would feel as they ought.

Stephen Van Rensselaer doubted if any man could stand against the popularity of Tompkins, " yet the accounts from the country induce me almost to believe in your success . . . If you were the Candidate, our best characters everywhere would be Candidates for the Legislature and with such men I think you could be of great service to the country." But one voice urged against it, that of Gouverneur Morris. The governorship as Jay and he had made it in 1777 was an office of some dignity, said he, but since Colonel Burr's convention in 1801 had cut it from a seventy-four to a razee it was not worthy of a first-rate man. King would leave the Senate with reluctance; he disdained the petty turmoil of state politics. He was at first indignant at the advantage that his friends had taken. Yet as in 1804 when from highest motives he declined the nomination which would have drawn him into a conspiracy, so now he accepted from the same compelling sense of duty. If he could rally once again to public service the old aristocracy, it was worth the sacrifices of his own ambition. After three weeks' hesitation, he accepted.[1]

The campaign was conducted with much spirit. The Federalists reviewed the record of the war, and claimed that with all the promises and fine professions nothing had resulted but a hundred million dollar debt; war had been a pretext to increase the patronage and power of the administration. Heavy taxes and depreciated paper made up its legacy. The Peter Allen legislature was the subject of their bitter scorn; " that a Council of Appointment should be chosen by the vote of a spurious member struck some minds with considerable force." The free negroes who had been the object of some Democratic legislation on elections, were complimented and defended.[2] Of Tompkins, the candidate of the Democracy, it was declared he had misapplied state funds in carrying on the war,[3] while as to King the foolish calumnies of 1807 were all revived.[4] Charles King as a commissioner to investigate the conduct of an English military prison had recently reported in a tone considered too magnanimous, and this was used against his father.[5]

---

[1] See letters to him from T. Dwight, Hermanus Bleecker and others, J. R. Van Rensselaer, James Kent, Jacob Morris, W. A. Duer, T. J. Oakley, D. B. Ogden, S. Van Rensselaer, Wm. Henderson, Zebulon R. Shepherd, W. W. VanNess, John A. King, Gouverneur Morris, *King Correspondence*, vol. ii, pp. 502-522. Gouverneur Morris refers to the convention that took away the governor's exclusive right of nomination to the Council of Appointment, and gave concurrent right to any Councillor.

[2] See Addresses in *Albany Daily Advertiser*, Feb. 14, *N. Y. Commercial Advertiser*, March 18, April 10, 19, *N. Y. Spectator*, April 24, 27, 1816; T. Dwight to King, *King Correspondence*, vol. v, pp. 502-503.

[3] *N. Y. Spectator*, Jan. 24, 1816.

[4] *N. Y. Columbian*, April 23, 1816; *National Advocate*, etc., see *King Correspondence*, vol. v, pp. 529-534.

[5] This was the incident of the shooting of the mutinous prisoners at Dartmoor, *cf.* (Charles Andrews) *The Prisoners' Memoirs* (N. Y., 1815).

In hope of catching votes from some Clintonians the Federalists complained that New York had not its proper hearing in the capital at Washington.[1] But since it was rumored Tompkins would accept the nomination to the Vice-Presidency, and would consequently resign within a year, such support could not be hoped for.

The Clinton interest will all be thrown into the scale against us [said "Field-marshal" William Coleman of the *Evening Post*]. At the same time they will, with Machiavellian cunning, probably aid our *assembly* ticket upon the cunning calculation that a federal Council of Appointment would prepare the way for reinstating Clintonians in office, by removing past incumbents which they would not dare to do. DeWitt being chosen governor next Spring, according to promise, to fill the vacancy occasioned by Tompkins being elected to the Vice-Presidency, will come into power in due time and federalists, cleansing the stables the ensuing year, will make way for a glorious state of things which is to succeed at a subsequent election; a fine arrangement.[2]

Though New York city went for King, he lost by nearly seven thousand votes through the state.[3] "The federal party in the sense of a party aiming at political power no longer exists," said he; "Victrix causa diis placuit, sed victa Catoni."[4]

Liberty is too dear to be voluntarily parted with [he wrote in

---

[1] *E. g.* address in *N. Y. Commercial Advertiser*, April 10, 1816.

[2] To King, April 21, 1816, King Mss., N. Y. Historical Society.

It was hoped that Tompkins' opposition to the canal would arouse resentment in the west (Wm. Coleman to King, April 21, 1816, *King Correspondence*, vol. vi, p. 20); at least the Federalists were resolved to check frauds in that region which they claimed had prevented Van Rensselaer's election in 1813. There had been more voters in some counties than the census warranted (T. J. Oakley to King, March 29, 1816).

[3] *N. Y. Spectator*, May 8, 1816; J. S. Jenkins, *Lives of Governors*, p. 198.

[4] *King Correspondence*, vol. v, p. 530.

his discouragement, to Christopher Gore] and it must therefore be gradually weakened by making the People jealous of
its wisest and most sincere Defenders; so that open force may
in the end be used to destroy it.   But why touch upon this subject to you, who have so often and so impartially considered
it?   We have been visionary men . . . It has probably become
the real interest & policy of the Country, that the Democracy
should pursue its own natural Course.   Federalists of our age
must be content with the past.   It would be most unworthy
to affect to have changed our opinions.   I would not suffer the
self-humiliation & reproaches of the changelings, I could name,
for the highest offices & applauses, that could be given them.[1]

The Federalists now no longer to be active as a party, their
opponents were sure to divide; the Federalists would be able
" to assist the true interests of Freedom and of Justice by
giving their influence to the least wicked Section of the Republicans." [2]   Even Gouverneur Morris came to this opinion; a few weeks before his death he wrote, " If our country
be delivered, what does it signify whether those who operate
her salvation wear a federal or a democratic cloak? " [3]
The northern aristocracy had come to realize that old times
were past.   With their professed regard for the people's
good they had joined a high indifference to the people's
will.   For appearances they thought that honest men should
cherish no concern.   It was permissible for them to oppose
a war which would interrupt their shipping; it was permissible for them to admire the English constitution; but
when in their keen desire to see the administration wrecked,
they celebrated the disaster at Detroit and ill concealed their
glee at the failures of Wilkinson and Dearborn[a]—was it a
marvel that the body of the people came to think that the
aristocracy were more British than American,

---

[1] May 8, 15, 1816, *ibid.*   [2] To Edward King, May 21, 1861, *ibid.*

[3] *Diary and Letters*, vol. ii, p. 602.

[a] General James Wilkinson (1757-1825) and General Henry Dearborn
(1751-1829), two American generals who failed in their invasions of
Canada during the War of 1812 and were relieved of command.

> " And universal patriots grown
> Feast for all victories—but our own?" [1]

It was clear that the party had no future; the leaders were discouraged by defections of two sorts. Many lesser chiefs had openly apostatized, renounced their creed and shouted raucous praises of democracy. These were visited with the ostracism of old friends. A meeting held in Washington Hall resolved:

That we are not disheartened by desertions which increase our purity more than they diminish our strength; and that we can have no wish to retain in the circle of our friends, whether political or social, any person who is capable of finding in the power, the pleasures or the emoluments of office, an adequate compensation for the loss of his integrity. [2]

It was, besides, a matter of no little irritation to the leaders that many men of property and social station were beginning to shun the forum of political debate. The indifference of this class to official honor at the hands of a democracy had begun to be observed. They who had so eagerly petitioned for such preference when it was the king who was the fountain of bestowal, now gave up old aspirations and seemed content to choose as ministers of their government men whom they would never think of welcoming to dinner. " Whence is it," inquired Egbert Benson, " that the same thing which was so sought, should now, and by the same class, those desirous to be distinguished for their wealth and otherwise for their condition, be so slighted? I leave this question to the learned scribe and the wise disputer." [3]

---

[1] J. K. Paulding, *The Lay of the Scottish Fiddle: A Tale of Havre de Grace* (supposed to be written) by Walter Scott (N. Y., 1813), canto ii, stanza iv.

[2] *N. Y. Commercial Advertiser*, April 29, 1816.

[3] Egbert Benson, *Memoir*, read before The Historical Society of the State of New York, Dec. 31, 1816 (N. Y., 1817), p. 52.

CHAPTER VII

CLINTON, DIVIDER OF PARTIES

WHEN in 1815 Mr. Clinton was turned out of the mayor's office, his prospect seemed completely dark. His numerous foes had read him out of the Democracy, his Federalist friends seemed likely to continue in their helplessness. Financially embarrassed as he was, and bred to no career save that of politics, poverty might soon enforce humiliation. His personal adherents were men of such reputation that they injured more than aided him.[1] In the winter of his discontent he was accused of seeking, with the pitiful aspiration of a ruined man, some understanding with the Federalists, whereby he might be named again for President;[2] but he was, in truth, too shrewd a man to take the major rôle in a fiasco. He managed to get himself put up as an elector and voted for Monroe and Governor Tompkins, both of

---

[1] J. D. Hammond, *Political History*, vol. i, pp. 399-400, 423-424.

[2] Roger Skinner to Clinton, March 21, 1816, Clinton Mss., answering a challenge to prove a statement which Skinner was reported to have made: "With respect to you being a candidate for the next President of the United States, and of your having an understanding with the federal party for the attainment of that object, I have no knowledge, neither have I informed any one that such was the fact. It is, however, true that I have heard the subject mentioned and calculations made on the probability of success by a gentleman warmly attached to you and who appeared resolved on the measure, and in his calculations he placed to your credit all the federal strength of the Union, and although a professed republican, he appeared to regret that the federal [strength] was not greater." See also in *ibid.*, letters to Skinner, Nov. 14, and to J. D. Hammond, April 19, 1816.

whom he cordially disliked, to make a good impression on the Democratic party. He must if possible win Federalist support without offending his old followers.[1]

There was hope for Clinton because he could conceive and carry out great projects. He now organized meetings in New York and Albany to make popular the scheme of the canal that he and Morris had surveyed; legislators were addressed in memorials, well-written and convincing, that bore the trace of his connection. Such a man could not be kept in Coventry. The Federalists, whose interests lay in great land-holdings and in commerce, came to him for counsel on the project he had made his own. The west was deeply interested; liberal-minded men throughout the state were glad to offer their support. The Tammany Society, or Martling Men, who worked against the enterprise because of its promoter, soon realized that they had made an error.[2] An element of strength for Clinton was found in the Irish of the state. Old predilections had been strengthened by the decision of the recent mayor when presiding as a judge, that a priest as a witness might withhold the secrets of the confessional.[3] The immigration which had come from Ireland in the last years of the European war and since, despite the restrictions of Great Britain, made this support important.[4] It was clear that Clinton's star was rising; even his brother-in-law, Judge Ambrose Spencer, partly through Mrs. Spencer's mediation, now sought an interview, and a reconciliation was announced.[5]

The strength of Mr. Clinton, founded thus on popular

---

[1] J. Emott to R. King, Dec. 28, 1816.   [2] *Cf. supra*, ch. v.

[3] J. G. Shea, *History of the Catholic Church in America*, vol. ii, pp. 165-167.

[4] W. J. Bromwell, *History of Immigration to the United States*, p. 13, note.

[5] Hammond, vol. i, p. 430.

support, was more general through the state than in the legislature. In consequence the gentlemen who favored him to take the place of Tompkins, when the latter should become Vice-President, planned and carried through a Republican state convention held at Albany, with delegations from each county, the first conforming to the modern standard. This was preferred by his adherents to a legislative caucus of the party, because it was well known that in most counties which sent Federalists to Albany, the Republicans desired Clinton. These would have their word in a convention. Judge Spencer's influence was rightly counted on to secure the proper delegates, and Clinton was nominated, in spite of Martin Van Buren and the men from Tammany Hall;[1] and though these recusants insisted on supporting Peter B. Porter of Black Rock,[2] their candidate received less than two thousand votes at the election. The strong man with an idea had won his way from humiliation to the highest honor of the state. It was significant that Van Ness, J. R. Van Rensselaer, Jonas Platt, Elisha Williams and other Federalist leaders gave strong support not only to Clinton for governor but also to Clintonians for the legislature. The *New York Evening Post* declared

In short, that in the western district federalism is abandoned. In explanation of their views, they say, that the democratic party having adopted federal measures of the Washington administration have thus reluctantly acknowledged these measures were right, and that there is therefore no longer anything to differ about . . . The requisite capacity for government is, on all hands, acknowledged to be found in those who are about

---

[1] Hammond, vol. i, pp. 436-444.

[2] This was Van Buren's policy, though other leaders of the old Madisonians objected; see E. T. Throop to Van Buren, March 15, 1817, Van Buren Mss.

to succeed to power in this state . . . To say more at this time would not consist with sound discretion.[1]

In the summer of 1817, then, party prejudice seemed softening. The program of the Democratic Congress with its projects of the bank, the bonus bill, and the high protective tariff, was made up of Hamiltonian measures to be carried out in a Jeffersonian spirit. Federalists could not easily object; it was for their opponents to meet the charge of inconsistency.[2] In Albany as well, old Federalists found no little satisfaction. Clinton's inaugural address as governor, delivered when the legislature came together in January 1818, attracted more attention than was usually bestowed on such pronouncements.[3] The new executive was nothing if not bold in his conception of the duties of the state. He urged the generous support of education from district school to college; agriculture and the arts should be encouraged by subventions; the militia must be drastically reformed upon new models of efficiency; the poor laws must be changed; far-reaching legislation with respect to banks was needed; the financial system of the state itself must be re-arranged. His most effective phrases were reserved to recommend his favorite scheme of inland navigation.[4] " To do " was the watchword of this leader now come to official power. The Federalist squires applauded his

[1] See in *N. Y. Herald* (edition of *Evening Post* " for the country ") May 17, 1817. " In this State, after a good deal of jockeying & much of extraordinary coalition among men who have censured each other in the coarsest and bitterest language, Mr. Clinton will be chosen without opposition." R. King to C. Gore, April 17, 1817.

[2] King to Gore, June 26, 1816. Gouverneur Morris had complained the previous year, that Calhoun and Clay went much too far. *Diary and Letters*, vol. ii, p. 595.

[3] D. Hosack, *Memoir of Clinton*, p. 75.

[4] *Messages from the Governors* [*of New York*] (Albany, 1909), vol. ii, p. 897 *et seq.*

remarks on agricultural societies; land holders in the west
and north beheld their friend in the champion of canals.
The fact that Clinton was not considered orthodox by the
Virginia School in Washington made Federalist support
more natural and appropriate.[1] Opposition centered within
Tammany Hall in New York city, and soon Clintonians
and Federalists in consequence, issued warnings to the
commonwealth against corruption from the great town by
the sea. " A great commercial capital is seldom the chosen
seat of liberty," they said in an address. " She oftener de-
lights in the mountain fastnesses and in the cultivated
plain." [2] The feud between " up-state " and " the city "
was begun.

Those Federalists who had worked for Clinton in the
canvass of 1812, of course again declared their friendship.
Judge Jonas Platt exchanged most fulsome compliments
with the governor, and worked for all his measures.[3] Chancellor Kent and Clinton visited each other's homes and were
on terms of confidential friendship.[4] Josiah Ogden Hoffman was Clinton's firm supporter in the city, where support
was needed.[5] Thomas J. Oakley and the " Columbia Junto "
—Williams, J. R. Van Rensselaer and Van Ness—were
all Clinton men.[6] Troup as a lawyer found enjoyment in

[1] J. Savage to Clinton, March 18, 1818, M. B. Tallmadge to Clinton,
Jan. 6, 1819, DeW. Clinton Mss.

[2] *Address of the* [Clintonian] *Republican Members of the Senate and
Assembly Adopted at a Meeting . . . April 4, 1820,* pamphlet (Albany,
1820).

[3] Clinton's Letterbook V, Jan. 14, 1822, Fr. A. van der Kemp to
Clinton, March 20, 1823, Jonas Platt to Clinton, Oct. 4, 1823, T. Eddy
to Clinton, Oct. 4, 1823, Clinton Mss.

[4] DeWitt Clinton's Diary (N. Y. Hist. Soc. Coll.), numerous entries.

[5] Wm. A. Duer, *Reminiscences,* p. 27.

[6] John Duer to Van Buren, March 27, 1819, Van Buren Mss.; M. B.
Tallmadge to Clinton, Jan. 6, 1819, Clinton Mss.

the governor's speeches, and as a western man he anxiously
encouraged the movement for the canal.[1] Cadwallader D
Colden was his intimate correspondent.[2] The Patroon,
with whose family Clinton soon became connected by marriage, thought him satisfactory, though Federalism in Albany was quite strong enough to stand alone.[3] The governor exchanged friendly letters on politics and agricultural
societies with the Jays at Bedford, including many expres-
sions of esteem.[4] William L. Stone, who had edited the
Northern Whig of Hudson and the *Albany Advertiser,* and
who took charge of the *New York Commercial Advertiser*
in 1820, was among his most valuable supporters.[5]

But it was not the leaders only who took up with Clinton;
much of the body of the party in the counties could be
counted on as well. After 1816 it was only in the ancient
strongholds that Federalist candidates were presented under
the old party name.[6] Elsewhere the faithful were exhorted
to vote for the best man (provided he would stand with
Clinton), and in many counties there was a frank and open
coalition.[7] Clintonian and Federalist were often inter-
changeable terms, and the word Republican was reserved
for followers of Van Buren and his coadjutors of the
Tammany Society.[8] Sometimes the factions which sup-

---

[1] Troup to King, Feb. 4, 1819, *King Correspondence.* It is true Troup
deplored the necessity of supporting a Democrat.

[2] DeWitt Clinton Mss. *passim,* but especially Dec. 20, 1813.

[3] S. Van Rensselaer to Clinton, Jan. 6, 1819, *ibid.*

[4] July 27, 1818, Letterbook IV; Aug. 6, 1820, *ibid.,* V.

[5] "We have been attentive observers of Mr. Clinton's administration
and measures," he wrote on coming to the city, "and frankly declare,
that in general, both have met with our approbation," *N. Y. Commercial
Advertiser,* April 11, 1820.   [5] *Albany Gazette,* April 13, 27, 1818.

[7] *Albany Advertiser,* March 31, 1818; *Albany Gazette,* April 13, 23,
1818; M. M. Noah to Van Buren, July 13, 1819, Van Buren Mss.

[8] George McClure to P. G. Childs, Feb. 13, 1822, Isaac Pinson to
Childs, Feb. 7, 1822, John Rugen to S. A. Talcott, Feb. 13, 1822, Childs
Mss. (N. Y. Public Library).

ported Clinton were combined under strange and startling names, like the " Low Salary Men " around Cayuga Lake.[1] Through the state there was no question where the chief part of the old Federalists had gone. There were fourteen counties in the state which had voted for Van Rensselaer for governor in 1813, and three years later for Rufus King. In the hotly fought election of 1819, eleven of these were registered for Clintonians.[2] Yet even in this triumph there were murmurings of opposition.

When in 1817 Clinton was carried to the state house on a wave of popularity, he might have stayed a universal favorite had he learned the arts of affability. He was formed to be admired and obeyed, but not loved. In the designs of his imagination he was a mighty architect, but he failed to take account of means; he forgot that execution must depend on whims, on human loyalties and prejudices. He would not pause to make friends with men. A correspondent put the case concisely :

And let me tell you, Sir, if no one else has the candour or boldness to say it (I mean among your friends) that the charge of a cold repulsive manner is not the most trifling charge, that your political enemies have brought against you—you have not the jovial, social, Democratical-Republican-how-do-you-do Suavity of a Root;[3] nor the honied and cordial, or even the complaisant, manners of a " beloved Tompkins." [4]

Judge Hammond, who long served him as attorney, writes that petitioners who came to Albany had declared that they

[1] J. S. Jenkins, *Lives of the Governors*, p. 508 *et seq.*

[2] See tables in *Albany Advertiser*, June 7, 1820.

[3] Gen. Erastus Root of Delaware Co., an Anti-Clintonian leader.

[4] John Brennan to Clinton, postmarked Sept. 23, 1823, Clinton Mss. Another writes (*ibid.*, no date) of Clinton's enemies:

" Some of whom do accuse thee of being full proud,
There's some truth in this it must be allowed."

preferred to be graciously denied by Tompkins, to having favors granted by the bearish Clinton.[1]

But his methods were as harshly criticized as were his manners. All deplorable devices which made New York politics a scandal were charged to his invention, because, no doubt, he was unusually adept in their employment. Rightly or wrongly, he was charged with having been the first to make public office family property.[2] A hostile paper printed an elaborate catechism

calculated to show the faculty of providing for a family in an elective government, by the discovery of a drop of Clintonian blood; and how it qualifies a man for office or for any number of offices to the exclusion of his fellow citizens, whatever be their talents or merits. [Two samples out of thirty questions will suffice]. Question: Why is Pierre C. Van Wyck Recorder of the City of New York, (and) Commissioner in Bankruptcy, and why is his brother Notary Public? Answer: Because his mother was the sister of Pierre Van Cortlandt, who married the daughter of George Clinton, who is the brother of James Clinton who is the father of DeWitt Clinton. Question: Why is Charles D. Cooper Clerk of the county of Albany? Answer: Because he married the adopted daughter of John Tayler, who is cousin of George Clinton, who is uncle of De Witt Clinton.[3]

His personal adherents who had followed him through lean years of defeat were largely men of broken fortune and dark reputation, and it was generally charged that they retained his good will by playing a constant stream of compliment to satisfy his vanity.[4] It seemed to many that the leader confused the success of republican principles with applause of himself.

[1] *Political History*, vol. ii, pp. 269-272.

[3] *Cf.* H. L. McBain, *DeWitt Clinton and the Spoils System.*

[3] *Poughkeepsie Political Barometer*, April 24, 1811.

[4] Hammond, vol. i, pp. 399-400, 423-424.

The great governor in his appetite for praise was not discriminating, yet he found peculiar satisfaction in literary fame. He was eager for distinction as savant as well as statesman, claiming fellowship as near with Aristotle as with Pericles. In 1817 the Germans had not yet preached the doctrine that scholarship to be respectable must be confined, and Clinton tried to run the range of learning. It was not by chance that his first biographer was a botanist, a physician and an F. R. S. and that the second was a professor of natural and experimental philosophy.[1] The bewildering diversity of his scientific interests is illustrated by his correspondence. People wrote to him of new varieties of meteors and new varieties of clams; they sent him drawings of ships that could sail sidewise, of moundbuilders' remains, and of wonderful keyed harps; he was questioned on the arts of Athens, the theology of Calvin, the tribal dialects of Indians, blue clover and the recipes of cures for hydrophobia; gentlemen whom he had never seen wrote careful and minute descriptions of their travels, others proved the earth was hollow, and one sent a " confidential plan for the amelioration of mankind " by means of a society.[2]

This last proposal was fittingly addressed to him, for he was at least vice president of all such enterprises in the state and corresponding member of nearly all of those outside its bounds. He delivered long orations before the New York Historical Society, the Literary and Philosophical Society of New York, the American Academy of the Arts, the Society of Phi Beta Kappa and many others.[3] In these discourses there was some contribution to the several

[1] David Hosack, *Memoir of DeWitt Clinton* (N. Y., 1829); James Renwick, *Life of DeWitt Clinton* (N. Y., 1840).

[2] These letters grow in frequency after 1817, see Clinton Mss.

[3] See pamphlet collection in N. Y. Public Library.

sciences, but much of vain pomposity and parade of
erudition. Frequently his illustrations and his classical
quotations were traceable to common manuals and handy
dictionaries. And there were graver faults, as we shall see,
which critics who disliked his manners and the methods of
his party management, were quick to seize upon. The
societies, they said, which let themselves be gulled by such
transparent fraud, were themselves fair butts of ridicule.
It is not surprising that among these keen lampooners the
most conspicuous was "Abimelech Coody," Gulian C.
Verplanck.

As Verplanck had listened to the mayor's stinging rebuke
in the famous trial for riot, he had resolved to devote his
pen from that day forth to the disgrace of Clinton. The
coalition by which Federalists gave their votes to make the
mayor President was abhorred by Verplanck, and he felt
chagrined when Federalist councils of appointment retained
this enemy in office. In 1814 he wrote a series of attacks
printed in a political sheet called *The Corrector*,[1] but words
were not his only weapons. The Federalist party, he declared,
must be made clean of this defilement, and joined by Hugh
Maxwell and the Radcliffes, who had been snubbed in ap-
plications for the mayor's office, he published a schismatic
ticket for the assembly. The "Washington Federalists"
was the name assumed by the associates in this enterprise;
but by the hostile *Evening Post* they were hailed derisively
as "Coodies." Judge Spencer, then at war with Clinton,
thought he saw some possibilities in this little party, but
the ticket was supported by a few score voters only, and the
movement toward a new party was for a time abandoned.[2]

In 1815 there appeared another Coody pamphlet called *A*

[1] W. C. Bryant, *Discourse on Verplanck*, p. 18.
[2] *N. Y. Commercial Advertiser*, April 26, May 2, 1814; Hammond, vol.
i, p. 398.

Fable, wherein Clinton was portrayed as " a young Irish greyhound of high mettle and exorbitant pretensions." [1]   In the *Analectic Magazine* Verplanck and certain colleagues described in an irreverent humor the publications of the mayor's learned societies, and ridiculed their members, whose long lists of honorary degrees, they said, were monuments of vanity.[2]   Although the author had no word of praise for Tompkins or his Virginia overlords, the Tammany Society was much delighted by this round abuse of Clinton.

The object of all these attentions had not the gift of silence. He responded with a *Letter from a Traveller,*[3] first berating James K. Paulding, whose recent *Lay of the Scottish Fiddle* had contained some bitter satire on the friends of Clinton in New England.[4]   Other writers in the group were then attacked, but the most savage thrust was saved for young Verplanck.   This man (the letter ran) who had made his first exhibition in life as a rioter in a church and since, like Hannibal upon the altar, had sworn revenge upon the arm that punished him, was now

the head of a political sect called Coodies, of a hybrid nature, composed of the combined spawn of federalism and jacobinism, and generated in the venomous passion of disappointment and revenge; without any definite character, neither fish nor flesh,

[1] *A Fable for Statesmen and Politicians of All Parties and Descriptions, by Abimelech Coody, Esq., Formerly Ladies' Shoemaker* (N. Y., 1815).

[2] *Analectic Magazine,* vol. iv (1814), pp. 349-350.

[3] (DeWitt Clinton) *An Account of Abimelech Coody and other celebrated writers of New York; in a letter from a traveller to his friend in South Carolina* (N. Y., 1815).

[4] See especially canto ii, stanzas iii, iv, xi (note 9) ; canto iii (note 3) ; canto v, stanzas xvi, xxvi and notes 9 and 12.   The fact that these young writers took remuneration shocked Clinton: "Almost in every other place men write for amusement or for fame—but here there are authors by profession, who make it a business and a living."

bird nor beast, animal nor plant, but a non-descript made up of

> All monstrous, all prodigious things,
> Abominable, unutterable and worse than
> Fable . . . . . [1]

After the unkindest caricature of his enemy, the "The Traveller" described himself: " Mr. Clinton, amidst his other great qualifications, is distinguished for a marked devotion to science—few men have read more, and few can claim more various and extensive knowledge. And the bounties of nature have been improved by persevering industry." Such self-appreciation would be beyond belief had not the manuscript in his own hand been preserved by the printer.[2] After this performance he was, for a time, allowed to rest, for Verplanck spent the next two years in Europe.[3]

[1] Pages 12, 14-15. Clinton's unpleasant temper is revealed by his description of Verplanck, touching on physical peculiarities, such as are by custom immune from the pen of satire: " When I saw Abimelech Coody, he arose from his chair as I was announced and did not approach me in a direct line, but in a sidelong way, or diagonally, in a kind of *echelon* movement, reminding one of Linnæus' character of a dog, who he says always inclines his tail to the left. This I attributed at first to diffidence, but I no sooner had a full view of him, than I instantly saw

> . . . ' the proud patrican sneer,
> The conscious simper, and the jealous leer.'

His person is squat and clumsy, reminding one of Humpty Dumpty on the wall. A nervous tremor is concentrated at the end of each nostril, from his habitual sneering and carping, with a look as wise as that of Solomon, at the dividing of the child, upon an old piece of tapestry."
That Verplanck deeply resented this indecorous attack is shown by his reference to Clinton as one who would

> " —sneer at crooked back or gibbous breast; "

see his *Bucktail Bards* (noticed *infra*), p. 134, and note p. 150.

[2] I have not seen this manuscript, but Chief Justice Daly, in his *Biographical Sketch of Verplanck*, speaks of its existence in 1870.

[3] On this journey he was accompanied by his wife, the sister-in-law of J. O. Hoffman. Mrs. Verplanck died in Paris in 1817.

So far, among the Federalist party, the active opposition
to Clinton had been limited, for the most part, to literary
men, but they were soon supported by recruits from among
the politicians.   J. O. Hoffman had supported Clinton in
1812, and since that time had been a constant worker in his
interest.   Having been appointed recorder of the city by the
Federalist Council in 1810, and turned out by the wheel of
change, he looked for restoration when Clinton came to
power.   But though the governor professed his gratitude
for Hoffman's many services, the office was bestowed upon
another Federalist.   No fault could be found with Peter
A. Jay to whom he gave it, but this did not solace the defeated candidate who now joined the opposition.[1]   Several
other Federalists were disappointed.   The charge that
Clinton favored Federalism would hurt him with old friends
among Republicans, and the Council seemed extremely
chary as to honoring the gentlemen of the " old party "
even though their help produced Clintonian majorities.
Most Federalists accepted this condition.

Let us await calmly and tranquilly a better state of things
[admonished " Senex " in a letter to the *Albany Advertiser*] ;
talents and virtue will be certain to attract attention and gain
notice.   Gov. Clinton can scarcely be considered a free agent
as regards those who have borne the name of federalists ; the
least indication of even a liberal treatment of one of us is seized
upon as evidence that he is turning federalist.[2]

The Federalists were secretly welcomed by Clintonians, but
except for a few like Peter A. Jay, they were officially ig-

[1] Wm. A. Duer, *Reminiscences*, pp. 27-28; *N. Y. Commercial Advertiser*, April 9, 14, 1819; *N. Y. American*, April 14, 24, 1819.

[2] March 11, 15, 1819. "And would you," sarcastically answered a
Federalist opponent of Clinton, "would you have Mr. Clinton subject to
the possibility of incurring such a vile imputation?" *N. Y. American,*
March 20, 1819.

nored. Yet the Coodies and their friends would have it that
the party had been sold out for offices by the Columbia
Junto; the voters had been duped. Upon Oakley and his
accomplices who hoped for personal reward, they fixed the
name of Swiss, who fight for pay.[1]

The final, formal break within the Federalist party came
upon the question of the re-election of Rufus King as
senator. When, with the assembling of the legislature in
1819 the matter was considered, it was assiduously whis-
pered here and there by Tammany men that King was
favored by the governor, those artful plotters hoping thus
by bringing in a Federalist name to spread unrest among the
old Clintonians. Some who had criticised Clinton for indifference to his Federalist allies relented on this rumor, but
were undeceived when they investigated.[2] The governor
had not forgotten King's speech in 1812; even if he had
determined to extend the patronage to others than Republicans (which he feared to do), Rufus King would have
been most carefully neglected. The malcontents, led by
John A. King, the senator's son, and William A. Duer,
declared this was enough to establish Clinton as the very
monument of perfidy and selfishness. Henceforth the
Coodies had energetic friends in Albany. There seemed
hope that some Federalists, who had been supporting
Clinton, would rally to their older leader, and Rufus King
was nominated as an old party candidate. The Martling
Men were glad to see the coalition threatened, and young
King believed that he might count on some New York Republicans to support his father's interest;[3] but he was over

---

[1] This name was first applied by Gen. Root in the legislature of 1819,
see *Bucktail Bards*, p. 59.

[2] Hammond, vol. i, pp. 482-483.

[3] J. A. King to R. King, Jan. 14, 1819, and R. King to J. A. King,
King Correspondence, vol. vi, p. 191.

sanguine; conditions were not ready for this strange alliance. As the Clintonians named John C. Spencer, the son of Ambrose Spencer, so Van Buren and his Martling followers selected Colonel Samuel Young, who was quarrelling with the governor about the canal funds.[1] The votes were taken on February second; King had but twenty-eight, yet neither of his rivals had commanded a majority; the election was seen to be impossible in that legislature, and it was postponed until the following year.[2]

Most Federalists took the outcome calmly and helped to elect a Clintonian council of appointment in hope of a supreme court judgeship,[3] but some were not so tolerant.

The manner in which the federal party [wrote John A. King] has been treated upon all occasions and most especially in the nomination of the Senator, by Mr. Clinton and his adherents, decided me never to give my support to a Council of his selection; not willing therefore to throw away my vote, and willing to bear my testimony against that gentleman's conduct, as well as to evince my disapprobation of the direction which has been given to the sentiments of the majority of the federal party by some of its interested and artful leaders, I voted for the Martling Council—Mr. Duer and Carman were the only federalists who voted with me.[4]

But the Clintonian Federalists determining on a closer coalition were ready to excuse the slight on Rufus King. The *Hudson Whig,* which voiced the opinion of the Columbia Junto, asked if a man who curried favor with the cabinet and justified the atrocities of General Jackson in Florida could deserve the honor of his party.[5]   Oakley and

---

[1] *Cf.* Clinton Mss. during 1819.   [2] Hammond, vol. i, p. 486.

[3] J. A. King to R. King, Feb. 3, 1819. In this hope they were disappointed.

[4] *Ibid.,* also J. A. Hamilton, *Reminiscences,* p. 44.

[5] Quoted in *N. Y. American,* May 1, 1819.

James Emott of Dutchess County deprecated all the unpleasant agitation for King. It was obvious that unity was past.

While John A. King was gathering supporters one by one in Albany, his brother Charles—the ebullient Charles, surnamed " the Pink " [1]—was planning out another enterprise. Gulian C. Verplanck, now returned from Europe, his cousin Johnston, and some others of the same age and social station, joined with Charles King to found a newspaper. They were to call all honest men to their support, recreate the party of the talents and proscribe the venal Swiss, who had usurped the rule and maintained it by intrigue. These young men would not sit with their " hands folded while the character and best interests of the state are sacrificing at the shrine of a few profligate and ambitious leaders." [2] Thus the *New York American* was begun on March 3, 1819, a small semi-weekly sheet with large type, no advertisements and little news—chiefly editorials against DeWitt Clinton and his band of followers.

Disapproving of the conduct of all parties in their native state [announced the editors] they will do their utmost to overturn a system of fraud and venality, and to rescue the character of New York from the disgrace, and its power from the abuses, consequent to the control of men, whose means are corruption and hypocrisy, whose ends are the gratification of their petty and selfish ambition.

The credulity of those poor dupes who made up the Fed-

---

[1] G. K. Schuyler, "A Gentleman of the Old School," *Scribner's Magazine*, vol. lv, p. 612. References to his manners and his conversation can be found in numerous entries in Philip Hone's *Diary*.

[2] Charles King to Rufus King, Feb. 8, 1819. This letter is not published in full in C. R. King's edition of *The Life and Correspondence of Rufus King*, but was consulted in the King Mss., in the N. Y. Hist. Soc. Collections.

eralist majority, they averred was pitiful; even Clinton's major triumph, the project of the canal, was the legacy of Gouverneur Morris. Clinton was but " the step-father of internal improvement." He had scorned them as traitors in 1808, then flattered them in 1812 and since. Now after gaining the support of many and again in power he refused to requite any of his obligations.[1]

The other Federalist papers, attached to Clinton's interests, looked on with amused contempt.

A little, meagre, drivelling, skewing Tammany paper [scornfully remarked the *Albany Advertiser*] has been got up in the City of New York, by a knot of scribblers, who consider that the universe rests upon their shoulders, and the state of New York is a foot-ball which they can kick about with their neat little pretty morocco pumps . . . We are told that Alexander Hamilton, the present leader of the Tammany delegation, and James A. Hamilton (another son of the late General Hamilton) are two of the editors. Mr. Barent Gardenier has declined. Mr. Hugh Maxwell and G. C. Verplanck, who we believe are both Tammany now, but who lately pronounced two Washington Benevolent Orations,[2] we are told are among the editors. . . . The number of editors who conduct the *American* is not far from twelve or fifteen.[3]

The young editors resented all these charges of desertion to the enemy; they tried at first to be as independent of Van Buren as of Clinton. They desired a third party to which true Federalists might rally—the " high-minded descendants of the great men "—and put forth in March a ticket to attract such a following. But they were embarrassed by the applause of Clinton's foes within the Democratic party; a

---

[1] *N. Y. American*, March 3, 1819.

[2] Maxwell had spoken before the Hamilton Society, *N. Y. Statesman*, Feb. 26, 1814. For Verplanck's oration see *supra*, ch. iv.

[3] March 9, 1819.

common enemy makes strange friendships, and the sympathy proved irresistible. It was not pleasant to go to Tammany Hall, for the sachems had been unwilling to join them in the fight for Rufus King, but it was inevitable. In April they compounded a mixed ticket; a new coalition was forming.[1] Throughout the state at the election of 1819, a surprising number of Federalists were chosen for the legislature. Yet the *American* was not sanguine that these victories would stimulate the party to self-reliance or that the trend toward Clinton would be checked. To co-operate with all opponents of the governor was deemed the editors' only course, since their own old partisans were so indifferent to their call. " Which side the majority of the Federal representatives will take, is, we hope, at least, doubtful; although we fear honesty will be no match for intrigue."[2]

Clinton realized that some recognition now was necessary, and Thomas J. Oakley from Dutchess County, a Federalist leader in the legislature, was appointed to the lucrative and influential office of attorney-general. The Coodies and their colleagues were outraged; if Clinton was to win the loyalty of the Federalists by offices, why pass by the great King in February and pick out Oakley in July? " Answer ye timid creeping things, who fear the winter frosts, but whose activity and venom is warmed into life by the summer heats —answer if you dare."[3] Anything that the Clintonians would do or could do, simply proved a signal for more acrimonious philippics. Indeed as one reviews the writings of these young gentlemen, he is irresistibly drawn to the belief that they hugely enjoyed these opportunities for plain and ornamental rhetoric,—for literary self-expression with Clinton taken as the theme. One suspects they founded

---

[1] *American*, March 10 , April 7, 21, 24, 1819; J. O. H[offman] to W. P. Van Ness, Feb. 25, 1819, Van Ness Mss.

[2] *American*, May 19, 1819.   [3] *Ibid.*, July 21.

their newspaper not so much that certain things should get done, as that they should have a chance to urge them in fair periods. Nor does this question their sincerity; youth in its egotism yearns to be of service, conspicuously and theatrically, but still honestly. The Verplancks, the Kings, the Duers, the Hamiltons, loved to do the service of unrestrained writing.

A sample of their style, it is believed, will not be wearisome: [1]

But quickly the election returns [of 1819] presented to the money changers a new and unexpected result: a return to the assembly of Federalists in number and character altogether un-looked for and unknown. It required the whole extent of the exercised talent of these versatile actors [the Clintonians] to adapt their language and their conduct to the new state of things. The old song of the absolute necessity of the dissolu-tion of the Federal party could no longer be usefully said or sung; without a flush of shame they resolved to chaunt their palinode. But as the reputation of Lord Bacon [Elisha Wil-liams?] was rank, and as the two other Bondsmen were not in sweet odour, the gentleman from Dutchess, the secret hand, was selected at the May term to sound the trumpet and beat the drum for the Federal muster; the ranks were thin—the service seemed not promising; and even among the known devotees of the Junto—among some of the enlisted lobby agents, the money changers,—there arose the voice of discon-tent, and a murmuring sound of dissatisfaction. It rang in the ears of the by-standers something like " point d'argent—point de Suisse." [But Oakley's appointment silenced all] . . . . How idle it is to talk of words when Ecce homo—ecce signum, is an argument that speaks to the senses, and sets at naught the orator's art or the poet's power. Alas, Walpole, wert thou to arise, how wouldst thou weep to see thyself undone. Every

[1] *American,* May 19, 1819.

man with thee had his price: yet even Walpole never knew
the infinite advantage of having his own proper person a standing example, a speaking argument of the merit of recent works,
and of the benefits of conversion. The device is ingenious, the
effect ought to be assured, and the practice recorded. It is
worth tomes of casuistry and volumes of newspapers. . . . .
Religious aspirants have no glimpse vouchsafed them of heaven
but through promise and description; but the rulers of the State
of New-York work not after ancient models, nor by types and
figures and words; they point to the man, they show you with
their fingers the cause and the effect. They scorn the coldness
of a verbal description, and distrust the uncertain power of
promise; they put their seal of office on the forehead of their
late convert and now proselyting minister, to give efficacy to his
calls, warmth to his words, and point to his arguments. In the
same manner the Justice [Spencer] that worketh unseen, and
hath power and might for a day and a year and a season, points
to his creature as the proof of his dominion: it is a sign for
the times, nor is it unreasonable to expect from such a sign
the gathering of both Jews and Pagans, the Clintonized Federalists and the unadulterated Clintonians.

Where such duplicity could flourish was no place for
honest men. The loyalties of the Federalists, they said,
could not be sold; the faithless leaders and their dupes
should be abandoned and the honorable remnant join with
Clinton's enemies; men like Martin Van Buren would
properly appreciate their purpose and their service. By the
middle of the summer it was generally known that there
had been a thorough-going coalition between the Federalist
malcontents and the sachems of the Tammany Society.[1]

There now appeared a pamphlet called *A Martling Man,
or Says I to Myself—How is This?*,[2] a satire which, with

---

[1] *American*, July 3, 14, 21, Aug. 14, 1819.

[2] The series of letters comprised in this pamphlet was first printed
in the *N. Y. Columbian* in the spring of 1819.

incisive wit like that of Abimelech Coody, presented an
innocent inquirer to make the enemy absurd. But this was
written by an old Clintonian, Pierre C. Van Wyck, with
some revising, it was charged, by the governor himself.[1]
It took up one by one the strangers who had been received
at Tammany Hall. Josiah Ogden Hoffman was the first,
it said, because he had not been made recorder; Barent
Gardenier, Philip Brasher and some others had followed
for like reasons; Richard Hatfield and the Hamiltons had
been persuaded to come in by promises and flattery, to gain
the value of their names; Hugh Maxwell and " Gilley "
Verplanck, who had hounded Clinton since the riot in
Trinity Church, now tired of guerilla fighting had brought
their Coodies to the Martling army. William A. Duer and
some others had joined with General Root, the old Madisonian chief, at Albany, " to go thorough in their opposition
to Mr. Clinton." The Democrats of Tammany were eager
to extend a welcome to all the apostates; these, they said,
were true patriots; whenever Mr. Bayard or General Clarkson said a word of praise for the governor, it was
complained that such Federalists had purchased Clinton.

But in the literary contest the Martling Man was destined
to be far outmatched. If he (as well as Abimelech Coody)
suggests successors like Major Jack Downing[a] and Hosea
Biglow,[b] a rival came into print far more pretentious, who

---

[1] The copy in the N. Y. Public Library is endorsed " by Pierre Van
Wyck "; see also *The Bucktail Bards* (see *infra*), p. 48:

> " Retouched and interlined was here
> A *Martling Man*; 'twas sent by Pierre;
> Hoping his Magnus would be willing
> To help the wit, and *mend the spelling*."

See also *ibid.*, note, pp. 73-74. He was at that time District Attorney,
having been Recorder of the City of New York. He is described by
Judge Hammond as poor and dissipated, but a man of talents, *Political
History*, vol. i, p. 423.

[a] Major Jack Downing, the pen name of Seba Smith (1792-1868) whose
letters published in the Portland *Courier* were nationally known for their
pungent and satiric comments on politics.

recalls the Augustan age of Pope and Swift. Gulian C.
Verplanck, with some aid from John Duer and from Rudolph Bunner, a politician and a scholar who had been at
one time a trusted colleague of the Columbia Junto,[1] published in the *American* during 1819 a series of seven poetic
satires on Clinton and his friends. Such was the interest
they aroused that before the year was done, Verplanck had
reproduced them in a volume of some two hundred pages
entitled, from the ancient Tammany emblem, *The Bucktail
Bards.*[2] Possessing the urbanity and easy grace of the
Knickerbocker school, replete with grave quotations from
the lines of the Æneid, the Horatian Odes, Macbeth, Ab-
salom and Achitophel, and the Dunciad, it was obviously
written for an audience of cultivated men, in hope, no doubt,
of winning them away from Clinton. The satire of the
poems is so apposite and sharp, that they might have been
important in the history of American literature were it not
that their allusions are so hopelessly obscure to all but those
familiar with New York a hundred years ago. It were
pleasant, were there time, to regale the reader with the de-
licious foolery of Scriblerus Busby's Prolegomena, wherein
the author with waggish impertinence pays respects to the
critic Jeffrey, to Charles Philips, the Irish orator, and to
Dr. Parr, the classicist, who is supposed to have sent a bit
of doggerel, impressive in Greek transliteration, or to the
excursus concerning the Ελαφονερκοι—or Bucktails, which
so cleverly pokes fun at the pedantic Clinton and his learned
societies.

---

[1] W. C. Bryant, *Discourse on Verplanck*, p. 18; J. A. Hamilton,
Reminiscences, p. 42.

[2] The tail of the buck worn in the hat was adopted as the official badge
in 1791, and the name "Bucktail" had been fastened on the party; E. P.
Kilroe, *Saint Tammany and the Origin of the Society of Tammany or
Columbian Order in the City of New York* (N. Y., 1913), pp. 114, 147,
148, 164, 165.

---

[b] Hosea Biglow, the pen name of James Russell Lowell (1819-1891)
for a series of humorous political poems written in Yankee dialect under
the title, *Biglow Papers* (1848; 1867).

The first poem portrays " The State Triumvirate," Clinton, St. Ambrose (Judge Spencer) and Fallacio (Judge Van Ness), and tells the story of an office-seeker, Dick Shift, who played to win their patronage by the demonstration of his talent in hypocrisy:

> " 'Corruption?' True, his forte, his trade,
> And yet no word, no look betray'd
> His guilt; but acts of baseness name,
> He was the first to cry out, 'shame';
> Though prudent, doubting still the fact,
> The vice he blam'd, was vice abstract;
> He held the maxim quite sublime,
> To spare the sinner, lash the crime—" [1]

The hero is presented to the stern St. Ambrose, who is won by flattery, he is brought within the chilling gloom of Clinton's presence, and gains Fallacio's ear by cunning plans for a conspiracy. Verplanck deplores the fall of Judge Van Ness, who has been Clintonized—

> " O that a mind,
> Form'd to instruct or mend mankind,
> By noblest arts to rule a state,
> Or King's pure fame to emulate,
> By use, by habit, long deprav'd,
> To low intrigue should be enslav'd!"

—and sometimes in anger or in shame at the disgrace to which Clinton and his men have brought the state, leaves far behind the sportive vein of satire.

There are three " Epistles of Brevet Major Pindar Puff," in heroic verse, supposed to have been written by the governor's salaried panegyrist, whose confessions, inserted here and there within the fulsome flattery assumed to be enjoyed by Clinton, envenom the point of the poet's sarcasm.[2] Clinton's vain show of his learning and the solecisms

---

[1] Page 35.

[2] " Of praise a mere glutton, he swallow'd what came,
  And the puff of a dunce, he mistook it for fame;
  Till his relish grown callous, almost to disease,
  Who pepper'd the highest was surest to please," (p. 140).

of his turgid prose are subjects of the satire.[1] For one who valued himself upon his literary reputation, this merciless dissection of his masterpieces was doubtless painful, but the Major must go further to admit the plagiarism of his hero in

> " That fam'd discourse, of patches fram'd
> From authors.
>   Quoted?
>   No, not named;
> The stolen thoughts, the skill that suits,
> The art that ' pilfer'd tropes transmutes,'
> The passage chang'd, to nonsense leaning,
> Retains the words, and drops the meaning;
> The flow'rs he seiz'd from Johnson—,
>   Well?
> He caught the stalk, the blossoms fell!"[2]

He offers in a deadly parallel a dozen excerpts from the learned lexicographer and Dr. Clinton to prove the latter's much too profitable reading.[3]

Of course the governor's fellow scientists like Dr.

---

[1]   " His skill in conch-shells, and his Indian lore;
          His wondrous wisdom in our state affairs,
          His curious knowledge of the tails of bears," (p. 104).

See especially the comment on Clinton's ineptitude in classical allusion, on pages 143-144. The author in a note thus characterizes Clinton's style; " His wit has a sort of partridge flight, always low, never light, gay or airy, or of long continuance, yet still with a good deal of activity and whirring vigor, as long as it is on the wing" (p. 173). The American printed an " account " of a paper upon " the Clintonian crab-apple, which is produced by a graft of the Pyram Toricum, or blue-light pear, upon the Malum Jacobinum, or Jack-Cade pippin. It was for this discovery that Dr. Clinton was elected a member of the London Cockney Historical Society, as announced by Messrs. Lang [of the N. Y. Gazette], Lewis [of the Commercial Advertiser], and Spooner [of the Columbian]."

[2] Bucktail Bards, p. 47; see also pp. 104, 131 and 155.

[3] Pages 141-146. A reference to like borrowings from Hume and Burke appears on page 131. The Albany Argus accused him of plagiarizing Frederick the Great (Dec. 18, 1819).

Mitchill, Dr. Hosack, Mayor Colden, and the rest, are likewise cleverly lampooned as partners of his pedantry, and the poet then speaks

> " Of learn'd Societies, that nothing need,
>   In every walk of Science, to succeed,
>   Save more attention, and some more expense,
>   And some more learning—and a little sense." [1]

Other members of the literary group, besides the Bucktail Bards, contributed good verses, as when Halleck's gentler muse, in *Fanny,* played

> " Around the many, whose exalted station
>   Has been attained by means 't were pain to hint on,
>   Just for the rhyme's sake—instance Cl*n*on." [2]

To defend the governor a number of his friends now sharpened their pens

[1] Page 133, and note on page 149. This phase of Clinton is satirized also in a poem called *The Pilgrims of Hope, An Oratorio for the Clintonian Celebration of the New Year,* which appeared first in the *N. Y. American,* Jan. 1, 1820, and afterwards in pamphlet form (N. Y. Pub. Lib.). The following quotation from Chief Justice Daly's *Biographical Sketch of Verplanck* will be interesting: " ' The Bucktail Bards' was at the time attributed to Mr. Verplanck, though it has since been supposed to be the work of several hands, and the names of Judge John Duer, and of Rudolph Bunner, an active politician and a man of vivacity and wit, have been named as connected with him in the production of it. He was himself always very reticent upon the subject. When called upon, at the dinner given in the Century [Club] to Fitz-Greene Halleck, to respond to a toast complimentary to this satire, he evaded the question of authorship, but on other occasions implicitly admitted his connection with it, but that was all. He probably felt (for he was not a man to bear animosities) that he had accomplished by his production at the time, all that he had desired, and was willing to let the controversy end with the causes that had produced it " (p. 46).

[2] This poem was published first at New York in 1819. See in 1839 edition, pp. 7, 14, 18, 21, 27. In " The Croakers" published 1819 *et seq.* by Halleck and J. R. Drake, there are many such references, see *Poetical Writings of Halleck and ...Drake* (N. Y., 1869), pp. 255-362.

" Against those rude and foolish, angry boys,
Who in th' American his fame assail,
Daring against our country's pride to rail," [1]

and none with more effect than Gideon Granger, who, after
thirteen years as Postmaster-General, now lived in Canandaigua. In a pamphlet signed "Epaminondas" he professed unstinted admiration for Clinton and his efforts in
behalf of agriculture and the Grand Canal.[2] (He was himself especially enthusiastic with respect to the latter project
and had given a thousand acres as his personal contribution,
though his ungenerous enemies would have it that the land
was scarcely worth the taxes).[3] He said the governor was
abused by small pettifoggers, extortioners and sharp prac-
ticers at law, because of some most salutary measures he had
carried through. He filled many pages with invective
against Tammany. To meet the charge that Clinton had
appointed Federalists he told of those appointed by Madison himself, beginning with James A. Bayard as peace
commissioner. Let there be no great concern as to this
matter;

we have lived to see the federalists disband as a party, and in
general retire from political strife. We have lived to see some
of their bitterest leaders join the opposition of Mr. Clinton, and
make the most vigorous efforts to excite your prejudices against
him, while at the same time a portion of the more thoughtful
and moderate have given an honorable support to the administration.[4]

Granger was too canny and too cautious in speaking of

[1] *Bucktail Bards*, p. 132.

[2] Gideon Granger, *The Address of Epaminondas to the Citizens of the
State of New York* (Albany, 1819).

[3] *Report of State Surveyor*, 1863, N. Y. Assembly Doc. I, p. 99; *Geneva
Palladium*, quoted in *N. Y. American*, Jan. 22, 1820.

[4] Pages 28-29.

the latter " portion," for they really constituted nearly all of the old party; they chose to vote for Clinton rather than court humiliation with a candidate of their own number. Clinton had become the leader of the aristocracy, with a few conspicuous exceptions, and with this group Granger was at heart right glad to be associated. He had grown rich by the proceeds of his fire-lands in the Connecticut Western Reserve, and with money invested in stocks and bonds, as well as land, he now lived near Federalist friends, in a mansion " full of servants." [1] His three sons married into Federalist families,[2] and one of them, Francis, became an able leader of the Whigs in the state and nation. By such evidences throughout the state, the firmness of the coalition was revealed.

When the legislature met, in 1820, Clinton knew that it would now be folly to deny his Federalist connections; his private spite against Senator King he straightway swallowed and in an address to the legislature announced himself a supporter of King's election. The interest focused on the

[1] Gideon Granger to Clinton, Dec. 13, 1820, Clinton Mss. As to his friends see article under his name in Appleton's *Cyclopedia*, checked with references to John Greig, William Wood in *N. Y. Commercial Advertiser*, March 18, 1816; he left his affairs in the hands of Jonas Platt. The author has examined Mr. Granger's will in Canandaigua, N. Y., and has computed that his property ran far above $100,000.

[2] See J. Granger, *Launcelot Granger . . . a Genealogical History*, Hartford, 1893. The eldest son, Ralph, married the daughter of W. W. Van Ness (see marginal correction in copy in N. Y. Pub. Lib., pp. 181-182) ; the second son, Francis, married a Van Rensselaer of Utica (p. 301) ; and the third, John Albert, a daughter of Amasa Jackson (p. 305). To check Jackson, *cf.* his toast at the Federalist banquet, New York city, *N. Y. Commercial Advertiser*, Feb. 23, 1815.

After Granger's quarrel with Madison, in which the redoubtable wife of the President was said to have had a share (see note to *Pilgrims of Hope*), he was attracted to Clinton as the champion of the north in the fight against Virginia domination within the Republican party (see, for example, his interesting letter to Clinton, March 27, 1816, Clinton Mss).

Bucktails. Would they dare to flout their new allies who wrote for the *American,* by neglect of their admired hero? Yet would they dare nominate a Federalist? Van Buren, Root, Young and others conferred with William A. Duer; all agreed that the Federalists had so far declined as a party, that he could safely be endorsed.[1] Van Buren, with the aid of William L. Marcy, the recorder of Troy, prepared a pamphlet in praise of King as a patriot who had stood by the President in the War of 1812.[2] And so, as John Quincy Adams recorded in his diary, " King, who after 10 trials last winter, could not get so many as twenty votes out of one hundred and fifty, now came in by a unanimous vote of the Senate and all but three of the Assembly." [3] This concession on the part of the Democracy was considered as another sign that Federalism in its old organization was dead.

In a caucus of the party on the question of the speaker, Elisha Williams announced the policy of the Columbia Junto: " A committee should be appointed in behalf of the gentlemen then present to meet and state to the friends of Mr. Clinton that the candidate of their choice should receive the cordial support of the federal party." T. J. Oakley and others cordially approved. John A. King at last arose, confessing his amazement at such hardihood. A fair proposal had been made to name a Federalist; it had been heard in silence by these once respected leaders. He announced his intention to vote for the Republican, or if gentlemen pleased so to call it, the Tammany candidate. He would never meet with Federalists again at the behest of the

[1] J. A. King to R. King, Jan. 8, 1820.

[2] Van Buren Mss., Dec. 13, 1819, for draft. *Cf. Albany Argus,* in discussion, quoted in *American,* Dec. 18, 1819, and E. M. Shepard, *Martin Van Buren* (Boston, 1888), pp. 60-62.

[3] J. Q. Adams, *Memoirs,* vol. iv, p. 517.

wretched junto from Columbia County. He moved adjournment; and thus came to its end the Federalist party in New York.[1]

A few days later there appeared *An Address to the Independent Federal Electors*[2] which declared the party broken up[3] and even the ties of private friendship which had bound its members now finally severed.[4]

It is, therefore, after deliberate reflection [said its signers] that we have resolved to unite ourselves, unequivocally, and without reserve, to the great republican party of the state and union . . . With republicans we entertain a deep-rooted distrust of the views and character of Mr. Clinton as a politician . . . He has endeavored to create a personal faction, and to surround himself with a band of low minded sycophants, and venal dependents . . . Let others prostrate themselves before their sultan, in humble adoration; we mean not to enroll ourselves in the Janissary corps. [As to those Federalists who join with Clinton] we confess our inability to account for this union upon any other principles than mutual private interests of the parties.

To this address there were some fifty signers, including, besides the young men of the *American,* such prominent Federalists as Morris S. Miller and Zebulon R. Shepherd, who had sat in Congress,[5] George Tibbits, who had been

[1] J. A. King to Charles King, Jan. 6, 1820, *King Correspondence.*

[2] *An Address to the Independent Electors of the State of New-York, on the subject of the Election of a Governor and Lt. Governor of the State* (Albany, 1820).

[3] This announcement was received with consternation and reproach in states like Maryland, where the Federalist party had some hopes. Rufus King was obliged to explain in letters to such objectors that conditions in New York were " very peculiar."

[4] This threat of social ostracism had been made on the other side in 1816, see *N. Y. Commercial Advertiser,* April 19, 1816.

[5] Mention had been made of Judge Miller's importance in chs. ii and iii.

the candidate for lieutenant-governor in 1816, and many who had served in Albany. Judge Hammond remarked that he believed that in the annals of political parties there could be found no like number of men of talent, wealth, social position and personal worth, so scattered through the state, who combined for a single political object and yet drew after them so few voters of the party, as did these men of 1820.[1] Their reasoning was dismissed as silly. While everybody knew that most good Republicans disliked the governor because he would consort with the Federalists, these protestants withdrew professing their belief that the Federalists, as such, had disappeared. In their florid rhetoric they had frequently referred to themselves as " high-minded men." The opposition mocked them with their own description; henceforth they were the " High-minded Federalists."

Their efforts, then, met small reward. Particularly anxious were the sons of Rufus King to have their father's blessing on their enterprise, but though several times addressed in terms affecting, but respectful, the seasoned statesman quietly refused to be a party to their plans. That he had a low opinion of the governor was certainly no secret, but he saw no cause to sow the seeds of bitterness between himself and Chancellor Kent, the Patroon, and Judge Platt and others of his friends who had joined with Clinton.[2] He would not have it seem that Van Buren and

Shepherd was a well known lawyer of Granville, Washington Co., see C. Johnson, *History of Washington County*, Philadelphia, 1878, pp. 202, 206, and *N. Y. Civil List*, 1882, p. 451. The name is variously spelled. Many of these men had attended the convention that had nominated King in 1816, *cf. N. Y. Commercial Advertiser*, March 18, 1816.

[1] *Political History*, vol. i, p. 529.

[2] He was no doubt influenced in this direction by a letter from Robert Troup, March 22, 1820. Van Buren's letter of March 23 to the senator

himself were trading favors. There were others of the old party who disliked Clinton heartily enough but could not bring themselves to vote for Tompkins, who was named for governor by the Bucktails. The Vice-President as governor throughout the late war had been careless in his accounts. The comptroller, Archibald McIntyre, drew up a lengthy statement of his derelictions, impressive in transcriptions from the ledgers.[1] The secretary of the navy, Judge Smith Thompson, was considered as a candidate by some Democrats, but to abandon the Vice-President would savor of disloyalty and he was retained in spite of criticism.[2] The High-minded Federalists who had professed so nice a sense of honor, could scarcely all be won to Tompkins while his reputation bore this stain. For example, at a meeting of such gentlemen in Madison County, resolutions were passed disapproving Clinton and the Federalists in the legislature who had endorsed him, but likewise opposing Tompkins, and, as between the two, declaring their neutrality.[3] It was doubtless these circumstances that made the schism less important. The majority of leading Federalists read the address of the seceders with boisterous derision.

Whereas, the fifty-one high-minded gentlemen [wrote "Jonathan Old School" in the *Albany Advertiser*] . . . have expressed a wish to be released from the federal party, and from all those who have heretofore been their political friends, in

is a model of courteous suggestion. John A. King's letters show dignity in disappointment; see especially that of April 13. Charles was less patient; see that of March 18. Wm. Coleman also earnestly but vainly sought King's active aid for Tompkins, see letter of March 11.

[1] See especially (A. McIntyre) *A Letter to His Excellency Daniel D. Tompkins Late Governor of the State of New-York*, 112 pp. and Appendix (Albany, 1819).

[2] R. King to Van Buren, Jan. 31, 1820, *King Correspondence*; Bennett Bicknell to P. G. Childs, Feb. 14, 1820, Childs Mss.

[3] M. S. Miller to P. G. Childs, March 6; Bicknell to same, March 17, 1820, Childs Mss.

behalf of fifty thousand voters in the party I do hereby release, quit claim and discharge the above high-minded gentlemen from all allegiance,

granting all right, title and interest to the Vice-President and his Bucktails.[1]

It was believed that the break would not be serious outside of New York city,[2] but there the Federalist friends of Clinton must be active. The *Commercial Advertiser* after observing that in the calm of the last four years the Federalist freeholders had not deemed it necessary to give themselves political concern, now warned its readers that that time was past.[3] At a meeting in Washington Hall, a motion to nominate an independent ticket was overwhelmingly defeated, and Clinton was endorsed with much enthusiasm.[4] Elsewhere in the state old Clintonians averred that now that the Federalist party had been purged of noxious slanderers they were more anxious for a coalition.[5] Judge Van Ness declared that, " There is not now an influential or respectable federalist who is not with us. The few few who have gone are objects of disgust and contempt." [6] The High-minded Men, or " Royal Party " as they were sometimes called, playing on the name of their chief leaders,[7] were said to have their hope of due reward; and, in-

---

[1] April 21, 1820.

[2] The Patroon to Sol. Van Rensselaer, March 7, 1820, Mrs. Bonney's *Legacy*, vol. i, p. 350.

[3] April 11; see also *Albany Gazette*, March 20, 1820.

[4] *N. Y. Spectator*, April 25, 1820.

[5] *E. g. The People's Ticket, For Governor DeWitt Clinton*, etc., pamphlet (Waterloo, N. Y., 1820), pp. 7, 11. Undoubtedly written under the influence of Elisha Williams, the founder of Waterloo.

[6] To Sol. Van Rensselaer, June 20, 1820, Mrs. Bonney's *Legacy*, vol. i, pp. 341-342.

[7] J. McKinstry, quoted in S. W. Williams, *The Family of Williams*, p. 143.

deed, they evidenced but little self-denial in taking office at
the hands of the Republicans. William A. Duer was made
a regent and then judge, when the Democratic party came
to power;[1] Hugh Maxwell was made district attorney for
New York. George Tibbits and Barent Gardenier carefully
negotiated terms,[2] while Gulian C. Verplanck, John A. King
and others were elected to the legislature.[3]

To all attacks the editors of the *American* responded
with full vigor. Elisha Williams, T. J. Oakley and J. R.
Van Rensselaer were riddled with what piercing epithets
ingenuity could furnish,[4] but their largest ammunition
was reserved for Judge Van Ness, an officer of greatest
dignity among the Swiss. Throughout 1819 they branded
him as an unjust judge devoted chiefly to the damning of
his enemies, truckling to the powerful, and always ready to
be purchased.[5] In May they spoke of an impending revela-
tion. " Like the sword of Damocles," said they, with stagey
mystery, " it hangs over you, and but a hair sustains it; it
will fall at a proper time; till then we bid you a temporary
farewell; ' we shall meet again at Philippi.' " [6] The long-
heralded exposure came at the last of January, 1820. It was
then charged that Van Ness, with Williams and J. R. Van
Rensselaer, had accepted a huge bribe in 1812 for their
support and influence in chartering the Bank of America.

[1] Mr. Van Buren to R. King, Feb. 2, 1820, *King Correspondence*;
John Duer to Mr. Van Buren, March 27, 1819, and Van Buren to
Joseph C. Yates, Dec. 10, 1822, Van Buren Mss.

[2] Van Buren to George Tibbits, Oct., 1820, and B. Gardenier to Van
Buren, Jan. 20, 1821, Van Buren Mss.

[3] *N. Y. Civil List*, 1881, pp. 304-305.

[4] *E. g.*, March 6, 10, 13, April 17, 28, May 12, 15, July 17, 1819.

[5] March 24, 27, 31, April 14, 24, 28, July 24, 1819.

[6] May 15, 1819. There were other hints as to what was coming, as
for example in notes to the *Bucktail Bards* and to *Pilgrims of Hope*.

The allegation was now direct and could not be ignored.[1] The Bucktails seized upon it and General Root, their leader in the legislature, proposed a formal inquiry, which in spite of protests from Van Ness and fellow Federalists, was provided.

Judge Hammond, who was then a member of the legislature, who later served two terms in Congress and made numerous visits to the English House of Commons, maintains that the debate upon this question surpassed any that he heard in those more famous halls.[2] It was developed in Elisha Williams' deposition that his own enthusiasm for the charter had been stimulated by an offer of a very advantageous loan to his bank in Hudson, but when war became more certain a higher interest rate had been requested. President Oliver Wolcott, of the Bank of America, for this consideration then offered Williams twenty thousand dollars, but the arrangement was contingent upon two good sureties being found to secure the loan. J. R. Van Rensselaer consented to be one, provided he was given five thousand dollars of the money paid to Williams. Judge Van Ness agreed to be the other, but with him there was no knowledge of the details of the contract or any word of compensation until about a year after the charter had been granted, when Williams insisted upon paying him a similar five thousand. The judge, then,

[1] Suggestions toward an investigation had been made by Alexander Hamilton as long before as March 9, 1819, see *Albany Advertiser,* March 10, 1819.

[2] *N. Y. Commercial Advertiser*, Feb. 4, 1820. Root claimed " public fame " sufficient to warrant such procedure, citing the case of Judge Chase. The Clintonian Federalists realizing that the inquiry was inevitable insisted only upon a committee large enough to insure them proper representation. Van Ness replied to the charge, in *Albany Advertiser*, Jan. 29.

[3] *Political History*, vol. i, pp. 522-523.

in his efforts for the charter, despite all charges by the Bucktails, had been innocent of any hope of personal reward.[1] On Williams' evidence he was finally acquitted, but the imputations were not soon forgotten, and his power in the state was much impaired.[2] Williams and Van Rensselaer by their own admissions lost much of their prestige, and the Columbia Junto did not again essay to play a leading rôle in politics.[3] Another testimony had been given that the political leaders of the aristocracy were not above the temptation to enlarge their fortunes.

With these leaders gone, Federalists could no longer, in any sense, be said to have a party organization in New York. Although in some districts like that of Albany the designation was retained, the members of the fallen party, like the other opponents of the Democratic organization, were known as Conservatives or, more frequently, Clintonians. Henceforth, until he yielded to Van Buren and abandoned Adams, Clinton could command the votes of most " old Federalists," but hardly the same enthusiastic loyalty that had been vouchsafed to Hamilton and Jay, true representatives of their interests and their class.

[1] *N. Y. Assembly Journal,* 1820, p. 833; Hammond, vol. i, pp. 520-521, note; F. Ellis, *History of Columbia County,* pp. 91, 177-178. Before the arrangement in Hudson was completed, a fourth beneficiary had been added, T. P. Grosvenor, Williams' brother-in-law and debtor; J. A. Hamilton, *Reminiscences,* pp. 48-53.

[2] Dr. Jeremiah Van Rensselaer to Sol. Van Rensselaer, March 1, 1820, Mrs. Bonney's *Legacy,* vol. i, p. 345.

[3] J. A. Hamilton, in his *Reminiscences,* p. 54, of course exaggerates Van Ness' humiliation.

CHAPTER VIII

PROPERTY OR PEOPLE?

IT was a favorite tenet of the Jeffersonian philosophy that no law should outlast twenty years without revision. Change is so normal in the modern world, that in any fundamental compact which elaborates the duties and the rights of man within the state, there is luck as well as foresight in the choice of words which will suffice more than a single generation. The constitution which gentlemen like Jay, Livingston and Morris had drawn up in 1777 to meet the needs of freeholders within the Hudson valley, did not content the workmen in the cities,[1] who after 1812 increased in number, or the farmers of the western counties who had taken up their holdings under mortgages withholding title until final payment.

In the three decades that followed the first census, the state of New York quadrupled in population—grew greater by a million — but more than four-fifths of this gain had come in lands that had been lately wrested from the Iroquois.[2] Enterprising towns, like Rochester and Buffalo,

[1] The workmen had been dissatisfied from the first; see the petition of " Mechanicks in Union" given by C. S. Lobinger, *The People's Law* (N. Y., 1909), pp. 156-161.

[2] See tables in H. L. Young, "A Study of the Constitutional Convention of New York State in 1821" (unpublished, but filed in the library of Yale University). This dissertation (Yale, 1910) is valuable in its analysis of the social forces behind the parties in the convention. The earlier chapters setting forth the conditions of settlement are especially interesting. *Cf.* O. Turner, *History of the Phelps and Gorham Purchase* (Rochester, 1851), and J. H. Hotchkin, *History of Western New York* (N. Y., 1848), chaps. i and ii.

already challenged cities of the east for rank in trade and industry. Settling evenly from north to south, the counties west of Seneca Lake could boast a hundred to each two mile square, while the middle region, centering in Oneida, was now more than half as thickly peopled as the old colonial counties on the Hudson. Only in the Adirondack country were there less than ten to a square mile. Since the second war with England, ever growing numbers had taken up the westward march; the traveler Bradbury reported in 1816 that wagons carrying the household goods of emigrants passed across Cayuga Bridge throughout the snowless months at the rate of four or five a day.[1]

The sudden creation of prosperous towns, and highly cultivated farms in the center of those forests, in whose solitudes, within a very few years, the Indian hunter pursued his game [remarked another Englishman], appears rather more like enchantment than the slow result of progressive efforts with which in the old world savage nature has been subdued.[2]

The city of New York had grown, chiefly in the " mechanic wards," [3] from thirty thousand to four times that number. It was a new people who, in the last years of the second decade of the nineteenth century, demanded a revision of the constitution framed some forty years before.

There was one reform upon which all disinterested men agreed. The men who framed the first state constitution had engaged upon a war of protest against tyranny, which throughout the colonies had had its agency in the executive. A governor was an object of suspicion, and the common-

----

[1] J. Bradbury, *Travels in the Interior of America* (second edition, London, 1819), p. 318. His informant stated that more than fifteen hundred had passed within the last eighteen months.

[2] Adam Hodgson, *Letters from North America* (London, 1824), vol. i, pp. 337-340.

[3] J. Macauley, *Natural, Statistical and Civil History of New York*, vol. ii, p. 89.

wealth would yield him power only with a niggard hand. He must not be allowed to fill the public service with his minions, and in consequence the power to name subordinate officers of state was entrusted to a Council of Appointment. By 1818 this body, chosen by the assembly, always on the strictest party lines, dispensed some fifteen thousand offices worth in fees and salaries more than a million dollars.[1]

> "Before its witchery, of late,
>   Our proudest politicians trembled,
> When the five Heads that ruled the State
>   Around the Council-board assembled."[2]

Often obscure men, raised to transient power by a chance majority in the assembly and flattered by a horde of office-seekers, they met behind closed doors and voted usually without a record of the ayes and noes.[3] "If the ingenuity of man," the governor admitted in a later message, "had been exercised to organize the appointing power in such a way as to produce continued intrigue and commotion in the state, none could have been devised with more effect than the present arrangement."[4]

To appreciate the standards of the public service under this régime, one must review the private correspondence of

[1] Governor Clinton's message of 1820, *Messages from the Governors,* vol. ii, p. 1019, and Carter, Stone and Gould, *Report of the Proceedings and Debates of the Convention of 1821* (Albany, 1821), p. 297. The record compiled by Messrs. Wm. L. Stone, of the *N. Y. Commercial Advertiser,* and N. H. Carter, of the *Albany Advertiser,* with the help of the stenographer Gould, is more complete than that by L. H. Clarke, published in Albany in the same year. Although Stone and Carter were strongly Federalist in politics, there was no criticism of partisanship against their work. Their edition will henceforth be cited as *Debates.*

[2] Fitz-Greene Halleck, *Writings* (N. Y., 1869), p. 323.

[3] J. D. Hammond, *Political History,* vol. i, pp. 468-470. Judge Hammond was a member of the council in 1818.

[4] *Messages,* vol. ii, p. 1043. He assigned this as the chief cause of the peculiarly malignant rivalry of parties in New York.

the members of the council. Special competence seemed the last consideration to be urged for an appointment; applicants were usually presented on the ground of party loyalty, though indigence and bodily affliction were oftentimes remarked to touch those councillors of " philanthropick views." " Please pardon the liberty I have taken," wrote one applicant; " my poverty is the only apology I can offer for it "; others asked for help against the coming of the sheriff.[1] Candidates for town and county offices, of course unknown in Albany, were recommended, or, in fact, appointed by local party leaders entirely without responsibility. This system cried loud for reform. The politicians with some reluctance joined in the demand, but neither Clinton nor Van Buren desired that the credit for improvement should go to his opponent.

In February, 1818, Ogden Edwards of the Tammany Society introduced a resolution in the legislature calling for a constitutional convention to provide a new arrangement for appointment.[2] Governor Clinton, hoping to control the council soon to be selected, against the advice of prudent friends refused to sanction this proposal.[3] General Root,

---

[1] B. Whiting to P. G. Childs, Feb. 24, 1822, and W. B. Jones to same, Jan. 10, 1822; see also letter from J. B. Pierce, Feb. 5, 1822, S. Beardsley and others, Feb. 27, 1822 (Childs Mss.), and numerous entries in the Clinton Mss. " As I have no business and cannot get anything of employ here, although I would be willing to do any labour to make an honest living for my family—but find I cannot make a living here and am obliged to spend what little I have, I have reluctantly undertaken to write you to acquaint you that a number of my friends in the county of Albany induce me to apply for the sheriff's office. . . ." G. G. Van Zandt to John Tayler, Dec. 18, 1818, Tayler Mss.

[2] A similar proposal had been made in 1811; *cf.* C. Z. Lincoln, *Constitutional History*, vol. i, p. 615.

[3] *N. Y. Evening Post*, Feb. 2, March 2, 1818; Hammond, *Political History*, vol. i, p. 469. Some Clintonians anxious to forestall the Bucktails were ardently urging reform; *e. g.*, C. G. Haines, *An Appeal* (pamphlet in N. Y. Public Library), and letter from same to Clinton, no date, Misc. Papers, Clinton Mss.

nothing daunted by rebuff, then moved further to revise
the fundamental law by amendments to abolish the Council
of Revision and to extend the right of suffrage.[1] Committees of correspondence in the towns and villages urged
on the movement; orators and editors reflected and increased the popular enthusiasm.[2] Clinton, silent for a year,
finally recommended a convention to consider the appointing power, but the proposition was rejected; the Bucktails
must have more.[3]

For many months the sachems in New York had hesitated in the matter of the suffrage; to qualify the landless
in that city would be to enlarge the influence of immigrants
from Ireland, and they well knew that Clinton had been
popular among that class.[4] But that politician, agile as he
was, could not safely ride two horses; he now leaned so
heavily upon his Federalist support that he could scarcely
hope to keep his hold upon the poor. The Tammany men
believed that they might win these forces to their standard
by taking up their cause, while, if they proceeded with
caution, they need not fear to lose the prosperous mechanics
and shop-keepers.[5]

The re-election of the governor in the spring of 1820
made it clear to all his numerous foes that his influence

---

[1] *N. Y. Evening Post*, April 1, 1818.

[2] *Albany Advertiser*, June 23, 1819; *N. Y. Spectator*, June 25, 1819.

[3] They demanded a thorough-going general reform, which Clintonians
in the legislature for a time successfully opposed. *N. Y. Commercial
Advertiser*, Jan. 26, 1820.

[4] G. Myers, *History of Tammany Hall*, pp. 67-68; *National Advocate*,
May 10, 1817.

[5] In this they were not disappointed; " after 1821, the Irish member-
bership and influence had become dominant, if the cordial toasts to
Ireland's sons and the popularity of St. Patrick, who well-nigh supplanted Columbus as a patron, may be ascribed to genuine sentiments."
E. P. Kilroe, *St. Tammany, etc.*, p. 145.

must be destroyed by some far-reaching means.[1] Already the " high-minded " *American* had come out for a general convention; now a meeting was convened in Tammany Hall and the policy determined. In September of that year the *National Advocate* spoke for the society, and the Democratic press throughout the state echoed with a cry for wide extension of the franchise.[2] When the legislature met in November to choose electors who would vote for James Monroe, the governor mildly recommended a convention for particular reforms, but the opposite party, in control, put through a bill providing for immediate election of the delegates with no limit as to powers.[3]

Clinton and the Federalists foresaw that a convention of some sort must be called; the next device of their defensive tactics had to be postponement. If they could but delay the project for a year or two, the census of 1820 might be made the basis of apportionment of the delegates, and this would weight the influence of western counties where Clinton, as the protagonist in the movement for the Grand Canal, could count on much support. In the elections which would intervene their party might be able to win back the legislature and the Council of Appointment. In case their prestige could be thus enhanced the bill might finally be drawn to protect those features of the old law which were

---

[1] " They feel their defeat to the pith of their bones and the core of their hearts, but are recovering from their discovery and hope to revolutionize everything. . . . They talk of dividing counties—calling a State convention—extending the right of suffrage—abolishing the Council of Appointment—districting the State for Senators anew—and many other schemes." C. G. Haines to Clinton, May 29, 1820, Clinton Mss.

[2] *N. Y. American*, March 13, 1819; *National Advocate*, Sept. 13, 1820: *N. Y. Evening Post*, Nov. 2, 1820.

[3] *N. Y. Evening Post*, Nov. 13, 14, 1820, and *N. Y. American*, Nov. 20, 1820.

so esteemed by men of property.[1] Most of all they feared to lose the Council of Revision which the Democrats had destined for extinction.

This body, made up of all the judges of the supreme court, the chancellor and the governor, had long been hated as the guardian of all old Federalist principles. While Chancellor Kent, Chief Justice Ambrose Spencer, Jonas Platt and William W. Van Ness, as a majority, could veto any law, democracy might well complain. To save their power for a season the council determined now to use it, and with Clinton's acquiescence the Federalist judges refused their indispensable assent to the convention bill. It was necessary, they declared, that the people should cast ballots to decide whether a convention should be called.[2] This objection, fantastic as it was, for no honest man could doubt the people's will, had in their eyes the merit of delaying the inevitable day of death. In their statement it was suggested, likewise, that the bill await the coming census.

This was not the first time that the judges had denied a popular demand. In 1809 they had disallowed a bill for setting off new districts in the state; in 1812 they had refused permission for enlargement of the court (by a Democratic Council of Appointment). They had checked the "war-hawks" in their drastic measures for conscription and the treatment of deserters. They had extended their

---

[1] "I am in favor of a Convention properly and fairly called, but not for one got up precipitately for bad purposes, under bad auspices, and with a view to shake society to its foundations in order to sustain bad men." Clinton to Henry Post, Nov. 25, 1820, in J. Bigelow, "DeWitt Clinton as a Politician," in *Harpers' Magazine*, vol. 1, p. 414.

[2] Judges Platt and Van Ness found it expedient to be absent; consequently to defeat the Republicans, Yates and Woodworth, Clinton was obliged to join the chancellor and the chief justice, and thus unmistakeably display his colors. The objections are set forth in A. B. Street, *The Council of Revision*, pp. 450 *et seq.* Clinton was no doubt anxious to prevent, if he could, a convention with general power.

protection to the negro allies of the Federalists.[1]   The council's temporary victory in 1820 but nerved the Democrats to fiercer resolution.   Not only must the council be abolished, but every one of these aristocrats in ermine must be driven from the bench.

The Federalist newspapers reopened the whole controversy.   The Council of Appointment only, they declared, should be discussed,[2] and addresses were prepared by the conservatives throughout the state.   " Our constitution was framed by wise and patriotic men," said one written in Poughkeepsie, and it maintained " that no alterations ought to be made, except such as experience had made absolutely necessary, that no wild plans of innovation ought to be indulged, [and] that party spirit ought not to be suffered to intrude." [3]   John C. Spencer rose in the assembly to present a measure of delay, but, for the first time in a score of years, the house refused to listen to the reading of a bill.[4] Michael Ulshoeffer, of the Tammany Society, reported on the action of the Council of Revision, in which he showed how inconsistent were some members in this matter of preliminary reference to the people; but to speed the process of convention their principle was granted and a plebiscite of all who had paid taxes or performed some service to the state was decreed for February, 1821.[5]   The Clintonians,

[1] A. B. Street, *The Council of Revision*, pp. 362-364.

[2] *Albany Statesman*, quoted in the *Albany Argus*, Jan. 2, 1821.

[3] E. Platt, *History of Poughkeepsie*, pp. 97-98, 310.   It is interesting to see the name of Morgan Lewis next to that of James Emott among the signers.

[4] He was joined in this movement by western men like Myron Holley and Samuel M. Hopkins, *N. Y. Commercial Advertiser*, Jan. 13, 1821.

[5] Ulshoeffer's long speech may be read in A. B. Street, *op. cit.*, pp. 455-476; see also *N. Y. Evening Post*, Jan. 13, 15, 17, 18, 1820.   All free males over twenty-one, who paid taxes or served in the militia or in work upon the highways, were given the vote for this election.

to save appearances, were thus obliged to vote in favor. A convention was demanded at the polls by a majority of more than seventy-four thousand votes.[1]

The campaign for delegates revealed how hopeless was the cause of the conservatives. The adherents of the governor assumed a tone of high disinterested patriotism and attempted, where they could, to have the nominations made without regard to party.[2] Where this stratagem was not availing, they took the name of Independents.[3] Matthew Clarkson, Nicholas Fish, Samuel Jones, Cadwallader D. Colden, John Wells and William North went to defeat in New York city, and Stephen Van Rensselaer, Ambrose Spencer, James Kent and Abraham Van Vechten to victory in Albany—all as "Independent Republicans"![4] Only in Columbia, a county where the "syren song of French equality" had never yet beguiled the freemen, could the proud old name of Federalist be safely flaunted in the press and on the platform.[5] Here the leaders warned against the passion for experiment and novelty that so marked the times. "Fluctuation," they averred, "in any system of government is a calamity."[6]

But the Democratic papers pressed the issue of the suf-

[1] *N. Y. Evening Post*, May 1, 5, 1821.

[2] *N. Y. Commercial Advertiser*, June 18, 1821; *National Advocate*, May 15, 1821; *Batavia Times* in *Albany Argus*, June 8, 1821.

[3] *Albany Argus*, May 18, 1821.

[4] *Ibid.*, May 29, June 18, 1821; *N. Y. Commercial Advertiser*, June 20, 1821.

[5] *Hudson Whig*, June 18-23, 1821. In Rensselaer County, also, the name was used (*Plattsburgh Republican*, in *Argus*, April 10, 1821), but here the ticket was unsuccessful. In Dutchess County a circular bore the name but it was sent out secretly. *Dutchess Observer* quoted in *Argus*, May 29, 1821.

[6] Address quoted in *N. Y. Commercial Advertiser*, June 18, 1821.

frage to the front. " Publicola," in his essays in the *Argus*, defined the faith on this important question.[1]

Why [inquired the official spokesman of the party] should the men who have had the good fortune to inherit property from their ancestors enjoy greater privileges than those honest and industrious citizens who earn their daily bread by the sweat of their brow? . . . As honest poverty is no disgrace, it ought to form no obstacle to the full enjoyment of our political rights.[2]

But this free talk of universal suffrage stirred up unnecessary opposition, thought Van Buren, and " apprehension that the rights of property would not be sufficiently guaranteed." Selecting the Patroon as the most important landlord in the state, he vouched to him through Rufus King, their common friend, that such was not the program of the Democratic leaders. Extension there would be, but not transcending all restriction.[3] Thus reassured, the Patroon had voted for holding a convention, a circumstance which now each party tried to use to its advantage.[4] Some hoped

[1] " Plain Thoughts on the Extension of the Suffrage," beginning May 29, 1821.

[2] *Albany Argus*, April 24, 1821.

[3] " The extent of his political influence furnishes a strong temptation to Mr. Clinton & his desperate followers to infuse into his mind the strongest apprehension. . . . I have observed with much regret that those efforts have been in some degree successful, and am very anxious that Mr. V. R. should be undeceived in this particular, & knowing your friendship for him and his respect for you, I hope you will embrace the opportunity presented by his visit to Washington to converse freely with him on the subject." Van Buren to King, Jan. 14, 1821, *King Correspondence*. Note Van Buren's text in enlisting King's aid ostensibly to circumvent the dishonest Clinton. Before the letter is ended he virtually asks King to try to make the Patroon a Bucktail. Van Buren's own caution with respect to universal suffrage is illustrated by a toast which he proposed, July 4, 1821: " The elective franchise; existing restrictions having proved to be as impolitic as they are unjust, it is the office of wisdom to correct what experience condemns." G. Bancroft, *Martin Van Buren* (N. Y., 1889), p. 67.

[4] *Hudson Whig*, quoted in the *Albany Argus*, May 25, 1821.

a compromise might be developed in the deliberations; the returns of the election, however, showed how meagre was the prospect of concession. The personal adherents of Mr. Clinton elected but three delegates and their Federalist colleagues but thirteen, while the Democrats with one hundred and ten could carry their reforms to whatever lengths they might desire.[1] There were many who now pledged " The Elective Franchise—The birth-right of every free citizen, to the enjoyment of which the law of nature and of nature's God entitles him." [2]

The convention, meeting on the twenty-eighth of August in the assembly chamber of the capitol, proceeded to elect the " Farmer's Boy," Daniel D. Tompkins, now second officer of the United States, as its president. Escorted to his high seat opposite the doors, he could regard with satisfaction a body whose " towering majority represented the interests, feelings and views of the friends of democratic government." [3] In the end seat on his right was Colonel Samuel Young, whom Tompkins in the late war had rewarded with a place upon his military staff in recognition

[1] The distribution of the Federalists and Clintonians elected was as follows: Westchester, 1 out of 3; Oneida and Oswego, 3 out of 5; Montgomery, 3 out of 5; Albany, 4; Columbia, 4; Schenectady, 1 out of 2. *National Advocate*, July 10, Nov. 16, 1821. The proportion of Federalists to Clintonian-Republican delegates was probably the same as that throughout the governor's supporters. " We felt that we were a mere handful of men dependent on the federalists for political existence, . . . but I confess I thought the federalists regarded us as an incumbrance upon them; or rather somewhat as the rich man regards his poor relations who have been cast upon his charity, and whom he feels in honor bound to maintain, although the expenditure for that maintenance goes to diminish an estate which he has a right exclusively to enjoy." Hammond, *op. cit.*, vol. i, p. 534.

[2] *Albany Argus*, July 6, 1821.

[3] The words of P. R. Livingston, *Debates*, p. 50. A large picture of the assembly chamber of the capitol of 1808 may be seen in P. A. Chadbourne, *The Public Service of the State of New York* (Boston, 1882).

of his trenchant satire on the Federalist sedition. In the prime of middle life and inclined to radical reform, he could be counted on for telling blows against all institutions that did not square with the new philosophy.[1] Two seats behind, there sat another stout reformer, General Erastus Root, much more renowned upon the field of politics as one who sought to break a lance with every champion of privilege. Forty-nine years old, he stood as yet unscarred by the dissipation that injured his good fame,[2] and ready to take up the battle in his gay and taunting way for all revolutionary theories of politics or of religion.[3] He would have graced the Mountain thirty years before in France. Behind him in the rear row and a little toward the center sat the third of this extraordinary trio, Peter R. Livingston, a philosophical democrat of considerable wealth, harsh and forceful in his utterance and steadfast in allegiance to the principles of Thomas Jefferson. These led the mad-cap democrats of whom Van Buren said, " They thought nothing wise that was not violent." [4]

In front of Livingston was Ogden Edwards, who represented Tammany and the influences of restrained reform; with him the president, in looking through the rows, might naturally associate the venerable Rufus King, sitting but a few feet distant, now the moderate spokesman of " high-minded men," and then turn swiftly to the left side of the house where, in an aisle seat near the front, sat King's colleague in the national Senate, Martin Van Buren, blond and smilingly benignant, whose soft words and subtle indirec-

[1] G. B. Anderson, *History of Saratoga County* (Boston, 1899), p. 510.

[2] M. M. Bagg, *Pioneers of Utica; N. Y. Commercial Advertiser*, Aug. 7, 12, Oct. 15, 1824; Misc. Papers, Clinton Mss.; see testimony in Root *vs.* Editors, *N. Y. American, Albany Argus*, Aug. 25, 1824, June 19, July 4, 1826, *etc.*

[3] *N. Y. Commercial Advertiser*, Nov. 2, 1821.

[4] Van Buren to J. A. King, Oct. 28, 1821, *King Correspondence.*

tions had charmed his way to leadership. No obstruction of the enemy would escape his notice, yet no vain enthusiasm would betray him to intemperance in speech. Doubtless Tompkins realized that here, and not in the stately presidential chair, sat the man whose prudent hand would hold the Democratic delegates in firm control.[1]

It was, as the president well understood, a delicate business. Although reforms might seem predestined by the June election, they would not be accomplished without meeting from the Federalists an opposition no less grim than skilful. As he looked upon that little company—less than a score of men, " commissioned," as a great historian has said, " to impede the onward movement to a government of all men by all men " [2]—he might well have suffered some misgivings; for their talent was far more impressive than their numbers. In knowledge of the law, of history and institutions, they outmatched any group of equal size that could be furnished by the Democrats.

Midway down the right aisle sat the chancellor in the ripeness of his eight and fifty years, short in stature, but so vivacious and alert that in all the room there was no man less likely to be overlooked. He had come resolved to dedicate his learning in political science, gleaned from tireless study of the ancient classics and the works of modern commentators, to the task of saving for posterity those principles and practices which had been tried and sanctified by time. The aptest pupil of Judge Egbert Benson, he had surpassed his master in determination to defend the old dominion of the wise and good.[3] Three seats from Kent,

[1] Van Buren's county, Columbia, being inveterately Federalist, he was elected by Otsego County.

[2] George Bancroft, *Martin Van Buren*, p. 66.

[3] J. Duer, *Discourse on James Kent* (N. Y., 1847), pp. 9, 73: Wm. Kent, *Memoir of Chancellor Kent* (Boston, 1898), p. 178.

looking toward the left, there sat the Patroon, younger by
two years than the chancellor and more fine of feature.
He was not accounted eloquent, but his probity and public
spirit, universally acknowledged, might so weight his simple
word as to outbalance the most labored rhetoric of many
an opponent.

In that same row, exactly in the center, towered the form
of Chief Justice Ambrose Spencer, master of the law, somewhat supercilious in his deportment, and suspicious of
political reformers. No man in the assemblage could cow
this august person, and none there could convince him of
an error in his logic; no man of small experience might
safely challenge him in a debate. Sitting at his right was
his associate upon the bench, William W. Van Ness, whose
brilliant, penetrating mind and ready wit have been remarked by readers of these pages; and beside Van Ness, his
old friend, Elisha Williams, still " the most celebrated jury
lawyer in the state and probably in the Union," inventive in
conception, rounded and graceful in utterance, fertile and
copious in diction, though now smirched in reputation and
discounted by many of his hearers as too clever to be great.[1]
Some seats further to the left side of the house was J. R.
Van Rensselaer, their colleague from Columbia County, and
on his right Judge Platt, then fifty-two years old, pious,
honest and intensely serious in his effort to check the ravages
of demagogues.[2] The president might turn away from such
a row where clustered his opponents, but looking toward
the rear he could not fail to recognize the formidable Abra-

---

[1] On Williams, besides the references in chapters ii and vii, *supra*, see
Levi Beardsley, *Reminiscences*, pp. 208-210; W. A. Butler, *Martin Van
Buren* (N. Y., 1862), pp. 10-11. The *Albany Argus*, May 25, 1821, had
paid its respects to Williams " of bonus memory."

[2] W. J. Bacon, *Early Bar of Oneida* (Utica, 1876) ; J. D. Hammond,
Political History, vol. i, p. 279.

ham Van Vechten, " full of solid learning and solid sense," but with all the horror of a good Low Dutchman at any innovations whatsoever.[1] What has been said of conservatives in general, might be observed of him, that " his pigmy hope that life would some day become somewhat better, punily shivered by the side of his gigantic conviction that it might be infinitely worse." [2]

There remained two men of some importance in that little group, Ezekiel Bacon and Peter A. Jay, both born in Independence year. The former has not figured in our narrative; he had entered politics a quarter of a century before in Berkshire County, Massachusetts, as an ardent Jeffersonian, and had once regaled the citizens of Williamstown with so strong an exposition of his doctrine that the college students burned a copy of his speech as a public condemnation.[3] He had served as an official under President Madison, but upon removing to the Mohawk valley, being a man of enterprise, like Gideon Granger, he had struck hands with Clinton, planned to build a packet boat to ply the Grand Canal, and stood out against all policies of its opponents.[4] As to Peter A. Jay, he was an able father's able son, inheriting his political philosophy together with his personal integrity, and called his adversaries quite impartially " the Jacobins," though certain radicals were singled out for

[1] D. D. Barnard, *Discourse on Ambrose Spencer*, p. 24, and J. D. Hammond, vol. i, p. 456.

[2] Morley's *Voltaire*.

[3] E. Bacon, *An Oration . . . at Williamstown*, July 4, 1799 (in N. Y. Public Library) ; F. B. Dexter, *Yale Annals, 1794.*

[4] He was a noted lawyer, and though in debate " not ready or fluent, speaking extemporaneously with embarrassment," when he prepared his discourse " he brought ample knowledge, sound logic and clear intelligible statement." M. M. Bagg, *Pioneers of Utica*, pp. 395-396; J. Q. Adams in H. Adams, *New England Federalism*, pp. 243, 301, *etc.;* E. Bacon, *Recollections of Fifty Years Since* (Utica, 1843).

special scorn.[1] Such a galaxy of talent might well cause the president to wonder if in numbers there was strength. As frequently in history, the conservatives had learning on their side.[2]

It was not surprising that the Council of Revision was marked as first to feel the power of the people. The judiciary, it was said, must be separated from the other branches, to supply the check demanded by the perfect scheme of Montesquieu;[3] the old council had acted *ultra vires* when they vetoed laws as inexpedient; they should have passed on constitutionality alone.[4] But the chief reproach was founded on their Federalism and their arrogant attempts "to stay the march of progress." Opposition to the will of the majority was hopeless, and the council was abolished without a dissenting vote, though not without a protest.[5]

Judge Platt reviewed its long career of more than forty years with the eloquence of deep sincerity: it had served the right without regard to censure or applause; its members had shared the frailties of nature, but " when," said he, " I see the axe laid to the root of the tree which our fathers planted, watered and defended, a tree which yielded much good and wholesome fruit, and has long afforded us shade and shelter, I confess, sir, that I witness its destruction with no ordinary emotions."[6] The chief justice and

---

[1] P. A. Jay to John Jay, Oct. 10, 28, Nov. 15, 1821, *Jay Correspondence.* His home town had been carried nearly three to one for "no convention." *Debates*, p. 679.

[2] In number they were about one-eighth of the whole, yet in Stone's list of those who took important parts in the deliberations their names make up a third. *Debates*, p. 690.

[3] Tallmadge, *Debates*, p. 86.

[4] Tompkins, p. 71.

[5] Sept. 4, p. 47.

[6] He warned his colleagues against those who applied their remedies with so little wisdom that "in curing one evil, they create others," pp. 53, 56. Van Vechten also pronounced a eulogium, p. 83; see for Kent and Spencer, pp. 87, 89.

the chancellor also voiced a sad resentment at the slurs the
council had received, but these threnodies were listened to
with some impatience; the council was despatched, there
let the matter rest. Some, like the president, would hide
the wound by saying that it had been done in kindness to
relieve the judges of these disagreeable distractions,[1] but
this was but a thin deception, for, as everybody knew, the
judges were themselves to be cashiered. Others of a
franker mind declared the action but a just rebuke to those
whose characters deserved it.[2]

The moderate committee, which had discussed this question, advised that the negative be given to the governor,
whose veto could be overridden by two-thirds of the legislature. Peter R. Livingston was for a mere majority.
"Keep the power with the people," he adjured his hearers,
"they will not abuse it." It appeared to him, he said, agreeing here with Bentham, "like a solecism to say that the
people would assent to measures which would be injurious
to their own good."[3] In this he had the aid of General
Root, who observed that

in all ages, where free governments have existed, those have
been found who would transfer to the minister or executive
more power than was expedient for the good of the people.
This tends to perpetuate the aristocracy which exists in the
constitution, and instead of being fostered, should receive the
firm opposition of those who advocate the cause of the people.[4]

Tompkins, the president, believed that no negative was
necessary. "There can be no use for a veto on the passing

[1] Tompkins, p. 81.

[2] Root, quoted p. 85.

[3] He desired a majority of those elected to the houses, not merely of
those present. Twenty-six were finally mustered for his plan, pp. 52, 59,
116.

[4] Pages 62-63, 100.

of laws," said he, " but to prevent violations of the constitution; and for this purpose your judicial tribunals are
sufficient." [1]   The conservatives, on the other hand, would
use the power especially in questions of expediency, but
admitted that the plan of the committee was adequate if the
governor were given a sufficient length of term to make
him independent.[2]   Van Buren's " moderate men " were
satisfied and the measure was adopted.

The " people's adversaries " [3] thus shorn of power, the
convention took notice of the Council of Appointment.
No one could say a word in its behalf.   The wanton partisanship of the Democratic council which had sat throughout that very spring had disgusted friend and foe alike; it
was abolished by unanimous vote.[4]   Following the spirit of
the times, the committee on this subject recommended that
militia officers, except the very highest, be elected by the
men-in-arms.   The Federalist press might argue that popular elections would destroy authority; [5] but what authority, it was replied, should be obeyed that did not spring

---

[1] Page 79.   Tompkins afterward proposed a separate council made up
of lawyers but not judges.   This proposition received no attention.

[2] Bacon, p. 120.   Mr. Dodge, of Montgomery County, took a middle
position; he proposed that the governor's veto be overridden by a two-
thirds majority on constitutional objections, or by a majority on those
of expediency, p. 116.   On Federalist opinion on the governorship, see
Spencer, pp. 47, 115; Van Vechten, p. 85; Kent, pp. 63-64.

[3] The characterization of the judges is John Duer's, the "high-
minded" delegate from Orange County, p. 105.

[4] B. F. Butler to Jesse Hoyt, Feb. 20, 1821, W. L. Mackenzie, *Life and
Times of Martin Van Buren* (Boston, 1846), p. 167; *N. Y. Commercial
Advertiser*, March 31, 1821.   It had swept out of office several men
who had survived many changes, like Solomon Van Rensselaer, adjutant general, Archibald McIntyre, comptroller, and Gideon Hawley,
superintendent of schools; for recorder of Hudson it appointed a man
recently convicted of a felony.   *Hudson Whig* quoted in *N. Y. Commercial Advertiser*, April 13, 1821.

[5] *N. Y. Commercial Advertiser*, Sept. 22, 1821.

directly from the people? Many civil servants likewise were to be elective, and cities were to choose their own; [1] certain officers of the state administration, like the treasurer, the comptroller and the secretary of state, were now to be selected by the legislature, while others, including all the judges, were to be appointed by the governor with the confirmation of the senate. [2]

This last proposal introduced the question of the governor's term. As a minority party, the Federalists had favored the provisions for home rule, but their theory of politics led them to desire the executive to be as independent as was possible in his vetoes and appointments. Spencer, Kent, Jay, Platt, Williams, the Van Rensselaers, Van Vechten and Van Ness, together with obscurer fellow-partisans, [3] voted for continuation of the three-year term. At the opposite extreme were Colonel Young, General Root, P. R. Livingston, and others who desired annual elections, following that " great principle of republicanism—rotation in office." [4] Again Van Buren, always anxious that the party

---

[1] P. A. Jay, however, warned the delegates of the danger of mob rule in cities, p. 391.

[2] The full proposal, which was in general adopted, may be found in *Debates*, pp. 160-161. 3,643 civil officers were left to be appointed as the legislature might direct, p. 297; only 453, out of the 14,943, were now left to the central appointing power, p. 162. The common councils of the cities were to select mayors, *etc.*, except in New York, where a special electoral council was provided. General Root's amendment providing for election of non-commissioned officers is found on pp. 300-301. Justices of the peace were to be appointed by local councils of officials. Election of judges, however humble, was not yet considered safe.

[3] *E. g.*, Elbert Jones of Queens, Rhinelander of Montgomery, and Van Horne of Herkimer. The last named, though not originally listed with the Federalists, voted almost consistently with the leaders, thus making their certain voting strength seventeen. The vote on the governor's term is on page 148.

[4] Pages 148, 158, 547, 550; on one vote the single-year men were successful, p. 177.

enterprise be not wrecked upon excess, came forward with a compromise:

As we have vastly increased the power of the governor, a strong desire is manifested to abridge his term, and in this sentiment I concur. But how abridge it? We wish the people to have the opportunity of testing their governor's conduct, not by feelings of temporary excitement, but by that sober second thought which is never wrong. Can that be effected if you abridge the term to one year? No, sir. . . . I hope the blank will be filled with two years.[1]

This provision was accepted by a scant majority.[2] P. R. Livingston, however, was still determined that the executive be curbed whenever possible. Still following Mr. Jefferson, he wanted it laid down in the constitution that the governor should address the legislature only by a written message— "the speech," said he, was " a relic of monarchy, founded in the love of pomp and splendour and show." [3]

But it was the question of the suffrage which elicited the great debates of the convention; it was held to be of more than local or temporary interest.

Mr. Chairman [solemnly remarked a member], the friends of rational liberty in all quarters of the globe have their eyes fastened upon independent, confederated America; in the front rank of this confederacy, in the most conspicuous station, stands the great state of New-York, and the result of this convention will decide her fate, perhaps forever.[4]

The discussion soon struck to the fundaments of politics

[1] Pages 147-148.

[2] Pages 551-552.

[3] Pages 173-174. General Root's motion that the right of proroguing the legislature be taken from the governor, was narrowly carried, pp. 135-136.

[4] E. Williams, p. 247.

and government. Problems of sovereignty, original and delegated, such as puzzled Plato and Rousseau, were reviewed at length by men who cherished theories as far apart as the poles. There were those to whom democracy was something more than a form of government—a destiny of perfection, indeed, proceeding " as uniformly and majestically as the laws of being and as certain as the decrees of eternity." [1] To these, man's right to rule himself appeared so natural and evident that instances and syllogisms seemed but impertinence. But there were others, whose fortunes we have traced for two decades, who declared this was a novelty to be received, if at all, after closest scrutiny. Their philosophy we may with profit here examine before the argument is broached.

More than a century before, John Locke had stated it as well as it is likely to be stated. When one reads the solemn judgment of that essayist that " the great and chief end, therefore, of men's uniting into commonwealths, and putting themselves under government, is the preservation of their property," [2] one has the kernel of their thought. They believed that government by the wise and good was better than by the ignorant and vicious. But a larger proportion of the wise and good was to be found among the men of property than among society at large. Those who had it by inheritance had therefore more of leisure to acquire wisdom and were immune from passions of cupidity, while those who earned it did so by the exercise of those abilities which might be serviceable to the state; *ergo*, government by the part was preferable to government by the whole. It might be urged that experience did not bear out this logic, that many men of property were indolent and unproductive.

---

[1] This is the phrase of Bancroft, *History of the United States*, American Revolution, vol. i, p. 1.

[2] *Essay on Civil Government*, chap. ix, par. 124.

But to this it could be answered that these, though numerous, yet were exceptional; it was better that some unworthy should enjoy the special privilege than to deny it to a class which as a whole would use it beneficially for all. In America estates were not entailed; [1] there was plenty of cheap land which able men could easily acquire to use for the benefit of themselves and of society. Possession of property might here, certainly, be called a proper test of talent. Locke had said that men possessed of property must have despotic power over those who were not; [2] Elisha Williams now explained that those in whose hands sovereignty was lodged were trustees for the rest. [3]

It was natural that such men should be satisfied with the old constitution which limited the franchise to those who held the requisite amount of real estate or rented tenements of a considerable value. The old system had worked well, they said; the state had grown in business and in population. [4] Was it, then, the " part of wisdom to substitute experiment for experience?" [5] Gentlemen were warned of " doubtful and dangerous innovations." [6] The delegates were there " convened to *amend* their constitution, not to *destroy* it." [7] Talk of social evolution showed a shallow understanding; " man has been," said J. R. Van Rensselaer, " and probably always will be, subject to the same passions and feelings, and under like circumstances the future will

---

[1] Entails were prohibited in New York by an act of July 12, 1782; see *Consolidated Laws of the State of New York* (1909), vol. iv, pp. 3379-3380.

[2] *Works* (edition of 1751), vol. ii, p. 217.

[3] *Debates*, p. 248.

[4] Kent, pp. 219-220.

[5] Van Vechten, p. 230.

[6] Van Ness, p. 266.

[7] E. Williams, p. 252.

strongly resemble the past." [1]   But the majority were not impressed with these sententious sayings.

The committee on the suffrage reported for a very liberal extension; every white male citizen twenty-one years old, who had resided for six months within his district and paid taxes, or on assessment had performed some work upon the public roads, or had been enrolled in the militia, might vote for any officer elected by the people.[2]   The chairman, Mr. Sanford, declared that this was what the electors had expected. The chancellor, however, voiced the protest of conservatives:

I cannot but think the considerate men who have studied the history of republics, or are read in lessons of experience, must look with concern upon our apparent disposition to vibrate from a well-balanced government to the extremes of democratic doctrines. Such a proposition as that contained in the report, at the distance of ten years past, would have struck the public mind with astonishment and terror.[3]

Yet everyone was well aware that much had happened in the last ten years. Chief Justice Spencer, hoping that a remnant might be saved, now offered an amendment providing that only those possessed " in law or equity " of a two-hundred-and-fifty-dollar freehold could vote for senators.[4] It was upon this proposition that the principal debate developed.

Although the holding specified was left unchanged, there was one element of novelty. Since the canal had actually

[1] Page 364. Compare J. R. Van Rensselaer's opinion of the French Revolution (p. 363) with that of P. R. Livingston (p. 224).

[2] Page 134. This is substantially the provision finally adopted, except that the new constitution required one year's residence within the state, p. 661.

[3] Page 219.

[4] Page 215.

been begun, the west was turning rapidly to Clinton; but
under the old constitution many in those counties were not
yet enfranchised. It was the custom there, especially upon
the Holland patent and the Pulteney estate, to purchase
land on long-term contracts wherein the title did not pass
until the entire obligation was fulfilled.[1] Spencer now proposed that all holders who had invested the required sum in
payments or improvements should be allowed the special
senatorial franchise: " they ought thus to vote, because
they represent portions of the soil, and because they have
that attachment to the preservation of all the rights incident
to real estate." [2]   Other Federalists came forward to praise
this feature of the proposition. Elisha Williams declared
his own opinion that this injustice might have easily been
remedied by a declaratory act of the legislature bringing
such equity within the definition of a freehold; but this sensible suggestion, he complained, had been unheeded by the
Democrats, who would not stop with moderate reform.
He believed that thirty thousand votes for the convention
were referable to this cause alone.[3]   Judge Van Ness could
not agree with Williams as to what might have been accom-

---

[1] This was true, likewise, in the case of settlers on the Hornby and
the McComb purchases. The contrast between east and west in this
respect was striking. In some counties of the older region, like Rockland, Richmond and Suffolk, the majority of adult males who would
be qualified by the committee, possessed a two-hundred-and-fifty-dollar
freehold, and in most others, such as Westchester, Ulster, Washington,
Saratoga, Montgomery, Schoharie, etc., the number was nearly half.
In the west, however, the ratio was low. A few counties may serve as
examples: Allegany, 325: 1797; Chautauqua, 629: 2266; Niagara, 276:
1421; Genesee, 1813: 6517; Livingston, 1086: 2420; Monroe, 1737: 3972;
Ontario, 4399: 7055, etc. In the state there were 100,839 who could
qualify under Spencer's provision and 159,262, admitted by the committee, who could not; see tables in *Albany Argus*, August 12, 1826.

[2] Spencer, p. 216.

[3] Page 247 *et seq.*

plished by a simple law, but he heartily approved the amendment which was now proposed, and pointed out how beneficial it would likewise be to those respectable citizens who held the almost endless leaseholds of Trinity Church in New York city.[1] Spencer pressed his measure as in accordance with the purpose of the founders of the state. The senate had been entrusted with the guardianship of property. Why have two houses if they did not represent two diverse interests?[2]

To the defense of the amendment in general there came an able champion. James Kent had fought throughout his whole career for the rights of the individual as distinguished from those of the people.[3] He could never forget that he was " Lord Chancellor," commissioned to uphold true legal principles however unpopular they might be.[4] Yet in all that company, when he arose, there was not one to sneer. " When I recall the suspicions that then prevailed," wrote a delegate in later life, " and the censure in which others were then involved, I doubt whether a similar case is to be found in history." [5] No abstract can do justice to the grave and solemn eloquence of the chancellor as he pleaded for the old order on that September afternoon in Albany. It demands quotation in long passages, for so complete and so sincere was his defense that it touched on nearly every point that later was developed. " It was," as a member afterwards remarked, " an elegant epitaph of the old constitution." [6]

[1] Pages 265-266. These would be qualified by the "improvement" provision.

[2] Pages 216-217.

[3] Wm. Kent, *Memoir of Chancellor Kent*, p. 180.

[4] Kent to Platt, Oct. 29, 1821, *ibid.*, p. 182.

[5] John Duer, *Discourses on James Kent*, p. 69. He said that the case of Sir Matthew Hale possibly afforded a parallel.

[6] Cramer, p. 237.

Dare we flatter ourselves [he asked, when he had painted the calamities democracy had brought upon republics of the old world] that we are a peculiar people, who can run the career of history exempted from the passions which have disturbed and corrupted the rest of mankind? . . . The men of no property, together with crowds of dependents connected with the great manufacturing and commercial establishments, and the motley and indefinable population of the crowded ports, may, perhaps, at some future day, under skilful management, predominate in the assembly, and yet we should be perfectly safe if no laws could pass without the free consent of the owners of the soil. That security we at present enjoy, and it is that security which I wish to retain. The apprehended danger from the experiment of universal suffrage applied to the whole legislative department, is no dream of the imagination. It is too mighty an excitement for the moral condition of men to endure. The tendency of universal suffrage is to jeopardize the rights of property and the principles of liberty. There is a constant tendency in human society—and the history of every age proves it—there is a constant tendency in the poor to covet and to share the plunder of the rich; in the debtor to relax or avoid the obligations of contract; in the majority to tyrannize over the minority, and trample down their rights; in the indolent and profligate to cast the whole burthen of society upon the industrious and virtuous; and there is a tendency in ambitious and wicked men to inflame those combustible materials. . . . New-York is destined to be the future London of America, and in less than a century that city, with the operation of universal suffrage, and under skilful management, will govern this state. . . .

Society is an institution for the protection of property as well as life, and the individual who contributes only one cent to the common stock ought not to have the same power and influence in directing the property concerns of the partnership as he who contributes his thousands. He will not have the same inducements to care and diligence and fidelity. His inducements and his temptation would be to divide the whole capital

upon the principles of agrarian law. . . . We have to appre-
hend the oppression of minorities, and a disposition to encroach
upon private right — to disturb chartered privilege — and to
weaken, degrade and overawe the administration of justice
[especially since the delegates are] already determined to withdraw the watchful eye of the judicial department from the passage of the laws. . . . We stand, therefore, on the brink of
fate, on the very edge of a precipice. If we let go our present
hold on the senate, we commit our proudest hopes and our
most precious interests to the waves.[1]

The sentiment that property rights must have particular
protection was general among the Federalists. " Life and
liberty are common to all," said Abraham Van Vechten,
" but the possession of property is not. Hence the owners
of property have rights which, in relation to those who are
destitute, are separate and exclusive." [2] Those should have
a greater voice who have a greater stake in society, remarked Elisha Williams.[3]

They are the patrons of your institutions, civil and religious
[added Judge Van Ness]. They build your churches, and defend your altars and the country of which they are the protec-
tors. They erect your school-houses, found and support your
colleges and seminaries of learning, establish and maintain
your charitable institutions, and construct your roads and
canals.[4]

The chancellor declared again that life and liberty were seldom jeopardized; it was property which must be walled

[1] Pages 219-222.

[2] Page 226. "Does it follow thence that a man who has only life and
liberty to be protected, needs protection to the same extent with one
who in addition to life and liberty possesses both real and personal
property?", p. 227.

[3] Page 252.

[4] Page 267.

against assault.[1] General J. R. Van Rensselaer conjured up the gloomy prospect of agrarian laws; the poor had always coveted the goods of the more prosperous, and if they had the power they would gratify their criminal desires by a general distribution.[2]

When Democrats declared that the franchise was *demanded* by the poor, Federalists became impatient. If they demanded thus what was not theirs, how long, if it were granted, before they would demand the property itself. " Sir," said one, " if it be just and safe to confer this right, it should be bestowed gratuitously; nothing should be yielded to this menacing demand." [3] " Are we jealous of property," inquired the chief justice, " that we should leave it unprotected?" [4] He was assured by Mr. Radcliffe of New York that gentlemen need not despair about the helplessness of property; it would always carry with it an influence quite sufficient for its own protection; to give it artificial aid was to make it dangerous to other rights. If property must specially be represented, why should there not be two votes for the holder of five hundred dollars' worth, and twenty for a man who held five thousand? Society was not a money partnership, but an association of all men for the common good.[5]

But it was freehold property for which the Federalists felt a singular concern. They assured their colleagues that here there was no danger of accumulation. Few estates would grow in size; on the contrary, by the operation of the laws for regulating descents, the holdings would grow smaller. Landowners, representing the most stable and im-

[1] Page 286.
[2] Page 363.
[3] E. Williams, p. 254.
[4] Page 218.
[5] Page 225.

portant interest, should have a distinct weight in one branch of the legislature. Personal property might elude the eye, but theirs was always there, imperishable and immovable and ready for the tax assessor. It was because of this that they were called upon to pay a disproportionate amount into the public treasury.[1] When danger threatened, the landless man might swing his pack upon his shoulder and disappear from sight, but the yeoman and his son must stay, abide the draft and defend the state.[2] They were the least dispensable of all society; prosperity was bottomed upon agriculture; its surplus products made possible the arts and the professions. Then, too, that ancient superstition that honesty is the peculiar quality of countrymen, was exploited in well-rounded periods. " Their habits, sympathies and endowments," said the chancellor, " necessarily inspire them with a correct spirit of freedom and justice; they are the safest guardians of property and the laws." [3] To hear the Federalists, remarked a Democrat, one would conclude that all rights were safe if thirty-two men from the sacred turf sat gravely in the senate. Knowledge or intelligence would not be needed if only they were chosen by the well-to-do landholders.[4]

In another argument of the conservatives can be seen a faint reflection of the rivalries in England; as in 1832 and 1867,[5] in the parliamentary contests, so here, was heard the warning that to qualify the landless would so increase the influence of selfish manufacturers as to create an aristocracy far more pernicious than that which it would supplant Single men employed in factories, and boarding here and there, would have the ballot; but, observed the chief justice,

[1] Van Vechten, pp. 226-231.

[2] E. Williams, p. 253.

[3] Page 220.

[4] Cramer, pp. 238-239.

[5] E. g., *Annual Register*, 1867, remarks of Lord Cecil. p. 90.

under the pretence of giving the right to them, we in fact give it to those who employ, clothe and feed them. I appeal to this convention whether they do not believe that a man who employs twenty, thirty or fifty of these persons, if on the approach of an election he tells them he wishes them to vote for this or that candidate — whether they will not feel themselves obliged to comply with his wishes. That man who holds in his hands the subsistence of another will always be able to control his will.[1]

It was the influence of this kind of property so concentrated, said J. R. Van Rensselaer (though one suspects him of a want of candor), that he dreaded as a source of evil to the state.[2]

Mr. Van Buren, on the other hand, declared the old arrangement most unjust; when three-eighths of all the property in the state was personal, why should real estate be so specially favored?[3] In rejoinder, Judge Van Ness affected to regard with dread the battening money interest. The lines were to be drawn as distinctly as between the sexes; witness how parties were aligning on the question of the tariff.[4] Commerce and agriculture, he declared, must intrench themselves against the manufacturers.[5] As for

---

[1] Spencer, pp. 196-197.

[2] Page 363. General Root scoffed at such apprehension: a manufactory was real estate and was assessed as such for taxes; its owner had his interest in land and buildings, p. 223.

[3] Page 257. "Large portions of the people, many of them persons of great intelligence and possessed of personal property . . . were, so far as regarded the choice of these officers, practically disfranchised." B. F. Butler, *Discourse on the Constitutional History of New York* (read before the N. Y. Historical Society, N. Y., 1847); G. Bancroft, *Martin Van Buren*, pp. 86-87. Van Buren was not averse to a small property qualification, *Debates*, p. 258.

[4] Page 267.

[5] He was answered that if personalty were made a basis for the franchise, it would benefit the commercial interests, allies of the agricultural as much as the manufacturing. Buel, p. 243.

the holders of securities and money whom Van Buren had commiserated, let them invest two hundred and fifty dollars in real estate, said Abraham Van Vechten;[1] nineteen-twentieths of them had done so already, added Van Ness.[2] But J. R. Van Rensselaer finally admitted that these interests in New York state were not so disparate, and proposed a new amendment in which personal estate of the required sum was mentioned as alternative to freeholds held " in law or equity."[3]

The Federalists found in the freehold qualification a stimulus to thrift.

If you *bestow* on the idle and profligate [asked Elisha Williams] the privileges which should be purchased only by industry, frugality and character, will they ever be at the trouble and pains to *earn* those privileges? No, sir; and the prodigal waste of this incalculable privilege — this attribute of sovereignty—like indiscriminate and misguided charity, will multiply the evils which it professes to remedy.[4]

It might be said, remarked Ezekiel Bacon, that property itself conferred upon its owner no talents and no virtue, but in this country, at least, " it was a safe and general rule that industry and good habits did, in almost every instance, conduct the man who practiced them to some moderate share of property."[5] As to those who failed, said Judge Van Ness,

[1] Page 227.

[2] Page 266.

[3] Pages 359-360. Van Buren confronted his opponents with a dilemma : " If they [the dependents of the manufacturers] were so influenced, they would be enlisted on the same side, which it is the object of the amendment to promote, on the side of property. If not—if they were independent of the influence of their employers, they would be safe depositories of the right," p. 263.

[4] Pages 253-254.

[5] Page 285.

by an irreversible decree of Providence, it was pronounced that " the poor ye have always with you." . . . But what was the character of the poor? Generally speaking, vice and poverty go hand in hand. Penury and want almost invariably follow in the train of idleness, prodigality, intemperance and sensuality. Was it not wise to discountenance these vices by encouraging their opposite virtues? [1]

General Stephen Van Rensselaer, the Patroon, would not insist upon two hundred and fifty dollars as a minimum for qualification, but the payment of some money tax he thought quite indispensable; [2] he opposed the clauses which would qualify under road work and militia duty. Yet, responded Dr. Ross of Genesee, this proposition would leave unenfranchised many, if not most, of those the general had commanded in the War of 1812. [3] In that trying day, who came forward into service? inquired ex-Governor Tompkins. " Not the priesthood—not the men of wealth—not the speculators: the former were preaching sedition, and the latter decrying the credit of the government to fatten on its spoil." [4] Mr. Sharpe explained the importance of the militia clause to the constituencies in the city of New York, where there was no public work upon the highways. [5] General Root, always disconcerting in his frankness, revealed a cogent reason for the Democrats' support: " They will not vote for peace-party men, but for men who are willing to bare their breasts to the arms of the enemy. . . . Not one in ten of these young militiamen would vote for a haughty, proud, domineering aristocrat; they will vote for *repub-*

[1] Page 268.
[2] Pages 183, 290.
[3] Page 182.
[4] Page 231; see also Cramer, p. 239.
[5] Page 359.

licans." [1] " The cry of aristocracy has been too frequently
addressed to this convention," complained Abraham Van
Vechten.[2] " I trust the old names of Aristocrat and Republican will persist," was General Root's response, " till
the former shall be bound to the footstool of the latter." [3]

Recurring in the Federalist argument, like the motif in a
fugue, came the fear of New York city. While among the
citizens of that community, they said, there were some who
had as much of virtue and more of wealth, talent, refinement and acquirements in literature than any corresponding number elsewhere in the state, there were also those
more ignorant, more wretched, more vicious and miserable,
the instruments of any demagogue.[4] And these by immigration would increase out of all proportion.

They have fled from oppression, if you please [said Elisha
Williams], and have habitually regarded sovereignty and tyranny as identified; they are men whose wants, if not whose
vices, have sent them from other states and countries to seek
bread by service if not by plunder; whose means and habits,
whose best kind of ambition, and only sort of industry, all forbid their purchasing in the country and tilling the soil.[5]

The chancellor and Judge Van Ness reviewed the city's
growth and contributed their dismal prophecies.[6] Van
Vechten said that the average of the senatorial votes under
the old system in the wards of the metropolis was some
four thousand; the proposed extension would increase this

[1] Page 360.

[2] Page 372.

[3] L. H. Clarke, *Report of the Debates*, p. 185. Practically all the conservatives voted against the militia clause, pp. 369, 554, and the highway clause, p. 554.

[4] J. R. Van Rensselaer, p. 362.

[5] E. Williams, p. 252.

[6] Pages 221, 268.

by more than threefold.[1]   The agricultural interest would be outweighed quite completely.

But the radicals were warmed by their own oratory and, impatient of obstruction by these voluble conservatives, they soon advanced to more extreme positions.   General Root brought in an amendment which would qualify the sons of those provided for by the committee,[2] and Melanchthon Wheeler, a member from Washington County, moved further to include all citizens who had been three years within the state, and one within the town in which they registered.[3]   In late September such confusion came to mark the voting that no man could prophesy what the next hour would bring forth.   Certain Federalists like Williams, Bacon and Van Ness fanned the flame that had been kindled by the root-and-branch Republicans, and apparently were willing to participate in any movement that would run to such absurdity as to disgust the voters at the polls with the whole constitution.[4]   " That gentleman," said Van Buren of Elisha Williams, " expressed a belief a few days ago that we had already made the constitution worse, and he probably would not regret to see us go so far as to have all the amendments rejected by the people." [5]

One day the convention voted to withdraw the franchise from those who merely worked upon the highways,[6] and

[1] Page 228. Of the adult males in New York city, 3,881 had a two-hundred-and-fifty-dollar freehold and 16,044 who would be qualified under the new provision had not. *Albany Argus*, Aug. 12, 1826.

[2] Page 202.

[3] Page 276.

[4] Pages 275, 278, 284, *etc.*

[5] Page 275.

[6] This was by a vote of 68 to 48, p. 283. General Tallmadge had previously introduced an amendment to qualify those who labored on the highway only if they also rented a $5-a-year tenement. It was not carried.

the next day voted by about the same majority to make it universal, on the plan of Mr. Wheeler.[1] The moderate Democrats expostulated at this "phrenzy." Van Buren said this would increase the electorate of New York city to twenty-five thousand men, enough to outweigh several counties in the west.[2] Ogden Edwards thought the time would come when those who now opposed demands for universal suffrage would be remembered as the benefactors of the state.[3] "High-minded men," like Duer, now counselled once again the exclusion of militia-men;[4] their organ, the *American*, warned solemnly against excess.[5] In a Sunday recess, Rufus King, weary of it all, wrote to his son Charles that "should the right of suffrage be made universal, the foundation of the constitution will be such as to impair my safe reliance on the superstructure."[6] Edwards finally was able to carry through a resolution to commit the whole question of the suffrage to a select committee, who might formulate an article more consonant with the deliberate judgment of the delegates.[7]

The committee brought in a proposal very similar to that

[1] This vote was 63 to 55, p. 287. Dr. Young, *op. cit.*, discovers that the country members carried this provision against those from the towns.

[2] Page 367. J. R. Van Rensselaer said this would increase the comparative influence of New York city to six times what it had been in 1814, p. 369.

[3] Page 282.

[4] Pages 271-272. General Root retorted: "It has been said that my amendment would not suit the sober-minded part of the community; I suspect it is more obnoxious to the high-minded than to the sober-minded," p. 272.

[5] *N. Y. American*, Oct. 20, 1821.

[6] Sept. 30, 1821, *King Correspondence*, vol. vi, pp. 405-406. He wrote Charles on Oct. 15, "I often wish that I had not come hither," *ibid.*, pp. 416-417.

[7] Pages 288-289.

which had originally been offered.[1] It was fought through, clause by clause, and finally carried by a vote of nearly two to one.[2] It was hoped by the conservatives that some privilege might still be kept for property by a requirement, which was once accepted by the convention,[3] that candidates for senator must have a thousand dollars' worth of real estate, but even this small relic of the old restrictions was denied them, for, by a resolution of Colonel Young, a simple freehold was at last declared sufficient.[4] The conservatives had again been routed.

Any who had stood between the people and their will were to feel the heavy hand of the convention. The judges who had made up the old Council of Revision must know their masters' scorn. Early in the discussion of the judiciary the plan for their dismissal was revealed.[5] Appointments to the supreme bench had run until the judge was sixty years of age; under this arrangement the eldest, the chief justice, had four more years to serve, while the youngest, Judge Van Ness, would not be superseded until 1836.[6] The chancellor would retire the following year, likewise at the age of sixty, unless considering his unique capacity the convention would extend the age of service in the equity court. But, in spite of Federalist appeals, there was apparently but little disposition so to do. In judicial duties he

[1] Page 329.

[2] Page 378. The final passage, in perfected language, came Oct. 29, p. 588.

[3] Page 582. Van Buren and his friends were not averse to this.

[4] Page 625.

[5] See discussion by Tompkins, p. 528, and Edwards, p. 534.

[6] The terms of the others would expire as follows: Yates, 1828; Woodworth, 1828; and Platt, 1829. C. Z. Lincoln, *Constitutional History*, vol. i, pp. 675-676. There was no injury to Woodworth and Yates when the judges were "constitutionalized out of office," as Woodworth was soon reappointed and Yates made governor.

was unassailable, admitted the "high-minded" Peter Jay Munro, but outside the court-room, retaining the prestige of his high office, he was a menace to the liberty and safety of the masses.[1] As to the other judges, a scheme was cunningly devised which provided for immediate retirement.[2]

It was in vain that Abraham Van Vechten protested that no man had understood that the convention had been called to turn out officers of government; a remedy was always ready for misconduct on the bench, in the process for impeachment. General Root responded that like other officers, if they merited the public confidence, they might expect a reappointment, and added with his scathing sarcasm: "The honorable chancellor has told you, and doubtless with truth, that he has no fear of an investigation. And if others have an equal security in the consciousness of rectitude, they are in no danger of being injured by the indignation of the people."[3] P. R. Livingston declared these Federalist judges had come into office by disgraceful coalition or by party treachery within the Council of Appointment; they had been well paid and had already had far more than they deserved.[4] The judges, on their own behalf, did what they could with dignity to stay the tide.[5] Henry Wheaton, a moderate from New York city, presented an amendment to protect the present judges, but it was voted down by the

[1] Page 615.

[2] Tompkins, p. 528; Edwards, p. 534.

[3] Pages 531-533.

[4] Page 520. Livingston's reference to coalition concerned the Quid council which had named Van Ness, and his reference to treason that of Robert Williams which had named Platt. Spencer had been appointed with the expectation that he would stay a Democrat.

[5] C. Z. Lincoln, *Constitutional History*, vol. i, p. 676. General Carpenter's amendment calling for an entirely new court was adopted, p. 624. This was said to have been suggested by Colonel Young and General Root, Hammond, vol. ii, p. 63. Some moderates, like Van Buren and Sanford, voted to retain the judges.

usual majority.[1] The Federalist party left high office in the state forever.

That some leaders were quite willing to exclude the remnant of that party from any influence in the legislature, is shown by a proposal of Van Buren. The Federalist majority in Columbia County would be sufficient to carry the third senate district as planned by the committee.[2] Van Buren moved to take Columbia away from Albany, Rensselaer, Greene, Schoharie and Schenectady, and attach it to the Democratic second district running down the Hudson River; and to take from this in compensation the safe and constant counties of Sullivan and Ulster, and transfer them to the third. A prompt remonstrance came from Elisha Williams (on whom Van Buren lavished no affection) : [3]

In the third district you have a Gerrymander. The monster will curl its tail on the mountains of Jersey—coil along the borders of Pennsylvania, wind its scaly and hideous carcass between the crooked lines of counties, and finally thrust his head into Bennington. Disguise it as you will, the object will be visible, and the people will understand it is to exclude federalism from every senatorial district.[4]

Van Ness presented an amendment to the prejudice of New York city, but both were soon defeated in the vote.[5]

Devices to humiliate the Federalists were scarcely needed; their favorite theories had been as thoroughly discredited as those of astral influence and the philosopher's stone. Al-

[1] Pages 621, 624.

[2] The new constitution increased the senate districts from four to eight.

[3] Page 264.

[4] Page 560. E. C. Griffith, in his *Rise and Development of the Gerrymander* (Chicago, 1907), pp. 56-61, discusses attempts at such redistricting in the first two decades of the century, but though he speaks of Bacon's proposal for single-member senatorial districts (Clarke edition of *Debates*, p. 213) he does not mention Van Buren's plan.

[5] Pages 560, 561.

though there was some carping at the constitution as not giving quite enough to popular control,[1] it was accepted at the polls by a majority of over thirty thousand.[2] So certain was the victory that many did not take the trouble to vote.[3]

The extension of the suffrage was not achieved by the eloquence of advocates; it came because it accorded with an American ideal. " From our cradles," said Judge Hammond, " we had been taught that a zealous support of equal rights and an extension of equal civil privileges to all was an evidence of our devotion to liberty and the true principles of a republican government." [4] The impulse was not wholly spent in the convention; four years later there were abolished what restrictions yet remained upon the manhood franchise.[5] No longer was there in New York a theory

---

[1] [Benjamin Romaine], *A Comparative View and Exhibition of Reasons opposed to the Adoption of the New Constitution, etc.*, by an Old Citizen (N. Y., 1822). This pamphlet speaks of " the princely prerogatives of our future governors," due to the appointing power (p. 5), checked only by an " aristocratic senate" without reference to the popular branch (p. 17). This critic may, be suspected, however, as he was a Clintonian, and therefore quite naturally opposed to this " child of the Republican Party." *Cf.* the following from P. A. Jay to John Jay, Nov. 15, 1821 (*Jay Correspondence*, vol. iv, p. 455) : " There seems to be a passion for universal suffrage pervading the Union. There remain only two States in which a qualification in respect of property is retained. When those who possess no property shall be more numerous than those who have it, the consequence of this alteration will, I fear, be severely felt."

[2] J. D. Hammond, *Political History*, vol. ii, p. 94.

[3] The *N. Y. Commercial Advertiser* on Jan. 21, 1822, apologized for having forgotten to print the news of the election when it had been received four days before. Albany, Columbia, Greene, Montgomery, Schenectady, Ulster and Queens counties voted against the constitution. In Ontario and Rensselaer the vote was very close; see *N. Y. Spectator*, Feb. 19, 1822.

[4] *Political History*, vol. ii, p. 49.

[5] *Albany Argus*, Jan. 21, 1825. Under this provision all adult males

that any class of men was wiser, abler or better than another in the public business. A political democracy had been established, that "perversion" of which Aristotle warned, "in which the mechanics and the hired laborers must needs be citizens." [1]   The ballot in the Jeffersonian opinion was a weapon of defense to protect the individual's rights; a decade must elapse before it was considered as an instrument of social progress. [2]   Yet to recognize and to define his rights, the young citizen must be enlightened by a systematic course of training, for Jefferson's whole theory rested on a "strong faith in the teachableness of the great mass of the people." [3]   The framers of the constitution realized that democracy and education must make their progress hand in hand, and their generation in New York showed an unexampled interest in the common school. [4]

---

who had lived a year in the state and six months in the county could vote. See *infra*, ch. ix. Of course, the qualifications concerning age and residence were retained. In 1833 the constitution was amended so that qualified voters in New York eity might vote for mayor, and in 1839 this provision was extended to all other cities of the state; C. Z. Lincoln, *Constitutional History*, vol. ii, p. 3.

[1] "Hence there is a particular polity, *viz.*, the extreme Democracy, in which the mechanics and the hired laborers must needs be citizens, while there are others in which it is impossible, *e. g.*, wherever there exists the polity commonly called aristocratical, in which virtue and desert constitute the sole claim to the honors of state; for it is impossible to live the life of a mechanic or laborer and at the same time devote oneself to the practice of virtue." Aristotle's *Politics*, J. C. Walden translation (London, 1905), p. 114.

[2] C. E. Merriam, *American Political Theories* (N. Y., 1903), chap. iv; E. D. Adams, *The Power of Ideals in American History* (New Haven, 1913), chap. v.

[3] John Fiske, "Thomas Jefferson, Conservative Reformer," *Essays, Historical and Literary* (N. Y., 1902), p. 145 *et seq.*

[4] Remarks of Mr. Buel, *Debates*, p. 242. "Obviously a society to which stratification into separate classes would be fatal, must see to it that intellectual opportunities are accessible on equable and easy terms. . . . Otherwise, they will be overwhelmed by changes in which they

They could fervently repeat the words of Danton: "Après le pain, l'éducation est le premier besoin du peuple."

are caught and whose significance or connections they do not perceive." John Dewey, *Democracy and Education* (N. Y., 1916), pp. 101-102. *Cf.* E. A. Fitzpatrick, *The Educational Views and Influence of DeWitt Clinton* (Teachers College, Columbia University, 1911).

NOTE ON THE NEGRO VOTE.—In an article entitled, "The Negro Vote in Old New York," *Political Science Quarterly*, vol. xxxii, no. 2, pp. 252-275, the present writer has presented the evidence which supports the following conclusions:

Slaves were introduced into the Hudson River region before Manhattan houses were a decade old. When the English took control a generation later the trade in "negears" was solicitously fostered by the government. They were scattered about in the houses of the aristocracy, who were Federalists, for the most part, in the early national period. Yet slave-holding did not pay, and was so expensive that Federalists themselves supported the Manumission Society, and finally by their party vote carried through a scheme of gradual emancipation. Their slaves, who had been well treated, stood by "the families" after freedom almost as faithfully as before; and as soon as any were qualified for the suffrage by owning $100 worth of property, they voted the Federalist assembly ticket. The mechanics had opposed emancipation, for they did not like to see the negro change his butler's coat for cap and jeans or his salver for a saw. The proportion of negroes in New York was then several times larger than now, and they were massed in doubtful wards in New York city and Brooklyn. In spite of all the Republicans could do, they actually decided the state election of 1813 in favor of the Federalist party. When in the convention of 1821 property qualifications were removed for whites by the Democratic-Republicans, a high qualification was retained for negroes, against the earnest protest of the Federalists led by Peter A. Jay. After this the negro vote was of less relative importance for a time, but it was steadily Clintonian, National Republican and Whig. In the preliminary discussion before the convention of 1846, Democratic papers and pamphleteers favored complete disfranchisement of the negroes, while the Whigs, as a whole, favored equal suffrage. The Whigs were almost unanimous, in the debates, against disfranchisement, but could not get equal suffrage provided for in the constitution, and had to be satisfied with a separate submission of this clause. A Democratic majority in the electorate defeated it. It was almost wholly a party question; abolitionist or free-soil sentiment had little or nothing to do with opinion

[*Note continued.*]

on negro suffrage. Tammany Hall, supported chiefly by mechanics, opposed any favors to the negroes, as they would attract others of that race to New York, and this would depress wages. The negroes voted Whig because of old loyalties and the fear of the mechanics. "For the last five or six years before I left New York," testified a witness in Iowa in 1851, in speaking of the negroes, "their votes were deposited sometimes for the third-party candidate, but most generally for the old Whig party." They were Whigs because their fathers had been Federalists. If there had never been a negro south of the Potomac, still the negro in New York would not have voted for the Democratic ticket.

CHAPTER IX

OLD COMRADES AND NEW BANNERS

THE sovereign people were exacting masters; they would not tolerate one souvenir of dynasts whom they had supplanted. Relics of prerogative, it mattered not how hoary their antiquity, were jealously resented by " the lordly mob of God-wise folk." After 1821, there being then no question as to the theory of government acceptable to New York state, the triumphant Democrats, like the Jacobins of 'ninety-three demanding heads, set out to purge the state of all those practices which might recall the old régime. The chief party contest of the legislature which soon followed, was on the question of the governor's speech. For a hundred and thirty years it had been customary for the executive to come in person to the legislature as soon as it was organized, a procedure which Clinton had recently defended as more deferential to the people's representatives than the sending of a message as had been proposed. On this the Democrats took issue with him, and refused to make the usual formal answer; these pomps and ceremonies they declared to be but " remnants of royalty," and won their point in a debate which exhausted almost an entire day and in bare abstract filled four columns of the *Argus*.[1]

The propriety of other old-time customs soon became the subject of discussion. The next year, Mr. Morss of New York city introduced a resolution, that the titles of

---

[1] *Albany Argus*, Jan. 15, 1822.

" his excellency," by which the governor was known, and
" honorable," bestowed on many officials of the state,
should " be discontinued and abolished, as incompatible
with the republican form and principles of the constitution." [1]   The resolution passed the assembly, but met derision in Clintonian newspapers. To the *Evening Post* it
seemed "degrading and ridiculous," [2] and Colonel Stone of
the *Commercial Advertiser* observed, in a sarcastic humor,
that equality would be extended soon to size and weight,
and in the interest of the new economy no one should grow
fat cheeks or double chin. [3]   But after some reflection the
legislators came to the conclusion that they had gone too
far, and within a week the precious titles were restored, to
the perennial delectation of humorists and foreign visitors. [4]
In February, 1823, the " high-minded " John A. King,
acting in the spirit of the time, attracted much attention
and support by a resolution in the senate to make the executive journal of that body a public record. [5]   The tendency
toward new ideals of popular control was plainly to be seen.

The vanquished Federalists realized the futility of any
protest; they had spoken all their mind in 1821, with
little more result than to intensify the prejudice against
them. Though some intransigents were never reconciled, [6]
most old-party men now joined with other followers of
Clinton as fully in accord with the new theory. For the

[1] *N. Y. Commercial Advertiser*, Jan. 13, 1823.

[2] *N. Y. Evening Post*, Jan. 18, 1823.

[3] *N. Y. Spectator*, Jan. 17, 1823. He had poked fun at the debate the
year before, see *N. Y. Commercial Advertiser*, Jan. 17, 1822.

[4] See the comment of Judge Hammond, *Political History*, vol. ii, p. 124.

[5] *N. Y. Senate Journal*, 1823, p. 129; J. A. King to R. King, Feb. 21,
1823, *King Correspondence; N. Y. American*, Feb. 24, March 3, 1823.

[6] See Wm. L. Stone, Jr., " Life and Writings of William Leete Stone,"
bound with Wm. L. Stone, Sr., *Life of Red Jacket* (N. Y., 1866), p. 25.

next few years in New York state, factions strove in their contentions each to prove itself more friendly to the people than its rival. We shall see conservatives assume the name of " People's Party " and demand of the reluctant Democrats the choice of the members of the electoral college by voters at the polls. " Resolved, That all power emanates from the People," ran a broadside issued by the leaders of Clintonians and Federalists, "and that they alone can safely be trusted with its exercise," [1] while another held that the doctrine " that the farther the appointing power was removed from the people the better," was opposed to all republican tradition. [2] In return, their enemies exhumed the past of Federalism. Its candidate in 1824 was scored as one who had vetoed the convention bill. [3] When, shortly after, a Senator of the United States was to be chosen, Silas Wright wrote Azariah C. Flagg: " Make a dash at Spencer in your paper for his conduct in the convention "; [4] it was important to remember that it was St. Ambrose who had argued for a landlord senate. [5]

To counteract the prestige of the People's Men, the Democrats in the spring of 1825 presented an amendment which provided for the popular election of justices of the peace and brushed aside the few restrictions on the general

---

[1] " Republican Fellow-Citizens of Albany," Dec. 23, 1823 (N. Y. P. L.). " Resolved, That the people, being the true source of power, are entitled to the enjoyment and exercise of that power in such a manner as they deem consistent with their interests and privileges," Broadside, "Albany County Convention . . . J. Alexander, Chairman," 1824 (N. Y. P. L.).

[2] Broadside, " Young Men's [Albany] County Convention," Oct. 18, 1824 (N. Y. P. L.). This same bill recommended DeWitt Clinton for governor and Stephen Van Rensselaer for senator.

[3] Broadside, " Calumny Refuted," 1824 (N. Y. P. L.).

[4] Feb. 1, 1825, Flagg Mss.

[5] Wright to Flagg, Jan. 18, 1825, *ibid.*

suffrage which had survived four years before.[1] These well-phrased resolutions introduced by Senator John Lefferts, though the work of Silas Wright (for " Brother Lefferts did not draw a long quill "),[2] were accorded a support almost unanimous, for few dared to vote against them, and, passed again in 1826, were then accepted at the polls. As when in 1822 it had been recalled by Democrats that Henry Huntington, named for lieutenant governor by the conservatives, had opposed extension of the right of suffrage,[3] so in 1826 Clintonians warned voters to beware of General Pitcher, a candidate for the same office, as he had stood against the election of the local justices.[4] In the arsenal of journalistic epithets, the word " aristocrat " was thought the deadliest of all, and when the contest grew most bitter it was hurled by either side against the other. New York state, as we have said, was now for all time committed to the doctrine of political democracy; this had ceased to be a question of debate. No leader could profess opinions such as those of Judge Platt sixteen years before; reputations were now searched as with a microscope to detect a trace of such a taint.

As the party of the landed aristocracy, the Federalists had been defeated and humiliated. Their name had such a

---

[1] Of course, a residential qualification was retained.

[2] Wright to Flagg, *loc. cit.*

[3] Broadside, " Falsehood Exposed " (N. Y. Historical Society).

[4] Broadside, " Republican Nomination [in Washington County] " (N. Y. Hist. Soc.). They also found some profit in berating Van Buren and his followers with respect to the electoral bill, and their organ, the *Albany Daily Advertiser*, printed editorials with the title-head, " The Aristocracy against the People " (*e. g.*, Oct. 20, 1826; *Albany Daily Advertiser, Extra*, Oct. 11, 1824; circular of *Albany Daily Advertiser* and *Albany Gazette*, 1824 (N. Y. P. L.). Van Buren was attacked in 1825 for having opposed the election of justices of the peace in 1821; see Broadside, " Caucus Mirror," Chenango Co., 1825 (N. Y. P. L.), and " Young Men's Convention," Coeymans, Oct. 14, 1825 (N. Y. P. L.).

woeful connotation that it was discarded. They declared their party lived in history alone, insinuating that they should now be enrolled as good Republicans, relieved from stigma and eligible to any office.[1] In the summer of 1822, the Clintonians by a general, though a tacit, understanding, for a time disbanded.[2] Its special enemies thus retiring from the field, the " high-minded " *American* joined in the opinion that the struggles in New York were at an end,[3] admitting that " the Federal party having no longer any ground of principle to stand on, has necessarily ceased to exist as a party." [4] The *Evening Post* and the *New York Gazette* declared that now the only contest was between the city and the country.[5]

But all this was far from grateful to the organizers of the Democratic party who had brought these things to pass. Were they, after years of planning and achievement, now to share their hard-earned fruits with those they had defeated? " This new-light political creed," scathingly remarked the *Argus*, " which pretends to disregard all political distinction, and to place all on the same footing, we regard as the offspring of the most detestable hypocrisy." [6] It had no patience with those smirking unctuous Federalists who prated of an era of good feeling. Let no one think that Federalism had passed away; the divisions in the body politics were not like village factions, formed in personal quarrels and dying in a year.

[1] *N. Y. Evening Post*, Nov. 2, 1822.

[2] J. D. Hammond, *Political History*, vol. ii, p. 91.

[3] M. Van Buren to R. King, Feb., 1822, *King Correspondence*.

[4] *N. Y. American*, Sept. 6, 1823.

[5] Quoted in the *Albany Argus*, Feb. 28, 1823.

[6] *Ibid.*, Jan. 18, 1822.

It is not so with the parties of which we speak. These, though they originate in single points of difference, take deeper root; they outlive the causes of their commencement, and those who constitute them are led to opposite sides upon all questions which may arise in the progress of public transactions. The classes of men of which they are composed, each alike, are bound together by a thousand affinities and antipathies; real or fancied persecutions rivet the bonds of union; the succession of generations renders them more enduring, and the transmission of sentiments and feelings of the father to the son is generally regular and unbroken. Notwithstanding the change of interests and of name, the same individuals and families have been found after the lapse of years, acting in concert on all questions of a public nature. Such has been the character and such the history of parties everywhere.[1]

The *Argus* in this editorial was not the first or last to set forth a philosophy of parties; yet why among the English-speaking peoples there should be two parties, apparently immortal, is a thorny problem which lies athwart the pathway even of the student of New York throughout the 'twenties. " The idea of an amalgamation of parties in a free state," said Judge Hammond, writing of an earlier condition, " is chimerical, and the notion that three parties can for any considerable time exist is ridiculous." [2] Long habit had played its part in enforcing this opinion. Englishmen had steadily developed an interest in their government some centuries before their continental neighbors; but soon after 1600 it became a question whether this interest should be kept and possibly increased, or should be wholly quashed by an officer of state who claimed to be above all human law. This question developed two important parties—the one, at least in name, standing for the country

[1] *Albany Argus*, Sept. 12, 1823.
[2] *Political History*, vol. i, p. 476.

and the diffusion of control, the other for the court and its prescriptive privileges — which with certain changes have persisted almost to today. Though some rivalries which strengthened this alignment were by their nature limited to England, the tradition of two parties was brought by colonists across the sea, was strengthened in the Revolution, when the voteless backwoodsmen and proletariat first tasted power, and was then transmitted to the nation, for a time to be deplored and then accepted as inevitable.[1]

These parties have endured while heroic leaders rose and fell. Antipathies so deep are only superficially explained by reference to the legal dialectics on a written constitution. The explanation frequently advanced, that they represent the cautious who rely on order and the bold who seek for liberty, conservatives who would not tamper with the major institutions — church, state, property and family — and reformers who see hope in change, has much to recommend it, yet the circumstances of the individual's position, whatever be his temperament, will oftentimes provide him with a secret bias. When property is not evenly distributed, it is the men who have the largest share who cherish a calm sense of legality, because as a minority they could not make appeal to force.[2] Yet with an open continent before them

[1] " In all free countries parties will exist; they necessarily arise from different views of public measures; and when confined within the bounds of moderation, they are calculated to awaken inquiry, to promote virtuous emulation, and to prevent the approaches of tyranny and oppression," *Address to the Republican Citizens of the State of New York* (pamphlet, Albany, 1813, N. Y. P. L.; supposed to have been written by DeWitt Clinton), p. 3. For a comment on the sectional character of party strife, see H. C. Hockett, *Western Influence on Political Parties to 1825*, Ohio State Univ. *Bulletin* (Columbus, 1917).

[2] That rich men were found in either party in the early nineteenth century, but that those whose property was in great plantations were, broadly speaking, in one party, along with the debt-burdened farmers, while those who held much personal estate were in the other, is the

the landed and commercial aristocracy had lost in relative importance and could not save their law in the face of the challenge of 1821. They must wait some years till, joining others in a reinvestment of their property, they found an economic issue in which their profit and the people's welfare seemed again to go together. Meanwhile as individuals they took up the name of those who had defeated them. It was, however, as Jefferson assured Van Buren, " an amalgamation of name but not of principle. Tories are tories still, by whatever name they may be called." [1] The Democratic leaders feared the Federalists bearing votes and were resolved to share with them no patronage.

An incident in 1822 contributed to keep alive this animosity. When the Albany post-office became vacant by a summary removal, Solomon Van Rensselaer promptly filed an application.[2] Tompkins, the Vice-President, and Senator Van Buren brought all their influence to bear to compass its rejection, solely on the ground that he had been a Federalist; but after grave discussion by the cabinet, the appointment was announced.[3] The conservative news-

thesis of C. A. Beard's, *Economic Origins of the Jeffersonian Democracy.* Of course many party men vote with economic interest sub-consciously apprehended, and a saving remnant in spite of it. As for the fact of there being parties at all, it is, perhaps, sufficiently accounted for in the natural combativeness of man.

[1] Jefferson to Van Buren, 1824, Jefferson's *Writings* (Ford edition), vol. x, p. 316.

[2] He had been turned out of his post as adjutant general the year before, was now in Congress and therefore had an advantage in proximity to the appointing power. His falling fortunes (for he belonged to a less wealthy branch of the family) would be repaired by the stipend of $2,000 and the patronage of $1,750. Solomon Van Rensselaer to the Patroon, Dec. 26, 1821, Mrs. Bonney's *Legacy*, vol. i, p. 369, and to De Witt Clinton, Nov. 22, 1824. Clinton Mss.

[3] " The principal charge against you, and I believe the only one, was that you were a Federalist, and opposed to what they called the Republican party " S. L. Gouverneur (Monroe's private secretary in 1822) to

papers were elated, but the Democratic officeholders gathered in Albany to protest.[1] " A more objectionable selection could hardly have been made," complained the *Argus*, " than that of General Van Rensselaer. He has always been a violent opposer of the republican party—republican men and republican measures have at all times been assailed by him, with the most bitter and acrimonious hostility." [2] A few days later the general's house was burned by some incendiaries.[3] Old party feeling had not passed away.

Though elections had been changed from April to November, the Democratic legislators met in caucus as was customary in the early spring, and fixed upon Judge Joseph Yates and General Root to head their ticket. Conditions being what they were, Clintonians withheld their chief from standing for a re-election, but did oppose Root for lieutenant governor, with Henry Huntington, a wealthy banker from Oneida County.[4] With no contest as to gov-

Solomon Van Rensselaer, March 23, 1839, Mrs. Bonney's *Legacy*, vol. ii, p. 110. Rufus King protested at first on the ground that it would interrupt the harmony of New York state, but after this statement he retired from the contest. *Cf.* R. King to R. J. Meigs, P. M. General, Jan. 3, 1822; to Charles King, Jan. 8, and Jan. 14, 1822; to Egbert Benson, Jan. 20, 1822; and W. A. Duer to R. King, Jan. 13, 1822, *King Correspondence*; D. D. Tompkins to Jonathan Thompson, Jan. 4, 1822, Mrs. Bonney's *Legacy*, vol. i, p. 373; Sol. Van Rensselaer to the Patroon, Dec. 26, 1821, *ibid.*, p. 370; and J. Q. Adams, *Memoir*, vol. v, p. 479. Judge Hammond, *Political History*, vol. ii, p. 96 *et seq.*, and Hugh Hastings, in his articles in the *N. Y. Commercial Advertiser*, Oct., 1883, scold King for his conduct, but in view of all the circumstances perhaps unfairly. Hastings, without mentioning his authority, says that the whole matter was quietly engineered by Clinton.

[1] *N. Y. Commercial Advertiser*, Jan. 10, 11, 15, 1822; *Albany Argus*, Jan. 15, 22, 1822.

[2] Jan. 15, 1822.

[3] *N. Y. Statesman*, February 20, 1822.

[4] *N. Y. Commercial Advertiser*, Oct. 26, 1822; J. D. Hammond, *Political History*, vol. ii, p. 231.

ernor, the campaign seemed to signalize the nadir of the
fortunes of conservatives, yet Huntington had more than
half as many votes as Root, scattered generally throughout
the state, and the old Federalist districts, as usual, sent
their opposition members to the legislature.[1] " The ship
and the crew are precisely the same that they were formerly," it was remarked, " with the same commander on
board; but without exhibiting any colours." [2] The new
governor, of a benevolent temper, sent a sapless message
to the legislature, intended to be soothing, and naïvely
nominated Jonas Platt and Ambrose Spencer as supreme
court judges, for confirmation by the senate.[3] They were,
of course, promptly and overwhelmingly rejected. The
governor must have had a genius for credulity to have
taken seriously the Federalist pronouncements as to amalgamation.[4] Because he had been unopposed it did not
mean the dawn of a millenium; it was fatuous to think
while Clinton lived that he would listlessly retire from the
field.[5]

[1] *Albany Argus*, Dec. 10, 1822; Solomon Southwick polled a few votes
for governor. *N. Y. Commercial Advertiser*, Nov. 7, 1822, Jan. 14,
1823; *N. Y. Evening Post*, Nov. 4, 7, 1822; *N. Y. Spectator*, Nov. 19,
1822; *Albany Argus*, Nov. 8, 12, 1822.

[2] *Albany Argus*, June 21, 1822. For a comment on the virulence of
party contests, *e. g.* in Canandaigua, where the *Ontario Messenger*
owned by J. C. Spencer, Granger, etc., disputed with the *Ontario
Repository*, see *N. Y. Commercial Advertiser*, Jan. 14, 1822.

[3] *Messages from the Governors*, vol. iii, p. 2; J. D. Hammond, *Political History*, vol. ii, p. 107; *N. Y. Evening Post*, Jan. 10, 1823.

[4] *Cf.* comment in *N. Y. Evening Post*, Jan. 27, 30, 1823.

[5] Clinton had retired with reluctance (J. D. Hammond, *Political History*, vol. ii, p. 98), for though his more intelligent and prudent friends
had discouraged him, others had given different counsel. Gideon
Granger had urged him to stand as the candidate of the west: " The
conclusion of the coming wheat harvest will be time enough to begin
to act. We should stand cool, easy & collected and when the season of
action arrives we should display an energy hitherto not exhibited. It

But a stronger influence toward vitalizing party spirit lay in the character and policies of the Democratic leaders. They desired an opposition firm enough to keep their followers in discipline. The " Holy Alliance " they were called at first, but this title did not indicate their permanence and mutual responsibility as well as one soon afterward bestowed upon them and accepted, the "Albany Regency".[1] Van Buren was, of course, their leader, a man uncommonly endowed with common sense and a shrewd and accurate judge of men; William L. Marcy should be numbered next, a bluff New Englander, who in intervals between his fighting in the war of 1812 had attracted notice by some able articles defending Tompkins, and had since instructed Rensselaer County in the doctrine through the columns of his *Northern Budget*.[2] Azariah C. Flagg, who had led his troops to battle by the Saranac as Marcy had by the St. Regis, had likewise served the party in his *Plattsburgh Republican*, and had come to the assembly marked for leadership.[3] Silas Wright, of St. Lawrence County, was elected to the senate in 1823; he had graduated from Middlebury College as one of four Republicans in a class of thirty, and

should be manifested by vigorous personal efforts rather than by newspapers vociferations. If it suits your convenience to explore the canal, the connexions between Seneca and the Susquehanah, the iron beds of the North and the reasonable evidence of the West, as well as the infant fishery on the East of Long Island perhaps it would not be without usefulness," April 4, 1822, Clinton Mss.

[1] E. E. Hale, Jr., in his interesting *William H. Seward* (Philadelphia, 1910), p. 44, note, states that the first use of this word that he had found was in the *Albany Advertiser*, Jan. 17, 1824, which speaks of " the cabinet council of Van Buren, or rather the regency whom he has appointed to govern the state in his absence."

[2] For sketches of Marcy, see J. S. Jenkins, *Lives of the Governors*, pp. 546-606, and J. B. Moore, "A Great Secretary of State," *Political Science Quarterly*, vol. xxx, pp. 377-396.

[3] *Appleton's Cyclopedia of American Biography.*

since risen to importance as a lawyer in his town of Canton. Competent and winning, and inflexible in his allegiance to the principles of Jefferson, though not conspicuously daring, he easily found place among the Regency.[1] The brilliant Samuel A. Talcott, a "high-minded" man from Utica, was three times attorney general after 1821, could argue as an equal with such advocates as Webster, and might have had a national career had he not mistaken dissipation for a sign of genius.[2] In this he was in contrast with his friend, Benjamin F. Butler, whose Puritan piety was mocked at by incredulous foes, and whose diligence and public spirit brought him high distinction.[3] Dr. Michael Hoffman, a German from the town of Herkimer, educated in the law as well as medicine, was of more importance in the group than has usually been recognized. The letters which he wrote from Washington, where he served eight years in Congress, are full of sound advice on large concerns of policy, while his financial plans and measures for the state, in their wisdom and consistency, should give him with historians something of the character of statesman.[4] Edwin Croswell, whose name concludes our catalogue, was the spokesman of the party. By his address and tact, aided by nice literary taste, he made the *Albany Argus* for a time the most influential paper in the northern states.[5]

[1] There are lives of Wright by J. D. Hammond (Syracuse, 1848) ; J. S. Jenkins (Auburn, 1847) ; R. H. Gillett, two volumes (Albany, 1874).

[2] Bacon, *Early Bar of Oneida County;* M. M. Bagg, *Pioneers of Utica,* pp. 418-424.

[3] W. L. Mackenzie, *Lives and Opinions of Benjamin F. Butler, etc.* (Boston, 1845).

[4] Letters from Hoffman to A. C. Flagg, constitute one volume in the Flagg Mss.; N. S. Benton, *History of Herkimer County* (Albany, 1856), pp. 323 *et seq.*; *American Almanac for 1850* (Boston) ; G. W. Smith, "The Career of Michael Hoffman," *Papers of Herkimer Co. Hist. Soc., 1896* (Herkimer, 1899), pp. 5 *et seq.*

[5] J. D. Hammond, *Political History,* vol. ii, pp. 154, 204, 524 n. The

That this group should stir opponents to a bitter condemnation, is not surprising, especially when in the absence of dramatic contests in national politics, attention was confined within the state.[1] They were formidable in solidarity. Wright in 1823 would have preferred John Quincy Adams for the presidency, while Flagg favored Clay, or possibly Calhoun;[2] but when their colleagues had decided, they were ardent Crawford[a] men. Flagg was for a popular election of electors until he was instructed,[3] and then became the chief defender of the older method; Hoffman later did not care for Jackson, but sank his prejudices in deference to the general party will.[4] If they could not always reach the Greek ideal of harmony, they could achieve a Roman concord. Yielding individually to what they thought the practical demands of leadership, they insisted on a like subordination throughout the party. They deplored self-nominations, and insisted on the authenticity of

N. Y. American, Feb. 2, 1827, charged that the "gentleman pensioners" of the Regency wrote articles which were sent out to affiliated papers in the state, from which later the *Argus* copied them as evidence of popular sentiment. The *Argus* denied this on Feb. 5, 1827. Benjamin Knower was called a member of the Regency, and also Roger Skinner, though he died in 1825. J. A. Dix, James Porter, T. W. Olcott, and C. E. Dudley were also regularly associated with the leaders; *cf.* Thurlow Weed, *Autobiography*, p. 103.

[1] See *N. Y. American*, Nov. 22, 1823. Van Buren seemed not quite able to understand why there should be so much hostile criticism: "Why the deuce is it," he wrote to Rufus King, "that they have such an itching for abusing me. I try to be harmless, and positively good-natured, & a most decided friend of peace," Sept. 21, 1822, *King Correspondence*.

[2] Wright to Flagg, Dec. 20, 1827; Flagg to Wright, Oct. 28, 1823; Flagg to Van Buren, Nov. 12, 1823.

[3] *Plattsburgh Republican*, Nov. 8, 1823; *N. Y. American*, Jan. 27, 1824.

[4] "I don't like the Jackson frolic very well, but I suppose we must have it," Hoffman to Flagg, Flagg Mss. He makes numerous other comments to the same effect.

[a] William Harris Crawford (1722-1834), U.S. minister to France, Secretary of War, Secretary of the Treasury, and in 1824 leader of the states' rights wing of the Republican party in an unsuccessful battle for the presidency against John Quincy Adams, Andrew Jackson and Henry Clay.

all done in a caucus.[1] To question this was wrong, they said; it had a bad effect on future contests: "an opposition on the ground of principle will be used to authorize an opposition on the ground of caprice."[2]

They did not look for harvest where they had not sown, and carefully apportioned their appointments.[3] The tough-minded William L. Marcy in debate with Clay admitted that, "They saw nothing wrong in the rule, that to the victor belong the spoils of the enemy."[4] They seemed to hold an absolutist, almost mystical, conception of the rights of the party, so important and so precious as to be beyond the laws of private ethics. "Don't be too fastidious," wrote Marcy; "when party feeling is strong almost anything that is done is right. I have not time to carry out fully my ideas on this subject, but a hint is enough to such a wise and experienced body as the *Albany Regency*."[5]

They were so successful that their bewildered enemies, in search of explanation, could think of nothing less than sorcery.[6] Silas Wright had little patience with the party managers he met in Washington: "They do not under-

---

[1] *E. g.* in *Argus*, Oct. 23, 1823. Adams men heartily approved of self-nomination; *cf. N. Y. American*, Oct. 4, 1825. "At no period before or since, has caucus law been more readily acquiesced in, and more promptly enforced than the present," J. D. Hammond, *Political History*, vol. ii, p. 114 (writing of 1823).

[2] W. L. Marcy and Edwin Croswell to A. C. Flagg, Oct. 20, 1825, Flagg Mss.

[3] "On the subject of appointments you well know my mind. Give them to good true & useful friends, who will enjoy the emoluments if there is any, and will use the influence to our benefit, if any influence is conferred by the office. This is the long and short of the rule by which to act," Silas Wright to A. C. Flagg, August 29, 1827, *ibid.*

[4] Marcy on Van Buren's nomination to England, *Annals of Congress*, vol. viii, pp. 1313, 1325, 1356.

[5] Marcy to Flagg, Feb. 6, 1830[?], Flagg Mss.

[6] Wright to Flagg, Oct. 10, 1827, *ibid.*

stand doing these things, after all," said he, "as well as the Albany Regency."[1]   Yet they were not often charged with gross corruption, and when taxed with having turned out officers whose competence could not be questioned, in order to make room for friends, they might correctly cite a long line of precedents.[2]   They exchanged the higher offices and honors of the state among themselves, but they faithfully performed the duties which attached to them. They were virtuosos in the arts of party management, but they had a theory of government and, as long as they remained together, a consistent policy.

The conservative party in the north, though it long opposed all social changes, has been the party of business enterprise, the party with a program, while the Democracy has been the party with a creed.[3]   It was to the latter that the Regency belonged, and hating public debt they steadfastly adhered to a policy of strict economy, to the disgust of the Clintonians and Whigs.[4]   They were not a mere cabal of politicians; three men of this small group took place among the able governors of the state and represented it as Senators in Washington; one became a President, and another refused a nomination for that office; four cabinet positions were distributed among them; the others were

---

[1] Wright to Flagg, Dec. 13, 1827, Flagg Mss.

[2] Proscription in New York goes back certainly to the times of Governors Fletcher, Bellomont and Cornbury,[a] when Leislerians[b] and their opponents were alternately turned out of office.   Marcy in the senatorial debate mentioned Spencer as a worse offender than the Regency in this regard.   It has been customary to trace the beginning of the practice to the Council of Appointment of 1801 of which De Witt Clinton and Spencer were members, but H. L. McBain (*cf. supra*, p. 6, note) has plausibly ascribed it to their Federalist predecessors.

[3] J. F. Jameson, *History of Historical Writing in America* (Boston, 1891), pp. 93-94.

[4] D. C. Sowers, *Financial History of New York State* (N. Y., 1914), pp. 64, 66, 67, 69.

[a] Benjamin Fletcher was colonial governor of New York from 1692 to 1698, Richard Coote, Earl of Bellomont, was colonial governor of New York from 1698 to 1701, and Edward Hyde, Viscount Cornbury, was colonial governor of New York and New Jersey from 1702 to 1708.

[b] Leislerians are named after Jacob Leisler (1640-1691), who led an

remembered as public men of principle and useful service. There was no possibility of " amalgamation " while such men determined otherwise; they had not long to wait before an issue was presented which silenced any talk of the catholicity of the great Republican party.

As the election of 1824 drew near, the contest for the presidential nomination grew exciting. Clay, Crawford, Adams, Jackson and Calhoun were all considered candidates, but Adams seemed to be the favorite in New York at first, by reason of his northern birth as well as of his public record; [1] since Virginia had furnished Presidents for eight administrations out of nine, many were determined to stand out for a northern man, who never had held slaves. [2] The Kings and their *American* brought most " high-minded men " to this decision. [3] The *Commercial Advertiser*, no doubt speaking for the majority of old Federalists, expressed regret that Clinton was not then available, and soon came out for Adams. [4] But agreement could

[1] *Albany Argus*, May 13, 1823.

[2] R. King's memorandum, *King Correspondence*, vol. vi, p. 508; Stephen Van Rensselaer to De Witt Clinton, Jan. 25, 1823, Clinton Mss. On the other hand, the *Argus* deprecated " the misguided attempts of the editors of the American to array the north against the south, and sow the seeds of disaffection and jealousy in the union," Aug. 15, 1823. On May 1, 1823, Johnston Verplanck retired from the editorship of the, *American* leaving Charles King in sole charge. On the matter of slaveholding, *cf. American*, August 15, 1823, and *Argus*, July 29, 1823.

[3] J. Verplanck to M. Van Buren, Van Buren Mss.; R. King to J. A. King, Jan., 1823, and to C. Gore, Feb. 9, 1823, *King Correspondence*. The *Argus* now begins to call the *American* a " Federal paper "; it was apparent, they observed, " that deep-rooted predilections were not easily controlled," Aug. 1, 15, 1823.

[4] Jan. 21, 1823; Aug. 13, 1824. It deprecated reference to " the now insignificant circumstance of his having been a federalist, or the still less important one, as concerns merit, of his now being a republican "; *cf.* likewise the *Poughkeepsie Journal*, and, according to the *Argus* (Aug. 26, 1823), all the other " ultra-federal " journals in the state.

insurrection in New York at the time of the accession to the British throne of William and Mary. Leisler gained control of the government despite the opposition of the aristocracy, but was later tried for treason and hanged. During the first part of the 18th Century the term "Leislerian" connoted advocacy of popular rights.

not be expected; the *Argus* now observed that true Democrats would leave the Secretary of State when they saw what kind of men supported him, while the Adams papers railed at Crawford as the candidate of Radicals and Jacobins.[1]

In national affairs, for more than twenty years, the New York Democrats had won their triumphs as the colleagues of Virginians. Disliking Adams for his friends, the leaders naturally chose Crawford as the candidate of their old allies, and because he stood for an authentic caucus nomination, a principle which they considered very precious. As early as January, 1822, they had come out strongly for this procedure, deprecating all irregular and premature announcements in the state.[2] The leader of the Regency long afterward explained that the Democratic party had always had more need of these devices than their adversaries, since the program of the latter would either fascinate the voters by its dramatic content or draw them by their economic interests.[3]

In 1823 it was apparent that the senators, most of whom

[1] *Albany Argus*, Aug. 24, 1824. " Mr. Crawford is the head and chief of the Radical party whose object it is to beat down and destroy all the most useful institutions of the Federal Government—the Army, the Navy, and fortifications, and Military Academy," *N. Y. Commercial Advertiser*, Nov. 4, 1823. The *American* printed much the same opinion, February 20, 1824. The name Radical had recently been introduced from England. " To prostrate the reign of jacobinism," wrote Clinton to C. G. Haines, on April 22, 1823 (Clinton Mss. Letterbook v), " we must arrange a party for the ensuing campaign on the ground of measure." The following day he wrote again of the levelling principles of the dominant faction. *Cf.* also John A. Dix's letters to Dr. George C. Shattuck, 1822-1824, *Mass. Hist. Soc. Proc.*, vol. 1 (Boston, 1917), pp. 143, 144, 147.

[2] *Albany Argus*, Jan. 29, 1822, March 25, 1823.

[3] Martin Van Buren, *Inquiry into the Origin and Course of Political Parties in the United States* (N. Y. 1867), pp. 4-5.

had been brought into office on the Democratic wave that followed the new constitution, were so completely under Regency control, that the majority of the legislature, no matter what the issue of the next elections, would probably declare for Crawford.[1] Since the presidential electors were then chosen by the legislature in joint session, this would surely mean the choice of Crawford by the state, which might turn the balance in the Union, and thus enormously increase the prestige of Van Buren and his coadjutors. Yet of all the candidates, Adams was no doubt most popular throughout the state, and his supporters, joined by those of Clay, Calhoun and Jackson, took counsel as to how such a triumph could be circumvented. By April a plan had been devised to change the law, if possible, so as to give the choice directly to the voters.[2] The personal followers of Clinton, who had been reticent upon the presidential question, but who here saw an opportunity to embarrass their chief enemies, instantly took ground in favor of this measure,[3] and there soon was organized a " People's Party " on the issue of the Electoral Bill.

The story of the ensuing contest is not unfamiliar; yet certain elements so clearly show how old partisan antipathies were strengthened, that it must not be passed over. While old Federalists maintained with all their eloquence

[1] A caucus of "regular Republicans," on Jan. 13, 1824, did formally support the congressional caucus proposals, *Albany Argus*, Jan. 16, 1824. The best account of this campaign is that of C. H. Rammelkamp, "The Campaign of 1824 in New York," in *Annual Report of American Hist. Ass'n., 1904* (Washington, 1905), pp. 117-201.

[2] J. D. Hammond, *Political History*, vol. ii, p. 127. "By offering the Bill now you are sure to attract attention." R. King to J. A. King, April 20, 1823. On this matter Rufus King and Van Buren parted company; *cf.* the courteous letter of Van Buren, May 2, 1823, *King Correspondence.*

[3] Hammond, vol. ii, p. 131.

that the common people must be trusted, the party known as Democratic declared that " intermediate elections were recognized as a general principle of our system," that instructions to assemblymen and senators were most improper, and that our institutions were not lightly to be changed.[1] This debate engaged the legislature through the winter of 1824. The Democrats, led now by Major Flagg, and still in the majority even in the lower house, entrusted the proposal to a committee safely hostile to a change.[2] An amendment to the federal constitution was recommended, but this could not be passed so as to affect the election of 1824; a shrewd Democrat brought in a plan by which if no candidate was given a majority at the polls, the matter would be settled in the legislature, knowing that among so many aspirants no one could get more votes than all the rest together; Senator Wright proposed a scheme complicated with such ingenuity that under it, as well, the legislature would have had the final choice. The session closed according to instructions, with nothing done.

These obstructions and evasions aroused a protest through the state that could not be mistaken, and the vacillating Governor Yates, who had in January counseled caution and delay, now, to the disgust of all the leaders of his party, called a special session for the coming August.

> " Like a war elephant, his bulk he shows,
> And treads down friends, when frightened by his foes." [3]

---

[1] *Albany Argus, e. g.*, June 27, Sept. 23, 1823; Wright to Flagg, Nov. 12, 1823, Flagg Mss.

[2] The report of the debate may be found in the *Argus*, Jan. 9, 1824, *et seq.*

[3] Toast at a dinner in Utica, *Argus*, July 9, 1824. For an example of the art of invective, one should read a two-column editorial in the *Argus* of June 8, 1824, beginning: " It is a painful duty to expose to the world the errours and the inconsistencies of a man in whom the com-

The sullen company that gathered on this summons in the sweltering midsummer of 1824 resolved to make their stay as short as could consist with parliamentary law. Silas Wright announced to Flagg that he expected "to be at Albany, God willing, Sunday evening with the Utica stage, at the capitol at 12 o'clock Monday, to adjourn on Tuesday, and to start for home on Wednesday morning at the farthest."[1] Yet in spite of resolutions introduced by Flagg, who complained that every extra day cost the state a thousand dollars, the session dragged on for a week.[2] Henry Wheaton of New York and Isaac Ogden of Walton, leaders of the People's Party, tried hard to force the question to a vote, but when at last the assembly passed the bill, the senate had adjourned, and joint action was impossible. Meanwhile excitement through the state grew day by day; it was clear that the election in November would increase the power of the People's Men.[3]

A caucus in the spring had chosen Colonel Young as candidate for governor, but it was unlikely in those troubled days that he could, like Yates, come unopposed to office.

---

munity has reposed confidence . . . ." The governor had in January advised waiting for a federal amendment; now he said that since Congress had adjourned, there was no hope of that. Thurlow Weed claims the credit for influencing the governor to his decision, *Autobiography,* p. 115.

DeWitt Clinton wrote as follows to Francis Granger, Jan. 25, 1824 (Granger Mss., Library of Congress): "The executive is hors de combat—Wotan's horse, Balaam's Ass, Livy's ox and Mahomet's Camel all harnessed together could not draw him out of the kennel of public indignation."

[1] July 24, 1827, Flagg Mss.

[2] *Albany Argus,* August 5, 1824.

[3] For a description of the extra session, see the *Argus,* Aug. 3-10, 1824, and letters from an Albany correspondent to the *N. Y. Evening Post,* Aug. 4, 6, 7, 1824. The letters have some interesting comment on the "high-pressure" oratory of "little Major Flagg."

Early in April the *Argus* bitterly remarked that those
malignants who could not rest content with regular nominations, had planned a "delegated convention," acting on
the single and unfortunate precedent of 1817.[1] This observation was correct; the delegates were soon chosen and
came to Utica the following September six score strong, to
settle on a nomination.[2] All but five counties in the state
were represented, though unfriendly critics poured derision
on the tiny local meetings, which in many places had commissioned these agents of the people.[3] Conventions, they
declared, were a favorite stratagem of Federalists; they
had held one once at Hartford.[4] But in fact the work of
the convention was not difficult, for there was little question
as to whom they would select.

The *personnel* of the new party had been no surprise to
Democratic leaders. "With scarcely an exception," wrote
Croswell of the *Argus* to Azariah C. Flagg, "those who
have been elected on the pretended '*People's ticket*' are the
one and implacable enemy under a new name. The enmity
will never die; and it is the more dangerous, because it is
insidious and comes under an artful disguise."[5] The cloak
could not conceal from them the hoof of Clintonism, and
unsteadied by alarm some now suspected the whole enter-

---

[1] April 6, 9, 1824. The *Argus* called this procedure "irregular," but
E. E. Hale, in his *Seward*, p. 65, points out that as the caucus method
is natural to a party in power, so the convention is a natural expedient
of an opposition.

[2] *N. Y. Evening Post*, Sept. 24, 25, 1824.

[3] *Argus*, Oct. 1, 1824.

[4] See toast at Hudson, reported in *ibid.*, July 16, 1824. Of course,
there had been quasi-conventions in the state before 1817. In 1792, for
example, George Clinton was nominated for governor at a Republican
meeting held in New York city, said to have been of "gentlemen from
various parts of the state;" see C. A. Beard, *American Government and
Politics* (N. Y. 1917), p. 128.

[5] Dec. 9, 1823, Flagg Mss.

prise as but a scheme to place their arch-opponent in the presidential chair. " I am fully satisfied," wrote one, " that if the law alluded to is changed, Mr. Clinton will get the vote of this state, and in that event he is sure of Ohio too." [1] Others, however, knew that though the majority of People's Men were old Clintonians and Federalists, a majority likewise, albeit these two segments might not coincide, were now supporting Adams to succeed Monroe. Yet these agreed that Adams and the electoral bill would lose prestige by any public joinder with a fallen hero. To force alignment of the People's Men with the former governor, just before adjournment they introduced a resolution to remove that gentleman from his office as canal commissioner.[2] Though the minority, excepting a small number especially opposed to Clinton, protested vigorously, the resolution was easily put through.[3]

This was the one capital blunder of the Regency. The act was so outrageous that it could not be defended under the most liberal interpretation of the common law of parties. Clinton had served gratuitously for fourteen years in this office, which he filled with a unique propriety. This wanton and vindictive stroke revealed how cunning had developed in these managers at the cost of their morality. The resentment of the personal followers of Clinton confirmed and strengthened their allegiance; old Federalists

[1] Roger Skinner to A. C. Flagg, Dec. 9, 1823, *ibid.* The *N. Y. American*, Feb. 3, 1824, ridiculed this fear, yet said that the principle was so important that no individual should be considered. Some Democrats feared the law would aid Clinton in 1828; see *Onondaga Repository*, quoted in *Argus*, Sept. 23, 1825. *Cf.* Thurlow Weed, *Autobiography*.

[2] A good account of this is found in W. L. Stone's letter printed in David Hosack, *Memoir of Clinton*, p. 48, *et seq.* The senate passed the resolutions with only three opposing votes.

[3] See Henry Wheaton (an Anti-Clintonian People's Man) to R. King, April 12, 1824, *King Correspondence*.

expressed a ready sympathy with their adopted leader who endured rebuke apparently for what they thought most honorable in his career; the western counties saw here another evidence that the Regency had no concern in their affairs. It was on this occasion that young William H. Seward threw off connection with the Democratic party.[1] Addresses of respect and confidence assured the late commissioner that New York would not content herself with those splendid services which he had rendered in the past.[2] In New York city the park was thronged with those who met to protest, and Matthew Clarkson, William Bayard, Nicholas Fish, Cadwallader D. Colden, Philip Hone and others drew up resolutions.[3] At Albany there was a similar meeting and committee.[4] Wheaton, Ogden, Tallmadge and some other People's Men who had sought to keep their party clear of Clinton, now realized that this could not be done.

At a meeting in the Tontine Coffee House in New York city his name was formally presented as a candidate for governor.[5] He had proposed an amendment to the federal constitution as long ago as 1802 embodying the principle of the electoral bill, and had recommended such a law in his

[1] Frederic Bancroft, *Life of William H. Seward* (N. Y., 1900), vol. i, pp. 17-19.

[2] See answers in May 19, 1824 in Letterbook vi, pp. 99, 103, and two addresses from Buffalo, May 10, 18, Clinton Mss.

[3] *N. Y. Evening Post*, April 19, 20, 1824.

[4] This included Samuel M. Hopkins, J. H. Wendell and other Federalists, as well as Clintonians like J. D. Hammond, Elisha Jenkins, Gideon Hawley, John Tayler, *etc.*, *ibid.*, April 21, 22, 1824.

[5] *N. Y. Evening Post*, Aug. 12, 1824. Clinton consented "from information that this measure will ensure victory, and with a view to crush intrigue," Clinton to Uri Tracy, Aug. 10, 1824. He had given up his presidential aspirations for the time being; see Stephen Van Rensselaer to Clinton, Dec. 25, 1822, Clinton Mss.

message of 1820.[1] The Clinton movement grew throughout the state,[2] and many delegates to the Utica convention were instructed to support him and no other. Consequently it was no surprise that, in spite of able opposition, he was given more than twice as many votes as his nearest rival.[3] There was then presented an address from the trenchant pen of Gerrit Smith, complaining that the insult of the Regency disgraced the great " state of New-York—the first in population, the first in commerce, the first in wealth and resources, possessing her full portion of talent, and deeply interested in the administration of our national government." He spoke of the ensuing election of a President, but cleverly avoided any odious comparison of the competitors of Mr. Crawford; " it would be idle and preposterous," said he, " to recommend candidates to disfranchised men." [4]

Positive proposals must always lose some members to a coalition, and this nomination, satisfying as it was to the majority, alienated certain elements. Whenever Mr. Clin-

[1] *Albany Daily Advertiser, Extra*, Sept. 27, 1824; *Messages from the Governors*, vol. ii, pp. 1039-1040. Clinton had written Francis Granger, Jan. 6, 1824: "An unhallowed attempt is now making to continue the usurpation of the election franchise from the people. How shall this be defeated? Let the people without reference to men but principles assemble at public meetings and speak in a language that cannot be misunderstood." See also to same, Jan. 18, 1824, Granger Mss.

[2] See, *é. g., Ithaca Journal* and *Cayuga Republican* quoted in *N. Y. American*, Aug. 18, 1824, and citations in *Albany Daily Advertiser*.

[3] On the first ballot Clinton had 76 votes; General James Tallmadge, 31; Henry Huntington, 13; with scattering votes to five others. A few discontented delegates seceded from the convention, *N. Y. Spectator*, Sept. 28, 1824. Sometimes the title " People's Men " was applied exclusively to those who opposed both Clinton and the Regency; see J. D. Hammond, vol. ii, p. 199. Tallmadge was selected for lieutenant governor.

[4] *Albany Daily Advertiser, Extra*, Sept. 27. 1824. There was also a set of resolutions.

ton was accepted as their leader by the old conservative party, he added his constructive and administrative talent to their treasury, but, with the exception of the western districts, he usually brought a personal following scarcely larger, if at all, than the number which he drove away. When the choice of the convention was announced, the *New York American* declared that it could take no further part in the campaign,[1] and there were others of the " high-minded " group who, having hesitated, now refused to vote the People's ticket.[2] Yet most of these anti-Clintonian Federalists were Adams men, and some Bucktails now complained that they had mingled with the Democratic party only to destroy it.[3] On the other hand, the *Evening Post*, which since it had been founded as a Hamiltonian paper had nursed a lively hatred of the Adams family, would not continue fellowship with those who preached the cause of the Secretary of State, whom they stigmatized as " the Benedict Arnold of Federalism." [4] Finding Clinton's fortunes linked with such as these, it regretfully abandoned him, to be an independent Democratic journal from that day to this.[5]

Nevertheless most People's Men were well content, and they began a spirited campaign. They held a multitude of meetings, in every county in the state, and issued broadside

[1] Sept. 25, 1824.

[2] *N. Y. American*, Oct. 27, 1824; *N. Y. Spectator*, Sept. 14, 1824. Others are mentioned in Clinton's Clippings, vol. iii, on the campaign of 1826. This scrap-book collection of clippings made by his own hand, if we may judge by the endorsements, is in the collection of the N. Y. Historical Society.

[3] *Watertown Independent Republican*, in Clinton's Clippings, vol. ii, p. 90.

[4] Oct. 29, 1824.

[5] *N. Y. Evening Post*, Aug. 11, Nov. 1, 12, 30, 1824. It favored Jackson but was content with Crawford.

manifestoes, in a tumid style of rhetoric then not quite yet out of fashion, shrewdly adding names of discontented Democrats whenever possible.[1] There was quiet work among canal contractors who had control of many votes.[2] Democrats recalled the record of the Federalists in the late war, and the shifting course of Clinton. That this candidate deserved appreciation for unpaid service as canal commissioner, they declared ridiculous; he had received state money since 1797 amounting to over a hundred and sixty thousand dollars.[3]

In return the People's Men cited with a proper pride their leader's efforts in the cause of education, his many contributions to science and the arts, as well as the beneficent design of the canals.[4] They said if the electoral bill had passed, the November special session to choose the electors would have been unnecessary and thirty thousand dollars saved the state.[5] They charged crimes against " King Caucus " in phrases with a reminiscent ring: " He has refused his assent to laws the most wholesome and necessary for the public good. He has forbidden his governors to pass laws of immediate and pressing importance. . . ."[6]

[1] E. g., " The Regency in Despair" (*Albany Daily Advertiser, Extra,* Oct. 19, 1824): "They will weep and wail and gnash their teeth, when the storm of popular fury shall overtake and utterly destroy them." See also "Republican Fellow-Citizen of the city of Albany," 1824 (N. Y. P. L.).

[2] J. C. Spencer to DeW. Clinton, Oct. 21, 1824. *Cf. National Advocate,* Oct. 4, 1823.

[3] *Albany Argus, Extra,* Oct. 15, 1824, answered in *Albany Daily Advertiser, Extra,* Oct. 16, 1824; *cf.* "Gratuitous Services," Oct. 18, 1824 (all in N. Y. P. L.).

[4] "Circular of the People's Committee, P. Cassiday, chairman," Albany, Oct. 22, 1824; "Thomas Jefferson's Opinion of DeWitt Clinton" (N. Y. P. L.).

[5] "Circular of People's Committee."

[6] *Albany Daily Advertiser, Extra,* Oct. 18, 1824.

This was the first campaign in New York state where an appeal was especially directed to young men, as only since the freehold qualification had been taken off the franchise could they play an important part in politics. There were "Young Men's Conventions" and "Young Men's Vigilance Committees" in many towns and counties, forming thus a precedent for years to come.[1] Likewise 1824 was the year when the convention system was accepted by the state. Seven years before, Republicans had gathered at Albany to name a candidate for governor, but delegates had been received without much scrutiny of their credentials, and the whole proceeding, looked upon as quite irregular, was not repeated in the next campaign. Now the People's Men in city wards and villages held meetings to name delegates to the conventions for the counties; at these, committees of correspondence were selected and ballots taken as to Congressmen and members of the legislature, as well as delegates to the great convocation at Utica. Here, after Clinton and Tallmadge had been chosen as the leaders, and an address and resolutions drawn and carried, there was appointed a committee whose duty it would be to call another state convention to meet in 1826. In that year we shall see their Regency opponents follow their example, and for decades Utica and Herkimer were known as the respective meeting places.[2]

[1] Advertisements in *N. Y. American,* Jan. 4, 1824; *Albany Daily Advertiser, Extra,* Oct. 18, 1824, "Young Men's [Albany] County Convention," speaks of similar conventions held by the Regency party in Schenectady and Troy. See also Broadside, "Young Men's Convention," 1825, which speaks of committees for towns and villages, and "Address of the Democratic Republican General Committee of Young Men," Albany, Oct. 1825 (N. Y. P. L.).

[2] Thurlow Weed, *Autobiography.* Popular ratification meetings were held; see, *e. g., N. Y. Commercial Advertiser,* Oct. 2, 12, 1824. Utica and Herkimer were respectively appropriate. "While the eastern population seated within Oneida County, almost unanimously acted with

The election gave a large majority to Clinton. It clearly showed what was the core of the new People's Party, in that the widest margins of this victory were in the old Federalist districts. In New York city the southern wards were registered for Clinton, and the northern wards for Young.[1] Albany went overwhelmingly for its old favorite.[2] The largest majorities were here, and in Columbia, Washington and Rensselaer counties, all Federalist strongholds, and in the west, Ontario, Genesee and Erie, where the canal made Clinton popular.[3] The *Argus* now found vindication of its claim that though the principles of Federalism had been repudiated, the members of that party still voted as a unit by a general understanding. It had been much the

the federalist party, the immigration to Herkimer seems to have been more equally balanced . . . " and to have followed the natural democratic tendencies of its early frontier life, N. S. Benton, *History of Herkimer County*, p. 259. The Germans were Republicans, *ibid.*, p. 261. The Democrats presented the following ingenious explanation for their adoption of the system: " The new constitution placing the election in the fall, has extended the interval between a legislative recommendation and the election, from a few weeks to more than half a year. The interval would be continued to be employed by our opponents, as heretofore, in intrigues and factious combinations to deceive the people. From notions of expediency, then, the mode of nomination has been changed," *Albany Argus*, Oct. 9, 1826. However they made no provision in 1826 for another convention in 1828, saying that the caucus system might be revived, *Albany Daily Advertiser*, Oct. 20, 1826.

[1] *N. Y. American*, Nov. 4, 1824. Federalists were elected aldermen and assistants in the first three wards, *N. Y. Evening Post*, Nov. 5, 6, 1824.

[2] *Albany Daily Advertiser*, Nov. 4, 1824.

[3] *N. Y. Evening Post*, Nov. 15, 1824. The following counties went for Young: Chenango, Delaware, Greene, Lewis, Orange, Otsego, Putnam, Rockland, Saratoga, Schoharie, Sullivan, Tompkins, Warren and Westchester, all old Republican counties; see *Albany Argus*, Dec. 7, 1824. The *Argus* in its editorials always called its opponents " the Federals."

same in 1823, and would be true again in 1825.[1] After the Albany city elections of the latter year, the state paper laconically announced: "Average majority for the aristocratic ticket for aldermen over the republican ticket, 246."[2] " There is not a prominent member of the party whom they serve in this city," it said, the following month, " who has not been member of the Washington Benevolent Society, and continued such during its existence."[3] It printed in its columns similar reports from many other papers.[4] All old leaders like Williams, Spencer, Kent, Platt, D. B. Ogden, Colden, Benson, the Jays, Van Rensselaers and Van Vechten were People's Men. A caustic writer of the town of Lansingburgh, in Rensselaer county, remarked: " The old Dutch power-proud aristocracy of the place are of the blue-light order of Federalists, real Tories in grain, call themselves what they may."[5]

The presidential contest in the legislature after the election was marked more by bargain and intrigue than by the ascertainment and expression of the public mind. Though some conservatives declared for Clay or Jackson,[6] most

---

[1] *N. Y. Commercial Advertiser*, Oct. 31, Nov. 6, 1823; *Albany Argus*, Nov. 14, 1823. *Cf. N. Y. Evening Post*, Oct. 30, 31, Nov. 4, 7, 1822, *N. Y. Commercial Advertiser*, Nov. 7, 1822, and *N. Y. Spectator*, Nov. 19, 1822.

[2] *Albany Argus*, Sept. 30, 1825.

[3] *Ibid.*, Oct. 20, 1825.

[4] See J. Platt to Clinton, Jan. 3, 1823; Kent to Clinton, Dec. 31, 1822, Nov. 9, 1824, Jan. 23, 1826, etc.; Clinton to Van der Kemp, Oct. 6, 1824 (Clinton Mss.) ; *N. Y. Evening Post*, April 20, 1824; and Clinton's Clippings, Oct. 16, 1826, vol. iii.

[5] H. G. Spafford to A. C. Flagg, March 3, 1826, and April 13, 1827, Flagg Mss.

[6] Most of Clay's support seems to have come from Republicans in the People's Party; but other conservatives stood for Jackson, *e. g.*, C. D. Colden, Robert Bogardus, J. B. Murray, *etc.* (see handbill of Jackson meeting over which Morgan Lewis presided, bound with Flagg

People's Men supported Adams, a preference now reflected in the legislature. But neither he nor Crawford could be chosen without the help of followers of Clay. How by printing a split ticket behind closed shutters on a Sunday morning, and promising some seven electors to the Kentucky candidate, in case they could be used effectively, Thurlow Weed secured these needed votes, is all set forth in his own remarkable account.[1] By a clever trick of this journeyman mechanic who held no public office, John Quincy Adams became sixth President of the United States. Yet the technical details of how a practical psychologist accomplished his first triumph need not concern us here; such *tours d'esprit* of party managers may for a time accelerate, retard or modify the tendencies of nations, but they cannot start or stop or permanently direct them.[2]

As one surveys the progress of political affairs in New York state throughout the early twenties, he observes that these years, as properly as any others in its history, deserve the well-worn title of " transition period ". The eighteenth century closed in 1821; its problems, most of them, had now been settled. What Mr. Madison believed " the most common and durable source of factions "—the various and un-

Mss.) ; Nicholas Fish, Ezekiel Bacon, *etc.* (*N. Y. Evening Post*, Nov. 12, 1824) ; J. C. Spencer and T. J. Oakley, W. A. Duer to R. King, Feb. 17, 1825, *King Correspondence.*

[1] *Autobiography*, chap. xiii.

[2] All factions (according to Weed) agreed in attributing to him the election of Adams, *ibid.*, p. 79. A somewhat similar stroke was accomplished in 1825 by the Democrats, whereby the senators of that party introduced so many candidates for United States Senator, that no nomination could be made in that house, and hence no joint ballot could be taken. Thus instead of Ambrose Spencer being chosen, the election was deferred until the following year, when with a Democratic majority the Regency secured the election. Though not generally known, this plan was wholly the work of Silas Wright; see Wright to Flagg, Jan. 28, 1824, Flagg Mss.

equal distribution of property [1]—still was present, and yet less clearly apprehended in those prosperous years when new land areas so welcomed settlers, than before or after. Parties were continued more from memory and habit than from calculated differences of interest; then, too, the joy of combat and the jealous competition for the honors of the state, guaranteed, as always, against an otiose contentment.   One harbinger of what the future would bring forth, however, was seen in the alliance of the surviving Federalist group, rounded out by moderate Republicans, with the voters of the growing west.

This region was no longer a frontier addicted to a doctrinaire democracy.   As a Puritan community, somewhat changed by transplantation, it still was earnest, active-minded and fond of enterprising measures; composed of immigrants from other states, it did not easily respond to state-rights sentiment; and with each new mile of the canal, its farmers and its millers felt more sympathy with the commercial men along the sea-coast.   Here were the bases of permanent co-operation.   How economic issues were developed which deepened the divisions of the electorate with respect to sections, classes, temperaments and legal theories, is to be the theme of the next chapter.

[1] *The Federalist*, no. x.

CHAPTER X

Manufacturing Becomes Respectable

" The internal concerns of New York," remarked an editor in 1822, " extensive as it is in territory, and with new resources unfolding themselves to public view, appear like those of a mighty and flourishing empire." [1]   The simile which was to furnish the great commonwealth with its accepted name already seemed appropriate.   The following year, when the eastern section of the Grand Canal had been completed, Albany received the first small tow-boat with acclaim, as it previsioned what prosperity and dignity to New York state this simple herald announced.[2]   In 1825, as the *Seneca Chief* brought Clinton through the last lock to the Hudson, " the thunders of cannon proclaimed that the work was done, and the assembled multitude made the welkin ring with shouts of gladness." [3]   When the governor's party finally reached Manhattan Island, the demonstration, with parades, illuminations and exulting oratory, came to its climax.

[1] *N. Y. Spectator*, Jan. 8, 1822.

[2] Broadside, " Celebration of Passage of the first Boat from the Grand Canal into the Hudson, at the City of Albany, on Wednesday, October 8, 1823 " (N. Y. P. L.). See also J. Munsell, *History of Albany* (Albany, 1867), vol. ii.

[3] *Albany Daily Advertiser*, Nov. 4, 1825. See the excellent account of the celebration along the canal, in W. L. Stone, *Narrative of the Festivities in Honor of the Completion of the Grand Erie Canal, etc.* (N. Y., 1825), and A. B. Hulbert, *Historic Highways* (Cleveland, 1904), vol. xiv.

" Such strains shall unborn millions yet awake,
    While with her golden trumpet, smiling Fame
Proclaims the union of the Main and Lake
    And on her scroll emblazons Clinton's name; "

handbills setting forth these florid sentiments were struck
off from a press mounted on the printer's float drawn in the
pageant, and were scattered through the admiring crowds.[1]

The profits of the western farmers soon surpassed their
expectations. Whereas before it took a hundred dollars
and about three weeks to bring a ton of goods from Buffalo
to New York city, now eight days and fifteen dollars were
sufficient.[2] Land west of Seneca Lake almost immediately
advanced in price four-fold.[3] The number of lake ships
clearing from the port of Buffalo doubled in a year or two.[4]
Rochester grew quickly from a little hamlet to a thriving
city, and while visitors in their astonishment recalled the
stories of Scheherazade, shrewd speculators who had
marked the woodland into building-lots amassed considerable fortunes.[5] The pioneer who had cut his painful way

[1] " Ode, by Samuel Woodworth, Printer," Emmett Collection, no.
11,422 (N. Y. P. L.).

[2] E. L. Bogart, *Economic History of the United States* (N. Y., 1914
ed.), p. 211.

[3] James Renwick, *Life of DeWitt Clinton* (N. Y., 1840), p. 268. Julius
Winden, " The Influence of the Erie Canal upon the Population along
its Course," a Mss. Thesis, University of Wisconsin, shows how much
greater changes in population followed from the canal in the western
counties than in the Mohawk region. Property value likewise increased
relatively toward the west, and over a wider area than the population.
Because shipments may be made from any point on a canal the influence
in property value was fairly continuous. Many foreigners settled in
the towns because of the opportunity for unskilled labor.

[4] *Buffalo Gazette*, in Clinton's Clippings, vol. iv, p. 20.

[5] James Stuart, *Three Years in North America* (Edinburgh, 2nd
edition, 1833), vol. i, p. 81; Basil Hall, *Travels in North America in the
Years 1827 and 1828* (Edinburgh, 1830), vol. i, p. 53. It had " sprung

into the wilderness had lived to see a mighty transformation. "He can close his eyes," declared an orator, "and the unbroken forest is dark and waving before him; he wakes and the fruit of every clime is proffered for his acceptance."[1] Two and a half million bushels of wheat now found their way to Albany each year.[2] In the decade after 1820 the increase of population in New York surpassed that in New England by over half a million, but the growth in the western counties was twice as rapid as in the older Hudson River region.[3]

More than two hundred boats, by 1826, were towed each week into the Albany basin from the Erie and Champlain canals, while a dozen steamers plied on scheduled time between that city and New York, some of which could make the journey entirely within a summer's day; yet neither these nor tugs and barges could exclude the white-sailed sloops from their accustomed pathway.[4] But if Albany, now seventh city in the country, profited by trading with the west and Canada, and occasionally despatched a brig to the Antilles,[5] the metropolis at the river's mouth by its new connection with the teeming hinterland beyond the Alleghanies, became the foremost city of the western world.

up like Jonah's gourd," remarked Col. Stone as he visited here in 1829, W. L. Stone, "From New York to Niagara," in *Buffalo Historical Society Pub.*, vol. xiv, p. 233. The gain in population between 1820 and 1830 for Rochester was 421 per cent; Buffalo, 314 per cent; and Syracuse, 282 per cent; see L. K. Mathews, "The Erie Canal and the Settlement of the West," in *ibid.*, p. 195.

[1] Speech of Judge Timothy Child, *Rochester Telegraph*, quoted in *Albany Argus*, Jan. 17, 1826.

[2] *Albany Patriot*, in Clinton's Clippings, vol. ii, p. 23.

[3] U. S. Census, 1870, vol. ii, p. 3.

[4] *Albany Argus*, April 12, June 14, 1825, Sept. 12, 1826; H. G. Spafford, *Gazetteer of the State of New York* (Albany, 1824), pp. 15-16.

[5] *Albany Patriot, loc. cit.*

The years of painful readjustment following the Peace of Ghent,[a] were now forgotten, and prosperity had come. When, in the spring of 1824, the canal had penetrated only through the Mohawk valley, three thousand houses were erected in the city of New York in anticipation; and the following year the papers spoke of capitalists moving hither in considerable numbers from the other states.[1]   A sanguine young man hazarded a prophecy, that with the passing of the generations New York might reach a population of five hundred thousand, and in a century, perhaps, a million.[2] The merchants, clearly realizing the benefit of cheap carriage of commodities, sent a large committee under Philip Hone to Albany to take a part in the formal opening of the canal,[3] and then expressed their gratitude to Clinton in a present of two handsome silver vases.[4]   With the resources of the state and nation waiting for conversion into wealth through any agencies that could command sufficient credit, the men of business might well be expected to endorse improvements through the government's co-operation, with small regard to constitutional objections.[5]

When the governor, in his almost endless message of 1825,

[1] Francis J. Grund, *The Americans in their Moral, Social and Political Relations* (Boston, 1837 edition), p. 276; *N. Y. American*, Jan. 4, 1824, Sept. 10, 1825. The value of imports at New York in 1821 was $24,-000,000, and in 1825, when the canal was completed, $50,000,000. F. J. Turner, *Rise of the New West*, p. 35.

[2] C. G. Haines in Washington Hall, *N. Y. Commercial Advertiser*, Nov. 13, 1823.

[3] J. D. Hammond, *Political History*, vol. ii, p. 205.

[4] D. Hosack, *Memoir of Clinton*, pp. 190-192.

[5] The confidence thus developed was probably an important reason why the American merchants weathered the English panic of 1825; see Broadside, "To the friends of internal improvement generally," 1826 (N. Y. P. L.). "I am told that property has Rissen in New York very considerably in consequence of the Cannal," wrote John Jacob Astor in Switzerland to DeWitt Clinton, in Oct. 1824, Clinton Mss.

[a] Peace of Ghent signed on December 24, 1814 in Ghent, Belgium and ended the War of 1812 between the U.S. and Great Brtiain.

advised the building of a dozen new canals at state expense, with a turnpike and a railway here and there between, the merchants knew that they would profit by each enterprise, and were confirmed in their Clintonianism.[1] With lateral canals branching from the Erie, and those connecting lakes and river systems, the prospect of development seemed limitless; Delaware Bay, the Gulf of Mexico, the St. Lawrence and the Hudson could interchange their commerce through the waterways of New York state.[2] A convention was arranged at which enthusiasts discussed these possibilities.[3] Railroads were considered by some forward-looking men as a means of conquering space perhaps superior to canals, and John Stevens published an announcement that he planned to organize a company which with state subventions would lay tracks along the Hudson.[4] " This will doubtless be stigmatized by some as a wild, impracticable project," he admitted, " but before pronouncing judgment, let the thing be tried." And although this enterprise was long delayed, in 1826, a road was chartered between Albany and Schenectady,[5] soon followed by another built from Ithaca to Owego, where horses for a time supplied the motive power.[6]

[1] *Albany Argus, Extra*, Jan. 5, Jan. 21, 1825; James Renwick, *Life of Clinton* (N. Y., 1840), pp. 274-276, 292.

[2] See papers of " Hercules," reprinted from the *Western Star*, in the *Albany Daily Advertiser*, in Sept., 1836, particularly Sept. 13.

[3] Broadside, " Convention Notice to the friends of Internal Improvement throughout the State," dated at Angelica, Oct. 22, 1827 (N. Y. Hist. Soc.). The convention was held at Utica, Dec. 5, Le Ray de Chaumont, of Chaumont, chairman, *Albany Argus*, Dec. 13, 1827.

[4] *N. Y. American*, April 4, 1825.

[5] See *Albany Argus*, March 30, 1826, for the debate. Clinton was much interested in railroads; see his Clippings, vol. ii. See also S. Dunbar, *History of Travel in America*, vol. iii, chaps. xxxix-xlii.

[6] *Report of the President and Directors to the Stockholders of the Ithaca and Owego R. R.* (Ithaca, 1838) in Cornell University Library. When the Syracuse and Auburn R. R. was opened in 1838, the rude cars were drawn by horses; see W. H. Seward, *Autobiography*, p. 356.

As far as parties in the state took sides upon these numerous requests for grants of money, the Regency were less enthusiastic than Clintonians. Erastus Root, the speaker of the assembly for three terms after 1826, opposed with skill and firmness such appropriations, though he made exception of a state road which would run across his county.[1] Silas Wright suspected many if not all these projects, and other leaders tried to narrow the expenditures whenever possible.[2] It was claimed, upon the other hand, that the People's Party were more favorable to business men who wanted charters for their corporations, than suited the best interest of the state. While the Democratic legislature of 1824 would grant but three bank charters,[3] the assembly of the following year, controlled by People's Men, allowed eighteen, though most of these were negatived when offered to the hostile senate; twenty-five insurance charters met a like fate.[4]

The *Argus* scornfully referred to opposition papers as the

[1] He had voted against the Bonus Bill ten years before in Congress, and had steadily opposed the Erie Canal plan, J. D. Hammond, *Political History*, vol. ii, pp. 242, 262, 319, 325. We shall see that local projects frequently brought sectional rather than partisan alignments. *N. Y. Commercial Advertiser*, Oct. 18, 1823; Fitz-Greene Halleck, *Writings*, p. 265.

[2] *Albany Argus* (supplement), Feb. 20, 1824, and M. Hoffman to A. L. Flagg, *passim* in Flagg Mss. The *Argus* claimed to be impartial.

[3] Thurlow Weed, *Autobiography*, p. 106. Two of these were granted under extraordinary conditions. It must be remembered that from 1791 to 1838 banks were chartered by special acts of the legislature, D. C. Sowers, *Financial History of New York State*, pp. 48, 49. R. E. Chaddock, *History of the Safety Fund Banking System of New York* (Washington, 1910), p. 247, shows that notwithstanding the growth of the state, from 1821 to 1825, when the Democrats controlled the legislature, there were only 10 banks chartered.

[4] See comments in *Schenectady Cabinet*, quoted in *Argus*, May 15, 1825, and *Oneida Patriot*, *ibid.*, May 13, 1825. The *Argus* credited Wright with successful opposition, Oct. 30, 1826. For insurance charters and for loan associations, see *ibid.*, Oct. 26, 1826.

servants of the monied corporations, and its editors warned loyal readers that no effort could be spared to insure a legislature " which will preserve us from an inundation of Banks and chartered speculations." [1]   Much was said about the " Lobby Party," and it was charged that Henry Post, the governor's confidential agent in New York, was too often found in Albany in the interest of some Lombard or insurance company, and was a master of " log-rollers." [2]   The Democrats declared that their opponents displayed the old Federalist recklessness with the people's money, and pointed out that their assembly had spent almost as much in one session, as had been spent by all the five preceding, which had been controlled by sounder counsels.[3]   Jeffersonians who held that governments are instituted among men solely to assure the rights of life, liberty and the pursuit of happiness, might well look askance at such active aid to business.

It was not surprising that such men should look upon John Quincy Adams with some disapproval.   In his inaugural address he called to mind the roads and aqueducts of Rome as among the imperishable glories of the empire, and suggested that this nation might well plan like means to great material development.   No sooner had the Congress met than he came forward with a program : Chesapeake Bay should be connected by canals with the Ohio and the Delaware ; Lake Memphramagog should be joined with the Connecticut ; the National Road should be extended, and another built from Washington to New Orleans ; islands should be sea-walled, lighthouses built, and harbors deepened.   Our commerce should be guarded by a stronger navy, and na-

[1] *Argus*, March 30, Aug. 17, 1826.

[2] *N. Y. American*, Nov. 31, 1825 ; John Bigelow, " DeWitt Clinton as a Politician," *Harper's Monthly*, vol. l.   Lombards were a species of loan association.

[3] *Argus*, Oct. 19, 1826.

tional defense should be secured by military schools and state militia equipped and trained according to the national prescription. A great university, surveys, observatories, and exploring parties, were to advance the cause of science at national expense. An item later added to the scheme was a Home Department which would superintend all these activities, encourage manufactures, and counsel states in their co-operation.[1]

With the announcement of these bold proposals, in New York, as elsewhere, papers took sides for and against the administration, and old cleavages were deepened.[2] Although a small minority of Federalists, like certain fellow-partisans of Boston, could not be reconciled to an apostate,[3] most of those who had composed that party now supported Adams, and pronounced against those politicians who would cramp the proper function of the central government in the interest of so-called states' rights.[4] At least three quarters of the Clinton following were for the President.[5] The voters of the western counties gave him their support, not alone because of their New England memories or their old suspicion of the Regency, but because they realized that his program

[1] Upon the publication of Adams's speech of Dec. 25 (J. D. Richardson, *Messages and Papers*, vol. ii, p. 319), Jefferson wrote to Madison, including a draft of "The Solemn Declaration and Protest of the Commonwealth of Virginia," which was to have been published, had not Madison advised against it; see Jefferson, *Writings*, vol. x, pp. 348-352, and Madison, *Works*, vol. iii, pp. 511-514.

[2] *Argus*, Dec. 17, 1825. M. Hoffman to A. C. Flagg, Dec. 22, 1826 and Jan. 8, 1827. Hoffman charged that Adams men favored internal improvement partly on account of patronage expected.

[3] The *N. Y. Evening Post* represented this minority. See for conditions in Massachusetts, J. T. Morse, *John Quincy Adams* (Boston, 1899), pp. 209, 217.

[4] *N. Y. American*, Jan. 1, 11, 14, May 1, 3, 16, 1826.

[5] J. D. Hammond, *Political History*, vol. ii, p. 252.

of appropriations for canals and roads throughout the farther west, would, if carried out, bring more commerce through their section and more grist to their flour mills.[1] If the city merchants had endorsed a policy of state improvement for the lower cost of transportation that it would bring, they enthusiastically approved these larger plans which promised much at small cost to themselves.

The orthodox Democracy of New York state regarded this broader American system with aversion, if not horror.[2] They cordially disliked the debts, monopolies, corruption, favoritism, and centralized control, which they alleged would follow from its operation.   In 1824, Senator Van Buren took his stand against the policy in Washington, and after Adams' pronunciamento in December, 1825, he introduced a resolution stating that the Constitution gave no power to Congress to construct roads and waterways within the states. In April, 1826, he said that Congress could not vote appropriations for such purposes, even if it left the building and the jurisdiction to the local legislatures.   In May, he said that it could make no permanent arrangements for or with those private capitalists who might undertake such enter-

---

[1] Clay men had followed their leader into the Adams ranks. Clay had liked Crawford, but disliked his principles, as far as he knew them, and had disliked Jackson's personality, though he had no great fault to find with his principles; see H. C. Hockett, *Influence of the West on Political Parties to 1825*, p. 139. It was typical that James Stuart, the English traveler, should find the canal agent with whom he talked an Adams man, *Three Years in North America*, vol. i, p. 75.

[2] This is true after 1823, though not so clear before. The *Argus*, Jan. 14, 1822, had said: " We rejoice to find that a bill making an appropriation for repairing this [Cumberland] road has passed the Senate of the United States by a vote of 26 to 9." The Democratic assembly of 1822 passed on April 10 a resolution asking government aid in improving the navigation of the Hudson. See also attempts to get aid for canal building, in D. Hosack, *Memoir of Clinton*, p. 102, and remarks, J. C. Spencer, *Argus*, Feb. 1, 1826.

prises.[1]   These views were shared by the other members of the Regency.[2]   " The very power claimed to make these canals," wrote one, " is opposed to our Democratic principles." [3]

The governor's opinion on these matters was the object of wide-spread interest and anxiety, especially among his followers, the great majority of whom endorsed the Presidential program.   Not only had he gone with Morris in 1811 to solicit aid in Washington, but the following year the legislature on his urging had persuaded Ohio to petition for a grant of federal money for the Grand Canal in New York state.[4]   Speaking to the senate and assembly in 1822, he had intimated that the western states then beginning waterways should be " assisted by the general government in carrying into effect the magnificent plans they had projected." [5]   In 1824, there had been a movement to name Clinton for Vice

[1] *Congressional Debates*, 1825-1826, vol. ii, pt. 1, cols. 20, 619, and 717-718. See W. N. Holland, *Life and Political Opinions of Van Buren* (N. Y., 1835), pp. 269-274, George Bancroft, *Martin Van Buren*, pp. 116-120, and E. M. Shepard, *Martin Van Buren*, p. 113; Van Buren to B. F. Butler, Dec. 12, 1826, Van Buren Mss.; Van Buren to J. A. Hamilton, Dec. 20, 1826, J. A Hamilton, *Reminiscences*, p. 63.

[2] Hoffman-Flagg correspondence, Jan. 8, 18, 22, 1827, Flagg Mss. Silas Wright, in the state senate, introduced a resolution similar in spirit to those passed in South Carolina and Virginia sustaining these contentions (see H. V. Ames, *State Documents on Federal Relations* (U. of Pa., 1906), no. iv,. He was successfully opposed by some old Federalists like C. D. Colden, and some People's Men like J. C. Spencer. Senator Jordan, a People's Man, then introduced a moderate resolution that Congress could not begin an enterprise within a state without the state's consent, and must yield the jurisdiction over the improvement to the state when finished (*Argus*, Feb. 2, 6, 7, 1826).   It seems never to have come to a final vote (*N. Y. Senate Journal*, p. 170).

[3] Hoffman to Flagg, Jan. 8, 1827, Flagg Mss.

[4] W F. Gephart, *Transportation and Industrial Development in the Middle West*, Columbia University Studies in History, *etc.*, vol. xxxiv, pp. 110-111.

[5] *Messages from the Governors*, vol. ii.

President, so that he could more conveniently assist in national development.[1]   But since the state, in answer to his perseverance, had built its own canal, he professed to see grave danger in any interference by the federal government in such concerns, and in his message of 1825, he bitterly complained of the new doctrine that Congress must control exclusively the commerce " among the states." [2]   It was not till 1827, however, that he spoke clearly on the power to construct canals and roads: " I think it due to a sense of duty and a spirit of frankness to say, that my opinion is equally hostile to its possession or exercise by, or its investment in the national authorities." [3]   But by this time, we shall see, Clinton and Clintonians had parted company; this pronouncement was one signal of the separation.

In 1826, however, the governor's prestige had suffered no decline, and the delegates who were convened at Utica nominated him by acclamation to continue in his office.[4]   The Democrats, at Herkimer, though some believed it inexpedient to name a candidate,[5] chose William B. Rochester, a

[1] B. V. Tyler to DeW. Clinton, Feb. 2, 1824, and T. A. Emmett to same, March 22, 1824, Clinton Mss.

[2] *Albany Argus, Extra*, Jan. 5, 1825. Clinton had spoken of himself as a states' rights man before, but not specifically upon this point (*e. g.* Clinton Clippings, vol. ii, p. 48).

[3] Message of 1827, *Albany Argus*, Jan. 2, 1827; Letter to Moses Hayden, Jan. 14, 1827, Clinton Mss.

[4] *Utica Sentinel and Gazette*, Sept. 22, 1826. The convention was attended by most of the same Clintonian-Federalist delegates that had met in 1824. Gen. Tallmadge was not renominated for lieutenant-governor, as he had ruined his prospects by his action in the senatorial contest the year before (Kingston *Plebeian*, Oct. 4, 1826), and Henry Huntington was finally selected for that office. C. D. Colden, P. A. Jay and James Emott were mentioned, among others, for the place. The *Argus* was outraged because the convention used the name " Republican" (Sept. 25, 1826).

[5] S. Wright to A. C. Flagg, Nov. 18, 1826, Flagg Mss.; Thurlow Weed to Francis Granger, July 5, 1826, Granger Mss.

young man from the town which bore his family name. He was known to favor all the doctrines preached by Henry Clay, and his selection was clearly in accordance with a principle, since oftentimes remembered, that a party by a nomination may, perchance, attract some whom its principles and record would repel. "Availability" was further illustrated in their choice for second place, Nathaniel Pitcher, who lived within the valley of the Erie Canal, but who had a following through the "southern tier" because of his recommendations as a state-road commissioner. Judge Hammond, the historian, who took an active part in the campaign, asserts that many politicians knew that Senator Van Buren, albeit outwardly agreeable, desired Rochester's defeat (though not that of General Pitcher), planning thus to form a coalition against Adams, with the re-elected governor. The "Little Magician," with clairvoyant apprehension, may have plotted the event which issued from the contest, but most of his associates, in ignorance or disapproval, gave their best support to Rochester and were chagrined when he was beaten.[1] As champions of the state road, Clinton and Pitcher were elected, though on opposing tickets, through the almost solid vote of certain southern counties.[2] Most old Federalist districts gave reduced majorities for the governor, and Rochester made inroads in the west. In account-

---

[1] S. Wright to A. C. Flagg, Nov. 18, 1826, Flagg Mss., shows that the Regency were not entirely in accord with Van Buren in this matter as implied by J. D. Hammond, *Political History*, vol. ii, p. 232. *Cf.* W. B. Rochester to A. C. Flagg, and all letters from Hoffman to Flagg, between Oct. 7 and the election, Flagg Mss. *Geneva Palladium* and *Monroe Republican*, quoted in *Argus*, Jan. 1, 1827. M. M. Noah, the Democratic editor in New York city, at that moment in charge of the *New York Enquirer*, was neutral in the campaign, see *Argus*, Nov. 6, 1826.

[2] *Cf.* return in *Schenectady Cabinet*, Nov. 23, 1826, and *Albany Argus*, Nov. 20, 1826.

ing for this change of sentiment, the student must take careful note of these suspicions that the builder of the Grand Canal did not longer represent the party of business enterprise.

Since his uncle had retired from the field of politics, Clinton's favorite candidate for President had been Clinton.   In 1822 and 1823, he had been hopeful of the nomination, and bitterly censorious of those who questioned his capacity for that exalted office; and for several years thereafter this possibility was ever in his mind.[1]   His tour through Pennsylvania, Ohio and Kentucky, in 1825, with its public dinners and receptions, was thought to serve these high ambitions. When, however, it was seen that the great contestants of the next campaign would be the President and General Jackson, he discountenanced for the time the hopeless efforts in his own behalf and came out strongly for the latter.[2]   Adams he considered as his rival in the north,[3] while the mutual esteem between the military chieftain and himself dated back half a dozen years.[4]   In this preference, the governor, Van Buren, and the Democrats of southern states, were now

[1] Letters in J. Bigelow, "DeWitt Clinton as a Politician," *Harper's Monthly*, vol. l, pp. 415-417.   The clippings collected by Clinton at this period show his assiduous interest.

[2] *N. Y. Statesman*, Oct. 2, 1827; DeW. Clinton to C. L. Livingston, Nov. 22, 1827, Clinton Mss.; J. D. Hammond, *Political History*, vol. ii, p. 256.

[3] W. H. Smith, *Charles Hammond and his Relations to Henry Clay and John Quincy Adams* (Chicago, 1885), p. 32.

[4] Clinton wrote compliments to Jackson in 1819, and defended him against the strictures of General Scott (Clinton Letterbook, vol. iv, pp. 366-377), while Jackson replied: "To receive such an expression of friendly feeling from so distinguished a man as yourself is peculiarly gratifying" (March 9, 1819, Clinton Mss.).   In 1819 the general as the guest of the Tammany society threw the meeting into consternation by a toast to Clinton; see Gustavus Myers, *History of Tammany Hall* (N. Y., 1917 edition), p. 52.

in accord; the *Argus*, which in 1824 had charged Jackson with designs to ruin the Republican party,[1] the following year expressed a complimentary judgment, though earnestly deploring, here again with Clinton, all premature discussion of the presidential contest.[2] For two more years it held to this position of benevolent neutrality.[3] The " Federalist charges " of Van Buren's secret aid to Clinton in the state campaign, however, seemed substantiated in unwonted favors now exchanged between the old antagonists, and by 1827 the coalition was divested of its clouds of mystery.[4]

But it was a personal arrangement. If Clinton thought the great majority of his adherents who had applauded Adams and his enterprises, would follow with docility to the support of one whose policies were well suspected to be different,[5] he merely evidenced again his old confusion as to his party and his person. Only a few old Federalists had favored Jackson in 1824, and, since Adams' program had been understood, these few had grown still less.[6] The edi-

[1] May 18, 1824.

[3] May 20, Nov. 11, 1825, March 30, 1826, and Clinton's Clippings, vol. iii, p. 31.

[2] *Argus*, Jan. 30 (supplement), April 12, June 2, 30, July 4, August 14, 20, 1827. It finally came out definitely as a Jackson paper on Sept. 27, 1827.

[4] W. C. Bouck to Van Buren, Nov. 17, 1826, Van Buren Mss. Van Buren endorsed Clinton's appointments to important judgeships, and by the support of Clinton, Van Buren was re-elected to the federal Senate; see J. D. Hammond, *Political History*, vol. ii, pp. 212, 214, 246, 255.

[5] Silas Wright wrote to Flagg, Dec. 20, 1827 (Flagg Mss.), after consulting with Van Buren, Hoffman and two other New York congressmen that it was understood that Jackson would oppose the American System and appoint orthodox Democrats to cabinet positions. He said the appointees of Adams in New York state had nearly all been Federalists.

[6] See *supra*, chap. ix; *cf. N. Y. Commercial Advertiser*, Jan. 14, 1822, and Hoffman to Flagg, Dec. 22, 1826 and Jan. 8, 1827, Flagg Mss. Thurlow Weed for a time feared otherwise; see to Francis Granger, March 29, 1827, Granger Mss.

torial pen of Thurlow Weed betrayed a trace of gall when he observed: "If we could for a moment credit the story that the Governor cherishes a thought of support for both parties, we would admonish him of the folly of such hopes." [1] Papers like the *Albany Advertiser* and the *New York Statesman*, whose personal loyalty to the governor had resembled vassalage, now announced that this relationship had passed, and printed "Adams" at their column heads. [2]

There is no room for hesitation [decided the *Buffalo Journal*], for however an exalted opinion the people of the state may have for the talents and services of Mr. Clinton, they cannot, in a question affecting the prospective welfare of the nation, sacrifice their own judgments in a blind reliance on his preference — honestly formed, perhaps, but evidently founded in errour. [3]

Of sixty "federal newspapers" in the state, fifty-one remained with Adams. [4]

It is clear that Federalists, and most of those associated with them, were disappointed in the governor. For ten years they had understood him to be pledged to policies according with the interests and philosophy (tempered now by some experience), which had been theirs time out of mind. Whatever Van Buren may have thought, at least some members of the Regency quite clearly saw how futile was the hope of winning Clinton's party to the cause they stood for.

[1] *Rochester Telegraph*, quoted in *Albany Argus*, March 30, 1826.

[2] *Albany Daily Advertiser*, June 22, 1827; *Argus*, June 23, July 2, 1827.

[3] Oct. 9, 1827.

[4] *Argus*, March 10, 1828. This paper said that of 49 Bucktail papers all but 7 were for Jackson. It spoke of the Adams party being made up of Clintonians and old Federalists like Elisha Williams, the Van Rensselaers, Col. Stone, Mr. Dwight, of the Hartford Convention, Charles King, of Dartmoor memory, and thousands of others. The *Evening Post* was a Clinton-Jackson paper; see on Sept. 24, 1827, and Wm. Coleman to Van Buren, ——, 1827, Van Buren Mss.

To some the course of caution and neutrality, by which this merger was to be effected, was obnoxious; such subleties bewildered honest Democrats, and merely for the gain of Clinton, even though he might be followed by a "little band," they were not worth the hiding and the plotting they entailed.   Some questioned the integrity of their old enemy and thought at last he would announce himself for Adams These were for a bold profession of the principles of 'ninety-eight, and to let those join them who found these attractive.   If their party came to power it would have to be with the old creed acceptable to the south.   They believed that Jackson could be easily converted to this faith, if he did not cherish it already, and urged an early caucus to present his name.

Van Buren yielded slowly (delay, though never dalliance, marked his technic), for he thought these very notions as to Jackson's orthodoxy were percolating through the state, and he had learned in 1824 that caucuses can follow better than they can command.[1]   On the thirty-first of January, 1828, a Democratic caucus nominated the Old Hero.[2]   No one knew precisely what were his principles, but the party

---

[1] Charles Butler to Flagg, Geneva, Dec. 15, 1827. " Even Adams himself will for our sake *read* the doctrines of Thomas Jefferson—and Mr. Jackson rather than not be President will reduce them to practice. Let us assert our principles. If it had been done when it ought to have been, we should have been followed by Virginia, S. Carolina & Georgia. Let us not wait until we *must follow* either C. & his Brotherhood—or the *old Feds*." " The *Argus* man is in favor of neutrality. Ask him which he will follow. Write me a categorical answer to that question," Hoffman to Flagg, Jan. 2, 1827; see also same Dec. 22, 1826, Jan. 8, 22. Dec. 21, 1827. " If Clinton is going to come out Adams as I have expected he would, in God's name let him do it soon, and then we can put our rudder," Silas Wright to Flagg, Aug. 29, 1827. For Wright's impatience of neutrality, see letter to Flagg, Dec. 20, 1827; Flagg's like feeling is mentioned in Hoffman to Flagg, Jan. 22, 1827. See also *N. Y. Evening Post*, Sept. 24, 1827, and *Albany Argus*, Sept. 26, 1827, and Coleman to Van Buren, April 17, 1828, Van Buren Mss.

[2] J. D. Hammond, *Political History*, vol. ii, p. 281.

leaders had assured themselves by this time that he shared their deep antipathies, and that his sympathies were with the frontier farmers and town laborers, rather than with the commercial capitalists and the old professional ruling class.[1] As to the manufacturers, recently observed to have an interest in the game of politics, these leaders had hestitated for a time, but with the influence of allies in the south, they were coming to a definite conclusion.

Steam and steel, which in the last years of the eighteenth century, had brought to England sudden wealth and want, cheapening goods and men, were introduced on this side of the Atlantic somewhat later with less convulsive readjustments of society. As household industries were crowded out in country districts, fertile land was readily available to use the energies released. Yet because no cataclysm marked those years, one must not overlook the changes in the life and thought of common men that followed from the great development of manufacturing in New England and the middle states throughout the quarter-century after the embargo. Cotton spindles, for example, could not be increased from eight thousand to half a million in seven years,[2] without some economic consequences which would sometime register themselves in politics.

In this development New York was second only to its neighbor, Massachusetts. In 1808, the Oneida Manufacturing Society set up at Whitesboro the first cotton-spinning mill in New York state,[3] while two years later woolen yarn

---

[1] See Hoffman-Flagg correspondence, January to April, 1827.

[2] E. L. Bogart, *Economic History of the United States* (N. Y., 1916 edition), p. 164. This gain was between 1808 and 1815.

[3] M. M. Bagg, " The Earliest Factories of Oneida and their Projection," in *Oneida Historical Society Publication,* 1881, pp. 112, *et seq.,* " The New Hartford Centennial," *ibid.,* 1887-1889, pp. 52-53. The first woolen mill in this section was begun in 1811, and the first power-loom in 1817, Bagg, p. 117. See also Evarts and Ferris, *History of Oneida County,* pp. 243, 623.

was spun in two mills near Poughkeepsie.[1] Although no revolution was immediately effected, and in 1822 the governor could still report that the leachers in their asheries furnished the chief export of the state,[2] the progress was continuous and steady till, with the middle 'twenties when canals and roads brought the material to mills and finished articles to customers, it was clear that a new epoch had begun. New industries were introduced even in the west and north, where the clangor of the factory bell, shattering the morning peace, might startle some stray panther roaming through the purlieus of the forest.[3] No one could tell how great a change could yet be wrought, or what unsuspected energies could be applied. It was a proud day when, in 1824, the *Commercial Advertiser* could announce that Mr. Ayres of Ithaca, who manufactured imitation Leghorn hats, would soon employ " one hundred females, some of whom are not more than eight years of age." [4]

Industrial enterprise, especially in iron, hats and textiles, combined with lower cost of transportation to bring prosperity to Albany, where in the three years after 1823 rents

[1] E. Platt, *History of Poughkeepsie*, pp. 83-85.

[2] *Messages from the Governors*, vol. ii, p. 1093.

[3] After the Erie Canal was opened the western counties began to manufacture somewhat for the New York city market, V. S. Clark, *History of Manufactures in the United States, 1607-1860* (Washington, 1916), pp. 347-349. Watertown grew rapidly because of the new cotton and woolen mills built there by Le Ray de Chaumount, *Jefferson Republican*, quoted in *N. Y. American*, Feb. 21, 1823. *House Documents*, 22nd Cong., 1st sess., no. 303, shows the influence of the Erie Canal on the distribution of industrial plants by 1833.

[4] In Clinton's Clippings, vol. ii, p. 51. Ithaca at the head of Lake Cayuga had a position not unlike that of Chicago, and it expected that the construction of railroads and of the canal to Sodus Bay in Lake Ontario, would make it the important center for central New York and Pennsylvania. But the hilly country immediately to the south deterred the railroad builders and they later surveyed easier routes and laid their tracks to make connection with Rochester and Buffalo.

advanced by half, and four-story business buildings were put up as fast as laborers could be secured.[1]   By 1827 there were sixteen textile factories in Oneida County giving work to seven hundred hands;[2] in five more years there were twenty cotton mills alone, with three times as many employees,[3] and though Utica itself contained but few, " every stream from the neighboring hills was covered with such speculations."[4]   Rensselaer and Dutchess Counties were not far behind. Auburn might have seemed like Goldsmith's loveliest village of the plain, observed an English traveller in 1828, " but for its numerous manufacturing establishments."[5]   The Genesee at Rochester ran spinning-mules and power-looms, as well as flour mills.[6]   Industrial statistics do not fascinate the general reader, but when in scanning the long columns of the census figures, one notices that while the total ouptut of the state was more than doubling in the decade after 1825, the *per capita* production of textiles in the households fell from 8.95 yards to 4.03, he has come upon a fact of some significance.[7]

[1] *Albany Daily Advertiser*, Sept. 1, 1826; *Albany Argus*, Sept. 9, 12, 1826.

[2] From a table in a Utica paper noticed in the *Rochester Telegraph* and quoted in *Argus*, July 4, 1827, 600 of these hands were children.

[3] In Oneida, 2,354 were employed; Dutchess, 1,974; Rensselaer, 1,621; Columbia, 1,285. Dutchess had also 6 woolen mills, Orange 6 and Rensselaer 5. T. F. Gordon, *Gazetteer of the State of New York* (Philadelphia, 1836), pp. 334, *et seq.* See also C. Benton and S. F. Barry, *Statistical View of the Woolen Manufactures* (Cambridge, 1831), p. 124.

[4] E. T. Coke, *A Subaltern's Furlough* (N. Y. edition, 1833), vol. i, p. 215.

[5] James Stuart, *Three Years in North America*, vol. i, p. 81.

[6] *Ibid., loc. cit.*; also Basil Hall, *Travels in North America*, vol. i, p. 53.

[7] R. M. Tryon, *Household Manufactures in the United States* (Chicago, 1917), pp. 304-307. The decline in household manufactures was naturally most sudden in Oneida County, where the figures ran

Iron manufactories—bloomeries, blast furnaces, and mills for nails and hoops—so grew in number that soon after 1830 about ten thousand people were dependent on their operation.[1] In 1827 there was opened in the city of New York the first hardware store dealing mainly in American goods.[2] After 1825, it was seen that " fossil coal " would soon come into common use, making possible new processes and increased production, while charcoal-burners working in the woodland, one by one allowed their pits to cool and whiten, and in disgust sought out some other means of livelihood.[3] Fertile land so cheap and so accessible in New York necessitated higher wages than in many other states, and these in turn gave stimulus to the invention of machinery.[4] In the

from 12.65 yards to 4.83. Other counties where the change was rapid were Schenectady, Columbia, Orange, Washington and Ontario. Statistics for 1820 are also given by Tryon, p. 288.

[1] T. F. Gordon, *Gazetteer*. The iron workers in the decade after 1825, doubled in number, increasing especially in Essex County. At the same time capital was withdrawn from old-fashioned industries like asheries (due to easier transportation of the lumber itself by canal), distilleries, grist and oil mills.

[2] J. L. Bishop, *History of American Manufactures* (Philadelphia, 1864), vol. ii, p. 387, note.

[3] F. J. Grund, *The Americans*, p. 284, quotes a Pennsylvania state senate report of March 4, 1835: 9,541 tons were used in 1824; 33,699 in 1825. This sudden increase was due to the opening of the Schuylkill mines; another sudden increase came in 1828 when the Lackawanna mines were made available. Anthracite was first used in the iron industry itself in 1838, C. Wright, *Industrial Evolution of the United States* (Meadville, Pa., 1897), chaps. x, xi.

[4] In Massachusetts and New Hampshire, only, were wages higher. Fishing and shipping doubtless had an effect similar to the Genesee lands in New York; also the greater development of manufacturing made a greater demand for labor. In New York the average wage was $1 per day, Timothy Pitkin, *Statistical View of the Commerce of the United States of America* (Hartford, 1835 edition) ; see charts in textile industry. See also F. J. Grund, *The Americans*, p. 274; Bishop's lists of patents for 1830, cited in J. R. H. Moore, *Industrial History of the American People* (N. Y., 1913), p. 415.

last years of the 'twenties it was realized that industry was changing; in the closely settled districts spinning-wheels and cottage looms were carried to the garrets, and apprentices and journeymen gave reluctant place to " hands ". [1]

In the constitutional convention the chancellor, J. R. Van Rensselaer and Van Ness, had spoken their opinion of the manufacturer as a menace to the established order of the state, not as safely to be trusted with political influence as the merchant and the landlord.   He could not then be counted on as an ally of Federalists.   He was not as yet the personage that he became a generation later.   He was not as yet a gentleman distinguished by inherited wealth, family portraits and a liberal education, but was still a glorified mechanic, merely, who had worked up from the bench.   The prominent manufacturers like Benjamin Knower, who made hats in Albany, Peter Sharpe, the whip-maker, and Clarkson Crolius, the potter, were then thorough-going Democrats.[2]   Federalists, it would appear, were not yet interested in the enginery of mills.   But in the middle 'twenties, when industrial profits became the subject of the gossip of the court-house and the banking office, their attitude was changed, and such old partisans as J. R. Van Rensselaer, Ambrose Spencer, Robert Troup, Platt, Gold and Philip Hone, began to take a part in the movement for " domestic industry," [3] and George Tibbits wrote an *Essay on the Home Markets*, charged with high enthusiasm.[4]

[1] As late as 1815 upon satisfactorily completing apprenticeship, a young man without property might be received as a freeman of the city of New York, *N. Y. Historical Society Collections*, 1885, p. 399, cited by R. F. Seyboldt, *The Colonial Citizen of New York City* (Univ. of Wisconsin, 1918).

[2] *Albany Argus*, Jan. 25, 1825; G. A. Worth, *Random Recollections of Albany*, p. 52.

[3] *Argus*, April 9, 1824.

[4] *Essay on the Expediency and Practicability, of Improving or*

The sentiment was soon reflected in the press. In April, 1825, William O. Niles published a prospectus of a paper to be known as the *Albany Journal and Mercantile Adver- tiser*, and to have for its concern " the encouragement of Commerce, Domestic Industry and Internal Improvement," [1] while at Saugerties some three years later there appeared the *Ulster Palladium and Manufacturer's Journal* devoted to the news about canals, machinery, railways and the tariff.[2] The Patroon, catching the new spirit, determined to devote a portion of his hundred-thousand-dollar income [3] to the founding and endowment of a Rensselaer School in Troy to instruct young persons in the " application of Science to the common purposes of life," an enterprise begun in 1825.[4] Others urged that New York follow Massachusetts in work- ing out a system of public instruction in the uses of ma- chinery.[5] It was, then, the decade after 1825, that saw the rise of manufactures, as well as the great development of commerce; [6] and it was in this decade, we shall see, that the old conservatives, supplemented by some others, reorganized their party and took on the name of Whig.

Creating Home Markets for the Sale of Agricultural Production and Raw Materials, by the Introduction or Growth of Artizans and Manu- factures, etc. (Philadelphia, 1829), in Library of Congress.

[1] *Argus*, April 29, 1825.

[2] Vol. i, no. 1 (May 3, 1828), is in the library of the N. Y. Historical Society.

[3] "Letters of a Traveller" to *National Intelligencer,* letter of June 16, 1825; T. F. Gordon, *Gazetteer of New York*, p. 651.

[4] See "constitution" of the institute in the *Albany Argus,* April 29, 1825.

[5] See *Livingston Journal,* quoted in *Argus*, April 8, 1825, commenting on the commission recently appointed by the Massachusetts legislature.

[6] The commercial progress of New York was continuous in this decade, though elsewhere there was a depression till after 1830; see Emory Johnson and others, *History of the Foreign and Domestic Commerce of the United States* (Carnegie Institution, Washington, 1915), vol. i, p. 220.

While this interest was deepening among the men of wealth and business enterprise, the legislature, where the Democrats were generally controlling, gradually withdrew its patronage, in spite of all appeals. There had been at first a hearty disposition toward encouragement. In January, 1817, eight essays signed by "An American" appeared in the *Commercial Advertiser*, proving that the manufactures of the state deserved subventions from the government at Albany, and the following month an act was passed exempting textile mills from all taxation and their employees from certain jury and militia service.[1] By 1823 this law had met with some objection from supporters of the Regency,[2] and their senators in 1824 put through a bill providing for repeal, though the People's Men, who then had a majority in the assembly, refused their sanction.[3] But the following winter, despite the opposition of John C. Spencer and his colleagues, the act was passed leaving woolen manufactures only as exempted from taxation.[4] Even in a few short

[1] Passed Feb. 28, 1827; *Laws of the State of New York*, 40th session, chap. 44. There had been a temporary law passed June 19, 1812, for the encouragement of woolen manufacture, many sections of which were revived in an act passed April 15, 1817, *ibid.*, chap. 240. A law appropriating $10,000 for the encouragement of household manufactures was passed in 1819, *ibid.*, 42nd session, chap. 107. On the American Society for the Encouragement of Domestic Manufacture, see Thomas Jefferson to Dominick Lynch, Jr., Monticello, June 26, 17, *Correspondence of Thomas Jefferson, 1778-1826* (Boston, 1916), p. 230.

[2] Remarks of Mr. Auger in the assembly, *N. Y. American*, March 4, 1823. A new tax law made no mention of the exemptions (*Laws*, 46th session, chap. 262), and during 1823 and 1824 there was a difference of opinion as to whether they were still operative; see *N. Y. Senate Journal*, 1824, pp. 87-89, 121.

[3] The bill passed the senate, Feb. 17, 1824, *ibid.*, p. 129; see remarks of Mr. McIntyre, *Albany Argus*, March 4, 1825. It is interesting to note that five of the seven opponents of the bill were People's Men.

[4] *Argus*, Feb. 15, 25, March 1, 1825. In the course of the debate, Mr. McIntyre, a People's Man of Montgomery County, spoke in favor of

years, it seems, the Democrats had come to realize that factories, like banks and docks, were not to be their citadels of strength.

Protection of American manufactures, for which there had been no considerable demand in the early days of the republic, was practically afforded on the most extensive scale by the restrictive laws that marked the eight years after 1807.[1]   When the signing of the Peace of Ghent had cleared the seas for commerce, the manufacturers prayed for artificial aid to keep their factories running; and the farmers, especially in the fertile western counties of New York, who found themselves unable to supply the English market by reason of the corn laws, joined in the demand for high protective duties on manufactured goods.   This seemed to them a measure of retaliation against England, and possibly a means to build up large industrial communities at home where their food-stuffs would be needed.[2]   Their flocks, which grew in number year by year and gained in value with improvements from Merino crossings, gave them so direct an interest in the progress of the woolen manufacture, that they cordially supported the tariff of 1824.   For a short time they were apprehensive lest the demand for factory hands should raise the wages of farm labor, but were soon assured that the mills would hire chiefly girls, and

continuing the exemptions, showing the famer's need of a home market in manufacturing towns, especially for his fine Merino wool; see *ibid.*, March 4, 1825. Mr. Vanderheuval, of St. Lawrence also made a vigorous protest; *N. Y. American*, Jan. 17, 1825. In many districts the manufacturing was still chiefly in the households.

[1] Of course, the principle was familiar in the eighteenth century, but except for Hamilton's report, " other subjects so absorbed the attention of public men that no distinct opinion appear in their utterance for or against protective duties," F. W. Taussig, *The Tariff History of the United States* (N. Y., 1914 edition), pp. 11-17.

[2] V. S. Clark, *History of Manufactures in the United States* (Washington, 1916), pp. 268-279.

thus instead of vying with the farmer would afford employment to his daughters. Immigration and the farm machinery coming into general use also helped prevent antagonism between the wool-growers and the manufacturers until the eighteen-fifties.[1] Yet the small farmer who had no such close connection with industries and cities listened more respectfully to true Democratic doctrine on the tariff. As to what this doctrine was and how it was developed we must now inquire.

[1] Clark, p. 279. See also E. Stanwood, *American Tariff Controversies in the Nineteenth Century* (Boston, 1903); O. L. Elliott, *The Tariff Controversy in the United States* (Palo Alto, Cal., 1892); Stephen Van Rensselaer to Van Buren, May 14, 1824, Van Buren Mss., and Silas Wright to Van Buren, vol. vii, pp. 96-99, *ibid*.

CHAPTER XI

POLITICAL DISTRACTION

IN 1824 but little opposition to protection had developed among the New York Democrats; objection to such measures on the ground of legal right as well as of expediency, found expression only in an unimportant group of thoroughgoing Jeffersonians.[1] While England preached the principles of Adam Smith but kept up tariff walls, the leaders readily admitted that America should give no heed.[2] Indeed it was the *American*, Federalist in all but willingness to work with Clinton, which most bitterly opposed the tariff, for, it said, the patronage now held out to the manufacturer would be withdrawn from commerce. Higher prices would be paid by farmers, making up the great majority of the consumers, to pay profits to mill-owners, whose evident prosperity, increasing with each year, required no sacrifice from trade or agriculture.[3] If farmers " have occasion to purchase anything of foreign growth or manufacture, and are able to pay for it, they can be quite independent whether the articles are manufactured in Old or New England, or elsewhere." [4] Protective tariff laws would stir resentment against the section where the manufacturing was carried on, and jeopardize the Union; even in that section they

[1] Remarks of Mr. Mallory in the N. Y. Senate, *Argus*, Feb. 27, 1824.

[2] *National Intelligencer*, quoted with approval by the *Argus*, Sept. 12, 1823; *N. Y. American*, Feb. 23, 1824.

[3] *N. Y. American*, Jan. 27, 1823.

[4] *Ibid.*, Jan. 31, 1824.

would cause complaint against those who would seem to be the special beneficiaries.[1]   Protective schedules on this article and that would be included quite against the public interest, by the vicious practice of " log rolling." [2]   Handicraftsmen would be out-competed by the great protected mills, which would draw their labor from the foreign rabble, cheap men devoid of skill, now flocking to our ports.[3]   " In good time," lamented "A Consumer," " we shall become a nation of machines and machinery—a Chinese community, a *manufacturing nation*, nobly and exclusively aspiring to rival Brummagem and Sheffield in the manufacture of pepper boxes and crown glass." [4]

Not all correspondents echoed the *American's* opinion: " Hamilton," to name but one, contributed a letter to show that moneyed men properly desired home industries in which their capital could be advantageously applied, while fathers welcomed steady employment for their sons, a condition which encouraged marriage.[5]   But the editors went on writing free-trade argument about producing where production was the cheapest without regard to arbitrary lines upon a map; no one could persuade them, they declared, that " the vast ocean which rolls almost before our eyes was meant not for a highway, but for an impassible boundary to the intercourse of nations." [6]   They indicated Mr.

---

[1] *N. Y. American*, Feb. 18, 1823; Feb. 17, 23, 1824.

[2] *Ibid.*, Feb. 17, 1824.   This is the first instance I have seen of the use of the expression "log-rolling."   It is used again in this paper, November 31, 1825.

[3] *Ibid.*, March 5, 6, 1824.

[4] *Ibid.*, Feb. 21, 1824.   " Brummagem " was, of course, the derisive epithet for Birmingham.

[5] *Ibid.*, Feb. 22, 1823.   He wrote also of the need for a balance of trade in America's favor, rather than the extravagant importations of 1822.

[6] *Ibid.*, Feb. 25, 1823; March 4. 1824.

Webster, who then in Washington preached the doctrine of low tariff, as their ideal of statesmanship,[1] and cordially supported Gulian C. Verplanck, who strove in the assembly to control more strictly the incorporation of manufacturing companies.[2] The *Evening Post*, then still reckoned as a Federalist paper, joined in the complaint that " nearly seventy persons concerned in manufacturing establishments had been elected to the present Congress," where they had carried through " an anti-commercial and mischievous bill." [3] Federal votes assisted to elect three anti-tariff Congressmen in November, 1824; it was clear that the shipping element within the conservative party in the state was prejudiced at first against the manufacturers.[4]

But there were several reasons why the New York merchants could not comfortably hold this attitude. In the first place, their fellow-partisans within the upper Hudson and the Mohawk valleys found the new investments very profitable, as we have seen; by 1828 the *Argus* was complaining that the Albany central committee formed by tariff men was but a " Clintonian-Federal caucus," since out of twenty-five, but three were genuine Democrats.[5] Their New England colleagues, also, soon decided that commerce, important as it was, could not wisely check the growth of industry; Daniel Webster in the vote of 1827 signalized this change of sentiment. The western farmers, with whom the city merchants had co-operated under Clinton, likewise wished a tariff. The *New York Society for the Promotion of the Arts and Manufactures* declared its object was to give " re-

[1] *N. Y. American*, Jan. 11, May 1, 3, 1826.

[2] *Ibid.*, Feb. 23, 1824; *Argus*, March 12, 1824.

[3] *N. Y. American*, Oct. 29, 1824; see also *National Advocate*, Nov. 1, 1824.

[4] *N. Y. Evening Post*, Nov. 6, 1824.

[5] March 17, 20, 25, 27, 1828.

lief to the agricultural interests of the state, by encouraging the growth, introduction and stationary residence within it, of a manufacturing population adequate to the consumption of its agricultural produce and to the fabrication of its raw materials." [1]   The staple farmers of the west who were near enough to the canal to market their surplus, it seemed, might seek to swing their party to support protection.

Then, too, the New York merchants were pledged to Adams and his Secretary, Clay, who favored cheapening the inland transportation.   But the administration more and more accepted the protective tariff as the leading feature of a broad program. [2]

While the planter and the merchant and the shepherd and the husbandmen [averred the President] shall be found thriving in their occupations under the duties imposed for the protection of domestic manufactures, they will not repine at the prosperity shared with themselves by their fellow-citizens of the professions or denounce as violations of the Constitution the deliberative acts of Congress to shield from the wrongs of foreign laws the native industry of the Union. [3]

The historians of American ideals have given less attention than they should to the enthusiasm for material prosperity which characterized the devotees of the American system, not only in the times of Clay and Webster, but likewise in the later years when a new Republican party exalted the full dinner-pail. [4]   " An ideal," remarks a recent

---

[1] *Argus*, April 9, 1824; see also letter from a Mr. Tod, of Greenfield, Saratoga Co., in *N. Y. American*, Feb. 22, 1824.

[2] *Cf.* comments of the *Troy Sentinel* and *Northern Budget*, quoted in *Argus*, June 11, July 9, 1824.

[3] J. D. Richardson, *Messages and Papers of the Presidents*, vol. ii, pp. 413, 414.

[4] E. D. Adams, *The Power of Ideals in American History* (New Haven, 1913) ; A. B. Hart, *National Ideals Historically Traced* (N. Y., 1907).

writer, "is an emotionally colored conception of a state of things which would be better than the present." [1]   Now the merchants of the great metropolis, as we have tried to show, belonged to the dynamic party with the program of development by intelligent extension of the sphere of government. If the tariff was a necessary item of this program, they must take it.   They also, very likely, calculated on a benefit; if manufactures made the country rich, as had been claimed, there would be a brisk demand for unprotected articles imported from abroad.   Whatever was their course of reasoning, the merchant wards in New York city in the election of 1828 cast their votes for Adams although he was a tariff man. [2]

That a considerable portion of the capitalist party should seem willing that the tariff should be made a campaign issue, was a matter of some interest to the Regency.   They became ingeniously evasive, and were accused of " non-committalism " by their adversaries. [3]   They replied that the question of domestic industry and its protection had no connection with party politics, and their newspapers reported the many tariff meetings without comment. [4]   They deprecated all attempts of Adams men to claim the measure as their own. [5]   When the Harrisburg Convention was announced, Marcy, who for some time was an advocate, warned the delegates through the columns of his *Budget* to " keep aloof from all party considerations; let them attend solely to the object for which the convention is called." [6]

But this was ignorant advice, since Clay had planned the

---

[1] C. D. Burns, *Greek Ideals* (London, 1917), pp. v-vi.

[2] *N. Y. Commercial Advertiser*, Jan. 1, 1828. On the straight tariff vote of 1828 the New York congressmen voted against; see F. J. Turner, *Rise of the New West* (N. Y., 1906), pp. 242, 320.

[3] *Albany Daily Advertiser*, June 27, 1827.

[4] *Argus*, June 23, 30, July 4, 21, 1827.

[5] *Ibid.*, July 16, 1827.

[6] *Ibid.*, July 17, Nov. 29, 1827.

meeting as a nucleus of a reorganized, revitalized American party, and he and other leaders were quite willing that protection should become the leading question of political debate.[1]   Van Buren avoided reference to the tariff when he could, but was known to be against protecting manufactures.[2]   Wright, Flagg and Hoffman favored tariffs for the farmer, if at all, while Marcy found his views so moderate that he opposed the high-protectionists.[3]   The Democrats in the assembly resolved that the woolens bill of 1827 was too favorable to mill-owners.[4]   Some manufacturers within the Democratic party, like Benjamin Knower, indignantly protested against this attitude and stanchly fought each proposition to investigate industrial profits, but they were impotent to change the party policy;[5] Peter R. Livingston left the party largely on this issue.[6]

[1] F. W. Taussig, *Tariff History*, p. 85. The *N. Y. Evening Post*, now Democratic, on Aug. 1 and 9, 1827, charged that the convention was a political measure, though it admitted on Aug. 11, that many who went were unaware of it.   Clay's intentions are set forth in a letter to B. W. Crowninshield, March 18, 1827; see *Quarterly Journal of Economics*, July, 1888, pp. 490-491.   When the convention's proposals were introduced in Congress, there were 78 Adams men and 12 Jackson men for, and 14 Adams men and 100 Jackson men opposed, *Niles' Register*, vol. xxxv, p. 57 (quoted by Taussig).   Clay's first important speech in the campaign dealt largely with the tariff (C. Colton, *Life and Works of Henry Clay* (N. Y., 1904), vol. i, pp. xiv-xvii), though the "bargain and corruption" charges subsequently played a large part.

[2] Gabriel Mead to Van Buren, Feb. 13, 1827, Van Buren Mss.; George Bancroft, *Martin Van Buren*, p. 146.

[3] J. D. Hammond, *Life of Silas Wright*, pp. 105-108; Wright said able men could sustain themselves, but some manufacturers who had made mistakes "want Uncle Sam to help them out," Wright to Flagg, Jan. 16, 1828; Hoffman to Flagg, Feb. 3, 1828, Flagg Mss.

[4] *Argus*, Feb. 1, 1828.

[5] Knower, Dudley and Olcott signed a circular letter calling for a tariff on the Harrisburg lines; for this controversy see Flagg to Wright, Jan. 10, 22, 1828 and Wright to Flagg, Jan. 16, 28, 1828, B. Knower to M. Van Buren, Jan. 27, 1828, Van Buren Mss.

[6] Hoffman to Flagg, Feb. 3, 1828, *ibid.*, J. D. Hammond, *Political History*, vol. ii, p. 323-324.

When a protectionist convention at Albany, in 1827, declared it could not " but regret the zeal with which a portion of our southern brethren oppose a protection to other essential interests embracing vastly greater territory and population," [1] it touched the Democratic leaders where they were most sensitive. In March, the legislature of Virginia had called the tariff laws, " unconstitutional, unwise, unjust, unequal and oppressive," [2] and if the New York Democrats would hold their fellowship with the Virginians, it was clear that they must be an anti-tariff party. Yet the protective principle was so widely cherished through the north, that no politician from that section would essay a definite and open opposition on the floor of Congress. To meet the situation, the reader will remember, a hodge-podge of absurdities was carefully contrived upon a plan which Clay declared originated in Van Buren's fecund brain, [3] and by which what seemed to be a measure of protection would have to be rejected by the votes of real protectionists, with no stigma fastened to the friends of Jackson.

Silas Wright, then a member of the House committee on manufactures, explained the trick to southern representatives. [4] To win support (for to achieve success it must get votes from all except the honest friends of the American System) he called it an agricultural tariff, and declared, " The struggle is, no doubt, to be between the *farmer* and the *manufacturer*. [5] But the manufacturers, who perceived

[1] *Argus*, July 18, 1827.

[2] *Niles Register*, vol. xxxii, pp. 167-170.

[3] Clay's *Works*, vol. ii, p. 13.

[4] F. W. Taussig, *Tariff History*, p. 96, and his authorities.

[5] Wright to Flagg, March 21, 1828. On Van Buren's request Wright prepared quotations on the tariff from Washington, John Adams, Jefferson, Madison, etc., and an estimate of the condition of the wool trade in New York state. He estimated that there were 30 or 40 woolen factories employing $30,000 or $40,000 and between 15,000 and

the springs within the trap, decided to accept the bill, although its schedules were ill-balanced and embarrassingly high, so that the principle of a protective tariff might be saved. The law was passed, to the disgust of its ingenious architects. From widely different causes, then, the support from New York state was unanimous, except for New York city and some counties on the lower Hudson.[1] From that time forth the Democratic leaders threw off all pretence of protectionism.

But the slowly formulating sentiment upon the tariff was not the sole consideration of the Regency and their opponents. There were other factors which delayed a straight and strict alignment of two parties in the state—a rivalry of sections for grants of public money, a strange fanatical enthusiasm, and a personal loyalty — each of which must briefly be reviewed.

In 1809, a correspondent writing Clinton on the prospects of a state canal, said that he had been informed of " an attempt to embarrass that project by a petition which originated in Kingston for a turnpike," and deplored " that contemptible locality of calculation " which cursed the plans of wise and able statesmen.[2] When the subject was debated in the legislature, " those opposing were the southern and middle counties, including Delaware." [3] Yet as the work proceeded to completion and success, opposition in those sections which would not be served, changed into a

---

20,000 hands. He said there were probably 5,000,000 sheep in the state, making about 30,000 men directly interested in selling wool. See Van Buren Mss., vol. vii, pp. 96-97.

[1] F. J. Turner, *Rise of the New West*, p. 242 (map).

[2] From H. N. Butler, March 12, 1809, Clinton Mss.

[3] George Tibbits to Benjamin Tibbits, June 13, 1828, in D. Hosack, *Memoir of Clinton*, Appendix, pp. 488, *et seq.* Tibbits mentions opposition also from the eastern parts of Rensselaer and Washington Counties, with parts of others.

strong desire for some similar accommodation. The achievements of Macadam in the north of England had aroused considerable attention in this country,[1] and with promptings from the southern counties, Governor Clinton in his message of 1825 recommended the construction of a great state road to join the lower Hudson with Lake Erie. Opposition was immediately forthcoming. In the valleys traversed by the Erie and Champlain Canals the residents were satisfied with what the state had done and disliked to pay their share of taxes to build a turnpike through the " southern tier "; if Clinton had engaged to get the votes of the canal men for a road, as was alleged,[2] he could not keep his bargain. However, a commission of inquiry was provided and a tentative survey begun.[3] Mass-meetings and conventions, labored essays and long editorials, attested public interest in the southern counties;[4] but when the commissioners reported in 1826, the northern members of the legislature were all the more confirmed in opposition.[5]

Partisan connections seemed forgotten in this all-absorbing contest. While Gamaliel Barstow, a People's Man from Tioga County, and General Root, whose home lay on the line surveyed, were leading advocates,[6] Francis Gran-

[1] *Albany Argus*, Sept. 4, 1826.

[2] C. E. MacGill, *History of Transportation in the United States to 1860* (Washington, 1917), p. 163.

[3] Hammond, who was one of the three commissioners, gives a full account of the matter in his *Political History*, vol. ii, pp. 201, 209, 219-225, 233, 235, 245.

[4] *Albany Argus*, March 1, June 16, July 15, 1825; May 29, June 2, 21, Aug. 30, Sept. 4, 1826; *Albany Daily Advertiser*, May 26, 1826.

[5] The charge that the canal party had managed that the survey be run through difficult and impracticable country, where the road would be of little service, which is accepted as true by Miss MacGill, *loc. cit.*, seems to rest on slight evidence; *cf.* Hammond's account.

[6] *Albany Daily Advertiser*, Jan. 31, Feb. 1, 1827; *Albany Argus*, Jan. 20, 1827.

ger, an Adams-Clinton member of assembly from Ontario County, and Colonel Young were the severest critics of the measure. Granger favored lateral canals which would connect not only the central lakes, but the Susquehanna, the Chenango, the Chemung, and even the Alleghany rivers, with the great trunk waterway from Buffalo to the Hudson. Road transportation, he maintained, was too expensive.[1] Colonel Young addressing the Phi Beta Kappa Society of Union College, could feel no sympathy for southern farmers; if their holdings were sequestered, they had probably been purchased at a price appropriately low; if values would be raised by such development, let private enterprise assume the risk. " Works of labor," asseverated this ex-commissioner of canals, "and the accumulation of wealth appertain to individuals, and not to governments. A government might manage a farm, a manufactory, or a mercantile concern; but it would always be a losing business."[2] The southern members naturally accused him of some prejudice in his political economy, and were not convinced. In 1826 they voted for Clinton, who had espoused their cause, and the Democratic candidate for lieutenant governor, Nathaniel Pitcher, who had pleased them as a road commissioner; their support, as we have seen, made possible success for both.

Each party tried to claim the project of the road, as well as those of the canals that were to lead to Pennsylvania, or to connect the St. Lawrence with the Mohawk or, across the north, with Lake Champlain.[3] They searched for ideal

[1] Speech in the assembly, *Advertiser*, Feb. 12, 1827.

[2] Samuel Young, *Discourse, delivered at Schenectady, July 25, 1826, before the New York Alpha of the Phi Beta Kappa* (Ballston Spa, 1826).

[3] *Advertiser*, May 26, 1826, and *Argus*, May 29, 1826; Wright to Flagg, Nov. 19, 1826, Flagg Mss.; N. E. Whitford, *History of the Canal System of New York*, vol. i, pp. 610, 741, 742.

candidates who might be thought exclusively in favor of each local scheme, and who could, as the phrase went, ride all the hobbies.[1] But the state road did not perplex the party managers for long, as in April, 1827, the measure was defeated.[2] Judge Hammond, counting over the sixty-four opposing votes in the assembly, found that fifty-five were cast by representatives of districts bordering on the great canals.[3] The southern counties were obliged to wait some years till with the building of the Erie Railroad they gained access to the markets of the world.[4]

But this distraction was as nothing in comparison with one which soon succeeded it.

On the 11th of September [runs a letter To the Public, printed by a citizens' committee of Batavia in the autumn of 1826] William Morgan, a native of Virginia, who had for about three years past resided in this village, was, under pretext of a Justice's Warrant, hurried from his home and family, and carried to Canandaigua. The same night he was examined on a charge of Petit Larceny, and discharged by the Justice. One of the persons who took him away immediately obtained a warrant against him in a civil suit for an alleged debt of two dollars, on which he was committed to the jail of Ontario County. On the night of the 12th of September he was released by a person pretending to be his friend, but directly in front of the Jail, notwithstanding his cries of *Murder*, he was

---

[1] Governor Clinton is accused by Hammond of recommending in his message more improvements than could possibly be accomplished, so as to please all sections, *Political History*, vol. ii, p. 244. See Michael Hoffman to Flagg, July 30, 1828, where there are indecorous jests about " the all-yielding Lady Granger."

[2] *Albany Argus*, Feb. 15, April 7, 8, 1827.

[3] *Political History*, vol. ii, p. 245.

[4] Miss MacGill in stating that DeWitt Clinton presented a report in favor of the railroad in 1832 (p. 595), like many others, confuses the governor with DeWitt Clinton, Jr.

gagged and secured and put into a carriage, and after travelling all night he was left (as the driver of the carriage says) at Hanford's landing, about sunrise on the 13th, since which he has not been heard from.[1]

This paragraph with its nightmare thrills, sounding like an extract from a penny-dreadful, describes an incident which changed the politics of half a dozen states.

While the authorities were searching for a motive for the crime, a rumor was recalled by neighbors in Batavia, that Captain Morgan had been about to issue from the press a book revealing the Masonic secrets. On the strength of this suspicion, writes a witness, some

implicated the whole masonic fraternity. This, however, was not at first the general public sentiment, but when, as the investigation proceeded, it was found that all those implicated in the transaction were masons; that with scarce an exception, no mason aided in the investigation; that the whole crime was made a matter of ridicule by the masons, and even justified by them openly and publicly; that the power of the laws was defied by them, and committees taunted with their inability to bring the criminals to punishment before tribunals, whose judges, sheriffs, jurors and witnesses were masons; that witnesses were mysteriously spirited away, and the committee themselves personally vilified and abused for acts which deserved commendation, the impression spread and seized a strong hold upon the popular judgment, that the masonic fraternity was in fact responsible for this crime.[2]

---

[1] This broadside, dated Oct. 4, 1826, is mounted with the Clinton Clippings, vol. iii. It seems particularly inappropriate that this should have taken place in "Sweet Canandaigua," remarked by all travelers for its tranquil loveliness; see Francis Lieber, *Letters to a Gentleman in Germany* (Philadelphia, 1834), p. 264, James Stuart, *Three Years in North America*, vol. i, p. 291, Basil Hall, *Travels in North America*, vol. i, pp. 42-43, 152, etc.

[2] J. D. Hammond, *Political History*, vol. ii, p. 373. The author having

A conviction thus arrived at that the Masons felt a live-lier concern as to the fortunes of their order than as to the common safety of society, a movement toward political proscription made its way throughout the west. The reputation of this great fraternity in the Continental countries as a force opposed to true religion was remembered in America; the year before in Illinois a Baptist minister had been driven from the church because he held to Masonry.[1] The Masons seemed to take too prominent a part in public matters. It was estimated that most office-holders were members of the local lodges; they assumed the right to lay all corner-stones;[2] a few years since at a convention of the order in Albany, the capitol building was reserved for their exclusive use, and none but Masons were allowed to enter.[3] On that occasion the governor, with great solemnity, resigned the dignities of his grand-mastership to the greatest landlord in the state; power joined to mystery was dangerous.

Why were these tylers, sentinels and masters of the veil?

little immediate personal knowledge of this movement, secured a friend who had lived through it to contribute this chapter to his history. Ten chapters of Thurlow Weed's *Autobiography* form the most circumstantial general account of the early history of the Anti-Masons, though it is colored by the writer's desire to present himself as consistent in his leadership in this cause from 1826 to 1834. Hammond's informant says: " It is impossible, too, to say whether these movements were first commenced by opponents of freemasonry to put down the institution, or by the free masons to put down the committee," vol. ii, p. 378.

[1] *Albany Argus*, July 8, 1825. Perhaps the New England communities in New York and elsewhere remembered the suspicion of secret societies which had developed in the Illuminati controversy in Massachusetts in the 1790's; *cf.* Vernon Stauffer, *New England and the Bavarian Illuminati* (Columbia University Studies in History, *etc.*, 1918).

[2] *Rochester Telegraph* quoted in *Argus*, July 8, 1825.

[3] Handbill in Clinton's Clippings, vol. iii, p. 68, and *Albany Gazette,* Oct. 4, 1825.

What dire secrets could not bear the light of day? There were tales of high priests in their sacerdotal splendor, kings in velvet, " royal " officers of one name and another. Did not these things smack too much of monarchy? Such men could not be trusted with the people's liberties; they should be voted out of office. In many towns throughout the western counties in the spring of 1827 committees were appointed to conduct the agitation; and tickets from which Masons were carefully excluded gained considerable success in spite of the desperate efforts of the order.

Missionaries took the " blessed spirit " into other sections of the state, and into parts of Massachusetts, Rhode Island and Connecticut, all through Vermont, into southern New Jersey, western Pennsylvania and northeastern Ohio; everywhere that the New England conscience was present to receive it, anti-Masonry became a power.[1] For it was an idealistic movement, often taking up with revivalist religion, anti-slavery, temperance, nativism and other similar enthusiasms, and spreading its strange gospel by means of lecturing and preaching, and tons of tracts and papers. Hysteria is not a lovely thing to contemplate, yet the historian who follows this infatuation knows not whether to be saddened or amused.   " It is almost impossible," remarks a modern writer, " to believe that the actors in that curious extravaganza were our fathers, sober, earnest, God-fearing men." [2]

Masons in the western counties, hopeless of elective office by the suffrages of neighbors, cried out in distress to Albany to be furnished with appointments by the Regency that they

[1] Charles McCarthy, " The Antimasonic Party," *American Historical Association Report*, 1902, vol. ii, pp. 365-574, is a thorough monographic study of this movement in its political aspect.

[2] A. W. Tourgee, *Letters to a King* (N. Y. and Cincinnati, 1888), letter ix, p. 118.

be not lost beneath the overwhelming wave.[1] A man in Rochester wrote Major Flagg: " In your part of the state the Anti-Masonic projects may appear chimerical—they are not thought so here." [2] But the Plattsburgh editor was soon receiving papers in exchange that showed how formidable was the invasion even in his section: the *Republican*, which worried Marcy in the town of Troy; the *Herald*, at Potsdam, where New-Englanders showed eager interest, and the *Anti-Masonic Champion* of Sandy Hill.[3] Yet it was, of course, within the " infected district " in the west where this influence was strongest. Here delegates from several counties were convened in 1827, nominations made, and fifteen men elected to the assembly.[4]

At first both parties shared in consternation, but circumstances soon combined to identify the Anti-Masons with the Adams men. The agitation started in a district where the President was popular, and naturally the majority of the new enthusiasts had been his followers; other Adams leaders through the state, hard-driven by the Regency, welcomed any aid however unexpected. When Francis Granger carried through a resolution in the legislature to inves-

[1] S. Starkweather to Flagg, Dec. 27, 1827, Flagg Mss. (Misc. Papers),

[2] Ebenezer Griffin to Flagg, July 30, 1828, *ibid*.

[3] J. H. French, *Gazetteer of the State of New York*, pp. 553, 573, 678; F. B. Hough, *History of St. Lawrence and Franklin Counties*, p. 346.

[4] These were distributed as follows: Chautauqua 2, Monroe 3, Otsego 1 of 3, Ontario 2, Orleans 1, Genesee 2, Seneca 2, Wayne 2 of 3, Yates 1; see *Albany Argus*, Nov. 21, 1827. There were only 13 " Federal" members elected. This was the campaign when Thurlow Weed, whose story that a body found in Lake Ontario was that of Morgan was widely doubted, was reported as saying that it was " good-enough Morgan till after election." Weed denied using these words (*Autobiography*, p. 319), but admitted that he had said too many things he could not prove (Weed to Francis Granger, March 29 [1827], Granger Mss.).

tigate the crime, it was thought the Democratic state administration did not show a proper sympathy. Jackson and the governor, now joined in politics, were high " adhering Masons," while the President was not. Indeed, it was not long before the conscientious Adams was proposing to help tear off the veil that sheltered such fraternities by publishing the harmless secrets of Phi Beta Kappa.[1]

Among the leaders, Thurlow Weed, Francis Granger and William H. Seward soon recognized that Anti-Masonry might serve some other ends besides discrediting a ritual. Weed, who in 1826 was still working as a journeyman in Rochester, not far removed from poverty, had been active in the movement from the first, and was a member of the central committee who directed propaganda. Supported by a fund contributed by converts, he had started the *Anti-Masonic Enquirer*, which now preached the gospel to thousands of subscribers. When a meeting at Le Roy in March, 1828, with many "seceding Masons" in attendance, decided to form a general party and hold a state convention, Weed was sent out on a roving commission to stir up interest and secure appointed delegates wherever possible.[2]

The eastern Adams men, who saw what depletions the "blessed spirit" had accomplished in their party ranks, determined to recapture these western voters as soon as might be. They held their convention at Utica before the Anti-Masons, and, possibly on Weed's suggestion, they proposed for governor, Judge Smith Thompson, who took no stand on Masonry, with Francis Granger, an enthusiast, for second place. When the Anti-Masons came together they resolved, however, in spite of all that Weed could do,

---

[1] J. Q. Adams, *Letters on the Masonic Institution* (Boston, 1847 edition).

[2] T. Weed, *Autobiography*, p. 341.

" wholly to disregard the two great political parties," [1] and in recognition of his work in the assembly, named Granger as their candidate for governor. On Weed's advice, that gentleman declined, choosing the nomination by the Adams men, as first received. The radical element, disgusted with Weed's compromising, temporizing policy, nominated a fantastic person, Solomon Southwick, a seceding Mason; yet his following was but a remnant. It was obvious to Democrats that Anti-Masons were now numbered with their foes; by May, the *Argus* was complaining loudly of their menacing activities, and soon referred to them as " Federalists." [2] The first days of bewilderment were past, and it was clear that the struggle in the state between the two old parties would not be interrupted, but would instead grow more intense.

One other cause of the confusion in the party politics of 1826 and 1827 was, as frequently before, uncertainty as to the position and the plans of Governor Clinton. How thoroughly and how long he could co-operate with Van Buren, and just how many personal followers he could count upon, were favorite themes of speculation in the lobbies of the capitol and in the country stores. It was felt that his hegira to the Regency would date no epoch, that his position was unstable and promoted anything but peace. The Democratic leaders found that his presence in the Jack-

---

[1] Hammond, vol. ii, p. 387. " The Anti Masonic convention has just taken a recess of an hour to make up their minds on a resolution submitted by a committee appointed last evening ' that it is expedient for the convention to disregard all national & State politics & to make an antimasonic nomination of Governor & Lt. Governor.' This is the substance, I quote from memory. The resolution was reported by a *decided majority* of the committee, notwithstanding it is believed that they were pressed to a different course by Weed & Wm. A. King," John Willard to Flagg, Aug. 5 [1828].

[2] *Albany Argus*, May 12, 1828, Feb. 26, 1829.

son forces chilled the loyalty of many who had long been trained to hate him. But in February, 1828, these wranglings were unexpectedly concluded. On the eleventh of that month, while after a day's labor he sat talking with his sons, his head fell forward and he died; " his departure was as quiet as if he had dropped asleep." [1]

Mingled with the awe at such a sudden taking off, there was an understanding that the future of the parties in the state could now be read more clearly.

A great change must necessarily take place in the politics of our State dependent upon the death of Gov. C. [wrote Silas Wright]; the greatest obstacle with our best men in taking the side of Gen'l Jackson was the fear that his success might incline to the elevation of Mr. Clinton, and but for that impression they would long since have espoused the Jackson cause openly. He has added something to the numbers, but unless I am much mistaken you will now find many a strong man's scruples at an end, and his hands loosed, and that the strength of Gen'l Jackson and of Democracy will be co-extensive in New York.[2]

On the other hand, the cause of the " high-minded " schism in the old Federalist party was removed. And some Clinton men, who had hesitated when their leader had proclaimed himself for Jackson, could now rest content with old associates. Perhaps no other event could have restored the clear distinctions of a dozen years before.

The historian, however, cannot dismiss the great governor with such words as these. He has oftentimes been numbered with the most successful politicians of our his-

---

[1] James Renwick, *Life of Clinton*, p. 296. Francis Granger, who arrived a few minutes after Clinton's death, wrote a graphic account to his mother, Feb. 12, 1828, in Granger Mss.

[2] To Marcy, Feb. 18, 1828, with Flagg Mss.; see also *Albany Argus,* Feb. 27, 1828.

tory,[1] but this estimate is founded on a hasty view of his career. When compared with Thurlow Weed, that master of adjustments, or with Van Buren, the suave and "noncommittal," his deficiencies in this respect are patent. Persuasiveness, the first requisite, he sadly lacked. He despised intrigue, and when he tried it, as in 1812, he fumbled so ineptly as to make him lasting enemies. He served no apprenticeship in politics, but by reason of his uncle's favor sprang to prominence at once; his natural hauteur was, therefore, never softened, and owning no superiors, his sarcastic wit went unadmonished. He was sparing in his thanks, and showed but small concern that his supporters should be favored; they were usually made to know that he could do without them. Personally incorruptible, he took no pains to hide a cynical belief that most other men were not. In his self-confidence he let the impression spread that every loyalty must center in himself. "His own aggrandizement," observed John Quincy Adams, "has been the only test of his party attachments, and he has, consequently, been a mere man of coalitions."[2] In all the arts which qualify a politician he was indifferent or singularly clumsy. A close associate admitted that he was "personally unpopular."[3]

Yet another friend declared him "the most popular man of his time."[4] And both were right, if "popularity" may have two meanings, since a man who cannot win affection

---

[1] *E. g.*, S. P. Orth, *Five American Politicians* (Cleveland, 1906), chap. ii; and J. Schouler, *History of the United States of America* (N. Y., 1894 edition), vol. ii, 409; E. Channing, *History of the United States*, vol. iv (N. Y., 1917), p. 397.

[2] *Memoir*, vol. v, p. 38.

[3] J. D. Hammond, *Political History*, vol. ii, p. 270.

[4] Ambrose Spencer, *Defence of Judge Spencer*, quoted by J. S. Jenkins, *Lives of the Governors.*

may yet be universally admired. Few public men could more deserve respect than he, for if he was no politician, he was more, a statesman; his interests were in measures, not in majorities. He stooped to low devices on occasion, not because he liked them, but that great ends might be served. Of his splendid services to New York state no recapitulation here is needed; by intellect and faith and perseverance, he built great public works, improved the common schools, encouraged every art that supported or embellished life, and devised fair laws as to the revenues and their expenditure, the military forces of the state, the careful supervision of the banks, sanitation in the cities, the care of the unfortunate, and the discipline and labor of the prisoners.[1] He had the gift of prescience. Carried forward by no Shelleyan passion to renovate the world, he yet summoned all his valiant energies to the creation of the common wealth, and showed the liberal's optimism in his confidence in education. His messages presented the program of a man who knew. As an administrator, both as mayor and as governor, he was resourceful and efficient. Such accomplishments entitle him to rank with the American statesmen, the only one, it may be said, who played no part of much importance in the federal government.

That he cannot be included with the greatest may be accounted for in a certain lack of composition in his principles and policies. Though he generally confessed a Democratic creed, he essayed to lead the Federalists, and, indeed,

---

[1] All these subjects were presented in the governor's messages in such a way as to result in legislation, see *Messages from the Governors,* vols. ii and iii, *passim,* especially the notes by the editor C. Z. Lincoln; also E. A. Fitzpatrick, *The Educational Views and Influence of DeWitt Clinton,* S. L. Mitchill, *Discourse on the Character & Scientific Attainments of DeWitt Clinton* (N. Y., 1828), G. de Beaumont and A. de Tocqueville, *Du système pénitentiaire aux États-Unis* (Paris, 1836), p. 6, *etc.*

in that time and place, his tastes associated him more naturally with the aristocracy. He expressed himself on all occasions, and no doubt sincerely, as the steadfast friend of states' rights, yet other interests that he cherished, such as the internal development of America and the growth of manufacturing, would prosper better under another theory of government; merchants, engineers and capitalists cannot see the boundaries of states. Having long disliked Virginia, he could not be successful in the Democratic party; yet had his principles allowed him he could not rise to leadership among the National Republicans, since that entailed a close co-operation with Adams, of whom he was inordinately jealous as his competitor for honors in the north. Death came, perhaps, when he had done what he was fitted best to do.

The campaign of 1828 was said by many to be the most exciting in the history of the state.[1] It was the first in which the people had participated so directly in the election of a President; it presented a choice between two well-marked personalities, whose differences in governmental policies were defined more clearly than had been the case in any other closely fought political contest since the Revolution of 1800. It was apparent to observers that Jackson was more popular than Adams, because he was " considered the sterner and more inflexible republican;" [2] he was, as the public were assured in an elegant inscription on the campaign banners, prepared to " go the whole hog." [a]

His partisans accused the administration of intrigue to defeat the people's will, of extravagance, and of maintaining an aristocratic civil service. They deplored the cunning

[1] James Stuart, *Three Years in North America*, vol. i, p. 233.

[2] *Ibid.*, vol. i, p. 76.

[a] Thomas Hamilton, *Men and Manners in America* (Philadelphia edition, 1833), vol. i, p. 18.

by which the guileless Anti-Masons had been hoodwinked into a disgraceful coalition in the state.[1] On the other hand, the Adams men expressed their admiration of the bold constructive platform of their leaders. At Ballston Spa, for instance, a meeting praised the high protective tariff, and drew up an address entitled " The American System ":

The present administration of the general government [they declared] is at the head of a great system of policy that promises to elicit the enterprise,—enlarge the resources,—increase the wealth,—and promote the independence of our country. . . . . It is for its adherence to this system of policy, so congenial to our situation,—so inseparable from our prosperity,— and so honorable to our character,—that the present administration has been assailed.[2]

The Regency, concerned as deeply in the outcome, at their Herkimer convention brought forward their best candidate for governor, Van Buren, the tactful chief who made no enemies; and they associated with him on the ticket Judge Enos T. Throop, who had lately sentenced the luckless kidnappers of Captain Morgan, but who disapproved of Anti-Masonry. The nomination of lieutenant governor was considered of unusual importance, since if Jackson were successful, it was well known that Van Buren would be summoned to his cabinet.[3] The canvass proved the

[1] *E. g.*, the resolutions of a Republican meeting at Edinburgh, N. Y., in *Saratoga Sentinel*, Oct. 7, 1828.

[2] *Ballston Spa Gazette.* Nov. 3, 1828.

[3] Silas Wright was considered for governor, but was dismissed as too young; see Ebenezer Griffin to A. C. Flagg, Rochester, July 30, 1828. Nathaniel Pitcher desired renomination, but he had been too much involved in the state road controversy, and was now in ill health. The Regency's experience with Mr. Crawford led them to attach importance to the latter consideration; see letters from Hoffman, July 30, 1828, from R. H. Walworth, Nov. 17, 1828, and from John Targee,

wisdom of the choice, for Van Buren was elected governor
by a margin of some thirty thousand votes, though not by
a majority, for of the total Solomon Southwick had about
an eighth.[1] The counties in the east voted on the old lines;
"the real Federal counties have gone against us," wrote
Michael Hoffman,[2] and Van Buren acridly complained
about the "manor influence."[3] The whole region around
Albany, together with Montgomery and Oneida, the north
and northwest slopes (excepting Clinton), and Queens, were
registered for Thompson, while of the country west of
Cayuga Lake each party had about a third.[4] In the city of
New York, the three southern wards, constant in their
Federalism from the first, now cast their votes for Thomp-
son and the President.[5] Adams and Rush,[a] throughout the

Feb. 10, 1829, Flagg Mss. Judge Hammond understood it was because
of Pitcher's deficiencies in education, *Political History*, vol. ii, pp.
287-288.

[1] It was said that if the extreme apostles of the "blessed spirit" had
been content to vote for Thompson, Van Buren would have been
defeated; but this combination was impossible as they would have
insisted on a thorough-going program which the adhering Masons
among the followers of Adams and Clay would have refused to support. Hammond's judgment on this matter is uncharacteristically hasty;
see *Political History*, vol. ii, p. 289. Weed had realized as early as
August that there was little hope for Adams (Weed to Francis
Granger, Aug. 26 [1828], Granger Mss.), and was certain of defeat
when the Adams men would not nominate Granger for governor.
Gerrit Smith wrote Judge Carroll (March 14, 1828, *ibid.*) that Granger
was too young, and this may have weighed with the Judge in bringing
forth Thompson (see Weed to Granger, Oct. 26, *ibid.*).

[2] To Flagg, Nov. 8, 1828, Flagg Mss.

[3] "The Manor influence here was exerted to an extent unknown for the
last 20 years," Van Buren to C. C. Cambreling, Albany, Nov. 7, 1828,
Van Buren Mss. He said the Federalism of '98 seemed risen from the
dead.

[4] See maps in Charles McCarthy, *The Antimasonic Party*.

[5] E. Williams, *New York Annual Register, 1830*, p. 218; *N. Y. Evening Post*, Nov. 10, 1828; *N. Y. Morning Courier*, Nov. 11, 1828.

[a] Richard Rush (1780-1859), negotiated the Rush-Bagot Agreement
regarding the Canadian border and in 1828 ran unsuccessfully for the
vice-presidency on the National Republican ticket with John Quincy
Adams.

state, received only five thousand less than Jackson and Calhoun.[1] The last President to be chosen on his record as a first-class statesman soon left the White House.

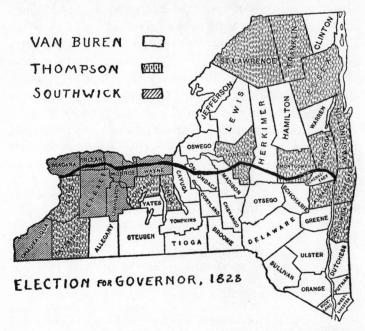

VAN BUREN

THOMPSON

SOUTHWICK

ELECTION FOR GOVERNOR, 1828

For all the bitterness of the campaign—the "Coffin Hand-bills," which set forth the cruelties ascribed to Jackson when he invaded Florida, the slanderous broadsides dealing with the General's marriage, and the reckless charges as to " bargain and corruption," were outstanding features [2]— travelers remarked how decently the country elections were conducted; no Scotch drunkenness or shameless English bribery disgraced the voters at the polls.[3] After the hurri-

[1] See comment in J. S. Jenkins, *Lives of the Governors*, p. 439.

[2] See Thurlow Weed's *Autobiography*, pp. 307-308, for that politician's honorable course regarding these handbills.

[3] James Stuart, *Three Years in North America*, vol. i, pp. 233-238.

cane of oratory and deluge of print, society resumed its
wonted way. " The morning after election all is quiet, the
sea is calm as if a heavy rain had fallen upon it. There
hang the staring handbills with their enormous imputations
and caricature exaggerations, now lifeless, tasteless, and
without any farther effect or use than haply to point a
moral." [1] Yet many felt that the campaign, with its talk
of the American System on the one hand and Democratic
simplicity on the other, had drawn a clearer line between
the parties.

The Aristocracy and the Democracy are arrayed against each
other [wrote Michael Hoffman the week the victory was an-
nounced]. If we will now avow our principles and reduce
them to practice in a judicious system of reforms in the state
and federal governments, the country will prosper and the
Democratic party prevail. We must reduce both the number
and the salaries of officers, civil, naval and military. Make
them work harder, live more economically, and, of course, live
longer. I fear only the excess of Government, and consider
occasional reforms as indispensable. [2]

But the " excess of Government," as Hoffman chose to call
it, would nevermore be charged against the old aristocracy,
as such, with their theories of political privilege and social
precedence. [3] The aristocracy was already being rapidly
transformed into a business party, who took political equality as an accomplished fact.

[1] F. Lieber, *Letters to a Gentleman in Germany*, pp. 25-26.

[2] Michael Hoffman to A. C. Flagg, Nov. 8, 1828, Flagg Mss.

[3] *Cf.* C. L. Becker, " Nominations in Colonial New York," *American
Historical Review*, vol. vi, p. 261. " The principal difference between
the federalists and the Adams republicans was, that the former intended
to be the guides, and the latter the exponents, of the people in carrying
out the policy specified," Alexander Johnston, in Lalor's *Cyclopedia*,
vol. iii, p. 1101.

CHAPTER XII

TOM, DICK AND HARRY TAKE A HAND

IN the great debate of 1821 the Federalist delegates had warned their innovating colleagues that novel and perplexing problems to the state would follow from a grant of universal suffrage, and that the newly enfranchised rabble of the towns would lay a spoiling hand upon the guaranties of property. Those who had survived in 1829 believed they saw a melancholy vindication of their fears. Industrial wage-workers, whose number had increased with such rapidity, had discovered that the " equality thus far attained was only equality before the ballot-box, not equality before the conditions of life, or even equality before the law." [1] It was noticed that they felt themselves already a considerable portion of society, expected more importance, and were determined to exact some legislation in their own behalf.

There was a tendency, observable among employers, to standardize the working day in industry as from sun to sun, unfairly following the precedent of agriculture, while the workers claimed that more than ten consecutive hours at the bench partook of slavery. They wanted laws not only to insure these proper limits, but special statutes with respect to woman and child labor; they must have legal security of wages by mechanics' liens and protection against

---

[1] The section by Miss Helen L. Sumner in the *History of Labour in the United States,* by John R. Commons and associates (N. Y., 1918), vol. i, pp. 169-335, sets forth the principal facts about the labor movement in New York politics between 1827 and 1833, and may be considered as superseding previous accounts.

352

seizure of their tools to satisfy their creditors. A broader interest, which was given the foremost place in all their tables of demands, was their zeal for free and tax-supported schools.[1] In New York city nearly half the children did not go to school, because their parents could not pay tuition fees of private institutions or would not take the bounty of the Public School Society.[2] In spite of all the efforts of Clinton and his predecessors, eighty thousand children still remained unschooled throughout the state.[3] Equality of education could alone make sure a democratic government. " It is false, they say, to maintain that there is at present no privileged order, no practical aristocracy, in a country where distinctions of education are permitted." [4]

Another wrong the workers thought should speedily be righted was patent in the law and custom of imprisonment for debt. In 1830 five-sixths of those incarcerated in the jails of New England and the middle states were there upon complaints of creditors, the majority for debts of less than twenty dollars. In this oppression New York held a sad preëminence.[5] To give but one example, it was reported that in Monroe county in a single year there was about one imprisoned debtor for each ten families.[6] Called together by the *Spirit of the Age*, the radical paper of the

[1] Commons, *etc.*, vol. i, pp. 171, 181.

[2] W. O. Bourne, *History of the Public School Society of the City of New York* (N. Y., 1873), p. 111, and *Working Man's Advocate*, May 1, 1830.

[3] *Mechanics' Magazine*, August, 1833, quoted in Commons, *etc.*, vol. i, p. 182.

[4] Thomas Hamilton, *Men and Manners in America* (Philadelphia, 1833), vol. i, pp. 39, 161.

[5] F. T. Carlton, "Abolition of Imprisonment for Debt in the United States," *Yale Review*, vol. xvii, pp. 339-344, and *Reports of the Prison Discipline Society of Boston*, especially for 1830.

[6] *Working Man's Advocate*, Mar. 27, 1830.

town of Rochester, a convention of the Friends of Liberal
and Moral Principles bought the freedom of all debtors in
the jail.[1] It is hardly necessary to remark that a poor man
might any day be victimized through malice or revenge;
the reader will recall that William Morgan had been thrown
into a debtor's cell for a trivial sum.

The workingmen protested against the ruinous competition of prison labor, and the masons of the city of New
York refused to work with stone cut in the shops at Sing
Sing.[2] They bitterly complained of laws and doctrines that
stamped their unions as conspiracies, and opened prison
doors to those who struck for better wages or conditions.
The militia system they unreservedly condemned. Not
only were the training days a joke as far as military service
was concerned, and more important for conviviality than
for defence, but the loss of three days' wages was an item
in the worker's budget. The rich man could stay away and
pay twelve dollars fine, as many did, but the mechanic had
his choice between the drill-field and the jail. It was computed that the system cost the workingman four times as
large a fraction of his income as a capitalist who lived upon
the proceeds of a hundred thousand dollars.[3]

The laboring classes cherished a suspicion of all banks,
whose paper money of fluctuating value in their weekly pay
caused such uncertainty. Auctioneers' monopolies kept
prices higher than they should be, and were resented most
by those who had the least to pay.[4] Witnesses and jurors
should have a fairer compensation, and litigation should be

---

[1] J. B. McMaster, *The Acquisition of the Political, Social and Industrial Rights of Man in America* (Cleveland, 1903), pp. 106, 109.

[2] *N. Y. Evening Post*, June 22, 1830.

[3] Commons, *etc.*, vol. i, p. 180.

[4] *Cf.* H. Secrist, "The Anti-Auction Movement of 1828," in *Annals
of Wisconsin Academy*, vol. xvii, no. 2.

made more speedy and less costly.[1] All these survivals of
the old prescriptive privileges which barred the way to true
democracy and that universal justice which was certain to
come with it, must be swept away, else of what avail were
ballots? To insure these changes honest simple men must
be entrusted with the office, and wise laws enacted; then
crime and misery would straightway be diminished. "The
aristocracy or men nominated for their influence are unfit
to be legislators for the great mass of the people." [2]

In April, 1829, the workingmen in New York city held
some meetings to resist the movement of the employers to
extend the working day beyond ten hours, and appointed a
committee to effect their purpose. This common action was
so formidable that the employers soon desisted, and the
committee felt itself at liberty to use its prestige toward
accomplishing political reforms. A party soon was organized upon the precedent of one which had been formed the
previous summer in Philadelphia, the first labor party in
the world.[3] During October, resolutions were drawn up
which embodied most of the demands that have here been
outlined, and a ticket for the assembly was devised, consist-
ing of a printer, a house-painter, a brass-founder, a white-
smith, a cooper, a grocer, two machinists, two carpenters
and a physician; the *Working Man's Advocate* now appeared to preach the doctrines, with the motto: "All children are entitled to equal education, all adults to equal
property, and all mankind to equal privileges." Some in-
road was made into the ranks of Tammany, and one man
was elected from the ticket, while others had considerable
support, the physician being last.[4]

[1] Commons, *etc.*, vol. i, p. 282.

[2] *Working Man's Advocate*, Oct. 31, 1829.

[3] Commons, *etc.*, vol. i, pp. 169, 195.

[4] A good account, shorter than Miss Sumner's, may be found in F. T.
Carlton, " The Workingmen's Party of New York City," *Political Science
Quarterly*, vol. xx (1907), pp. 401-415.

The party first fell under the direction, or perhaps it were better said, the domination, of Thomas Skidmore, an admirer of Thomas Paine and an agrarian reformer of the most thorough-going type. In his plan " the equal division of the property of all who died in any given year was to be made among all those coming of age during the same year." [1] But most " Workies," as the members of the party were inelegantly called, had no such revolutionary purpose, and Skidmore, taking off about a hundred followers, yielded place to Robert Dale Owen, Frances Wright, and George H. Evans, the editor of the *Advocate*. Owen soon outlined a scheme of guardianship in education by which parents would resign control of their children to the state, after the Platonic theory, and this extreme proposal likewise alienated many who desired only simple practical reforms. [2] So there came to be three factions, each claiming to be orthodox and each in its own paper berating the two others.

But though disturbed by these internal quarrels, the movement spread, and in 1830 meetings were convened at Albany, Troy, Kingsbury, Lansingburgh, Hartford, Saratoga and Glens Falls, along the Mohawk at Schenectady and Utica, at Auburn and Salina, and in the western counties at Palmyra, Canandaigua, Ithaca, Geneva, Rochester, Batavia and Buffalo. [3] Several local tickets were surprisingly successful, and a state convention nominated candidates for governor and other offices. " Workeyism " in New York city daily grew more formidable. When the common council planned to celebrate Evacuation Day, the workingmen decided to parade in honor of the July Revolution which had

[1] Carlton, *op. cit.*, p. 402.

[2] For this period of R. D. Owen's career see his *Threading My Way* (London, 1874).

[3] Commons, *etc.*, vol. i, pp. 260-263, 281; J. D. Hammond, *Political History*, vol. ii, pp. 330-331.

lately been reported from Paris. The original proponents, with some reluctance, consented to a combination pageant, which is described in a somewhat mordant humor by the English Tory, Captain Hamilton:

Then came the trades. Butchers on horseback, or drawn in a sort of rustic arbor or shambles, tastefully festooned with sausages. Tailors with cockades and breast-knots of riband pacing to music, with banners representative of various garments, waving proudly in the wind. Blacksmiths, with forge and bellows. Caravans of cobblers most seducingly appareled, and working at their trade on a locomotive platform, which displayed their persons to the best advantage. . . . [1]

The captain could not approve of workingmen so consequential;

> A butcher on his steed so trim,
> A mounted butcher was to him,
> And he was nothing more. [2]

Yet this undeniably represented voting power, and voting power must be respected. The Anti-Masons, hopeful of attracting their support, soon declared for the abolition of imprisonment for debt and a thorough reform of the militia system. [3] But the Democrats could offer more than promises; their majority, in 1831, finally wiped out the debtor's prisons, despite the opposition of the pettifogging lawyers, the state printer (who profited by the necessary legal advertisements), and the business men, especially rum-sellers. [4]

---

[1] Thomas Hamilton, *Men and Manners in America*, vol. i, pp. 39-40. Chapter x of this work, giving the author's view of the political changes which must come from the development of manufacturing, is unusually interesting.   [2] *Ibid.*, p. 44.

[3] C. McCarthy, "The Antimasonic Party," *American Historical Association Reports*, vol. ii, pp. 404-405.

[4] F. T. Carlton, "Abolition of Imprisonment for Debt," pp. 343, 344. The Anti-Masons, not numerically important in the legislature, were solidly for this measure, W. H. Seward, *Autobiography*, pp. 191-192. There was a resolute but unsuccessful attempt in 1834 to repeal the law.

When Tammany came out for a mechanics' lien law, it is estimated that about four thousand voters returned to the Democracy, from whose ranks they had originally seceded.[1] An economist has observed that "the Democratic party from 1829 to 1841 was more truly a workingmen's party than has been the case with that party or with any other great party in the country since."[2]

Many Clay men who had no taste for Anti-Masonry, joined the Workingmen in an attempt to keep them independent of the Jackson party,[3] and preached the benefit to labor of high protective duties. The evils of an unrestricted competition with the pauper mill-hands of Great Britain and the continent, became a favorite theme of orators. Now and again some critic pointed out that tariffs increased prices, and that workers had to purchase clothes as well as make them; nevertheless the impression grew throughout the northern cities that the workingman's chief object of solicitude should be the thickness of the envelope that held his pay, and that in some way this dimension was in direct proportion to the height of the protective tariff wall.[4] So the wages argument found some favor for the American System among the laborers, as that of the home market had secured the grain- and wool-producing farmers, and a faction of Clay Workingmen in New York city in 1830 helped National Republicans to office, while elsewhere through the state there were coalitions. It was by such aid in Auburn that William H. Seward, though not yet thirty

---

[1] G. Myers, *History of Tammany Hall,* p. 99. The law that was passed, however, applied only to New York city, Commons, *etc.,* vol. i, p. 329.

[2] R. T. Ely, *The Labor Movement in America* (N. Y., 1900), pp. 42-43.

[3] J. D. Hammond, *Political History,* vol. ii, pp. 330-331.

[4] G. B. Mangold, *The Labor Argument in the American Protective Tariff Discussion* (Univ. of Wisconsin Economics and Political Science Series, vol. v, no. 2), pp. 35-36, 71, 79, 81.

years of age, was elected to the senate of the state by a considerable majority,[1] and in the campaign of 1832 a certain Samuel Stevens, a Workingman, was nominated for lieutenant governor by the Anti-Masons.[2] In 1834 Silas B. Stillwell was found by Whigs to be available for the same office, partly on the ground that he had been a shoemaker.[3]

Thus by quarrels among themselves, by the art of politicians, as well as by the imputations of religious unbelief as followers of the infidels, Skidmore, Owen, Evans and Miss Wright, the Workingmen were broken as a political organization, though, as is the case with most third parties, not until they had brought to pass or hastened several of the great reforms they earnestly desired. Besides the debtors' and mechanics' measures, which were actually enacted into law, educational reform received an impetus from their discussion, and the old militia system narrowly escaped annihilation by the legislature in 1830 and was reformed in 1831, although it survived in law till 1870.[4] The party could endure with equanimity the thundering denunciations of the old Federalist press, and the epithets of "mob" and "rabble" and the "dirty shirts," while they saw their efforts bring about such democratic gains.[5]

[1] E. E. Hale, Jr., *William H. Seward*, p. 80; F. W. Seward, *Life of Seward*, vol. i, p. 176.

[2] W. H. Seward, *Autobiography*, pp. 78-79; see also F. Granger to T. Weed, undated, pp. 28-29, in Granger Mss.

[3] D. S. Alexander, *Political History*, vol. i, p. 403.

[4] Chapter 80, Laws of 1870. All military laws before this provided for assembly of the reserve militia at least annually but after 1846 there was no such assembly, as a law of that year prescribed only a nominal fee, of fifty cents, for absence. This operated in fact as a general poll tax. See *Annual Report of Adjutant General for 1860*; Chapter 350, Laws of 1840; Chapter 270, Laws of 1846; and Chapter 447, Laws of 1862.

[5] See *N. Y. Commercial Advertiser*, quoted in *Working Man's Advo-*

Meanwhile the ancient war went on between the Regency and an opposition which was itself divided. Weed, in 1828, had managed something like a coalition, but the Clay men, or the National Republicans, as they began to call themselves,[1] had been hesitant, and the Democrats (officially persisting in the name Republicans) had won a sweeping victory. In 1830, Weed and Granger sought again to cast the blessed mantle of Anti-Masonry over all the discontented, after patching it with an assortment of new " principles ". Internal improvement and the protective tariff were extolled to keep the Adams interest;[2] flattering advances were made to Workingmen; New York city bankers might be won by promising to exempt their institutions from the Safety Fund law which had lately been put through by Van Buren;[3] a sturdy championship of the Chenango Canal proposal was counted on to hold the voters centering in the towns of Norwich, Oxford, Greene and Binghamton.[4] Thurlow Weed was brought to Albany at a salary of seven hundred and fifty dollars a year to edit an Anti-Masonic paper; and the *Albany Evening Journal*, on March 22, 1830, made its bow as thirty-third among the organs of that party in the state.[5]

cate, Nov. 7, 1829; citations in J. B. McMaster, *Rights of Man in America*, pp. 102-103, and "A Century of Social Betterment," *Atlantic Monthly*, vol. lxxix, p. 72; and Commons, *etc.*, vol. i, p. 271.

[1] Seward, in his *Autobiography*, p. 64, applies the name as early as 1826, but this is doubtless due to a confusion in reminiscence, as the first use is found in the papers of 1829; see E. E. Hale, Jr., *Seward*, p. 62.

[2] *Proceedings of the Anti-Masonic Convention in the State of New York*, August 11, 1830 (pamphlet, Columbia University Library).

[3] R. E. Chaddock, " The Safety-Fund Banking System in New York State, 1829-1866," *Sen. Doc. 61st. Cong., 2nd Sess.*, vol. 34, p. 267.

[4] C. McCarthy, " The Antimasonic Party," pp. 396-400.

[5] T. Weed, *Autobiography*, p. 434; Frederick Hudson, *Journalism in the United States* (N. Y., 1873), p. 398. There were at that time 211 papers altogether in the state.

But their hopes were vain, for the Masons in the eastern counties, though they read the *Daily Advertiser* and might have followed Adams, cast their votes for Throop, the Democratic candidate for governor. Francis Granger was defeated by eight thousand in a quarter of a million. "Old Van Rensselaer's name," wrote Weed to Granger, " acted as it was designed upon the Fraternity." [1]

Early in the following year the National Republicans took on a bold front, and gathered delegates at Albany, where they listened to a speech by their new convert, P. R. Livingston. The Patroon, Judge Spencer, and over thirty others were appointed to attend the national convention called to name Clay for the presidency, and some spirited resolutions were published by the secretaries, Oran Follett and Joseph Hoxie.[2] The later correspondence of these secretaries shows the trend of party sentiment. They desired first to found a new state journal in Clay's interest, but they could not find the funds.[3] Next they gravely talked of nominating as a candidate for governor, General Root, who had recently declared against the Regency, hoping thus to pose as independents with no more connection with the Anti-Masons than with Democrats, but due to certain indiscretions of the General, they could not get the press to advocate this policy.[4] But if the National Republicans could not organize their forces, the canny Weed was willing to attempt it. In the spring of 1832 he was writing hopefully to Follett that "All men opposed to Jackson and the Re-

[1] Nov. 13, 1830, Granger Mss.

[2] J. D. Hammond, *Political History*, vol. ii, pp. 336-337.

[3] Oran Follett to Joseph Hoxie, Feb. 6, 1832, Follett Correspondence, *Quarterly Publication of the Historical and Philosophical Society of Ohio*, vol. v, no. 2, pp. 53-54.

[4] Same to same, Feb. 13, 1832, *ibid.*, p. 56.

gency seem determined to act together," [1] and soon Hoxie wrote him of a conference at Albany where an arrangement had been made:

They did so meet, and the following plan was discussed and agreed upon, viz., that we lie still until the Anti[-Masonic] Convention shall have been held, at which an electoral ticket shall be nominated composed of ½ of *Antis* and ½ of *Clay men*, & probably Granger & Strong for Gov. & Lieut. Gov., the electoral ticket pledged to go against Jackson, and with the understanding that if the vote of New York will make Mr. Clay president, he is to have them all, if not the Antis may as well vote for Wirt [their presidential candidate] or not, as it will only send the choice to the House. This arrangement is satisfactory to our friends here [in New York city] generally, and I believe in the River counties. With a view to prepare the public mind for this you will have doubtless seen and observed the tone of our papers of late touching the " union of honest men," &c. *The Daily Advertiser* and the *E[vening] Journal* at Albany are no longer at logger-heads.[2]

This " Siamese-twin scheme " was none too attractive to the Buffalo editor, Oran Follett, who had only lately written in disgust of " Anti-Masons (Bah!)," [3] but leadership must rest with talent and the Anti-Masons could not be outpointed. The National Republicans had little to lose, at any rate; Hoxie said, "A wag observed to me a few days since he thought we were looking up, being flat on our backs we could look no other way." [4]

[1] He flattered Follett by referring to his paper, the *Buffalo Daily Journal*, as " the most leading and influential national paper out of the city of New York," May 10, 1832, Follett Correspondence.

[2] J. Hoxie to Follett, May 11, 1832. Granger and Stevens were again named for governor and lieutenant-governor.

[3] Follett to A. C. Flagg, in 1830, Flagg Mss.

[4] To Follett, May 11, 1832, "When Masons of our standing, can be induced from considerations of duty, to make the sacrifices we have, and are making, our opponents must give us credit for devotion," Follett to H. D. Chipman, Aug. 6, 1832.

The plan was carried through and the National Republicans officially endorsed the ticket of the Utica convention, though careful to set forth " that though they adopted Anti-Masonic nominations, they were not anti-masons." County meetings and committees of correspondence sought to stir enthusiasm where they could.[1] But the arrangement whereby the electors might cast their votes for Clay or possibly a part of them for William Wirt, was mocked at by the Regency, and did not please extremists in the two wings of the opposition. Thoroughgoing " Morgan men " asked inconvenient questions; Chancellor Kent, whose name was first upon the electoral ticket, soon was interrogated by enthusiasts like D. C. Miller, the Batavian printer, from whose press " The Book " had issued in 1826, but he vouchsafed no answer. The New York Central Committee enjoined a cautious silence upon all the candidates associated with the chancellor, for kind words to Anti-Masons as to Wirt might be offensive to the Masons of the older faction. They admonished everyone that the time was not thought suitable to declarations or confessions, and wrote that " this Committee thinks it prudent that the communications with the electors should be oral and not by correspondence." [2] Already, then, among those who were soon to take the name of Whig, there was prescribed a smiling reticence as to the future.

But the Democratic party in the state was then better disciplined than ever before or since. Sagacious politicians had been sent into Chenango and Broome Counties to promise a canal, thus depriving Granger of an issue, and Senator

[1] H. Ketchum to State Corresponding Committee in Buffalo, Follett Correspondence, pp. 66-67.

[2] National Republican State Central Corresponding Committee to the State Corresponding Committee in Buffalo, Sept. 14, 1832. Follett Correspondence.

Marcy, who had been named at Herkimer for governor, as well as Jackson and Van Buren, were voted into office by a large majority.[1]

The paramount issue of the campaign, and a fatal one to Anti-Jackson men, had been the question of rechartering the Bank of the United States. Besides the general prejudice against monopolies, by no means limited to Workingmen, and the reliable antipathy of poor men toward the rich, there was in New York a special jealousy of that great corporation as an institution of a rival city, Philadelphia. Some local bankers who sought riddance of this great competitor gave their aid to Jackson in his " war," unaware, as yet, that in his heart he cherished a distrust of banks in general.[2] On the other hand, two " high-minded men " of much importance, Gulian C. Verplanck and Ogden Hoffman, who had remained within the Jackson party, now grew tired of "destructionists," and joined old friends among the National Republicans,[3] and some business men of Tammany, like Moses H. Grinnell, R. C. Wetmore and Dudley Selden,[4] realizing that a blow at credit anywhere was a dangerous beginning, likewise left the Democrats. But the opposition's greatest gain was in the *Courier and Enquirer*, the leading Jackson paper of the city, whose editors, Colonel Webb and Major Noah,[a] were heavily concerned in bank

[1] J. D. Hammond, *Political History*, vol. ii, pp. 423-424, 429.

[2] " I do not dislike your Bank any more than all banks. But ever since I read the history of the South Sea Bubble, I have been afraid of banks," Jackson to N. Biddle, in 1829, R. H. C. Catterall, *The Second Bank of the United States* (Chicago, 1903), p. 184.

[3] L. B. Proctor, *Lives of Eminent Lawyers and Statesmen of the State of New York* (N. Y., 1882), vol. i, p. 12, Verplanck was a debtor of the Bank; see Catterall, pp. 253, 273.

[4] G. Myers, *History of Tammany Hall*, pp. 106, 140-141; and Proctor, *op. cit.*, vol. i, p. 10. Selden had borrowed $8,000 of the Bank. See "Apostrophe to Dudley Selden, by a Poor Man," in the *Man*, March 22, 1834.

[a] James Watson Webb (1802-1884), editor of the *Morning Courier* and Mordecai M. Noah (1789-1851), editor of the New York *Enquirer*, merged their newspapers in 1829 to form the *Courier and Enquirer*, a pro-Jackson journal until the Bank War when both men became Whigs.

stock speculations and had largely benefited by the institution's subsidizing loans.[1] The Anti-Masons, for the most part, earnestly inveighed against the policy of the administration; Seward and Maynard in the senate and John Young and John C. Spencer in the assembly spoke zealously and often in the Bank's defense, while Fillmore and others framed memorials for public meetings.[2]

But the vote in 1832 showed conclusively that whatever financiers or party leaders thought about a bank, the people would not have it. This was no surprise to Thurlow Weed. He believed as firmly as any of his colleagues that a Bank was " necessary to the commercial, manufacturing, mechanical, and agricultural interests of the country, and as a means of regulating its currency and exchanges," but he likewise realized how hopeless it would be as a campaign measure, and what opportunity its discussion would give the Regency for fanning up the hatred of the poor against the "moneyed aristocracy." When Chief Justice Spencer urged that Webster's arguments be published in the *Journal*, Weed admitted them unanswerable in the light of justice or of reason, but declared that the two sentences in Jackson's veto message that touched on European stockholders and the wickedness of special privilege, would win ten votes to one secured by all the eloquence and logic of the God-like Daniel.[3] In general, he prevailed upon the Anti-Masons to put as little emphasis as possible upon this issue in the campaigns of the middle 'thirties.[4]

[1] Catterall, *op. cit.*, pp. 180-181, 258-263, 339, 345.

[2] W. H. Seward, *Works*, vol. ii, p. 223, and *Autobiography*, p. 151; J. D. Hammond, *Political History*, vol. ii, p. 352; *Buffalo Historical Society Publication*, vol. x, p. 86; *N. Y. Evening Post*, Feb. 7, 1832; T. Weed, *Autobiography*, pp. 372-373; L. L. Doty, *History of Livingston County* (Genesee, 1876), pp. 553-554.

[3] *Autobiography*, pp. 371-373.

[4] Horace Greeley, *Recollections of a Busy Life* (N. Y., 1873), p. 314.

Thurlow Weed devised few laws and seldom meddled in the large concerns of public policy. Leaving principles to Seward and others he could trust, he specialized in finding votes for what they recommended, advising only as an expert on the likelihood of popularity of any given measure. In his domain he was as close a student, as unselfish and as patriotic a man as they were in theirs. As a young boy, like Huckleberry Finn, he had shared the woes of an itinerant father who could never overtake prosperity; and, struggling slowly up from cabin-boy and printer's devil, he had learned the hopes and fears of the great mass of men better than the scholarly Seward or the courtly Francis Granger. He did, it is true, lend countenance to bribery at the polls, but this was a folk-way with the English-speaking peoples more accepted in his day than ours; when he had become the powerful Warwick of the state, he refused illicit profits for himself and had the confidence of honest men. His keen concern for popular opinion as to the policies of government, though the leader of a party not distinguished for democracy, shows how far had been the progress since the days of Jay and Hamilton and Colonel Varick and Judge Benson, when the mob were not consulted, and insolence went unrebuked.

By·1833 Weed had come to realize that if ever the Regency could be put down it would have to follow from the closest unity among its divers foes. Masonry had lost so many lodges that it now seemed a harmless thing indeed, and a party to combat it had become quite useless,[1] while the name and the weird lingo of the blessed spirit, which

---

"The poor were almost all against us before, and this course [of championing the Bank] will make them unanimously so," Weed to Francis Granger, Nov. 23, 1834, Granger Mss.

[1] The statute of limitations made it futile to continue seeking for convictions in the Morgan case.

still now and then appeared in its pronouncements, was
offensive to many National Republicans. In consequence,
" the *Evening Journal* went diligently and zealously to
work organizing the elements of opposition throughout the
State into what soon became the ' Whig party.' " [1]   This
name, thought to be so apt for those who criticized " King
Andrew," and so bound up with the triumph of the Revolution as to be almost synonymous with " patriot," was
first suggested for the united opposition by Colonel Webb,
in his paper, the *Courier and Enquirer.* It was strongly
recommended, at a party gathering, by Philip Hone, the
former mayor and the leader of polite society in the city of
New York, gained acceptance by April, 1834, and was used
in the municipal elections of that month.[2] The name had
never disappeared from party controversy, and had been
employed by Federalists and Jeffersonians, though chiefly
by the latter. It had been affixed to newspapers and clubs
and party tickets; [3] and formally assumed by " Nationals "

[1] T. Weed, *Autobiography*, p. 425.

[2] T. W. Barnes, *Memoir of Weed*, p. 48; B. J. Lossing, *The Empire
State* (Hartford, 1888), pp. 477-478; A. Johnston in Lalor's *Cyclopedia
of Political Science* (Chicago, 1882), vol. i, p. 1103. The honor of
christening the party was also claimed by Philip Hone; see his *Diary*,
vol. ii, pp. 34, 42; F. W. Seward, *Life of Seward*, p. 446. Lossing errs
in the date. Nathan Sargent, in his *Public Men and Events* (Philadelphia, 1875), vol. i, p. 262, claims credit for suggesting the name, and
probably had much to do with its acceptance in Pennsylvania; but compare C. McCarthy, " The Antimasonic Party," p. 459.

[3] I. Thomas, *History of Printing in America* (Worcester, 1810),
vol. ii, pp. 517-524. A pamphlet, *Report of the Corresponding Committee of the New York Whig Club on the Communication of the
"United Whig Club" Referred to them; Together with the Resolution
of the New York Whig Club thereon* (N. Y., 1809), discusses a broadside of the United Whig Club, N. Y., March 28, 1809 (in N. Y. Pub.
Lib.), which was issued by the old Burr faction. T. F. DeVoe, *The
Market Book* (N. Y., 1862), vol. i, p. 299, mentions the use of the name
by Anti-Federalists in 1793, and Jonathan Cooley, in a pamphlet, *A*

and Anti-Masons, it seemed at last to exempt them from the state reproach of Federalism.

The charter elections in New York city attracted much attention, as for the first time the voters could express their choice directly as to mayor. Cornelius W. Lawrence, a merchant, had been named as a candidate by Tammany, though in standing for the policies of General Jackson he was considered recreant to the interests of his own class, while Gulian C. Verplanck, who had left the Democratic party after their attack upon the bank, had been selected by the Whigs. On the three days of election the merchants were tireless in their exertions; many closed their stores at noon in order to give more time to " the great business of reform at the polls," though some threatened with dismissal those of their clerks or workmen who openly campaigned for Lawrence.[1]   In the late afternoons they gathered in the Exchange to listen to reports, and vied in their huzzas with those of Jackson men who congregated in the streets. The Whigs secured the common council, and out of some thirty-five thousand votes they lost to Lawrence by about two hundred only. Such a demonstration of their power was considered as an earnest of greater fortune in the future, and thousands came together for a fête at Castle Garden, where three pipes of wine and forty barrels of beer were drunk in celebration.[2]   One hundred

View of Governor Jay's Administration (Goshen, 1801), p. 11, by the Republicans. The latter party in the campaign of 1810 sometimes used the designation "Independent Whigs" (see *N. Y. Journal*, April 24, 28, 1810), and, when in 1813 Federalists were suspected of British sympathies, the name was popular again; see Address in *Albany Argus*, April 9, 1813, and Richard Riker to P. R. Livingston, April 11, 1818, in Emmett Mss., N. Y. Public Library. An example of Federalist usage is found in a pamphlet, *An Appeal to the Old Whigs of Massachusetts* (Boston, 1806).

[1] The *Man*, March 29, April 1, 1831.

[2] Philip Hone, *Diary*, vol. i, pp. 97-98, 100-101, 104.

guns were fired in Albany at the news; Buffalo made a gay
affair with salvos from the battery and illuminations;
Orange County Whigs gathered in great numbers in the
town of Goshen; there was a general festival of hope among
their fellow partisans throughout the state, as well as elsewhere.[1] It was, they said, the Lexington of a new war
against aggression.[2]

The new mayor's wealthy friends expressed their sympathy rather than congratulation on his coming to the office
by the suffrages of the ignorant and unwashed rabble, and
when somewhat later, on following the ancient custom of
receiving New Year calls, he was forced to lock his doors
against a friendly mob who sought to " use his house as a
Five-Point Tavern," gentlemen shook their heads in sor-
row.[3] They grieved because democracy had brought in not
only vulgar manners, but unbounded ignorance as well,
and, as in the bank affair, a reckless enmity to property and
business. Where is the power, mournfully inquired Philip
Hone, " which can bid the delicate machinery of individual
credit and public confidence to resume its harmonious functions when once deranged and put out of tune by the hands
of ignorance and misdirected power?"[3]

The Whig hopes that were centered on the fall elections
proved delusive. The Democrats were not insensible that
new " huzza strength " had been developed by the opposition in all its fulminations on the tyranny of General Jackson and the sycophantic flattery that he received from his
supporters in New York state. The rejuvenated party, they
realized, was held together by a common economic theory
agreeable alike to the business men, the manufacturers, the

[1] Hone, *op. cit.*, vol. i, p. 103.

[2] D. S. Alexander, *Political History*, vol. i, p. 401.

[3] Philip Hone, *Diary*, vol. i, p. 241.

staple farmers and the millers of the western counties, all of whom desired a government faithful in protecting credit and energetic in developing the natural resources.

Yet the politicians of the Regency apprehended quite as clearly that dissension might be sown between the Anti-Masons of the west, whose late crusade had had its democratic elements, and the Federalists of the eastern cities, cool conservatives with antique prejudice against those really powerful persons, the Toms, the Dicks and the Harrys. They realized that a broadside of invective against the Whigs would drive the parts to closer union in a common feeling of resentment; so they struck their sharpest blows against their eastern enemies and poured their pity on true Anti-Masons, the honest stalwarts, who had been cheated by the faithless Weed and Granger, when in 1832 the Siamese-twin electoral ticket would have sacrificed their strength to Clay had victory allowed. Let none of those deluded enthusiasts who had once been Republicans presume that their Federalist leaders cared a straw about the blessed spirit.

If [they said] the democratic Anti-Masons will take the trouble to make a list of the state senators and representatives in Congress, and to the State Legislature, who have been elected by their votes, we venture to predict that they will be astounded by the very inconsiderable number of their own class, who have in these respects found favor in the eyes of their own party. It is in perfect keeping with the aristocratic feelings of their federal allies, to confine the democratic Anti-masons to the enjoyment of town offices, whilst they themselves are permitted to fill the high places within the reach of the Anti-masonic votes.[1]

---

[1] Address to the Republican Voters of the State of New York, drawn up at the state convention in 1834, by John A. Dix and others, in *Albany Argus, Extra,* Sept. 14, 1834.

This adroit cajolery doubtless was of some effect, but it is not to this that the Democratic victory must be attributed. The argument with Andrew Jackson had rubbed and frayed the patience of Nicholas Biddle, president of the Bank of the United States, till by the end of 1833, in a rash temper, he determined to let the people suffer with the bank, by withholding loans, especially in New York, whose Congressmen had cast their votes against him. The bank's own friends could not defend this new manœuvre, and its enemies could ill conceal their glee at the general sense of wrong. Governor Marcy got the legislature to appropriate six millions, as a special credit for state banks, the very promise of which so stabilized the markets that the Whigs could rail at this measure, which they dubbed the " Monster Mortgage Bill," with only half a heart.[1]

As the public feeling grew during the summer of 1834, the prospect of the Whigs grew darker. They nominated the young senator William H. Seward, to the profound astonishment of Auburn, his home town, and the derision of the Regency, who poked fun at the youthful John Doe, candidate for governor.[2] The contest went again for Marcy, who had been renominated, and seven senators of eight elected were Democrats. Thurlow Weed, who on the declination of Gulian C. Verplanck, had suggested Seward, was so disheartened that he made some plans to move to Michigan.[3] He stayed but to encounter fresh perplexities.

It will be remembered that for several years after 1806, Rufus King and other Federalist leaders had found impla-

---

[1] W. H. Seward, *Autobiography*, pp. 153, 154. It was not necessary to draw on this fund, J. D. Hammond, *Political History*, vol. ii, p. 441.

[2] Address in *Albany Argus, Extra*, Sept. 14, 1834; see also F. Bancroft, *Life of William H. Seward* (N. Y., 1900), vol. i, p. 54, and E. E. Hale, Jr., *Seward*, pp. 110-112.

[3] E. E. Hale, Jr., *Seward*, pp. 110, 113.

cable opponents in the Irishmen.[1]　These immigrants had come in greater numbers in the hard times after Waterloo, bringing wives and children oftener than was the case with other racial groups,[2] and in the early 'twenties there came more, many of them seeking work upon the Grand Canal, along which they ultimately settled.　By 1829 there were thirteen Catholic churches in the state, of which five were in New York and Brooklyn and seven in the towns along that waterway.[3]　During the next decade the number of their parishioners more than doubled.[4]　Thrift and sobriety are not the outstanding virtues of the Irishman, and he was soon accused of adding far more than his quota to the burden of crime and pauperism that New York city, in particular, had to bear.[5]　It was there complained that the cost of its almshouses, bridewell and penitentiary was more than half caused by the foreign element.[6]　But this condition was not confined to the metropolis; in Wayne and Niagara counties there were protests, and in Rochester the overseer declared that seven-eighths of those who sought relief had come from Europe.[7]

[1] See *supra*, chapter iii.

[2] W. J. Bromwell, *History of Immigration to the United States*, pp. 13, 14; Edward Young, " Special Report on Statistics of Immigration," with Ninth Census.　This was despite Great Britain's attempts to limit emigration by law.

[3] J. G. Shea, *History of the Catholic Church in America*, vol. ii, pp. 181, 204, 205.　These of course were placed among three million Protestants, *ibid.*, p. 495.

[4] Commons, *etc.*, vol. i, p. 413.

[5] L. D. Scisco, *Political Nativism in New York State*, p. 20.

[6] The state enacted that any ship-master who knowingly brought in a convict immigrant should be fined or imprisoned, *N. Y. Laws of 1830*, Chapter 230, and N. Y. Assembly Documents, 1830, No. 260, quoted by Scisco.　Many citizens now wished to apply this provision likewise to paupers.

[7] J. B. McMaster, *History of the People of the United States* (N. Y., 1883—), vol. vi, p. 427.

In reflection of the contest which had recently been waged in England over giving Catholics seats in Parliament, clergymen and others in 1830 were beginning to inveigh against the menace of the Pope. Here was an alien church, they said, with alien loyalties, supported by a clannish people who refused to adopt American ways, except to insist that in a land of liberty they had a right to do as they might please. Newspapers began to warn their readers of the danger in extending citizenship and the right of holding office to such a separate people.[1] Considering the disparity in their objects of allegiance, and the gross and patent inequalities in standards of necessities and comforts,[2] which gave such gloomy prospect of continuance, here seemed to be the beginning of separate social castes, which yet, with universal suffrage, enjoyed political equality. Antagonisms such as these awaited only organization to make themselves the motives of effective force in politics.

In 1834, S. F. B. Morse, the artist, who had recently returned from Europe, announced that in Vienna he had discovered a propaganda for forwarding the Roman Church in the United States, and published letters calling on all patriotic men to stand against the growing power of the hierarchy in our political affairs.[3] Riots and violent en-

---

[1] See quotation in McMaster, vol. vi, p. 85.

[2] Even among the Catholics, it was said, there were some "who did not wish to be annoyed by the presence of an Irish mob," among which their servants were to be found, and who built a little church for their own use. *Aristocracy in America, From the Sketch-Book of a German Nobleman*, edited by F. J. Grund (London, 1839), vol. i, p. 208.

[3] Morse had long shared with his friend Lafayette the dread of the Catholic Church as a political influence; see E. L. Morse, *Samuel F. B. Morse, Letters and Journals* (N. Y., 1914), vol. ii, pp. 35-37, 330. His articles were first published in the *N. Y. Observer* during January and February, 1834, and the following year were printed in a small volume entitled *Foreign Conspiracy*. This work passed through seven editions. Morse regarded the St. Leopold foundation, referred to in the text, as a semi-political instrumentality of the Holy Alliance.

counters " between the Irish and the Americans " in that year gave a fiercer aspect to the controversy,[1] and there soon was formed a Protestant association, which naturally stirred up more rioting, till on one occasion it was necessary to call out a regiment and troop of horse to put it down.[2] During March, 1835, in some wards caucuses of nativists were held to draw up tickets wholly on this issue, while at a public meeting they considered " means to counteract the undue influence foreigners now possess over our elections," and eulogized the Revolutionary fathers. By October they had perfected a city organization supposed to be non-partisan as to the general issues of the state and nation.[3]

Nevertheless the movement was regarded as a hostile one by Democrats, who since 1827, when universal suffrage was at last in force, had assiduously cultivated immigrants, establishing a " naturalization bureau " where aid and counsel had freely been dispensed. In Tammany Hall special meetings were arranged for Irish, French and Germans, and the sachems put some influential Irishmen upon their local tickets, remembering others in the disposition of the humbler posts in departmental offices and in labor contracts for the city.[4] In the middle 'thirties, one-third of the eighteen thousand who made up their voting strength were said to be of foreign birth.[5] In 1841 it was charged against Van Buren, by one who thought he was possessed of special information, that the President had systematically intrigued to draw support from Catholic priests.[6]

---

[1] Philip Hone, *Diary*, vol. i, p. 100.

[2] *Ibid.*, and L. D. Scisco, *op. cit.*, p. 22.

[3] Scisco, *loc. cit.*

[4] See account of meeting of Adopted Citizens, Dennis McCarthy, chairman, in the *Man*, March 31, April 1, 5, 1834.

[5] G. Myers, *History of Tammany Hall*, pp. 87, 119, 139-140, 151-154.

[6] James A. Hamilton, *Reminiscences*, p. 314.

On the other hand, most Whigs were of a station in society where contrary opinions and practices were certain to prevail. A contemporary book preserves a conversation which may well illustrate with what surprise in such exclusive circles any sympathy with poor foreigners was generally received:

" Why, what singular notions you have, Mr. ———!" exclaimed the lady; " I hope you are not an advocate of the *rabble?*"

" Certainly not; I represent the people of my township."

" You do not understand me. When I speak of ' the rabble,' I mean those who have no interest in our institutions,—foreign paupers and adventurers, and particularly the Irish. I have no objection to liberty in the abstract. I think all men, with the exception of our negroes, ought to be free; but I cannot bear the ridiculous notions of equality which seem to take hold of our people. . . ."

" I have always been a democrat."

" Oh! You are a dem-o-crat, are you?" [1]

It was to be expected that Whigs would offer their encouragement to those whom they could well consider as allies.[2] In some districts they deferred entirely to the nativists, while in others they engrafted anti-foreign resolutions

[1] F. J. Grund, *Aristocracy in America*, vol. i, pp. 250-251.

[2] " In the meantime the Native American Association made up of different parties, and having no other bond of union than the total exclusion of foreigners from office, have had a meeting and nominated an Assembly ticket, of whom I do not know an individual; but I like the ostensible object of this association, and am of an opinion that times may come and cases occur in which this influence may be favorably exercised," Philip Hone, Diary, vol. i, p. 169. Hone doubtless reflected the sentiment of his class when he complained that " These Irishmen, strangers among us, without a feeling of patriotism, or affection in common with American citizens, *decide the elections in the city of New York*," *ibid.*, p. 184.

upon their own.[1] A fusion was effected with success on the nominations for the common council in 1836, and the patronage pertaining to that body was appropriately distributed. At the general elections in November, the nativists presented a congressional ticket including good Whig names, which the older party in a caucus formally endorsed in lieu of separate nominations, and in 1837, by complete co-operation, they succeeded in depriving Tammany of the chief magistracy of New York city. In the hour of triumph the weaker organization was absorbed;[2] indeed, it was the Whig encouragement which first had made it formidable. The latter party's gain consisted in some religious enthusiasts and some workingmen who worried lest wages be depressed by the influx of cheap labor;[3] but chiefly they had benefited by a rallying cry for their own party.[4]

The up-state Whigs were less stiff-necked in their conservatism than their colleagues in the city. Weed's attitude upon the bank, we have remarked; and he and Seward, together with their ally, Horace Greeley, who soon came into prominence, disliked the movement of proscription launched against poor foreigners. Governor Seward, a few years later, defiantly proposed a scheme which was interpreted as calling for a vote of money to the Catholic schools.

[1] L. D. Scisco, *Political Nativism*, pp. 27-28. They refused support to Morse as Native American candidate for mayor, because he was a Van Buren Democrat.

[2] *Ibid.*, pp. 29-31.

[3] This was not the attitude of most of the old Workingmen's Party; their leading organ, now the *Man*, was sympathetic toward the Irish, *e. g.* on March 31, June 24, 1834, June 23, 1835. The nativist movement abated after 1837 for a time due to the reduced immigration following the panic; see Commons, *etc.*, vol. i, p. 413.

[4] " The political leaders of the Native American party are opposed to naturalized citizens solely on the ground that these citizens do not uniformly vote on their side," O. A. Brownson, *Essays and Reviews* (N. Y., 1852), p. 426. His comment was written in 1844.

His supporters in the great metropolis were incensed, drew up statements in their meetings and wrote him stinging letters; [1] when the bill was signed, though pruned of most of its offensive features, they threw party discipline aside and were nativists again. This was irritating to Seward, Weed and Greeley, who had hope of some support from Irishmen who lived along the Grand Canal, though even in those towns they met with disappointment. [2]

The internal improvement policy, Seward declared, required unskilled labor quite as much as capital, and nothing should be said or done to check its flow from Europe. [3] Doubtless his concern, as well as that of Weed and Greeley, that foreigners should be received on equal footing with old settlers, sprang from an honorable and sympathetic spirit, and when a Whig legislature passed the Registration Bill, which made it difficult for such new voters in the city of New York, he signed it with unfeigned reluctance, [4] and

[1] F. W. Seward, *Life of Seward*, vol. i, pp. 471-472; H. Greeley, *Recollections of a Busy Life*, p. 129.

[2] Julius Winden, " The Influence of the Erie Canal," quoted at length by A. B. Hulbert, *Historic Highways*, vol. xiv, pp. 176-177; see also A. B. Johnson, *Thoughts on the Necessity for, and Actions of, The Approaching State Convention* (Utica, 1846), pp. 25-31.

[3] *Messages from the Governors*, vol. iii, pp. 727-728.

[4] " This right hand drops off before I do one act with the Whig or any other party in opposition to any portion of my fellow-citizens, on the ground of the difference of their nativity or their religion," Seward, *Works*, vol. iii, p. 388; H. Greeley, *Recollections*, p. 313. Greeley favored the bill. In 1834, the Whig common council in New York city considered a proposal to put a similar measure into force, but it was objected that it was contrary to the constitution of the state for them to do so; see the *Man*, April 12, 15, 17, 1834. Seward and Weed were both active in " Repeal meetings," *i. e.* to express sympathy with Daniel O'Connell's fight in Parliament for the repeal of the Act of Union, and the establishment of home rule for Ireland; see F. W. Seward, *Seward*, vol. i, pp. 697-698, and T. W. Barnes, *Memoir of Weed*, pp. 114-115.

was glad indeed to see it soon repealed by Democrats.[1]
When the Whigs were beaten in 1844, followers of these
leaders charged it to the folly of the nativists, while their
critics in the party claimed that they had themselves brought
on humiliation by their fatal friendship for the foreigners
and abolitionists.[2]

The last-named preference was imputed to the leaders in
the rural counties, but very seldom to the wealthy merchants of New York, who thrived on trade connections
with the south.[3] While the great Whig papers of the city
were accused of stirring up anti-negro riots,[4] their inland
partisans were lecturing on the crime of slavery. Many
abolitionists in the New England regions of the state supported Seward in 1838.[5] A letter of inquiry was addressed
to both the candidates, and though Seward's reply was not
considered satisfactory, it was less objectionable to his ques-
tioners than Marcy's, and his anti-slavery friends were vindicated in their faith by his firm stand with Virginia after
his election. Luther Bradish, of Malone, whom the Whigs
had nominated for lieutenant governor, came out strongly

[1] F. Bancroft, *Life of Seward*, vol. i, p. 117.

[2] F. W. Seward, *Seward*, vol. i, p. 734; H. Greeley, *The American
Conflict* (N. Y., 1864-1866), vol. i, p. 168. " I assure you we have no
strength to spare, especially since Charles King and other antediluvians
of our party will not permit the Irish or the Dutch [Germans?] to
vote the Whig ticket. Apropos, I am exceedingly indignant at this
Native American movement, and the folly of our people in giving aid
and countenance to disorganizers," Washington Hunt to Weed, quoted
in *Memoir of Weed*, p. 121.

[3] Philip Hone, *Diary*, vol. i, pp. 79, 109, 150, 157, 167, 174-175, *etc.*

[4] *N. Y. Courier and Enquirer*, quoted in the *Man*, June 9, July 12,
1834; see *N. Y. Journal of Commerce's* comment on *N. Y. Commercial
Advertiser*, June 20, 1834, and the *Man*, July 17, 1834.

[5] H. Wilson, *Rise and Fall of the Slave Power in America* (Boston,
1872), vol. i, pp. 408, *et seq.*

as an abolitionist.[1] A number of their Congressmen from western districts in the later 'thirties, like Abner Hazeltine of Jamestown,[2] S. M. Gates of Warsaw,[3] Philo C. Fuller of Geneseo,[4] and Mark C. Sibley of Canandaigua,[5] were well known as leaders of the movement, while even the Websterian Millard Fillmore then advocated freedom for the slaves within the District of Columbia and abolition of the trade between the states.[6] The Whigs were taunted in the West as being made up of " combined factions of Federalism, Abolitionism, and Conservatism,"[7] but it was recognized that the country leaders were hardly as conservative as the " antediluvian " Federalists in New York city.

But the new wine of democracy had made sad havoc with the legal bottles of the eighteenth century; some witnessed the result with the sincerest consternation, while others welcomed it almost in ecstacy. Workingmen whose fathers had had no political existence, had come to have an equal share in sovereignty along with those who cherished many-quartered coats-of-arms; strong in numbers and in resolution, they had demanded that their fetters be struck off, and had seen with what alacrity their will was executed. Irishmen who had brought little with them to this country

---

[1] F. Bancroft, *Life of Seward*, vol. i, pp. 71-72.

[2] *Centennial History of Chautauqua County* (Jamestown, 1904), vol. i, p. 612.

[3] *Bench and Bar of New York* (N. Y., 1897), vol. i, p. 334.

[4] L. L. Doty, *History of Livingston County*, vol. i, p. 539.

[5] *Ontario Messenger*, Nov. 20, 1839.

[6] E. B. Morgan, *Mr. Fillmore's Political History and Position* (pamphlet, Buffalo, 1856).

[7] *Ontario Messenger*, Nov. 13, 1839. They were charged with bargaining for abolitionist support, though they denied it; see *Ontario Repository*, May 6, 1840. The Whigs even in the 'thirties suffered losses to the independent tickets; see letter from Francis Granger, undated, pp. 26-27, Granger Mss.

besides a high regard for freedom and equality had jauntily refused to pay the slightest homage to the " natural leaders of society," and had permanently cast their lot with those who formally professed a different set of principles. But this spirit of democracy had penetrated quite beyond the party with which it was associated, and, on the other hand, as we have seen, it had already forced out of that party certain elements that would not be imbued. Others were to follow.

CHAPTER XIII

Two Views of Vested Rights

The Military and Civic Hotel, formerly located on the S. W. corner of Bowery and Broome Street, was a frame building of the olden time, not quite two stories high, and it appeared to have a friendly leaning towards the adjoining house, probably of long standing. Before entering the door, it was necessary to descend two or three steps below the pavement of the street to bring you on a level with the threshold. When you entered the door you would see that the Hotel was one of the most unostentatious of hotels in the world, for there was not the least appearance of aristocracy in the equipments of the bar, the unassuming landlord, or the guests to whom his services were devoted. Passing round the bar, you would find yourself at the foot of humble-looking stairs, lighted of evenings by a very humble-looking dark japanned lamp. . . . If you were desirous of seeing the temple of Loco-Focoism, and would go up the stairs, you would by ascending some six or eight steps, find yourself at the door of the sacred room. On crossing its threshold, you would find yourself under a low ceiling, and surrounded by walls of a smoky antique appearance. Two or four candles were wont to be stuck up around the room in tins attached to the walls, and, in the early days of the Loco-Foco party, two candles graced the table, until they were superseded by an embrowned lamp suspended from the ceiling, which sent up its columns of rich smoke, as if to indicate the aspiring fortunes of the Loco-Focos. There was a platform large enough for a small table and three or four chairs to stand on, and this humble enthronement was the only aristocratic or monarchic furnishment of the sanctorum. Yet it was here that true democracy was preached. . . .

So writes the Recording Secretary, F. Byrdsall, in his *Origin and History of the Loco-Foco Party*, a tiny black-bound volume issued to the world in 1842.[1]

Those who now and then foregathered in this little "great room" were Democrats, distinguished for strict orthodoxy. They were enthusiastic partisans of Jackson in his assault upon the Bank of the United States, but felt that this was but a good beginning of a great crusade against all monopolies and chartered business institutions. They believed that their own party in its long control at Albany had forgotten its true principles, and that politicians in chartering scores of banks had sold the liberties of the people for shares of stock. The scandal of the Seventh Ward Bank, when thousands of such shares had been distributed, to each Tammany senator among the rest, was but a bit more glaring than the many others.[2] "The cormorants could never be gorged," as Judge Hammond wrote;[3] one had but to glance across the pages of the legislative journals to realize how far the tendency had gone.[4] These banks but added to the public burdens; paper money, the reformers said, was but a sign of fraud.

Individuals by special acts were granted their monopolies of receiving on deposit a quantity of hard-earned gold and silver, and then issuing to the public a mass of paper of face value greatly in excess of what it really represented in the vaults. And the few restrictions were disregarded; witness the bank at Ithaca where an investigation had disclosed hardly one dollar to redeem a hundred on a possible

[1] Pages 44-45.

[2] G. Myers, *History of Tammany Hall*, p. 115; the *Man*, Feb. 27, 1834.

[3] *Political History*, vol. ii, p. 448.

[4] *Cf.* index in *N. Y. Assembly Journal*, 1834 and 1835; see also summary in the *Man*, March 1, 1834.

demand.[1] When bankers solemnly explained the needs of credit, these critics were impatient. Credit, they replied, should rest entirely upon the reputation of the borrower, which anyone might learn; let the creditor beware.[2] These views had lately found expression in the *Evening Post*. In March, 1834, it had presented a flattering review of Gouge's[a] *History of Banking* — a work which argued to the point that, " The very act of establishing a money corporation destroys the natural equilibrium of society " [3] — and had maintained that the government should take its money out of banks, institutions which produced more harm than good.[4] Admonitions from the other Democratic papers proved of no avail, and the *Post*, with its Utopian editors, was for a time disowned by the party.[5]

The Tammany Society was disturbed. The " anti-monopoly faction," in March, 1835, had wrested the control of a party caucus from the bankers, Gideon Lee and Preserved Fish,[6] and might again prove formidable. The ticket, which the regular committee had planned to offer for endorsement at the county meeting in October, was not free from bankers, and a contest was expected. On the appointed evening, the committee and a company of their supporters early gained an entrance by a back door to the hall,

[1] *Ithaca Chronicle* and *N. Y. Courier and Enquirer*, quoted in the *Man*, Feb. 20, March 20, 1834.

[2] F. Byrdsall, *History of the Loco-Foco Party*, pp. 148-149.

[3] W. M. Gouge, *A Short History of Paper Money and Banking in the United States* (Philadelphia, 1833), p. 229. This book acquired influence with the national administration, and its author is said to have suggested the Independent Treasury system; see D. R. Dewey, *Financial History of the United States* (N. Y., 5th edition, 1915), p. 235.

[4] See comment in the *Man*, March 17, 24, May 20, 1834.

[5] *N. Y. Evening Post*, Sept. 19, 1835.

[6] G. Myers, *op. cit.*, pp. 115-120.

[a] William M. Gouge (1796-1863) opposed banks and paper money. His *A Short History of Money and Banking in the United States* (1833) is the classic description of the early banking system in America and was extremely influential in the Bank War during Andrew Jackson's administration.

and a bank president nominated as the chairman a well-known bank director. But the opposition came in greater numbers, tore away the chair, placed within it a working-man who stood against monopolies, and claimed the meeting for themselves. The disgruntled leaders yielded to this force, and retired from the hall with their adherents; but as they left the building they gave a little vent to their enormous indignation by turning off the gas. The insurgents in their victory were not unprepared, for, having had some inkling of this stratagem, they had supplied themselves with candles and some " loco-foco " matches, then just coming into use, so that by this weird illumination they brought to a conclusion the business of the evening. Next day the *Courier and Enquirer* dubbed the faction which had held the hall, the Loco-Focos, a name that never lost its prominence for ten years or more.[1]

The victory, however, was short-lived, for the committee, disdaining facts, gravely published that its candidates had been accepted, and the party discipline was such that ward committees dutifully followed; " the ligatures of self-interest were drawn tight, and fears of extrusion from the party were awakened." [2] The protestants soon concluded that if their theories were to gain support by any organization, it would have to be their own, and consequently at a formal gathering at the Military and Civic Hotel, in January, 1836, they took the name of " Friends of Equal Rights." At the same time they drew up a Declaration which, after due reference to the natural rights and duties of mankind, set forth their " uncompromising hostility to bank notes and paper money as a circulating medium, because gold and silver is the only safe constitutional currency;" likewise it condemned monopolies and vested

---

[1] F. Byrdsall, pp. 23-28; *Niles Register*, Nov. 7, 1835.

[2] Byrdsall, p. 31.

rights, and declared that all charters of incorporation could be altered or repealed.[1] Two months later they put up their candidates for mayor and the common council, and in the spring election they polled almost half as many votes as did the Whigs, though Mayor Lawrence was re-elected. Yet in all this they disclaimed the purpose of founding a new party. They were, they said, good Democrats, more orthodox than the Tammany leaders; and, as it came about, these perfectionists were indeed the leaven which permeated the whole lump, and their very name at last was fastened on the party throughout the nation.[2]

"And now, gentle reader," quaintly writes the secretary, "you are requested to contemplate the glorious spectacle of a little band of men contending against two great political parties for the sake of principles only."[3] It was made up largely of those undistinguished amateur political economists of robust conscience and unquenchable idealism who make a valuable constituent of society; their drastic criticism is wholesome, and for the questionable remedies by which they would reform the body politic, hard-headed men are forced to find a practicable substitute. Small grocers and shop-keepers who had felt the pinch of wholesale prices, together with mechanics who read books on Sunday, were most numerous, though there were some disgruntled office-holders, and at least a half-dozen physicians were important in their counsels.[4]

Though somewhat broader in its *personnel*, the Loco-Foco movement had its impulse in the agitation of the

---

[1] Byrdsall, pp. 39-40.

[2] The independent ticket of the Loco-Focos drew off enough Democratic votes to be in part responsible for the Whig and Native American victories in 1836 and 1837.

[3] Byrdsall, p. 50.

[4] The *Man*, May 12, 1834, and Byrdsall, *passim*.

Workingmen five years before. The old organization had been broken up in 1831, as we have seen, and its members brought into the Tammany Society. The sachems, in return, sent several Workingmen to Albany and one, Eli Moore, a trade-union president, to Congress. The hall was opened now and then specially for gatherings of " useful citizens," [1] and " workeyism " seemed absorbed. But the radicals had not been soothed into forgetfulness by all this hospitality. By 1834 they had come to meet sometimes outside the party temple, and there were comments in the press about a Military Hall Democracy, as well as that of Tammany.[2] George H. Evans founded in their interest a penny paper called the *Man*, which advised them to remain together; " workingmen," he said, " must not only become politicians, but they must unite as politicians." [3] They pledged the local Democratic candidates for office in the state to oppose the chartering of monopolies and to labor for a law prohibiting bank bills of less than twenty dollars, but all but four forgot their promise.[4] The Workingmen were still loyal, and in 1834, when hickory poles were raised, they sang as lustily as anyone the praises of the President, yet their tone was sometimes ominous:

> Mechanics, Carters, Laborers,
>> Must form a close connection
> And show the rich Aristocrats
>> Their powers, at this election . . . .
>>> Yankee Doodle, smoke 'em out,
>>> The proud, the banking faction.
>> None but such as Hartford Feds
>> Oppose the poor and Jackson.[5]

[1] *E. g.* the *Man*, April 2, 4, 1834.

[2] *Ibid.*, May 16, 19, 22, 1834.

[3] *Ibid.*, 1st number, Feb. 18, 1834.

[4] *Ibid.*, May 17, 19, 1834; G. Myers, *History of Tammany Hall*, pp. 122, 131.

[5] The *Man*, March 25, 1834.

They were not much concerned in 1834 when the Bank of the United States attacked the credit of its rivals in the states; it was to them only " the old alligator eating the little ones." [1] Governor Marcy's six-million-dollar loan they grudgingly endorsed with an astonishing resolution:

Resolved, That, under the existing circumstances, the Mortgage Loan was needful to the State Institutions in order to paralyze the intended attack meditated by the British Bank. We, therefore, refrain from complaint. Still we believe that the act so direfully needed was *a gross, flagrant, unconstitutional* abuse of power—an act in turpitude like that of a gambler in desperate circumstances who blows out his brains rather than see his ruined family.[2]

The Regency were welcome to make out of this what they could!

In the fall campaign the radicals were an element of much importance in the city, where Marcy's large majority was brought together with their help. But the Whigs consoled themselves with the shrewd observation that pure democracy would prove unpalatable to many respectable Democratic leaders.

The agrarian party, who have had things pretty much their own way [wrote Philip Hone] will not stop at Martin Van Buren. . . . The battle had been fought upon these grounds of the poor against the rich, and this unworthy prejudice, this dangerous delusion, has been encouraged by the leaders of the triumphant party, and fanned into a flame by the polluted breath of the hireling press in their employ. . . . " Down with the aristocracy !" mingled with the shouts of victory, and must have grated on some of their own leaders like the croakings of an evil-boding raven.[3]

[1] The *Man*, March 29, 1834.
[2] *Ibid.*, May 17, 1834.
[3] *Diary*, vol. i, p. 119.

Whatever is, must prove its right to be—such might have been the Nihilist maxim of the Loco-Focos;[1] it was, as Hone had said, a restless day for Democratic leaders. Evans, toiling in his narrow, murky office at No. 1 Mott Street, as editor, compositor and pressman, was one of the most influential men in New York city. Every issue of the *Man* contained a challenge. It deprecated aristocracy within the army, and published articles against West Point as a useless institution which fostered swaggering bravos.[2] His paper was consistently and strongly anti-clerical; he desired to place church property upon the tax list, and would rid the prisons of their chaplains.[2]

In this he but continued what had been begun by Miss Wright and R. D. Owen. The former in the later 'twenties had suspected that a union of church and state might be effected by the Protestant clergymen.[3] The controversy as to carrying mails on Sunday, she considered the beginning of a bitter contest, and in her lectures organized Christianity was analyzed with little sympathy. The address which Owen had delivered *On the Influence of the Clerical Profession*,[4] had been exceedingly offensive to the pious, and when he and Miss Wright elaborated all the points of atheism in their newspaper, the *Free Enquirer*,[5] there was con-

---

[1] Professor Edgar Dawson, in an article entitled " Beginnings in Political Education," presently to appear in the *Historical Outlook,* states his opinion that it was apprehension of fearful consequence of the ultra-Democratic movement that led authorities to introduce the formal study of politics into the schools in the late thirties.

[2] The *Man*, Feb. 26, May 14, June 12, 18, 27, 1834.

[3] S. A. Underwood, *Heroines of Free thought* (N. Y., 1876), p. 213. Miss Wright became Mme. D'Arusmont in 1833, but continued to be called Fanny Wright by the press. On her life see *Memoir of Frances Wright* (Cincinnati, 1855).

[4] In the Hall of Science, Oct., 1831 (N. Y., 1831).

[5] N. Y., 1829-1832.

siderable comment on the infidel agrarians who preached subversion of our institutions.[1]   Thomas Hertell, a radical, whom the Democrats in New York city had sent to the legislature,[2] after arduous debate finally carried through the assembly a bill providing that, " No person shall be deemed incompetent as a witness in any court, matter or proceeding, on account of his or her opinions on the matter of religion," but the senate could not be convinced.[3]   It

[1] See especially Abner Cunningham, *An Address to the Consideration of R. D. Owen, Kneeland, Houston, and Others of the Infidel Party in the City of New York* (N. Y., 1833), which tells of the tragic death of infidels in scores of cases, chiefly by violence; see also L. J. Everett, *Exposure of the Principles of the " Free Enquirer "* (Boston, 1831).   The Workingmen in other sections of the state had formally repudiated these religious views as forming any part of the party creed (see Utica *Mechanics' Press*, July 17, 1830), and the atheistic leaders themselves had tried to keep the religious question free of politics (e. g. *Working Man's Advocate*, Jan. 16, 1830).   Yet those who found their religious opinions according to the *Age of Reason* were mostly members of the faction.

[2] J. R. Commons, *etc., History of Labour*, vol. i, p. 267.

[3] *N. Y. Assembly Journal*, 1835, pp. 49, 81, 747, 870; 1836, pp. 130, 137, 149, *etc., etc.*   It passed the assembly Jan. 31, 1837; *ibid.*, p. 184.   Scores of petitions were received on this matter.   A specimen of Hertell's argument as to legislation on opinion is worth quotation : " Human thoughts are impressions made on the mind by evidence presented through the medium of the senses and the intellectual faculties.   Man cannot avoid thinking, to a greater or less extent.   He cannot resolve what he will not think, without instantly seeing the folly and the futility of the attempt to execute it; for then he will think the more.   Human thoughts, therefore, are involuntary and irresistible.   Man cannot govern his thoughts or restrain them.   How can the legislature derive authority to do that which their constituents have not the power to do? "   The requirement of the law which he wished to supplant was professed " belief in the existence of a Supreme Being and that he will punish false swearing."   When it was charged that without religion there was no morality, Hertell replied that " rogues seldom professed unpopular creeds," and that infidelity was rare in Sing Sing; Thomas Hertell, *Rights of Conscience Defended* . . . (N. Y., 1835), pp. 7, 16, 29, 31, 34, 51.

was a Democratic legislature which ended the remuneration to the chaplains;[1] it was in Tammany Hall that the "infidels" held their Sunday exercises.[2] When a petition from the central counties was presented to the legislature, to exclude clergymen from the schools, it was observed that the signers were nearly all of them Democrats.[3] Under all these circumstances, it was not surprising that the Whigs could claim to be defenders of religion from the threatening "fannywrightism" of their enemies.[4]

As long as the old Democratic leaders were willing to play at radicalism, the mechanics gave them their political allegiance, while they worked for an improvement in industrial conditions through trade unions. When in 1835 and 1836 the active trading market had forced prices to new heights, many strikes were called throughout the state, by tailors, caulkers, iron-workers, carpenters and others, in hope of readjusting wages on a fairer scale.[5] But a rude shock came to those who placed their hopes in combinations. At Geneva, in Ontario County, the journeyman shoemakers had formed a union and demanded higher compensation. A suit at law was instituted to test their right to do so, and after an appeal it came to trial in the supreme court of the state. There in 1835 the union was adjudged to be a confederacy wrongfully to injure others, and hence a misdemeanor.[6] "If journeyman boot-makers," asked Chief Jus-

[1] N. Y. Laws, 1833, chap. 87; see also Moulton's *Report in the New York Legislature Against the Employment of Chaplains* (N. Y., 1833).

[2] N. Y. *Journal of Commerce*, July 16, 1834.

[3] *Springfield Republican and Journal*, Feb. 17, 1838.

[4] Byrdsall constantly defends his wing of the radicals from this charge. The disestablishment controversy in New England, of course, had its bearing on these later contests.

[5] N. Y. *Evening Post*, Feb. 11, 12, 24, 27, March 2, 5, 7, 1836.

[6] People *vs.* Fisher, *et al.*, 14 Wendell 10 (1835).

tice Savage, " by extravagant demands for wages, so enhance the price of boots made in Geneva, for instance, that
boots made elsewhere, in Auburn, for example, can be sold
cheaper, is not such an act injurious to trade?" According
to the court the New York law, in as much as it accepted
the old English custom, prohibited all price-fixing unions,
though eleven years had passed since they had been legal-
ized by statute in England.[1] A few months later, in New
York city, Judge Edwards took the same view and twenty
tailors were sentenced to a heavy fine.[2] Excitement ran to
a high pitch and riots were narrowly avoided by the vigilance of the police.

The *Evening Post* pronounced it all a travesty of justice;
it said that under this interpretation any temperance society,
as a conspiracy against the rum trade, was illegal. Why
should there not be " labor companies " as well as those of
capitalists for manufacturing? The law must speedily be
changed.[3] But the Whig newspapers of the city expressed
themselves as gratified that the majesty of the law had
been vindicated. The *American* was glad to see a pause to
those destructive tendencies traceable to Fanny Wright, and
the *Star* and the *Commercial Advertiser* took the same
view.[4] Many of the strikers were a dirty, loutish, foul-
mouthed set, remarked the *Courier and Enquirer* (apparently with much truth), and Judge Edwards had done good
service to the country (which, as the logicians say, was a
non sequitur).[5]

---

[1] The decision was based on a phrase of the English common law, which
had been written into the statutes of New York in the codification of
1829. See comment of *N. Y. Courier and Enquirer*, March 8, 1836.

[2] The charge is found in full in *N. Y. Journal of Commerce*, May 31,
1836, and the sentence, *etc.*, in the *N. Y. Evening Post*, June 13, 1836.

[3] *Evening Post*, May 31, June 1, 6, 7, 1836.

[4] All of June 15, 1836.

[5] May 31, 1836.

If the law was to be changed, the workingmen decided, it must be done through party politics. On June 13, 1836, at a great meeting in the park, it was determined to form a " separate and distinct party, around which the laboring classes and their friends can rally with confidence," and a state convention was summoned to meet in Utica the following September.[1] A committee soon published an address calling for the election of delegates, and declaring against chartered combinations, prison labor, " forced constructions of the statutes " and reliance on the precedents of British courts. They complained " that the leaders of the aristocracy of both the great political parties of the state . . . have deceived the workingmen by false pretences of political honesty and justice." [2] The Loco-Focos found themselves so heartily in accord with these sentiments that they joined the Workingmen at the Utica convention, and a coalition was effected in the name of the Friends of Equal Rights.[3]

The philosophy of politics professed at the convention was one of rights, natural and equal, and never vested by a special act of government; " no man has a natural right to commit aggression on the equal rights of another, and this is all from which the law ought to restrain him." [4] The state, then, was the individual's weapon of defense, not his instrument of construction, and certainly not existing for itself. Yet they charged the state with the responsibility for free and equal education; also, for a little time, it might be called upon energetically to redress the wrongs which it

[1] *N. Y. Evening Post*, June 14, 1836.

[2] *Ibid.*, July 23, 1836.

[3] Byrdsall, *History of the Loco-Foco Party*, chap. v. It was first called a " convention appointed by the farmers, mechanics, and others friendly to their views," p. 71.

[4] From the Declaration of Rights, *ibid.*, p. 68.

had fostered. All wealth they thought to be the accumulation of surplus labor, and should remain available to the producing classes.[1] They took comfort in the spectacle of the decline of feudal privilege that marked the times in England, and were hopeful that the golden age throughout all Christendom could be restored.

Colonel Young, whose sharp rebukes to his associates in the state senate had won him the regard of Equal Rights men, was invited to become the candidate for governor. He refused, but with such a strong endorsement of their principles that they used his letter as a tract. He knew, he said, that these principles were steadily advancing in the state, and wished them all success, but feared that in adopting a separate organization they might retard their progress.[2] They did not follow his advice, but took a less distinguished leader. In the fall campaign they pledged their candidates for the assembly to work for the repeal of the restraining law and thus abolish the chartering of banks by special acts, and for the exclusion from circulation of all bank notes of less than ten dollars in value. They were obliged to vote for the election of judges by the people, and for short terms in office; for the repeal of any and all laws forbidding working-people to combine to fix their wages; and for an amendment making more effective the mechanics' lien law. They were also to obstruct all measures tending to restore imprisonment for debt; and to labor for a " more extended, equal and convenient system " of public school institutions.[3]

The Equal Rights men took a hand in national affairs by submitting their " Declaration of Principles " to Martin Van Buren and Colonel R. M. Johnson, the national can-

[1] Byrdsall, pp. 59, 62, 75.

[2] *Ibid.*, p. 62; J. D. Hammond, *Political History*, vol. ii, p. 457. They did nominate Isaac S. Smith, a Buffalo merchant.

[3] Byrdsall, p. 88.

didates in the campaign of 1836. The former's answer
they declared evasive, but the latter's was deemed all they
could desire. Colonel Johnson had long been a favorite
with the workingmen. His efforts on behalf of debtors,
and his views of banks in general, were most satisfactory,[1]
and they had frequently expressed the hope that he would
be the nominee for President.[2] Now they would gladly
have cast their ballots for him as the second officer, while
withholding them from his more illustrious colleague; but
of this the electoral system did not admit, and in consequence they came out for a constitutional amendment that
would allow the popular election of President and Vice
President with separate indication.[3]

The *Evening Post* sent forth its daily fulminations
against stockjobbing and monopolies. It took the Jeffersonian view that laws should not be framed for more than
twenty years, and maintained that this should certainly
apply to charters of incorporation. At any rate they
should be freely altered when the public weal demanded it.[4]
The editors' enthusiasm in this matter sometimes befogged
their sense of fitness; when Chief Justice Marshall, the
steward of the Constitution, died in 1835, they remarked
that on the whole his removal was a cause of rejoicing.[5]
They gave tables of the profits of insurance companies, and
expressed a deep abhorrence of these gambling enterprises.[6]

[1] "A Kentuckian," *Biographical Sketch of Col. Richard M. Johnson*
(N. Y., 1845).

[2] *E. g.* the *Man*, Feb. 26, 27, March 10, April 17, 23, 29, July 10, 22, *etc.*,
1834.

[3] Byrdsall, pp. 58-60.

[3] *Evening Post*, Jan. 7, 11, Feb. 19, June 15, 1836.

[5] *Ibid.*, July 8, 1835; see comment of Philip Hone, *Diary*, vol. i, pp.
148-149.

[6] *Post*, June 16, 1836.

They classed all banks with lotteries, and exhibited a holy passion in delivering their sentiments on the currency, such as marked the later greenback and free-silver days. So William Cullen Bryant and his brilliant partner, William Leggett, penetrated with heroic and most useful zeal, together with some nonsense, gained their title to the name of radicals, and reached readers that were not accessible to penny papers like the *Transcript* and the *Man.*[1]

There were pamphlets also in which the universe was fearlessly explored and shrewd suggestions made for its re-ordering. Clinton Roosevelt, whom the Loco-Focos sent to the assembly, wrote upon *The Mode of Protecting Domestic Industry Consistently with the Desires of Both the South and the North by Operating on the Currency,*[2] criticizing tariffs with considerable perspicacity, and showing that a specie system which abolished all bank money, by lowering prices here would lessen the desire to buy commodities abroad because of their apparent cheapness. The chief service of his little monograph, which seems to have been widely read, was in calling the attention of mechanics to the falseness of the favorable comparisons between their wages and those of countries where the currency was not inflated. Wages made a variable standard with which to gauge prosperity, he said; it were as well to measure lumber with an india-rubber tape. But though his propositions pointed to free-trade in general, he had no use for the self-interest arguments advanced by writers like McCulloch; let the community be served, he said, and individuals would not want.[3]

[1] Parke Godwin, *Biography of William Cullen Bryant* (N. Y., 1883), vol. i, pp. 253-262.

[2] N. Y., 1833.

[3] Pages 4, 5, 7, 9, 13, 37, 43. He objected to banks on seven points. He had a personal animus against them, as his family's extensive property had been lost, he thought, because of unsound business conditions

William H. Hale, who published *Useful Knowledge for the Producers of Wealth*,[1] agreed with Roosevelt as to banks, tariffs, currency and corporations, but, alarmed at the concentration of wealth, went forward (while Karl Marx was still in grammar school) to condemn all "usury" to capital.[2] Indeed, the Loco-Foco candidate for governor, Isaac S. Smith, of Buffalo, in accepting his nomination in 1836, averred that "No person possessing mental or physical ability can have a moral right to consume that which he does not in some manner contribute to produce," and on the labor theory of value he excluded capital acquired by inheritance, gift or speculation from a share of income.[3] The theory of class struggle had been clearly stated:

What distinguishes the present from every other struggle in which the human race has been engaged [Frances Wright had written], is that the present is evidently, openly and acknowledgedly a war of class. . . . It is the ridden people of the earth who are struggling to overthrow the "booted and spurred riders" whose legitimate title to work and starve them will no longer pass current.[4]

The Loco-Focos, by withdrawing their support from the regular Democratic tickets in the state, insured the election of many Whigs.[5] But the ferment they had generated had

due to banks. His social outlook had been much affected by Owen and Miss Wright. Byrdsall remarks of him that he had a mind "fertile either to construct systems, mechanical machines, or literary matter," *History of Loco-Foco Party*, p. 93.

[1] N. Y., 1833.

[2] Pages 7, 9, 17-18, 19, 22. He said that labor and the United States was actually taxed $50,000,000 to support the bankers.

[3] Byrdsall, p. 75; see also John Commerford, *Address to the Workingmen of New York* (N. Y., 1840).

[4] *Free Enquirer*, May 3, 1830.

[5] This together with the Native American movement was responsible for the victories and the capture of the common council in New York in 1836, and the election of a Whig mayor in 1837.

worked far within their own party; it spread to other states; not only Colonel Johnson, of Kentucky, but Colonel Benton,[a] of Missouri, discovered that the Loco-Foco principles were sound, and, " following in the footsteps of his predecessor," Van Buren became suspicious of all banks and proposed his Independent Treasury.[1] The panic of 1837 seemed sadly to confirm the radicals' evil prophecies; and Democratic leaders soon took up their tenets as to banks and currency as the doctrine of the party. The *Albany Argus,* which had anathematized them as " Jack Cades "[b] and " Carbonari,"[c] came to preach their major principles.[2] When, a few years later, President Van Buren visited New York city, he attended the Bowery Theater in company with Alexander Ming, but recently despised as the " agrarian " candidate for mayor, and other leaders of the Friends of Equal Rights.[3] The amiable secretary, Byrdsall, might truly speak of the Loco-Foco Revolution, for the name and influence of the little group of " anti-monopolists " was for many years fastened on the Democratic party.[4] Considering the issue, the somewhat long analysis of their principles and program has, it is believed, been warranted.

It is scarcely necessary here to review the terrors of the panic, when fear bred fear as in some great catastrophe of nature. The President in his message to the special session of Congress, found the cause was the " redundancy of credit " which had marked the times, though he forgot the bank war and the specie circular, and might well, in the Democratic interest, have made some reference to the meagre crops and failures in Great Britain. When credit

---

[1] *Cf.* H. von Holst, *Constitutional History of the United States* (Chicago, 1878), vol. ii, pp. 202-203.

[2] Byrdsall, p. 54.

[3] Philip Hone, *Diary*, vol. i, pp. 365-366; Byrdsall, p. 17.

[4] Byrdsall, p. vi.

[a] Thomas Hart Benton (1782-1858), thirty years senator from Missouri, was a prominent Jacksonian and played an important role in the Bank War.

[b] Jack Cade (d. 1450) led a political uprising in England because of

tightened in New York, the city had not yet recovered from the fire which had demolished more than twenty million dollars' worth of property some fourteen months before. In the spring of 1837 the disaster seemed complete. The Whigs declared this the result of Jackson's meddling with the bank, and demanded that it be rechartered, but the new President sought escape in quite the opposite direction. When he saw that the deposit banks suspended specie payment, as we have said, he proposed a Loco-Foco remedy; he would take the government funds away from banks and lock them in the treasury vaults; he would refuse banknotes in all remittances to the nation and would not use them in payment to its creditors. It was this that made the Loco-Focos orthodox, and the Tammany Society and the Regency were forced to listen to their homilies with at least the affectation of respect.[1]

But when the message was read in Congress and Silas Wright brought in the independent treasury bill which would divorce the government from banks, there were some Democrats who expressed surprise and indignation. In the great forensic contest which lasted intermittently throughout the next three years, a half dozen influential Democratic senators and more than twice as many members of the House were steadfast in their opposition. They would not countenance the Whig scheme to restore the Bank of the United States, but desired a continuation of the state banks as depositories, though under more restrictions than before.[2] The leader of these men, who, with their followers throughout the country, were called "Conservatives," was

---

[1] It may be said that in the summer the feeling was still bitter, and some Democrats joined with the Whigs in wrongly attributing the flour riots in the city to the Loco-Focos.

[2] *Niles' Register*, vol. liii, pp. 75, 126, 365, vol. liv, pp. 75, 79, 285; *Congressional Globe*, vol. v, App. 205, 211, 213. Wright had first suggested buying state bonds with the surplus funds.

military reverses in France. His men were eventually dispersed and Cade himself was executed.

c The Carbonari (charcoal burners) were members of a secret Italian organization in the early 19th Century which advocated political freedom.

Senator Nathaniel P. Tallmadge, who had begun the fight the previous June in the preliminary debate.[1] He now argued on eleven points against the bill, defending the whole credit system as indispensable to business.[2] The chief champion in the House of Representatives was John C. Clark of Bainbridge, in Chenango County. The movement largely centered in New York, where by July, 1837, Tallmadge's arguments were approved by many Democrats.[3]

The President's message of September had scarcely been reported, when a meeting of the Tammany General Committee of fifty-one was convened. When a resolution to endorse the independent treasury was presented, thirty-two walked out, but by the quorum that was left the motion was carried by a vote of eighteen to one.[4] The Democratic Republican Young Men's Committee then came together and expressed the heartiest sympathy with the President in his demands, and the bankers of the organization, who had kept the friendship of the legislature in recent years by contributions of their time and money, finally withdrew.[5] These Conservatives increased in number day by day as the settled purpose of Van Buren grew apparent. In November, before election, they held a meeting under Judah Hammond, and drew up a statement of grievance and reproach, which the Whigs hailed with delight.[6] At a well-attended gathering on the second of January, 1838, they organized a committee of their own, according to the custom, with a

[1] *Cong. Debates*, vol. xiii, p. 75.
[2] *Cf.* H. Greeley, *Recollections*, p. 123; *Niles' Register*, vol. liii, p. 75.
[3] Byrdsall, pp. 158-159.
[4] G. Myers, *History of Tammany Hall*, pp. 132-134.
[5] *N. Y. Evening Post*, Sept. 26, 1837.
[6] *N. Y. Commercial Advertiser*, Nov. 3, 7, 1837.

president, fifty-seven vice-presidents, fourteen secretaries, and a general committee of vigilance made up of representatives from every ward. They issued a stinging address against the Loco-Foco principles.[1]

But though the Conservatives were naturally stronger in the city, there were many scattered through the state. In October, Tallmadge, Clark and Hammond called a state convention, which met in Syracuse, and resolved by general vote firmly to support Seward, named by the Whigs for governor, against Marcy, whom they called the Loco-Foco candidate.[2] It was hinted that the bankers employed other means than those of oratory and resolves, and there was a general impression that they paid liberally for the fireworks and shouters.[3] Their influence the Whigs acknowledged as a potent factor in the victory that followed, and in grateful recognition of the service, whose continuance they might secure, they re-elected Tallmadge to the Senate for six years more, in spite of the remonstrances of Fillmore, John C. Spencer and some others of the faithful, whose ambitions were neglected.[4]

The following autumn the Conservatives again convened at Syracuse to pledge their loyalty to the Whig leaders in

---

[1] *Proceedings and Address of the Democratic Republicans, Opposed to the Sub-Treasury* (N. Y., 1838), pp. 1-16.

[2] J. D. Hammond, *Political History*, vol. ii, p. 486.

[3] See Tallmadge's reply in Senate, *Cong. Globe*, vol. vi, p. 620, and D. S. Alexander, *Political History of the State of New York*, vol. ii, pp. 24-25.

[4] T. Weed, *Autobiography*, pp. 460-461. Van Buren made out so plausible a case for the independent treasury that outside of New York state the Whigs generally lost ground. One factor besides the support of the Conservatives in securing Seward's victory was the resentment in the northern and western counties, who sympathized with the Canadian rebels of 1837, and thought Van Buren's attitude needlessly severe; see J. A. Haddock, *History of Jefferson County* (Philadelphia, 1894), p. 21.

the presidential campaign, with five hundred delegates, representing nearly every county. They felicitated New York state for rebuking the national leaders despite " the combined power of agrarianism and infidelity leagued in their support," set forth their arguments against the new financial policy and defended the state banks against the calumnies of the ignorant levellers. They referred to the inevitable sufferings of business if the nation's funds were withdrawn from investment and circulation. There would be a painful shortage if the government insisted on drawing a great part of the specie into its vaults. Trade demanded half a billion dollars in currency. " How much more freely will you breathe when the screw of the President shall have brought you down to sixty million dollars?" [1] Such reflections brought the Conservatives to build up county organizations and work effectively in favor of their old opponents. After 1840 many stayed among the Whigs as a business party, though some gave support to Tyler in his opposition to a national bank.[2]

---

[1] *Niles' Register*, vol. lvii, pp. 187-190. During this campaign Tallmadge made the charge, which though denied was widely quoted, that Marcy had privately expressed to him his strong disapproval of the administration's Loco-Focoism; see *New Haven Palladium*, Oct. 30, 1839, and *Albany Argus* quoted in the Canandaigua *Ontario Messenger*, Oct. 23, 1839.

[2] There is scarcely a movement in history more susceptible of the economic interpretation, than that of the Conservatives. Mr. C. C. Latour of Columbia University has found by investigation that most of the leaders in New York city were bank officers or heavy stockholders. *E. g.*, see list in *Proceedings and Address . . . January 2, 1838*, and the following: E. T. Perine, *The Story of the Trust Co.* (N. Y., 1916), p. 15; P. G. Hubert, *The Merchants' National Bank* (N. Y., 1903), p. 37; F. B. Stevens, *History of the Savings Bank Associations of New York* (N. Y., 1915), p. 569; Walter Barrett, *Old Merchants of New York*, vol. iii, p. 229; Byrdsall, *History of the Loco-Foco Party*, p. 26; J. D. Hammond, *Political History*, vol. ii, p. 478. N. P. Tallmadge was a director of the Poughkeepsie Bank; see E. Platt. *History of Poughkeepsie*, p. 107.

The Whig victory had begun in 1837, when besides the mayoralty of New York they gained a hundred and one assembly seats to their opponents' twenty-seven. Six of eight senators elected were also of their party, but in the upper house they could not claim a clear majority until after the election of 1839.[1] Many able men, like the scholarly D. D. Barnard, of Albany, General Porter, of Niagara, and D. B. Ogden, of New York, who had been in forced retirement for a dozen years, now were able to devote their talents once again to the affairs of state. They applied themselves to see what could be done for business. The Democrats in 1835, moved somewhat by radical influence, had passed a law prohibiting the circulation as currency of bank bills of less than five dollars face value.[2] In a country where there were few gold and silver mines, this was decidedly embarrassing to trade, and numerous petitions were presented praying for repeal, but the majority could not be moved.

Scarcely had the legislature come together in 1838, when a Whig brought in a measure to restore small bills, which was promptly endorsed by the assembly. But the Democratic senate would not yield the principle, and insisted on an amendment that suspended the prohibitory law for two years only.[3] In the campaign of 1838, the question figured prominently, as " small bill seward " was pitted against " BIG BILL MARCY," [4] and at the following session when the senate was more favorable, the old law was entirely re-

[1] J. D. Hammond, *Political History*, vol. ii, p. 517.

[2] Chap. 46, *Laws of 1835*; see also chap. 155 and resolution of April 20, 1835, *ibid.*

[3] Chap. 51, *Laws of 1838*; it provided for different dates of final retirement, $1, $2, and $3 bills before July, 1840. After Jan. 1, 1841, there were to be no bills between $5 and $10.

[4] F. Bancroft, *Life of Seward*, vol. i, p. 67.

pealed.[1] The Democrats in their long period of power had, as has been said, incorporated many banks; but the majority of business men were irritated that these monopolies of issue were parcelled out to faithful politicians, rather than to serve legitimate commercial needs.[2] The Whig assembly, therefore, in 1838, passed a general banking bill, devised by Willis Hall of New York city,[3] which, when the opposition in the senate had been overcome, became a law. The shameful bartering of credit privilege, which had so long disturbed the state, was now over.[4]

The ways and means committee of the assembly in that year, true to the tradition of the party, brought in a report which outlined an elaborate scheme of internal improvement. It was written by the chairman, Samuel B. Ruggles, the New York banker, whom the Democrats considered an amateur, " silk-stocking " politician, but who was finally recognized as a competent American economist.[5] He could not deny himself superlatives when he contemplated how trade would be benefited by more facilities for transportation, and was most optimistic as to the state's ability to furnish them. The success of the two principal canals had surpassed the boldest expectations; and while the revenues had been expended, they were not " gone," as Democrats maintained, but were " invested " in more public works. It was true that not all the creditors who had supplied the seven millions for the great waterway had been repaid, but this was due to their reluctance to accept their payment be-

---

[1] Chap. 30, *Laws of 1839.*

[2] R. E. Chaddock, *History of the Safety Fund Banking System,* p. 345.

[3] H. Greeley, *Recollections,* p. 126; the Democratic votes were cast against the bill; J. D. Hammond, *Political History,* vol. ii, p. 484.

[4] The restraining law had been modified under pressure of public opinion in 1837; see Chap. 20, *Laws of 1837.*

[5] F. W. Seward, *Life of Seward,* p. 439; *Appleton's Cyclopedia of American Biography.*

fore their bonds matured; the money had been put aside, and the constitutional objection that the further revenues could not be spent for other improvements till the last receipt was signed, was frivolous. Why not a ship-canal? Why should not the state construct more railroads?

Ruggles had no liking for the Jeffersonian maxim, that the government " should never borrow a dollar without laying a tax in the same instant for paying the interest annually, and the principal in good time." Jefferson had lived in a time when expenditure was usually for war, which was a waste; he had not realized that a government could make investments. If the state desired to be forehanded, the canal tolls would warrant an indebtedness of $40,000,000. " It is evident," he said, " that $500,000 of revenue will serve as a basis of finance for $10,000,000 debt." Commerce must be served.[1] Azariah C. Flagg, who was still the state comptroller, made a firm remonstrance. He maintained that the net revenues were overestimated and in Whig computations no account was taken of necessary canal expense and repairs. It was going to the verge of prudence, certainly, to borrow money with provision for the interest only.[2] But despite the protests of the comptroller and the governor, the Whig assembly virtually met the heavy demands of Ruggles, though the senate would allow a loan of but $4,000,000.[3]

[1] S. B. Ruggles, *Report upon the Finances and Internal Improvements of New York* (N. Y., 1838). A law of 1835 had directed the canal commissioners to enlarge the Erie Canal, setting no limit. The commissioners had felt themselves restrained, however, believing that constitutionally they could not contract for improvements for which they could not pay in cash from surplus revenues from the canal. An application to the legislature had produced Mr. Ruggles' report; see J. H. Dougherty, *Constitutional History of the State of New York* (N. Y., 1915), pp. 151-152.

[2] *Annual Report, Comptroller, 1838*, p. 21.

[3] Cf. *Messages from the Governors*, vol. iii, p. 544.

William H. Seward, elected governor in November, was not expected to be moderate when the development of natural resources was concerned. He had two heroes, Clinton and John Quincy Adams, both of whose biographies he wrote in terms of highest admiration for their " magnificent conceptions." It was one of the disappointments of his administration that Democratic opposition in the legislature prevented the erection of a monument to the great governor, in whose service he had entered politics.[1] As senator he had been tireless in advocating more improvements; when out of public office he had been actively concerned in the movement for the state-supported Erie Railroad;[2] now, as chief executive, he had his greatest opportunity to recommend his policy.

In the first message he advised the annual expenditure for ten years of $4,000,000, for which the tolls of the canal would furnish payment before 1865.[3] His hearers were responsive and voted generous appropriations, providing only for the payment of the interest,[4] and " owners of property, contractors, brokers, builders and expectants of all classes created a coalition strong enough to control the activities of the legislature, and plunged the state deeper and deeper into debt."[5] The Democrats before him had not entirely refrained from similar enterprises, but they had been stung to action most sharply by the taunts of parsimony

[1] F. W. Seward, *Life of Seward*, p. 426.

[2] *Ibid.*, pp. 341-344.

[3] *Messages from the Governors*, vol. iii, p. 735; Seward, *Works*, vol. ii, p. 609; F. Bancroft, *Life of Seward*, vol. i, p. 88.

[4] " To avoid the necessity of direct taxation, however small, the obvious and sound rule of our financial policy will be to adjust the loans of each year so that the annual interest on the whole debt may always fall within the clear income of the state," Senate Document, no. 96, 1839, p. 12.

[5] D. C. Sowers, *Financial History of New York State*, p. 66.

flung at them by their opponents. Public sentiment had been stimulated by a society which first met at Albany in January, 1836, and which was principally officered by Whigs.[1] Probably most Democrats, in 1838, approved the attitude of Comptroller Flagg, while some, like Colonel Young, were even more intolerant. " Man alone," said he, " sells his offspring to speculators and monopolists, and this by a gross desecration of terms is denominated Internal Improvement." [2]

In the campaign of 1840 the Whigs were called the " forty-million-dollar party," a name which they could not shake off for many years.[3] But the charges of extravagance could not defeat them. The larger cities, in the hope of trade, generally gave Whig majorities, and it has been ascertained that in those sections where the staple farmers most desired an outlet to the city markets, Governor Seward was overwhelmingly preferred.[4] As his party was returned to power, the "more speedy enlargement" policy was continued, but the heavy debts contracted depressed the credit of the state. Complaints from those who were not beneficiaries so grew in volume that the Democrats controlled the legislature of 1842, and Flagg, again appointed as comptroller,[5] declared that the state must abandon its reliance on the future tolls of the canals, or come to bankruptcy. Thereupon the " stop-and-tax law " was enacted

[1] J. D. Hammond, *Political History*, vol. ii, p. 457; *N. Y. Evening Post,* Jan. 19, 1836.

[2] F. Byrdsall, *History of the Loco-Foco Party*, p. 63. Hale in his *Useful Knowledge*, pp. 25-27, and the *N. Y. Evening Post*, Jan. 7, 1836, take a similar view.

[3] *Albany Argus*, Sept. 25, 1840; *Ontario Messenger*, July 21, 1839; *N. Y. Evening Post*, Oct. 31, Nov. 3, 1846.

[4] Julius Winden, " The Influence of the Erie Canal," pp. 171, 173-175.

[5] This and similar state officers were then appointed by the legislature.

under Michael Hoffman's leadership; the public works were soon suspended, and short-time bonds, well-covered by taxation, were issued to repay the debts the Whigs had brought upon the state.[1] That the people took a like view was evidenced in the elections of 1842 and 1844, and by their call for a convention to revise the constitution, which, among some other changes, would set a limit to the state debt.

The great enthusiasm for internal improvements at the public cost had run its course. In a country of magnificent distances, means of transportation were properly considered indispensable; men of enterprise could well regard delay in their construction as a kind of crime. Yet, however plausible the generalization, individual enterprises were oftentimes regarded as risky experiments. Much capital was required to complete them; rich men in America reasonably hesitated to entrust their money to local companies at a time when credit lists were not available; and even if they had been willing, there was not enough accumulated surplus wealth in this young country to have satisfied a half of the demands. But in Europe, and especially in England, where manufactures were so profitable, there was capital enough, which, now in times of peace when nations had cut down their borrowing, was ready to be loaned on good security. These capitalists, however, were naturally even more reluctant than the few American millionaires to lend to individuals or joint-stock corporations so far away. The solution was in government responsibil-

---

[1] *Annual Report, Comptroller, 1843*, pp. 11, 13, 21, 22; J. H. Dougherty, *Constitutional History*, p. 154. A portion of the Democratic party (the "Hunkers") in the next few years took a Whiggish view, and desired to devote the surplus to improvements rather than to the payment of the debt, but Gov. Silas Wright in 1846 prevented such a law by his veto; see J. D. Hammond, *Life of Silas Wright*, pp. 286, *et seq.* See also J. A. Roberts, *A Century in the Comptroller's Office* (Albany, 1897), pp. 40-41.

ity, which, after the Erie Canal commenced its phenomenal earnings, seemed sufficient for entire safety, and on this guaranty millions upon millions in foreign bills of credit had been issued for American improvements. Not only on financial grounds the state's initiative seemed necessary, but state control of stone roads and canals, which anyone could use who had a cart or boat, seemed quite appropriate.

But in the early 'forties conditions had changed. State responsibility was no longer the magic key to foreign coffers, since Mississippi and some other commonwealths had defaulted on their interest payments and talked openly of repudiation.[1] Now that the experimental stage was over, domestic capital, augmented by industrial earnings, was ready for investment in private enterprises, especially in railroads, which were destined before the decade was completed to supersede canals. A railroad with its special rolling stock, in spite of Governor Seward's opinion, could not be considered as an open highway. So for them state support no longer seemed necessary, nor state control appropriate, and business men instead of lobbying to induce the state itself to develop its resources, came to fear the state's curtailment of their profits, and after their charter privileges were received they resented legislative interference.

[1] See G. W. Green's article in Lalor's *Cyclopedia of Political Science,* vol. iii, pp. 603-613.

CHAPTER XIV

Who Were the Whigs?

THE campaign of 1840 began directly after the inauguration of Van Buren. The Whigs in 1836 had been able only to annoy the enemy with local candidates, but with their practice in co-operation they were determined that four years later the Jackson dynasty should end. It was learned with apprehension that Mr. Webster might resign his seat in the Senate and D. B. Ogden, Philip Hone, Chancellor Kent and others of his New York friends planned a demonstration to dissuade him. On March 15, 1837, he visited the city, and was escorted to the spacious " saloon " in Niblo's Garden, at Broadway and Prince Street, where before a large and distinguished audience he delivered one of the greatest campaign speeches of our history, and certainly the greatest of his own career.[1] His summary of the " reign of Andrew Jackson " was a model of partisan narrative. The " executive encroachment," the drilling of the office-holders, the destruction of the currency and the disturbance of exchange, he reviewed with dignity and seeming impartiality, avoiding stricture and invective, yet presenting his selected evidence with such consummate skill as to convict the administration of incredible stupidity. He recommended the internal improvement of the west by national aid, either by direct subventions or by a thoroughgoing distribution of the revenues from the sale of public

---

[1] H. C. Lodge, *Daniel Webster* (Boston, 1883), pp. 238-239; E. Ruggles, *A Picture of New York in 1846* (N. Y., 1846); D. Webster, *Writings* (National Edition), vol. ii, pp. 189-230.

lands, according to the population of the states.[1]   As soon as the compromise arrangement would allow, he favored a high tariff, which would protect the manufacturers and workingmen " against the cheaper, ill-paid, half-fed, and pauper labor of Europe."   In his grand style he defended the Bank of the United States, and implied that it should speedily be rechartered.

Not often were the Whigs so clear and frank in the outline of their policy, for south was south and north was north, and no program would be pleasing to both sections— in fact, the southern partisans, quite out of place in their association with old Adams men, did not take kindly to programs at all.   In the north, it was to be a campaign of criticism of the financial policy of the administration.   When the occasion seemed propitious, the orators spoke cautiously against the annexation of Texas, and condemned the Seminole War as merely an expedient to save the slaves of fron-

---

[1] This would, of course, enable the states more easily to pay their debts, many of which were owed to British creditors on account of loans for internal improvement.   The proposition afforded the ground, however slight, for the Democratic contention that Webster and his party were arguing for an assumption of state debts by the federal treasury.   " Because we saw that . . . British Bankers who had been foolish enough to speculate in them [the securities], became at first suspicious, then inquisitive, and at length clamorous on the subject of their final redemption, and were silenced only by the assurance of the ' God-like Daniel ' that the general government *could* assume the liabilities of the states . . . because we saw something suspicious in the mission to England at such enormous expense to his party [in 1839], and his sudden abandonment while at London of his claims to the Presidency . . . because we knew that such was the manifest tendency of the ' Distribution ' system, so zealously advocated by the party at large —for these and other reasons we more than suspected that the ' whigs ' were secretly in favor of a direct assumption of the State debts by pledging the credit of the country for their redemption." *Troy Budget, Extra* (Columbia University Library) ; see also *Rough Hewer,* Sept. 3, 1840, on " British gold." Seward had strongly favored the measure; see *Works*, vol. i, pp. 415-416.

tier southerners from capture by the Indians. The defalcations of the Democratic office-holders, in the New York customs house and in the western land-offices, was a grateful theme to discourse upon at intervals; but the chief and constant issue was the suffering of business, and the proved wrong-headedness and incompetency of those who had tampered with the delicate machinery of credit. That is, the financial argument was paramount so long as questions of governmental policy were seriously debated. But the campaign of 1840 was not distinguished for serious debate.

It is not necessary here to rehearse the story of how Harrison and Tyler were selected as the party candidates. Clay could not win the abolitionists and Anti-Masons of New York or the militant free-traders of the south, and Webster had offended state-rights men; Thurlow Weed, more than any other, brought about the choosing of the western general. But Webster was rejected on another ground; he was " aristocratic." This consideration showed how completely the old order had changed. The men of wealth well realized, now liberty and equality had shown their power, that in enthusiastic profession of fraternity lay their only course of safety. Property rights were secure only when it was realized that in America property was honestly accessible to talent, however humble in its early circumstances. The Whigs found it needful to disavow as vehemently as they could any and all pretensions to a caste superiority in political life. Mr. Webster, at Patchogue, offered to strike with his great fist any man who called him an aristocrat, though Benjamin F. Butler repeated this ugly charge without enduring any violence save that of Webster's thundering invective.[1]

A fierce rivalry in simplicity sprang up between the par-

---

[1] *Rough Hewer*, Oct. 8, 1840.

ties. Charles Ogle, of Pennsylvania, made a speech in Congress arraigning President Van Buren as a sybarite, who drank Madeira wine and had made a palace of the people's White House by his enormous expenditures for decoration.[1] This speech, spread broadcast through the country, was the Whigs' most effective tract. It was true, of course, that the presidential mansion had been gradually furnished since rebuilding after the " late war," and the papers, therefore, could point contrasts between the present state and that of former days when Adams had received his visitors in an East Room of almost Spartan bareness.[2] They circulated drawings of the President, pictured as the model of sartorial perfection, seated at his table heaped with massive gold and silver service.[3] What could be expected of a chief magistrate who was reputed to cologne his whiskers? John Quincy Adams shuddered as Van Buren grew inordinately fat.[4]

Administration men defiantly retorted that the " Democracy is principally composed of the tillers of the ground, and the mechanics," [5] and founded Rough Hewers' Associations to offset the Tippecanoe Clubs which were multiplying through the country.[6] But it was vain for Democrats to gibe at opponents as silk-stockings, for the Whigs immediately pointed to the offensively luxurious Van Buren, and sang:

[1] *Congressional Globe*, vol. viii, p. 327. On the early consideration of this policy among the Whigs, see J. C. Spencer to Weed, Sept. 21, 1832, T. W. Barnes, *Memoir of Weed*, p. 44.

[2] *E. g. New Haven Palladium*, April 10, 1840.

[3] *Ibid.*, Feb. 17, 1840; see also issues of March 20 and April 3.

[4] *Memoir*, vol. x, p. 176.

[5] Elder John Leland in *Rough Hewer*, July 16, 1840.

[6] *Ibid.*, April 23, 27, 1840.

" We've tried your purse—proud lords, who love
   In palaces to shine;
But we'll have a ploughman President
   Of the Cincinnatus line." [1]

Eminent statesmen sitting on the platform at the rallies swayed to the rhythm of such exalted strains; Joseph Hoxie, a distinguished New York merchant, grew famous as the greatest choral leader of the campaign.[2] The Regency in despair dubbed their opponents the " sing-sing party," and abandoned rivalry for criticism of such methods.[3]

When a Democratic paper in an ill-starred moment made a jest about the obscure Harrison, who, if left alone, would be content with his log cabin and hard cider, the Whigs realized that their opportunity had come. It mattered not that the general really was in fairly comfortable circumstances and had recently been drawing an annual stipend of six thousand dollars; he was to be the log-cabin candidate. It was observed that the Democrats should be discreet in choosing a vice-presidential candidate, for "Mr. Van Buren, in consequence of his course of luxurious living to which he is addicted, may pass off any day without a moment's warning." [4] Compare all this, exclaimed the outraged Whigs, with the severe simplicity of Harrison, the farmer of North Bend, whom visitors had recently discovered flail in hand, threshing out his grain upon his barn floor.[5]

I have been in his log cabin [said Webster]. He lives in it

---

[1] From " Should Good Old Cider Be Despised?", *Log Cabin Song-book* (N. Y., 1840), p. 15.

[2] D. M. Fox, *History of Political Parties* (Des Moines, 1895), p. 116; W. Barrett, *Old Merchants of New York*, vol. ii, pp. 114, 116-117.

[3] *Log Cabin*, June 13, 1840.

[4] *Richmond Whig*, Aug. 7, 1840.

[5] *New Haven Palladium*, Feb. 7, 1840.

still. And he has made an addition to it, as many of us do. He keeps a horse. Well, I found him to be a very hospitable gentleman; the string of his latch is not pulled in. And I gave him my confidence.[1]

It was useless to argue about treasury notes or the recondite details of public revenues; if they could keep this picture before the people by speeches, songs and drawings, they could win. In good hard cider they toasted

> " The hard-fisted Farmer,
> The honest old Farmer ;
> We go for the Farmer that's work'd the farm well." [2]

To qualify before the great electorate, Governor Seward traveled in an old green-painted wagon, and chose to ride in row-boats, even when steam ferries were available.[3] The Whigs erected their log cabins in nearly every village to dispense hard cider and enthusiasm, and they were enormously successful, though the Democrats referred to them as " groggeries,' and stirred the apprehension of the temperance societies at the amount of this liquor consumed, sometimes, they said, " diluted with whiskey." In rebuke they drank their toasts in pure cold water.[4]

Mr. Webster, in his Saratoga speech, apologized profusely because the house of his nativity had not been made of logs; but he was quick to claim that honor for his elder brothers and sisters. " If I am ever ashamed of it . . . ," he fervently exclaimed, " may my name and the name of

---

[1] *Writings*, vol. xiii, p. 141.

[2] From " Come to the Contest," *Log Cabin Songbook*, p. 29.

[3] *Ontario Messenger*, July 19, 21, 1829. Seward had suffered somewhat earlier in his career because of a report that while travelling in Europe he had met too many aristocrats; see F. Bancroft, *W. H. Seward*, vol. i, p. 44.

[4] *Rough Hewer*, May 26, Aug. 13, Sept. 10, and *Mohawk Courier*, quoted in *ibid.*, June 18, 1840.

my posterity be blotted from the memory of mankind!"[1]
In a country where most people still made their homes in
log cabins,[2] such sentiments were popular. It was felt to
be the blessing of America, not that all should stay log-
cabin dwellers through their lives, but that anyone beginning in humble circumstances could by dint of application
become as great a man as Mr. Webster. The log-cabin,
coon-skin pageantry expressed the feeling of fraternity
deepened by the confident individualism which characterized
American society in the nineteenth century.[3]

Confronted with so prevalent and indigenous a sentiment,
the theory of class war, advanced by Frances Wright,
seemed a curious exotic phenomenon, confined to industrial
cities which were then not typically American. In the victorious campaign of 1840, the old aristocracy surrendered
its pretensions to prescriptive rights, which had long since
become absurd. Some scions of old families came down

[1] *Writings*, vol. iii, p. 30.

[2] W. E. Dodd, *Expansion and Conflict* (N. Y., 1915), p. 208.

[3] It was an evidence of the democratization of American society that
women took so prominent a part in the campaign of 1840, being present
in large numbers at the great rallies and sometimes the object of special
attention from the orators; see T. H. Benton, *Thirty Years' View*, vol.
ii, p. 206; A. C. Coleman, *Life of John J. Crittenden* (Philadelphia,
1873), vol. i, p. 127; *N. Y. Express*, May 9, 1840. Clay dreaded the
influence of women on the abolition movement. He said: "I intreat
that portion of my country-women who have given their countenance
to abolition, to remember that they are ever most loved and honored
when moving in their own appropriate and delightful sphere" (*Works*,
vol. viii, p. 159). Women in politics presented a phenomenon bewildering to southern statesmen. "By the bye," wrote A. P. Powers to
Howell Cobb, Oct., 1840, "this making politicians of women is something new under the sun" (A. C. Cole, *The Whig Party in the South*,
Washington, 1913, p. 61). Possibly the new education for women was
making a difference; see *Albany Argus*, May 8, 13, 1828; A. W. Calhoun,
Social History of the American Family (Cleveland, 1917—), vol. ii, p.
188; *Memoir of Frances Wright*; Commons, *etc.*, *History of Labor*,
vol. i, pp. 354-356; F. W. Seward, *Life of Seward*, p. 388.

like commoners to fight their way in the political arena, while others, feeling that they stood no better at the polls than did their servants, withdrew to the secure serenities of inconspicuous but comfortable houses, filled with old mahogany, old wines, old friends, and memories of ancient power.

Such is the broad view which confronts the historian today, though, no doubt, few saw it then. They knew it only as a furious campaign, replete with novelty. And there was novelty enough! When old caste distinctions had been softened, and before the great immigration of the later 'forties, the American people were homogeneous, likeminded, and, in consequence, uncritical. They were thus susceptible to slight suggestions, which with cumulative force carried them to queer extravagances.

The aristocracy, as such, no longer took a part in politics. " As they cannot occupy in public a position equivalent to what they hold in private life," observed De Tocqueville, " they abandon the former, and give themselves up to the latter; and they constitute a private society in the state, which has its own tastes and pleasures." [1]   In New York, as in other large commercial cities, social lines were drawn by some with a ridiculous assumption of finality, and snobbery was practised as an art, though it brought a smile to old-world visitors.[1] It was fashionable to contemn the politics of the time, but many who took this pose made little

[1] A. de Tocqueville, *Democracy in America* (Cambridge, 1863), vol. i, p. 228.

[2] T. Hamilton, *Men and Manners in America*, vol. i, p. 65.   H. Martineau, *Society in America* (2nd edition, London, 1839), vol. i, p. 13; F. J. Grund, *Aristocracy in America*, vol. i, p. 161. Some who had recently acquired wealth, now by the ostentatious leisure and extravagant dress of their ladies set up pretensions as aristocrats; see A. W. Calhoun, *Social History of the American Family* (Cleveland, 1918), vol. ii, chap. x.

secret of their fond belief that democracy would finally overreach itself, and that talent, property and station would again be given proper influence.[1] With opinions unchanged, they did not, however, give them voice in public, lest they be insulted.[2]

Captain Marryat,[a] after visiting the United States, declared that this great society must disintegrate, unless a political aristocracy were reconstituted.

I do not mean an aristocracy of title; I mean an aristocracy of talent and power which wealth will give—an aristocracy which will lead society and purify it. How is this to be obtained in a democracy?—simply by purchase. . . . In a country like America where the suffrage is universal, the people will eventually sell their birthright. . . . I say it has been done already, for it was done at the last New York election. The democratic party was sure of success, but a large sum of money was brought into play . . . and the Whigs carried the day.[3]

[1] F. J. Grund, *op. cit.*, vol. i, pp. 27, 220-221, 309-311.

[2] T. Hamilton, *op. cit.*, vol. i, p. 156; F. Marryat, *Diary in America,* second series (Philadelphia, 1840), p. 121. Capt. Marryat says: "That the morals of the nation have retrograded from the total destruction of the aristocracy, both in the government and in society, which has taken place within the last ten years, is most certain," pp. 122, 149. He found the New York merchants nearest his ideal in America, pp. 133, 140. For an example of pessimism as to the political future, see J. Fenimore Cooper, *The American Democrat* (Cooperstown, 1838), p. 6.

[3] F. Marryat, *Diary*, second series, p. 156. The captain refers to the lavish expenditures by Moses H. Grinnell, R. M. Blatchford, R. C. Wetmore, and other business men, who hired about 200 "floaters" from Philadelphia at $22 each in the campaign of 1838. The business seems to have been thoroughly done. When in 1840 these leading Whigs were brought before the recorder's court, they pleaded that the Philadelphians had been engaged only to insure the purity of the election against Democratic floaters who were coming from New Jersey. On these representations the case was dismissed! See *Rough Hewer*, Oct. 30, 1840, and G. Myers, *History of Tammany Hall*, pp. 140-141. It is, perhaps, appropriate to speak a further word on Whig campaign finance.

[a] Frederick Marryat (1792-1848), an English novelist who wrote a critical book about American manners entitled *A Diary in America* (1839) which resulted from a trip he made to the U.S. in 1837-1839.

But the future of America as foreseen by Captain Marryat and the gentlemen with whom he had conversed came
no nearer to the truth than that which Frances Wright had
prophesied. In the middle of the nineteenth century we
were not to see a ruling gentry or a war of classes. The
aristocrats of birth, when unsupported by wealth or talent,
dropped into a respectable obscurity, while the well-to-do
among them were soon inoculated with the feverish desire,
common in a bounteous but undeveloped country, to accu-
mulate more property and by this means outshine their
fellows. As manufacturers, railroads and finance absorbed
their interest, they found the game too fascinating to allow
them leisure actively to take a part in politics. They, of
course, voted the Whig ticket, and ladies boasted that they
could easily convert a wealthy Democrat into a Whig; [1]
but they contented themselves with making the government
safe for business by generous contributions to the campaign funds. When, indeed, they did discuss affairs of
state, the great ideals of the anti-slavery crusade and "manifest destiny " elicited their praise or condemnation. The

Even then the conservative party drew large contributions into its chest.
" I hope our rich men will shell out," wrote H. Ketcham to Follett in
1832, and confident appeals were addressed to such men as General
Porter (Follett Correspondence, Sept. 13, 1832) ; in that campaign it
was complained that the National Republicans had unlimited resources
(G. Myers, *op. cit.*, pp. 107-108). Marcy wrote to Jesse Hoyt, that he
feared the U. S. Bank would use $50,000 in the state (D. S. Alexander,
Political History, vol. i, p. 395), Weed tells how R. B. Minturn, Grinnell,
Blatchford, and others brought him $8,000 for distribution, a few days
before the election of 1839, and pays tribute to the broad view taken
by the New York merchants, on this and other occasions (*Autobiography*, pp. 448, 476-477, 503, 504). On the other hand, the Whigs did
take great pains to check illegal voting in the interest of Tammany; see,
for example, mss. record of Fifth Ward Whig Committee of New
York City, Oct. 16, 1840 (N. Y. Pub. Lib.).

[1] F. J. Grund, *Aristocracy in America*, vol. i, p. 221.

economic questions which had stirred the yeasty thirties were for a time forgotten.

Although the wildest projects for rejuvenating all society marked the next decade, there was no concerted movement of artisans against the capitalists as had been loudly heralded by the Workingmen and Friends of Equal Rights. The expected crisis, whose frightful shadow had been cast upon the pulpit and the press, did not arrive. In the first place, many of the changes for which the workmen had contended in their parties, were vouchsafed them by shrewd Democratic and Whig leaders, eager for their votes. The panic of 1837 had temporarily deprived many of employment, but when those nervous days were over, the agitators, also, found that the Texas problem, the petitions of the abolitionists to Congress and their pamphlets in the mails, had fixed the attention of the public mind, in place of matters which a few years before had been engrossing. But agitation not only went unnoticed; it was unnecessary as well, for the condition of the working class steadily improved.

Despite the opposition of the eastern manufacturers, the western lands were made cheaper for the settler,[1] and railroads joining the canals or extending into the northwest made them day by day more easily accessible. Even distant and mysterious Oregon was opening to settlement. It was generally realized that labor had here an alternative, and before the great influx of foreigners later in the century, employers had to offer large inducements to meet the competition of the western opportunity. For a generation wages were advanced more rapidly than prices.[2] Then, too, thrown backward from the west, there was the influ-

---

[1] The preëmption laws became permanent in 1841.

[2] *Senate Documents*, 52nd. Cong., 2nd. Session, Report 1394 (Report of Mr. Aldrich from Committee on Finance, 1893), part i, pp. 10, 14.

ence of that fierce individualism of the pioneer, who has created wealth from wilderness, and who knows that the same economic opportunity awaits every man or family in the east who will take like trouble. Socialism is professedly a scheme to keep comfortable existence always within the reach of honest toil; it is plausible alone in those societies where there are many who seem permanently denied a share in property; in America with her free lands there was no such exclusion.[1]

In surveying the political conditions of New York state in 1800, we took occasion to analyze the composition of the Federalist party.[2] It is proper now, perhaps, to attempt a similar examination of the Whigs. They had assumed their name as resistants to " King Andrew," and, taking north and south together, this was, no doubt, their only bond of union. But in New England and the middle states their dislike of this executive encroachment was grounded chiefly on the fact that they were excluded from the executive offices.[3] As old Elder Leland, of Cheshire, put it, " Strip a man of office and he will talk like a whig; put him into office and he will be a tory." [4] This may account for the professions of the party in New York, but it does not reveal its constituent parts.

On no question, in the noisy days of 1840, was there more recrimination than as to where the old Federalists were to be found. The Democrats, of course, pinned the

[1] It may be said the laborers bettered their condition when they ceased attempting to reconstruct society, and through their trade union attended strictly to raising their own wages.

[2] See *supra*, chapters i and ii.

[3] For an explanation of the Whig party largely on this basis, see Edgar Dawson, "The Origin of the American Whig Party," *History Teachers' Magazine*, vol. ii, pp. 160-161.

[4] John Leland to G. N. Briggs, Jan. 12, 1836, *Writings of the Late Elder John Leland* (N. Y., 1845), p. 675.

black cockade of 'ninety-eight upon their enemies. But the great Henry Clay attempted to repel the charge that the Federalists had changed their name for that of Whigs, and instanced fellow senators who had once been followers of Hamilton and Adams, but who had now transferred their fealty to Jackson and Van Buren.[1] A New York congressman supported him by citations in the House of Representatives;[2] papers printed similar lists,[3] and a favorite campaign song rehearsed the names of fifteen Democratic leaders formerly members of the discredited party.[4] Willis Hall, speaking in the assembly, referred to eighteen Federalist families in the city of New York who now were represented in the ranks of the administration.[5] Conversely, General Root pointed to the seven survivors of the New York senators who had voted for Jeffersonian electors in 1801; six of them, he said, were Whigs in 1840.[6]

However, Hamlet's mother showed but common shrewdness when she said, " The lady doth protest too much, methinks." The Whigs, in their diligent researches for names of Jackson Federalists, evidenced a too violent desire to allay suspicion. In this they were not successful. As we have tried to show, the old group, though dwindling, had largely kept together in New York, and formed the core of the rechristened party of the 'thirties. Once, when a certain politician's orthodoxy was impugned, Greeley remonstrated, " Is it not monstrous that anybody should fear

---

[1] *Works*, vol. viii, pp. 205-206.

[2] *Remarks of Mr. Christopher Morgan of N. Y. . . . March 26, 1840* (N. Y., 1840).

[3] *E. g. Springfield Republican*, Sept. 29, Oct. 6, 13, Nov. 10, 1838, June 1, 1839.

[4] " When This Old Hat Was New ", *Log Cabin Songbook*, p. 66.

[5] Quoted in *Springfield Republican*, Feb. 10, 1838.

[6] Quoted in *New Haven Palladium*, June 1, 1840.

the man . . . who is heartily supported by such Whigs as James Kent, David B. Ogden, Philip Hone, John A. King, &c., &c.?"[1]   Denials of Federalist origin were distasteful to such staunch old partisans as Colonel Stone of the *Commercial Advertiser*, for they were as useless as they were absurd.[2]   The great majority of the Federalists of 1812, who had survived, were Whigs in 1840.

But this remnant never could have carried an election. Most Clintonian Republicans, like Archibald McIntyre and Pierre Van Cortlandt, had remained with Seward and Granger, as champions of internal improvement for the nation and the state.   Some People's Men, like Dr. Barstow, who was named for lieutenant governor in 1836, likewise stayed with those who fought the Regency.   Some Democratic Anti-Masons, like John C. Spencer and John Young, who was to be made governor, formed with Weed and others ties too strong to make it easy to rejoin their former party when the blessed spirit had subsided.   The Democratic leaders, who had been so long in power, had been unable to minister to the ambitions of all their party workers, and some disgruntled politicians, like General Root, General Pitcher and Major Noah, as well as Jesse Buel, an ex-state-printer, who was chosen as the candidate for governor in the hopeless campaign of 1836, came over to the opposition out of hopelessness or spite.   As men like General Porter and P. R. Livingston had developed economic interests which would be served by the American System and internal improvement, they naturally joined the party of the business man.   This was a kind of motive even more obvious in the case of those merchants, like Wetmore and Grinnell, who appreciated the useful service of the Bank of

---

[1] *N. Y. Tribune*, Nov. 3, 1846.

[2] H. Greeley to W. L. Stone, Jr. in the latter's "Life of William L. Stone," p. 98; *Rough Hewer*, Aug. 13, 1840.

the United States; or of those bankers, like Tallmadge and the rest of the Conservatives, who became convinced that private credit was not effectually protected by the Democratic party. It was but natural that the Whigs should welcome these accessions as they came, and grant distinctions to their new adherents which would possibly draw others to their standard. On the electoral ticket of 1840 in New York, for example, six places were assigned apparently with this in view.[1] Besides all these, of course, there were many other voters caught and sometimes held by argument or song, as the " Panic Whigs " of 1838 and the " Log-Cabin Whigs " of 1840.

That the solidarity of parties was maintained is, no doubt, in part to be attributed to the influence of leaders. Personalities like those of Seward, Weed and Greeley, are lodestones to attract the uncertain. The material and social interests of the northern counties, for example, were clearly similar, their farmsteads rising one by one as the New England pioneers cut back the great south woods. The Concord coach, that labored over the rough way from Lake Champlain to the St. Lawrence, satisfied the needs of travel, while ox-drawn carts seemed adequate to haul the infrequent freight. No pet bank, no state road or canal, no basic staples, claimed their local loyalties. Yet in the ten years beginning in 1832, St. Lawrence and Clinton Counties were steadfastly Democratic, while their intervening neighbor, Franklin, was as safely counted for the opposition. This cannot be explained unless one calls to mind that the former counties were the homes of Silas Wright and A. C. Flagg, and the latter of the popular and influential Luther Bradish, who presided over the two houses of the legislature, first one and then the other. However, few historians

[1] Isaac Ogden, Gideon Lee, P. B. Porter, Pierre Van Cortlandt, James Burt and P. R. Livingston.

would argue that personal factors were the chief cause of the party loyalties at large.

A thesis has lately been advanced and supported with much scholarly research, that the two great parties of our history represent respectively two kinds of property interest, personal and real. If a student will cast up the sums of the assessments in the thirty-three counties regularly Democratic in the times of Jackson and Van Buren, and with due reference to the population, carefully compare his figures with those he has obtained from twenty-four Whig counties, his laborious computation will convince him that this thesis is not supported by the statistics.[1] It should be said, however, that the test has not been fair, as the interpretation is intended to apply to the whole country broadly separated into economic sections.

But our student, by constructing state election maps, will observe how constant was the western section in its loyalty to Whig principles. Here were farmers of New England stock who brought their grain and wool to the canal at places such as Buffalo, Lockport or Rochester, consigning it to the " home market," which they believed the American System was developing in the east. Here, too, were wealthy and conservative communities like Canandaigua and Geneva, and other towns like Warsaw, Batavia, Angelica, Fredonia and Geneseo, whose citizens apparently had

[1] In the realty assessments the counties contribute to no striking parallels with the election returns. It is found that of the 57 "upstate" counties, approximately half show an average assessment on personal estate of $12 or more per person. According to the theory these should be Whig counties. But investigation shows that there are 19 of them which are Democratic, and only 10 Whig. The counties where personal estate is found in smallest quantity *per capita* are most of them among the staunchest Whig strongholds in the west: Chautauqua, Cattaraugus, Allegany, Broome, Erie, Genesee, Cortland, Niagara and Orleans. See E. Williams, *New York Annual Register* (N. Y., 1830-1843).

brought with them a loyalty to the policies of the Adams family, and who had cherished gratitude to Clinton for opening their county to world commerce. It had been the fire of Anti-Masonry which had fused the western counties into an almost solid section, but the allegiance to Weed's party was retained because the young industrial communities and the commercial farmers found Whig policy comported with their interest.

Separate from the mass of the people [ran a Democratic address to the voters] the tories of the revolution and most of their descendants—the Hartford Convention men of the late war and most of theirs—the church and state men—the bankites and monopolists of every description — the operators in money who see in government nothing but a business transaction, more or less valuable according to the share they get of the profits, and who find more virtue in a price-current than they can in the Declaration of Independence—in fine, all who stand ready booted and spurred to jump into the public saddle —and you have in the residue the Democratic party.[1]

One scarcely looks for justice from the enemy; yet it is interesting to inquire if property was, as they implied, unequally divided between the two parties.

" By whom was the general surrounded?" asked the *American*, when Jackson visited New York city in 1828. " Did the oldest and most respectable inhabitants crowd around him? Did the judges of the different courts, the leading barristers, the presidents of banks, the collector and others of the government flock toward him?" No, it answered; it was generally mechanics and not men from the better walks of life who shouted their applause.[2] " The merchants were generally Federalists, as were most of the

---

[1] *Albany Argus, Extra*, Sept. 14, 1834.

[2] Quoted in *Argus*, March 3, 1828. It is well to remember that officeholders were not necessarily partisans of the President as yet.

lawyers," wrote Thurlow Weed of New York city after 1815.[1]

It is a very common fact [declared a chronicler of trade, looking backward from the 'sixties] that for thirty-four years (since 1828) very few merchants of the first class have been Democrats. The mass of large and little merchants have, like a flock of sheep, gathered either in the Federalist, Whig, Clay, or Republican folds. The Democratic merchants could have easily been stored in a large Eighth avenue railroad car.[2]

It seems, then, that there was an economic line that corresponded with the borders of political opinion. The testimony is clear enough, though perhaps too slight to warrant a definite conclusion. But there is the far more certain witness of statistics.

The circulation lists of party newspapers in New York city repay examination. In the 'thirties the penny press, having proved its power in London, made its appearance in the United States.[3] The decent, ponderous, respectable " six-pennies "[4] were scandalized; their readers, no doubt, shared their contempt and disgust for these " scurrilities " hawked about by newsboys. But the penny papers multiplied in previously untilled fields, where there was room for anything that was cheap, and they soon spread in circulation to reach numbers far exceeding those of the class whose opinions followed the lines of editorial leaders from the pens of Colonel Stone and Colonel Webb, Mr. King and Mr. Bryant. If men are judged according to the company

---

[1] *Autobiography*, p. 55.

[2] W. Barrett, *Old Merchants of New York*, vol. i, p. 81.

[3] F. Hudson, *History of Journalism in the United States*, pp. 416-428.

[4] These papers, which had held the field practically unchallenged in 1834, were so designated from the price of the papers over the counter. The subscription by the year was $10.00; see E. Williams *N. Y. Annual Register, 1835*, p. 129.

they keep, an index no less nice as to their taste and thought and size of purse is found in the newspapers they buy. They reflect as well as form opinion. The circulation of the six-penny newspapers we may suppose to have been chiefly among the well-to-do, and thus by finding what they chose to read, we may infer with fairness how this sort of people thought and voted.

According to statistics compiled for 1842,[1] the circulation of the cheap dailies had reached 62,500. It was to work among this larger class that Greeley's *Tribune* had been started the year before, and had now about 10,000 readers, representing, probably, the proportion of Whig strength there to be found.[2] The circulation of the "Wall Street papers" was 32,200, or less than half of that reached by the other group.[3] What were the politics of those journals which were desired by this fortunate third? This is a

---

[1] F. Hudson, *Journalism in the United States*, p. 525.

[2] *Ibid.*, and H. Greeley, *Recollections*, pp. 136, 137. The party leaders had realized the need of propaganda, even if expensive, among the poorer voters, and in 1834 had proposed issuing a cheap edition of the *Albany Evening Journal* and the *N. Y. Courier and Enquirer* to compete with the penny papers, but the plan had not been carried out (The *Man*, July 25, 26, 1834). However, the panic offered hopeful opportunity to the Whigs; Thurlow Weed devised the scheme of the campaign paper for this purpose and brought young Greeley to Albany to edit the *Jeffersonian* (Feb. 17, 1838—Feb. 9, 1839; Greeley, *Recollections*, pp. 125, 133-134, 316), and in 1840 the same editor was entrusted with the *Log Cabin* (May 27, 1840—Nov. 20, 1841), which was made popular by means of music score and pictures as well as what is now called a "magazine page." D. D. Barnard edited a Whig campaign paper at Albany in that year, known as the *Minerva* (see Howell and Tenney, *History of Albany*, p. 367). The Democrats seeing that these papers were successful established the *Rough Hewer* (Feb. 20—Dec. 24, 1840) at Albany with A. C. Flagg as editor. There were *Log Cabin songbooks*, and a *Tippecanoe Text-book* (published by W. O. Niles at $10 a hundred).

[3] The merchants advertised almost exclusively in these ten-dollar papers; W. Barrett, *Old Merchants*, vol. i, p. 25.

question which presents no difficulty, since that was a time when to preach the party doctrine was the chief reason of a newspaper's existence, and when its bills were often paid by generous appropriations from the party chest.[1]

The *Journal of Commerce* wished to be considered neutral and emphatically commercial,[2] and, therefore, its 7,500 may be neglected. The *Courier and Enquirer*, edited by Colonel Webb, was at this time strongly Whig, and of the most conservative wing.[3] The *Express* had been founded in 1836 by Willis Hall, who later was attorney general under Governor Seward, and was considered as a leader of the party; the paper's circulation had lately been increased by the merging with it of the *Daily Advertiser*, which had been edited by Theodore Dwight, renowned as secretary of the Hartford Convention.[4] The *American* "belonged to the strictly aristocratic and financial circles of the metropolis,"[5] and edited by Charles King, the admired ideal of Federalist gentlemen, was, of course, consistently and firmly Whig. Of that party, also, was the old *Commercial Advertiser*, founded to support John Jay. Born in a New England manse, its editor, Colonel Stone, had never faltered in the political faith he there imbibed, and distin-

---

[1] F. Hudson, *op. cit.*, pp. 345, 397, 411 (I. C. Bray), *Memoir of James Gordon Bennett* (N. Y., 1855), pp. 160-163, 170-172; W. L. Mackenzie, *The Lives and Opinions of B. F. Butler and Jesse Hoyt* (Boston, 1845), pp. 90, 93; E. E. Hale, Jr., *William H. Seward*, p. 97. Oren Follett writes to Joseph Hoxie, Feb. 6, 1832 (Follett Correspondence, Quarterly Pub. of Hist. and Phil. Soc. of Ohio, vol. v, no. 2) : "And who is it gives voice to the people? It is the humble man of types and paper, who is himself controlled by cash. Plant deep the 'root of all evil,' and good will spring from it."

[2] Wm. Hallock, *Life of Gerard Hallock* (N. Y., 1869), pp. 63-64.

[3] F. Hudson, *op. cit.*, pp. 344-362.

[4] *Ibid.*, pp. 517-520.

[5] *Ibid.*, p. 442.

guished for the "spicy and vigilant vindication" of these principles, he had from time to time published party papers in five different towns.[1] (He spoke sarcastically of "universal suffrage folks": "I am no Jacobin—no democrat," he said; "I hate the mob.")[2] These four Whig papers served 19,800 subscribers. The others among these journals which satisfied New Yorkers who took less thought of pennies, the *Evening Post* and the *Standard*, which had supported Jackson and Van Buren, could muster only 2,900 on their lists. Indeed, the latter of these two had kept its hold on life wholly by grace of subsidies from Washington. Though one may perhaps claim more significance for such deductions than they warrant, from these premises it seems fair to conclude, that of those who could afford to subscribe for the more expensive party papers, seven-eighths were Whig.[3]

[1] W. L. Stone, Jr., "The Life and Writings of William Leete Stone," (published with W. L. Stone, Sr., *Life and Times of Red Jacket*, N. Y., 1866), pp. 9, 11, 12, 16, 18.

[2] "New York to Niagara," *Buffalo Hist. Soc. Pub.*, vol. xiv, p. 240; W. L. Stone, Jr., *op. cit.*, p. 25.

[3] The preponderance of Whigs among this class of readers recalls a like condition with their Federalist predecessors. In 1816 there were seven daily papers in New York city, reaching in all their circulation 8,890 subscribers (F. Hudson, *op. cit.*, p. 226). In that day an annual subscription to a daily newspaper was an indulgence afforded only by the rich. Subtracting from the seven the *Mercantile Advertiser*, which professed neutrality (I. Thomas, *History of Printing*, vol. ii, p. 519) and served 2,000 patrons with extracts from other journals, we find that of the remaining six, four, totalling 5,290 in circulation were Federalist, while there were 1,700 subscribers to the Republican dailies. In 1816, then, 76 per cent of those sufficiently well-to-do to subscribe patronized the Federalist papers, and 24 per cent the Republican. Indeed, many of the 825 readers of the *Columbian*, here credited to the Republicans, were probably not orthodox members of that party, as DeWitt Clinton, whom it supported, was very friendly to the Federalists. (*Ibid.*, and *Encyclopedia Britannica*, 11th edition, article "Newspapers"; *National Cyclopedia of Am. Biog.*, article on B. Gardenier, owner of the *Courier*, vol. xiii, p. 433; *American Almanac*, Boston, 1835, p. 282; Hudson, pp. 225, 282).

It is interesting in passing to cite the opinion of a contemporary observer, that the papers of that day which were published on a costly and ambitious scale tended to become Whig, because of the dependence on the merchants' advertisements, a source of income more reliable than subvention from the party:

You may always doubt a democratic editor's sincerity when his advertisements begin to increase. He is then sure of making himself agreeable to a certain portion of the commercial community, and to meet soon with the proper reward of his new political faith. You may then expect to see him promoted in society and on 'change; and ten chances to one he will be able to settle with his creditors. After that he begins to differ on one point or another with the leading principles of the democratic party (for it is seldom that a man changes *at once* from a democrat to a Whig), until by degrees he renounces the whole doctrine as unworthy of a " gentleman and a scholar." [1]

Fortunately there can be added other evidence as to the character of parties in the state eighty years ago. Our survey according to the counties did not contribute to support the economic hypothesis, but perhaps it was because within a section like a county it is impossible to find how property was distributed. An examination of the cities, ward by ward through several years, however, will yield more interesting results; for here we may safely infer a general economic character to each small locality.

If we turn attention to the metropolis of the state and of the country, we find no way of correlating the political sta-

---

[1] F. J. Grund, *Aristocracy in America* (1839), vol. ii, p. 125. Also on advertising see W. Barrett, *Old Merchants*, vol. i, p. 25. Grund says that there are generally considerably more Whig papers than Democratic in a city, "which I take for the best possible proof that talent loves to be rewarded, and in republics, as well as monarchies, naturally serves those who are able to reward it," *op. cit.*, vol. i, p. 311.

tistics of the wards throughout the dozen years from 1828 to 1840, except by use of maps;[1] for new wards, created from time to time within the interval, confuse the tables for the purpose of comparison. Yet the character of the residents in the various localities themselves, we are informed, generally remained about the same until after 1840.[2] Considering the wealth *per capita* in each ward together with its politics throughout the period, a striking parallel may be observed.[3] The " aristocratic " first three wards and the fifteenth were inhabited, in general, by the richest men— and the most stalwart Whigs. But lest in some wards wealth might have been very unequally distributed, it is well to seek some index as to the economic outlook of the individuals according to their occupations.[4]

[1] Note on data presented in accompanying maps: The elections of 1810 and 1816 were typical closely contested elections in the last days of Federalism as a party. The mayoralty elections of 1834 and 1840 were also closely fought, while that of 1837 is given to show the extent of the Anti-Tammany vote when the panic, and the Native American and Loco-Foco movements were factors. The authorities are as follows: Wards in 1810 and 1816, D. Longworth, *Explanatory Map and Plan of New York City* (N. Y., 1817); election returns, *N. Y. Evening Post*, April 30, 1810, and May 4, 1816. For wards 1828-1840: D. A. Burr, *Map of the City and County of New York* (N. Y., 1832), *Map of City of New York* (N. Y., 1840); D. T. Valentine, *Manual of the Corporation of New York* (N. Y., 1842). For election returns: E. Williams, *New York Annual Register* (N. Y., 1831-1840); O. L. Holley, *New York State Register* (Albany, 1843); *N. Y. Evening Post*, Nov. 10, 1828, Nov. 12, Nov. 26, 1836; *N. Y. Morning Courier*, Nov. 11, 1828. The presidential vote corresponded with the state ticket vote.

[2] W. A. Pelletreau, *Early New York Houses*, p. 78, and other authorities cited *supra*, pp. 22-25.

[3] The following figures are computed from the tables in D. T. Valentine's, *Manual of the Corporation of New York*, 1841, pp. 49, 184. See Table, page 432.

[4] From the Census of the State of New York, 1845, as given in O. L. Holley, *New York State Register, 1846*, page 109, excepting, of course, the column of percentages which are computed. See Table, page 432.

Footnote 3, page 431, continued

Wards.	Assessment Total Estate.	Population.	Wealth Per Capita.
1st	$59,778,549	10,629	$5623
2nd	16,856,412	6,406	2631
3rd	17,261,110	11,581	1490
4th	10,415,555	15,770	660
5th	12,506,445	19,159	652
6th	9,997,978	17,199	580
7th	15,291,846	22,985	665
8th	13,248,758	29,093	455
9th	9,776,585	24,795	404
10th	6,857,650	29,093	235
11th	3,897,591	17,052	222
12th	12,365,350	11,678	1059
13th	4,554,054	18,516	245
14th	8,762,273	20,230	432
15th	22,783,167	17,769	1282
16th	17,919,139	22,275	804
17th	10,564,699	18,622	567

Footnote 4, page 431, continued

Wards.	Colored Persons.	Farmers.	Mechanics.	Merchants and Manufacturers.	Learned Professions.	Percentage of Aggregate of Merchants, Manufacturers and Learned Professions.
1st	192	....	284	2,869	354	92 per cent.
2nd	275	....	463	283	60	50 "
3rd	530	....	994	624	165	44 "
4th	190	....	1,684	441	50	25 "
5th	2,433	8	2,025	568	137	27 "
6th	1,073	2	1,281	153	68	15 "
7th	368	5	2,431	751	96	23 "
8th	1,841	1	3,161	765	134	22 "
9th	367	1	2,586	607	162	23 "
10th	445	13	3,080	499	99	16 "
11th	540	13	2,757	141	60	7 "
12th	559	187	620	354	70	36 "
13th	669	6	2,045	193	42	10 "
14th	1,243	3	2,737	289	97	12 "
15th	712	3	786	635	274	54 "
16th	1,079	28	2,968	563	181	20 "
17th	397	5	2,093	418	121	25 "

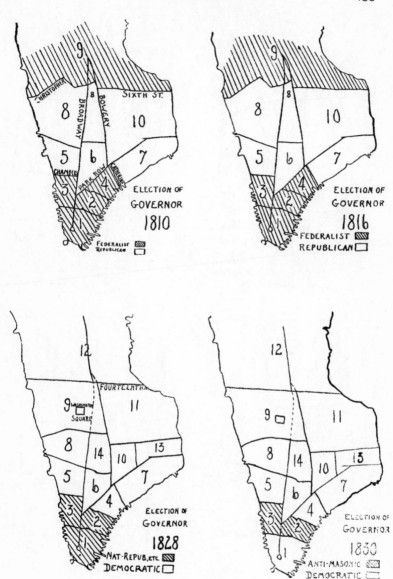

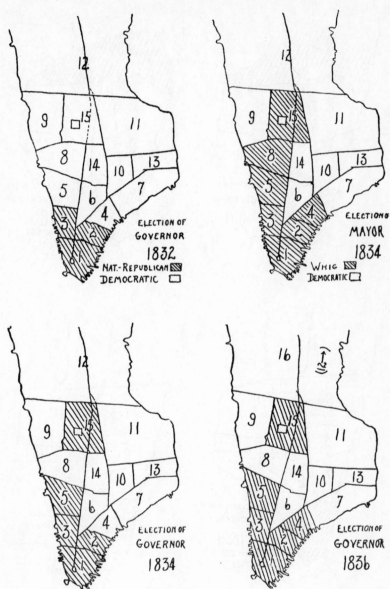

ELECTION OF GOVERNOR 1832

NAT.-REPUBLICAN
DEMOCRATIC

ELECTION OF MAYOR 1834

WHIG
DEMOCRATIC

ELECTION OF GOVERNOR 1834

ELECTION OF GOVERNOR 1836

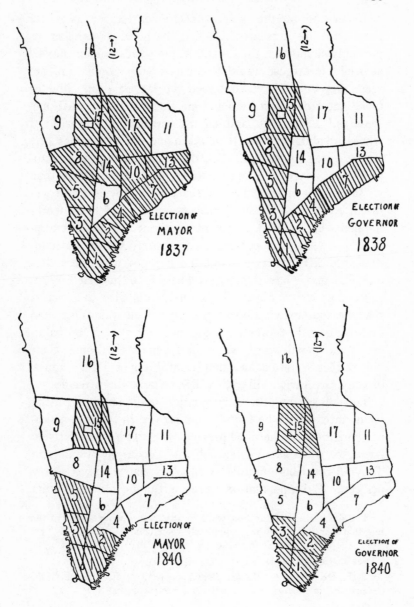

ELECTION OF
MAYOR
1837

ELECTION OF
GOVERNOR
1838

ELECTION OF
MAYOR
1840

ELECTION OF
GOVERNOR
1840

Depending on the figures of the nearest census where these data are presented, we find the previous conclusions perfectly supported; the reliable Whig wards, which showed as well the largest wealth compared with population, are seen likewise to have contained the largest proportion of merchants, manufacturers and members of the learned professions.[1] The fifth and eighth wards, the majority of whose inhabitants were poor mechanics, several times presented Whig majorities. But the residents here who actually voted were in more comfortable circumstances than would at first appear; for reference to another column will disclose that here a considerable proportion of these workingmen were colored, and hence without the ballot, except for those who were possessed of property worth two hundred and fifty dollars. And the negroes who were thus qualified, as we have seen, were likely from historic reasons to support the Whigs.[2] It is interesting also to observe, that the southern section of the city which was Whig, had likewise been Federalist, though many merchants and bankers of the fourth ward, when the fever of 1822 made their old residence untenable, had moved out to the " quiet, dreamy Greenwich village," which became the fifteenth.[3]

Turning to the other larger cities of the state and using what statistics can be found, we discover, in general, a similar condition. Where the property *per capita* was relatively large, the ward was Whig. Albany, Brooklyn, Buffalo and Troy all contribute figures to establish that wherever thirty per cent of the population were merchants, manufacturers

---

[1] The defalcation of the first ward in 1830 was doubtless due to the fact that "Anti-Masonry was completely repudiated in the city of New York," Seward's *Autobiography*, p. 78.

[2] See *supra*, note appended to chapter viii.

[3] T. F. De Voe, *The Market Book*, pp. 400-401; E. Bisland, " Old Greenwich," in *Historic New York*, First Series, pp. 290-291.

and professional men, the vote showed more Whigs than
were found in other wards. Conversely, where mechanics
made their home, Democratic candidates generally were certain of election.[1] Rochester, alone, refuses to yield support
to these conclusions; but the traditions of that city were so
strongly Whig that it scarcely furnishes the evidence for
our inquiry.[2]

It seems warrantable to conclude that, after due regard
for other factors, there remains an " economic interpretation " of the Whig party in New York state, as it was constituted in the early 'forties of the nineteenth century.

They had an interest in protecting property, but it was a
kind of property which was theoretically accessible to all
who had the industry and enterprise to gain it. Anything
that savored of the feudal system found small support even
from the Whigs. On the twenty-sixth of January, 1839,
Stephen Van Rensselaer, the last of the patroons, died,
mourned and eulogized by everyone who had known him.
The thousands of his tenants had tacitly agreed to refrain
from protest while he lived, but when his heirs attempted
to collect arrearages which he had allowed to grow, they
started a campaign of violence, which lasted for nearly a
dozen years. They claimed that during centuries of occupation of the land as lease-holders, hard-working farmers
had paid more than enough of quarter-sales and covenanted
fees, and had suffered more than was right from the oner-
ous restrictions as to wood and water, minerals and mill
streams. They refused to pay. Many men of property
realized that vested rights, in general, were jeopardized by
this defiance, and Governor Seward called out the militia to
coerce the tenantry along the Helderberg, near Albany.

[1] " Farmers " in a city are truck-gardeners or persons of small fortune,
who should be counted with mechanics.

[2] The tables and explanation for these five cities are printed in the
appendix.

But no gun was fired; even the most conservative Whigs, while lamenting Loco-Foco anarchy, admitted that huge estates in land did not serve the public welfare, and only deprecated the illegal form in which the tenants made their protest. The governor, himself, spoke of " their petitions for relief from tenures oppressive, anti-republican, and degrading." [1] The contemptuous resistance to undoubtedly legal claims spread to similar estates in other counties, notably Columbia and Delaware, and tenants, banded on the roads as " Injuns," reviled, belabored, and on some occasions killed the luckless constables who sought to arrest them. Yet the Whigs as a party did not protest, and Greeley's *Tribune* openly expressed its sympathy. It was a Whig governor who cleared the jails of anti-renters, and Whig legislators did not as a group oppose the measures by which the ancient privileges of the great landlords were diminished one by one. They were as willing to attract five thousand voters as were the Democrats. Not thus would Egbert Benson, Jonas Platt, Elisha Williams or James Kent have acted in their period of power. But times had changed; the rigid castes of the eighteenth century with all their " rights " were gone.

The influence of the old aristocracy as such had nearly disappeared, but its mantle had fallen upon capital and business enterprise, with their faithful pensioners of talent. Their party had no other steady principle than this: that business should go on. But in a country of such splendid possibilities as the United States, this was not necessarily mean and sordid, for it looked to a development that would, perhaps, bring comfort and prosperity to all, and prestige to the nation. Part of the legacy of Federalism to its successors was, of course, made up of some personal ideals—

[1] *Messages from the Governors*, vol. iii, p. 841.

distinction of deportment, appreciation of arts and letters, and other qualities of culture — and this gave the party a prestige beyond that of its numbers.

Of the two great parties [wrote Emerson], which at the moment almost share the nation between them, I should say that one has the best cause, and the other contains the best men. The philosopher, the poet, or the religious man will, of course, wish to cast his vote with the democrat for free trade, for wide suffrage, for the abolition of legal cruelties in the penal code, and for facilitating in every manner the access of the young and the poor to sources of wealth and power. But he can rarely accept the persons whom the so-called popular party proposes to him as representative of these liberalities. [The spirit of our American radicalism is destructive and aimless.] On the other hand, the conservative party, composed of the most valuable, most moderate, able and cultivated part of the population, is timid, and merely defensive of property.[1]

[1] Essay on Politics.

APPENDIX

(TO CHAPTER XIV)

STATISTICS OF PARTY POLITICS AND ECONOMIC INTEREST

ALBANY

WEALTH

Wards.	Aggregate Assessment on Property, 1849.[1]	Number of Voters, 1844.[2]	Average Assessment per Voter.
1st	$405,335	549	$738
2nd	618,740	605	1,023
3rd	912,515	963	958
4th	1,593,114	956	1,656
5th	3,708,546	547	6,780
6th	553,500	592	935
7th	531,935	604	880
8th	358,660	593	605
9th	877,993	867	1,012
10th	810,865	636	1,275

[1] Computed from tables in Joel Munsell, *Annals of Albany* (2nd edition, Albany, 1870), vol. ii, pp. 361-362.

[2] Computed from following table.

440

Elections 1842-1846 [1]

Wards.	1842 [2]		1844 [3]		1846 [4]		Anti-Slavery Vote.	
	Bradish.	Bouck.	Clay.	Polk.	Young.	Wright.	1842 [2] Stewart.	1844 [3] Birney.
1st	178	271	201	348	312	437	2	3
2nd	244	275	268	337	342	351	1	3
3rd......	480	400	516	447	468	518	5	11
4th......	545	339	572	384	624	504	10	8
5th......	337	230	299	248	338	249	5	8
6th......	305	195	359	333	478	406	7	10
7th......	216	251	262	342	324	416	1	4
8th......	222	286	219	374	316	462	1	5
9th......	471	274	520	347	625	364	3	6
10th.....	278	247	358	278	405	342	8	10

Percentage of Whigs

Wards.	1842	1844	1846	Average.
1st.........	39 per cent.	37 per cent.	42 per cent.	39 per cent.
2nd........	47 "	44 "	49 "	46 "
3rd........	55 "	52 "	38 "	48 "
4th	62 "	60 "	62 "	61 "
5th	59 "	55 "	56 "	57 "
6th........	61 "	52 "	54 "	56 "
7th	46 "	43 "	44 "	44 "
8th	43 "	37 "	40 "	40 "
9th	63 "	60 "	63 "	62 "
10th	53 "	56 "	54 "	54 "

[1] Elections for a somewhat later period are here considered than with New York and Brooklyn for want of assessment figures for the earlier years.

[2] From O. L. Holley, *New York State Register, 1843*, p. 69.

[3] From O. L. Holley, *New York State Register, 1845*, p. 69.

[4] The only data at hand on this election was the report in the *New York Tribune*, November 4, 1846 (received from *Albany Argus* message slip) which gave only the majorities by wards. Assuming the gain in all wards between 1844 and 1846 to have been at the same rate as between 1842 and 1844, the totals for 1846 were computed. From these, with the majorities given, the probable votes of each party were computed as well.

OCCUPATIONS, ETC., 1845 [1]

Wards.	Colored Persons.	Farmers.	Mechanics.	Merchants and Manufacturers.	Learned Professions.	Percentage of Aggregate of Merchants, Manufacturers and Learned Professions.	
1st	142	..	263	1	4	2	per cent.
2nd......	63	1	313	71	23	21	"
3rd	112	4	520	125	30	23	"
4th	71	..	446	220	62	39	"
5th	80	..	141	44	55	41	"
6th	33	..	260	117	40	38	"
7th	7	..	248	37	7	15	"
8th	38	..	201	11	10	10	"
9th	87	15	438	97	35	30	"
10th	155	20	379	82	31	25	"

Examination of the wards according to intensity of wealth shows seven wards, the 2nd, 3rd, 4th, 5th, 6th, 9th and 10th, where the average assessment was over $900. Turning to the table giving the average percentage of Whigs during these years, we find that 5 out of 7 of these regularly show a Whig vote of at least 4.5% (probably the sudden drop in the Whig vote in the 3rd ward is to be attributed to some local circumstance, for there is no other such eccentric fluctuation). In fact, all but the 2nd and 3rd are well above half. As a whole, where the property-holding average is high, the ward is Whig. The table setting forth the numbers engaged in four general groups of occupations (which may be supposed to include a very large proportion of the voters, as comparison with the total vote for 1844 will show), shows that wherever the proportion of merchants, manufacturers and professional men amounted to 30% or more, as in the 4th, 5th, 6th and 9th, the ward was Whig. But there are some Whig wards, as the 1st

[1] From the Census of the State of New York, 1845, as given in O. L. Holley, *New York State Register, 1846*, p. 107, excepting the percentages which are computed.

and the 10th, where the number in this class seems insufficient to account for the number of Whigs. But it may be seen that these two wards contain the largest number and the largest proportion of colored persons. Most of these did not vote, because of the peculiar franchise restrictions. Those who could qualify probably voted Whig; see *supra*, chapter viii, note. Only the second ward does not contribute support to the "economic interpretation."

BROOKLYN

WEALTH

Wards.	Aggregate Assessment on Property.	Number of Voters 1840.	Average Assessment per Voter.
1st	$2,720,150	303	$8,977
2nd..............	3,498,685	768	4,554
3rd	4,448,000	546	8,117
4th	3,077,575	964	3,191
5th	1,525,750	910	1,676
6th	5,331,310	480	11,107
7th	2,982,935	626	4,764
8th	970,060	117	8,291
9th	1,092,051	120	9,100

[1] Assessment figures are from the Tax Rolls, Series 1840, mss. in the office of the Deputy Receiver of Taxes, Borough of Brooklyn, Department of Finance, New York city. The number of votes is computed from table in O. L. Holley, *N. Y. State Register, 1843*, p. 82. No tax lists are available for years previous to 1840.

ELECTIONS 1834-1840 [1]

Wards.	1834 [2]		1836 [3]		1838 [4]		1840 [5]	
	Seward.	Marcy.	Harrison.	Van Buren.	Seward.	Marcy.	Harrison.	Van Buren.
1st	151	78	147	92	167	85	213	90
2nd.	227	322	282	300	273	243	359	409
3rd......	216	146	294	123	342	137	410	136
4th......	278	401	384	353	424	371	558	406
5th......	109	329	135	403	178	463	254	656
6th......	88	102	84	158	158	136	284	196
7th......	68	128	128	207	250	228	327	299
8th	21	68	21	63	28	52	35	82
9th	24	16	39	26	54	38	87	33

PERCENTAGE OF WHIGS

Wards.	1834	1836	1838	1840	Average.
1st	66 per cent.	61 per cent.	66 per cent.	70 per cent.	66 per cent.
2nd	41 "	48 "	44 "	46 "	45 "
3rd..	59 "	70 "	71 "	75 "	69 "
4th..	40 "	52 "	53 "	57 "	50 "
5th........	20 "	27 "	27 "	27 "	25 "
6th........	47 "	39 "	54 "	60 "	50 "
7th........	34 "	38 "	52 "	52 "	44 " [6]
8th........	24 "	25 "	35 "	30 "	28 "
9th........	60 "	60 "	60 "	73 "	64 "

[1] Figures are given for vote for president in 1836 and 1840, and for governor in 1834 and 1838.

[2] From Edwin Williams, *New York Annual Register, 1836*, p. 95.

[3] The only data at hand on this election was the report in the *N. Y. Evening Post*, November 4, 1836, which gave only the majorities by wards. Assuming the gain or loss in population to have been at the same rate between 1834 and 1838, the number of voters in 1836 was computed, and with the majorities given, the probable vote of each party was computed as well.

[4] From Edwin Williams, *New York Annual Register, 1840*, p. 222.

[5] From O. L. Holley, *New York State Register, 1843*, p. 82.

[6] If the table were continued, this percentage would be decreased as this ward returned to its former Democratic majority in 1842. See O. L. Holley, *New York State Register, 1843*, p. 82.

It is observed that there are five wards where the average assessment is relatively high and four where it is low. Comparing these figures with the percentage of Whigs, we find that in wards 1, 2, 3, 5, 7 and 9 the economic interpretation is supported, while the percentage in the 6th, and especially the 8th, seems too low, and that in the 4th too high. Six out of nine might be accounted a sufficient preponderance to establish a presumption, but the three cases which show contrary evidence are now to be examined again in connection with other data. In order to check any grossly unequal distribution of property within the wards, let us examine the table of occupations, etc., which affords a personal index.

OCCUPATIONS, ETC.[1]

Wards.	Colored Persons.	Farmers.	Mechanics.	Merchants and Manufacturers.	Learned Professions.	Percentage of Aggregate of Merchants, Manufacturers and Learned Professions.
1st	60	1	260	357	39	60 per cent.
2nd	134	5	555	203	11	28 "
3rd	141	1	307	474	57	63 "
4th	450	4	656	240	73	32 "
5th	203	4	945	90	7	9 "
6th	96	5	545	359	33	42 "
7th	336	51	922	131	26	16 "
8th	56	56	80	22	6	17 "
9th	397	41	66	28	..	21 "

Comparing the percentage of merchants, manufacturers and professional men with that of Whigs, we find a striking parallel. The apparent solidarity of this class was due to social tradition as well as community of economic interest. The 1st, 2nd, 3rd, 5th, 6th and 8th, in general, show quantities where

[1] From the Census of the State of New York, 1845 (the first where such data is presented), as given in O. L. Holley, *New York State Register, 1846*, p. 107, excepting the column of percentages which are computed.

they might be expected. In the 4th, 7th and 9th, there seems too few of this class to account for the larger percentage of Whigs, but they probably bore a higher ratio to the voting total than they do to the total of those listed in occupations, because of the large number of negroes in these wards.

BUFFALO

ELECTION OF 1844 [1]

Wards.	Clay.	Polk.	Birney.	Percentage of Whigs.
1st.......	282	487	4	37 per cent.
2nd	542	336	21	60 "
3rd	326	152	8	67 "
4th	325	602	14	34 "
5th	327	325	16	49 "

OCCUPATIONS, ETC., 1845 [2]

Wards.	Farmers.	Mechanics.	Merchants and Manufacturers.	Learned Professions.	Percentage of Aggregate of Merchants, Manufacturers and Learned Professions.
1st	356	798	461	15	23 per cent.
2nd......	3	474	263	67	40 "
3rd	8	351	148	39	34 "
4th	..	1011	2	38	4 "
5th	4	258	42	32	23 "

[1] The election of 1844 is chosen because it is the only one prior to 1845 (the date of the occupation statistics) available for the figures by wards. The data for votes is taken from O. L. Holley, *N. Y. State Register, 1845,* p. 76.

[2] O. L. Holley, *N. Y. State Register, 1846,* p. 103, excepting, of course, the percentage.

Here where the ward statistics show more than 30 per cent were members of the specified class, the ward was most heavily Whig. Where the mechanics were most numerous, in the 4th, the ward was most strongly Democratic.

ROCHESTER
ELECTION OF 1846 [1]

Wards.	Young.	Wright.	Percentage of Whigs.
1st.	269	235	53 per cent.
2nd	235	172	58 "
3rd.	281	218	56 "
4th	216	190	53 "
5th	210	227	47 "
6th	305	279	52 "
7th	153	117	57 "
8th	155	96	62 "
9th	153	172	46 "

OCCUPATIONS IN 1845 [2]

Wards.	Farmers.	Mechanics.	Merchants and Manufacturers.	Learned Professions.	Percentage of Aggregate of Merchants, Manufacturers and Learned Professions.
1st.	..	205	184	20	50 per cent.
2nd.	..	376	131	11	27 "
3rd.	7	250	56	38	27 "
4th.	10	395	77	36	22 "
5th.	7	140	17	10	15 "
6th.	52	382	53	22	13 "
7th.	35	127	4	3	4 "
8th.	16	165	3	7	5 "
9th.	27	312	42	6	12 "

[1] The vote here recorded is taken from the *Rochester Daily Advertiser*, November 5, 1846, on file in the office of the *Rochester Union and Advertiser*. The majorities, but not the total vote for 1848, are given in the *Rochester Democrat*, November 8, 1848 (Reynolds Library, Rochester). The Whig vote was then apparently much higher in proportion, the majorities for the first three wards being 161, 151, 162, *etc.* These figures in comparison with those of the following table show no connection between economic interest and politics. The traditions of this city, renowned for Anti-Masonry and manufacturing and anxious for a restoration of Whig canal policy, made its statistics hardly as useful as evidence, as those of other cities.

[2] From the Census of the State of New York, 1845, as given in O. L. Holley, *New York State Register, 1846*, p. 109, excepting the column of percentages which are computed.

TROY

ELECTION OF 1842 [1]

Wards.	Bradish.	Bouck.	Percentage of Whigs.
1st	234	241	49 per cent.
2nd	310	285	55 "
3rd	323	142	69 "
4th	322	231	58 "
5th	57	53	52 "
6th	107	67	61 "
7th	222	262	46 "
8th	107	63	61 "

OCCUPATIONS, ETC., 1845 [2]

Wards.	Farmers.	Mechanics.	Merchants and Manufacturers.	Learned Professions.	Percentage of Aggregate of Merchants, Manufacturers and Learned Professions.
1st	..	182	18	4	12 per cent.
2nd	8	285	104	42	31 "
3rd	1	190	47	32	29 "
4th	1	251	127	22	34 "
5th	10	107	325	4	74 "
6th	16	273	18	3	7 "
7th	..	167	..	2	1 "
8th	1	37	37	18	59 "

The evidence from Troy is not so striking as in some cities, as it seems to have been a Whig stronghold by tradition. Only once in the decade of the 'forties can we find more than one

[1] The election of 1842 is the only one in this period when more than one ward showed a Democratic majority. The figures for the votes are taken from the report in O. L. Holley, *New York State Register, 1843*, p. 92, excepting those for percentages which are computed.

[2] From the Census of the State of New York, 1845, as given in O. L. Holley, *New York State Register, 1846*, p. 114, excepting the column of percentages which are computed.

ward going Democratic. However, from this election, when the lines were most tightly drawn, deductions can be made which support the " economic interpretation." There were four wards which had more than 30% per cent of its workers engaged in manufacturing, commerce or the learned professions. These wards are all Whig. There are three wards which have less than 15% in this occupational class; the two Democratic wards are contained within this group. The seventh ward, which has the lowest percentage in this class, has also the lowest percentage of Whigs. It was the only ward which went Democratic more than once during the decade; see tables in E. Williams, *N. Y. Annual Register, 1840,* page 229, and O. L. Holley, *N. Y. State Register, 1845,* page 91.

INDEX

451

Revised November, 1964

harper ✦ torchbooks

HUMANITIES AND SOCIAL SCIENCES

American Studies

† The New American Nation Series, edited by Henry Steele Commager and Richard B. Morris.
‡ American Perspectives series, edited by Bernard Wishy and William E. Leuchtenburg.
* The Rise of Modern Europe series, edited by William L. Langer.
‖ Researches in the Social, Cultural, and Behavioral Sciences, edited by Benjamin Nelson.
§ The Library of Religion and Culture, edited by Benjamin Nelson.
Σ Harper Modern Science Series, edited by James R. Newman.
º Not for sale in Canada.

DANIEL H. HUNDLEY: Social Relations in our Southern States.‡ Edited by William R. Taylor   TB/3058

HELEN HUNT JACKSON: A Century of Dishonor: The Early Crusade for Indian Reform.‡ Edited by Andrew F. Rolle   TB/3063

ROBERT H. JACKSON: The Supreme Court in the American System of Government   TB/1106

THOMAS JEFFERSON: Notes on the State of Virginia.‡ Edited by Thomas Perkins Abernethy   TB/3052

JOHN F. KENNEDY: A Nation of Immigrants. Revised and Enlarged Edition. Illus.   TB/1118

WILLIAM L. LANGER & S. EVERETT GLEASON: The Challenge to Isolation: The World Crisis of 1937-1940 and American Foreign Policy   Vol. I TB/3054
Vol. II TB/3055

WILLIAM E. LEUCHTENBURG: Franklin D. Roosevelt and the New Deal, 1932-1940.† Illus.   TB/3025

LEONARD W. LEVY: Freedom of Speech and Press in Early American History: Legacy of Suppression   TB/1109

ARTHUR S. LINK: Woodrow Wilson and the Progressive Era, 1910-1917.† Illus.   TB/3023

ROBERT GREEN McCLOSKEY: American Conservatism in the Age of Enterprise, 1865-1910   TB/1137

BERNARD MAYO: Myths and Men: Patrick Henry, George Washington, Thomas Jefferson   TB/1108

JOHN C. MILLER: Alexander Hamilton and the Growth of the New Nation   TB/3057

JOHN C. MILLER: The Federalist Era, 1789-1801.† Illus.   TB/3027

PERRY MILLER: Errand into the Wilderness   TB/1139

PERRY MILLER & T. H. JOHNSON, Editors: The Puritans: A Sourcebook of Their Writings
Vol. I TB/1093
Vol. II TB/1094

GEORGE E. MOWRY: The Era of Theodore Roosevelt and the Birth of Modern America, 1900-1912.† Illus.   TB/3022

WALLACE NOTESTEIN: The English People on the Eve of Colonization, 1603-1630.† Illus.   TB/3006

RUSSEL BLAINE NYE: The Cultural Life of the New Nation, 1776-1801.† Illus.   TB/3026

RALPH BARTON PERRY: Puritanism and Democracy   TB/1138

RALPH BARTON PERRY: The Thought and Character of William James: Briefer Version   TB/1156

GEORGE E. PROBST, Ed.: The Happy Republic: A Reader in Tocqueville's America   TB/1060

WALTER RAUSCHENBUSCH: Christianity and the Social Crisis.‡ Edited by Robert D. Cross   TB/3059

HEINRICH STRAUMANN: American Literature in the Twentieth Century. Revised Edition   TB/1168

FRANK THISTLETHWAITE: America and the Atlantic Community: Anglo-American Aspects, 1790-1850   TB/1107

TWELVE SOUTHERNERS: I'll Take My Stand: The South and the Agrarian Tradition. Introduction by Louis D. Rubin, Jr.; Biographical Essays by Virginia Rock   TB/1072

A. F. TYLER: Freedom's Ferment: Phases of American Social History from the Revolution to the Outbreak of the Civil War. Illus.   TB/1074

GLYNDON G. VAN DEUSEN: The Jacksonian Era, 1828-1848.† Illus.   TB/3028

WALTER E. WEYL: The New Democracy: An Essay on Certain Political and Economic Tendencies in the United States.‡ Edited by Charles Forcey   TB/3042

LOUIS B. WRIGHT: The Cultural Life of the American Colonies, 1607-1763.† Illus.   TB/3005

LOUIS B. WRIGHT: Culture on the Moving Frontier   TB/1053

Anthropology & Sociology

BERNARD BERELSON, Ed.: The Behavioral Sciences Today   TB/1127

JOSEPH B. CASAGRANDE, Ed.: In the Company of Man: 20 Portraits of Anthropological Informants. Illus.   TB/3047

W. E. LE GROS CLARK: The Antecedents of Man: An Introduction to the Evolution of the Primates.° Illus.   TB/559

THOMAS C. COCHRAN: The Inner Revolution: Essays on the Social Sciences in History   TB/1140

ALLISON DAVIS & JOHN DOLLARD: Children of Bondage: The Personality Development of Negro Youth in the Urban South ‖   TB/3049

ST. CLAIR DRAKE & HORACE R. CAYTON: Black Metropolis: A Study of Negro Life in a Northern City   Vol. I TB/1086; Vol. II TB/1087

CORA DU BOIS: The People of Alor. New Preface by the author. Illus.   Vol. I TB/1042; Vol. II TB/1043

EMILE DURKHEIM et al.: Essays on Sociology and Philosophy: With Analyses of Durkheim's Life and Work. ‖ Edited by Kurt H. Wolff   TB/1151

LEON FESTINGER, HENRY W. RIECKEN & STANLEY SCHACHTER: When Prophecy Fails: A Social and Psychological Account of a Modern Group that Predicted the Destruction of the World ‖   TB/1132

RAYMOND FIRTH, Ed.: Man and Culture: An Evaluation of the Work of Bronislaw Malinowski ‖ °   TB/1133

L. S. B. LEAKEY: Adam's Ancestors: The Evolution of Man and his Culture. Illus.   TB/1019

KURT LEWIN: Field Theory in Social Science: Selected Theoretical Papers. ‖ Edited with a Foreword by Dorwin Cartwright   TB/1135

ROBERT H. LOWIE: Primitive Society. Introduction by Fred Eggan   TB/1056

R. M. MacIVER: Social Causation   TB/1153

BENJAMIN NELSON: Religious Traditions and the Spirit of Capitalism: From the Church Fathers to Jeremy Bentham   TB/1130

TALCOTT PARSONS & EDWARD A. SHILS, Editors: Toward a General Theory of Action: Theoretical Foundations for the Social Sciences   TB/1083

JOHN H. ROHRER & MUNRO S. EDMONSON, Eds.: The Eighth Generation Grows Up: Cultures and Personalities of New Orleans Negroes ‖   TB/3050

ARNOLD ROSE: The Negro in America: The Condensed Version of Gunnar Myrdal's An American Dilemma   TB/3048

HENRI DE SAINT-SIMON: Social Organization, The Science of Man, and Other Writings. ‖ Edited and translated by Felix Markham   TB/1152

KURT SAMUELSSON: Religion and Economic Action: A Critique of Max Weber's The Protestant Ethic and the Spirit of Capitalism.‖ ° Trans. by E. G. French; Ed. with Intro. by D. C. Coleman   TB/1131

History: Renaissance & Reformation

R. R. BOLGAR: The Classical Heritage and Its Beneficiaries: *From the Carolingian Age to the End of the Renaissance*　TB/1125

JACOB BURCKHARDT: The Civilization of the Renaissance in Italy. *Introduction by Benjamin Nelson and Charles Trinkaus. Illus.*　Volume I TB/40
Volume II TB/41

ERNST CASSIRER: The Individual and the Cosmos in Renaissance Philosophy. *Translated with an Introduction by Mario Domandi*　TB/1097

EDWARD P. CHEYNEY: The Dawn of a New Era, 1250-1453.* *Illus.*　TB/3002

DESIDERIUS ERASMUS: Christian Humanism and the Reformation: *Selected Writings. Edited and translated by John C. Olin*　TB/1166

WALLACE K. FERGUSON et al.: Facets of the Renaissance　TB/1098

WALLACE K. FERGUSON et al.: The Renaissance: *Six Essays. Illus.*　TB/1084

MYRON P. GILMORE: The World of Humanism, 1453-1517.* *Illus.*　TB/3003

FRANCESCO GUICCIARDINI: Maxims and Reflections of a Renaissance Statesman: *Ricordi. Trans. by Mario Domandi. Intro. by Nicolai Rubinstein*　TB/1160

JOHAN HUIZINGA: Erasmus and the Age of Reformation. *Illus.*　TB/19

ULRICH VON HUTTEN et al.: On the Eve of the Reformation: *"Letters of Obscure Men." Introduction by Hajo Holborn*　TB/1124

PAUL O. KRISTELLER: Renaissance Thought: *The Classic, Scholastic, and Humanist Strains*　TB/1048

PAUL O. KRISTELLER: Renaissance Thought II: *Papers on Humanism and the Arts*　TB/1163

NICCOLÒ MACHIAVELLI: History of Florence and of the Affairs of Italy: *from the earliest times to the death of Lorenzo the Magnificent. Introduction by Felix Gilbert*　TB/1027

ALFRED VON MARTIN: Sociology of the Renaissance. *Introduction by Wallace K. Ferguson*　TB/1099

GARRETT MATTINGLY et al.: Renaissance Profiles. *Edited by J. H. Plumb*　TB/1162

MILLARD MEISS: Painting in Florence and Siena after the Black Death. *The Arts, Religion and Society in the Mid-Fourteenth Century. 169 illus.*　TB/1148

J. E. NEALE: The Age of Catherine de Medici⁰　TB/1085

ERWIN PANOFSKY: Studies in Iconology: *Humanistic Themes in the Art of the Renaissance. 180 illustrations*　TB/1077

J. H. PARRY: The Establishment of the European Hegemony: 1415-1715　TB/1045

HENRI PIRENNE: Early Democracies in the Low Countries: *Urban Society and Political Conflict in the Middle Ages and the Renaissance. Introduction by John Mundy*　TB/1110

J. H. PLUMB: The Italian Renaissance: *A Concise Survey of Its History and Culture*　TB/1161

FERDINAND SCHEVILL: The Medici. *Illus.*　TB/1010

FERDINAND SCHEVILL: Medieval and Renaissance Florence. *Illus.* Volume I: *Medieval Florence* TB/1090
Volume II: *The Coming of Humanism and the Age of the Medici*　TB/1091

G. M. TREVELYAN: England in the Age of Wycliffe, 1368-1520⁰　TB/1112

VESPASIANO: Renaissance Princes, Popes, and Prelates: *The Vespasiano Memoirs: Lives of Illustrious Men of the XVth Century. Introduction by Myron P. Gilmore*　TB/1111

History: Modern European

FREDERICK B. ARTZ: Reaction and Revolution, 1815-1832.* *Illus.*　TB/3034

MAX BELOFF: The Age of Absolutism, 1660-1815　TB/1062

ROBERT C. BINKLEY: Realism and Nationalism, 1852-1871.* *Illus.*　TB/3038

CRANE BRINTON: A Decade of Revolution, 1789-1799.* *Illus.*　TB/3018

J. BRONOWSKI & BRUCE MAZLISH: The Western Intellectual Tradition: *From Leonardo to Hegel*　TB/3001

GEOFFREY BRUUN: Europe and the French Imperium, 1799-1814.* *Illus.*　TB/3033

ALAN BULLOCK: Hitler, A Study in Tyranny.⁰ *Illus.*　TB/1123

E. H. CARR: The Twenty Years' Crisis, 1919-1939: *An Introduction to the Study of International Relations*⁰　TB/1122

GORDON A. CRAIG: From Bismarck to Adenauer: *Aspects of German Statecraft. Revised Edition*　TB/1171

WALTER L. DORN: Competition for Empire, 1740-1763.* *Illus.*　TB/3032

CARL J. FRIEDRICH: The Age of the Baroque, 1610-1660.* *Illus.*　TB/3004

LEO GERSHOY: From Despotism to Revolution, 1763-1789.* *Illus.*　TB/3017

ALBERT GOODWIN: The French Revolution TB/1064

CARLTON J. H. HAYES: A Generation of Materialism, 1871-1900.* *Illus.*　TB/3039

J. H. HEXTER: Reappraisals in History: *New Views on History and Society in Early Modern Europe*　TB/1100

A. R. HUMPHREYS: The Augustan World: *Society, Thought, and Letters in Eighteenth Century England*　TB/1105

HANS KOHN, Ed.: The Mind of Modern Russia: *Historical and Political Thought of Russia's Great Age*　TB/1065

SIR LEWIS NAMIER: Vanished Supremacies: *Essays on European History, 1812-1918*⁰　TB/1088

JOHN U. NEF: Western Civilization Since the Renaissance: *Peace, War, Industry, and the Arts*　TB/1113

FREDERICK L. NUSSBAUM: The Triumph of Science and Reason, 1660-1685.* *Illus.*　TB/3009

RAYMOND W. POSTGATE, Ed.: Revolution from 1789 to 1906: *Selected Documents*　TB/1063

PENFIELD ROBERTS: The Quest for Security, 1715-1740.* *Illus.*　TB/3016

PRISCILLA ROBERTSON: Revolutions of 1848: *A Social History*　TB/1025

ALBERT SOREL: Europe Under the Old Regime. *Translated by Francis H. Herrick*　TB/1121

4

N. N. SUKHANOV: The Russian Revolution, 1917: *Eyewitness Account.* Edited by Joel Carmichael
Vol. I TB/1066; Vol. II TB/1067

JOHN B. WOLF: The Emergence of the Great Powers, 1685-1715.* *Illus.* TB/3010

JOHN B. WOLF: France: 1814-1919: *The Rise of a Liberal-Democratic Society* TB/3019

Intellectual History

HERSCHEL BAKER: The Image of Man: *A Study of the Idea of Human Dignity in Classical Antiquity, the Middle Ages, and the Renaissance* TB/1047

J. BRONOWSKI & BRUCE MAZLISH: The Western Intellectual Tradition: *From Leonardo to Hegel*
TB/3001

ERNST CASSIRER: The Individual and the Cosmos in Renaissance Philosophy. *Translated with an Introduction by Mario Domandi* TB/1097

NORMAN COHN: The Pursuit of the Millennium: *Revolutionary Messianism in medieval and Reformation Europe and its bearing on modern Leftist and Rightist totalitarian movements* TB/1037

ARTHUR O. LOVEJOY: The Great Chain of Being: *A Study of the History of an Idea* TB/1009

ROBERT PAYNE: Hubris: *A Study of Pride. Foreword by Sir Herbert Read* TB/1031

BRUNO SNELL: The Discovery of the Mind: *The Greek Origins of European Thought* TB/1018

ERNST LEE TUVESON: Millennium and Utopia: *A Study in the Background of the Idea of Progress.*‖ *New Preface by the Author* TB/1134

Literature, Poetry, The Novel & Criticism

JAMES BAIRD: Ishmael: *The Art of Melville in the Contexts of International Primitivism* TB/1023

JACQUES BARZUN: The House of Intellect TB/1051

W. J. BATE: From Classic to Romantic: *Premises of Taste in Eighteenth Century England* TB/1036

RACHEL BESPALOFF: On the Iliad TB/2006

R. P. BLACKMUR et al.: Lectures in Criticism. *Introduction by Huntington Cairns* TB/2003

ABRAHAM CAHAN: The Rise of David Levinsky: *a novel. Introduction by John Higham* TB/1028

ERNST R. CURTIUS: European Literature and the Latin Middle Ages TB/2015

GEORGE ELIOT: Daniel Deronda: *a novel. Introduction by F. R. Leavis* TB/1039

ETIENNE GILSON: Dante and Philosophy TB/1089

ALFRED HARBAGE: As They Liked It: *A Study of Shakespeare's Moral Artistry* TB/1035

STANLEY R. HOPPER, Ed.: Spiritual Problems in Contemporary Literature§ TB/21

A. R. HUMPHREYS: The Augustan World: *Society, Thought, and Letters in Eighteenth Century England*° TB/1105

ALDOUS HUXLEY: Antic Hay & The Gioconda Smile.° *Introduction by Martin Green* TB/3503

HENRY JAMES: Roderick Hudson: *a novel. Introduction by Leon Edel* TB/1016

HENRY JAMES: The Tragic Muse: *a novel. Introduction by Leon Edel* TB/1017

ARNOLD KETTLE: An Introduction to the English Novel. Volume I: *Defoe to George Eliot* TB/1011
Volume II: *Henry James to the Present* TB/1012

ROGER SHERMAN LOOMIS: The Development of Arthurian Romance TB/1167

JOHN STUART MILL: On Bentham and Coleridge. *Introduction by F. R. Leavis* TB/1070

PERRY MILLER & T. H. JOHNSON, Editors: The Puritans: *A Sourcebook of Their Writings* Vol. I TB/1093
Vol. II TB/1094

KENNETH B. MURDOCK: Literature and Theology in Colonial New England TB/99

SAMUEL PEPYS: The Diary of Samuel Pepys.° *Edited by O. F. Morshead. Illus. by Ernest Shepard* TB/1007

ST.-JOHN PERSE: Seamarks TB/2002

O. E. RÖLVAAG: Giants in the Earth TB/3504

GEORGE SANTAYANA: Interpretations of Poetry and Religion§ TB/9

C. P. SNOW: Time of Hope: *a novel* TB/1040

HEINRICH STRAUMANN: American Literature in the Twentieth Century. *Revised Edition* TB/1168

DOROTHY VAN GHENT: The English Novel: *Form and Function* TB/1050

E. B. WHITE: One Man's Meat. *Introduction by Walter Blair* TB/3505

MORTON DAUWEN ZABEL, Editor: Literary Opinion in America. Vol. I TB/3013; Vol. II TB/3014

Myth, Symbol & Folklore

JOSEPH CAMPBELL, Editor: Pagan and Christian Mysteries. *Illus.* TB/2013

MIRCEA ELIADE: Cosmos and History: *The Myth of the Eternal Return*§ TB/2050

C. G. JUNG & C. KERÉNYI: Essays on a Science of Mythology: *The Myths of the Divine Child and the Divine Maiden* TB/2014

ERWIN PANOFSKY: Studies in Iconology: *Humanistic Themes in the Art of the Renaissance. 180 illustrations* TB/1077

JEAN SEZNEC: The Survival of the Pagan Gods: *The Mythological Tradition and its Place in Renaissance Humanism and Art. 108 illustrations* TB/2004

HELLMUT WILHELM: Change: *Eight Lectures on the I Ching* TB/2019

HEINRICH ZIMMER: Myths and Symbols in Indian Art and Civilization. *70 illustrations* TB/2005

Philosophy

HENRI BERGSON: Time and Free Will: *An Essay on the Immediate Data of Consciousness*° TB/1021

H. J. BLACKHAM: Six Existentialist Thinkers: *Kierkegaard, Nietzsche, Jaspers, Marcel, Heidegger, Sartre*°
TB/1002

ERNST CASSIRER: The Individual and the Cosmos in Renaissance Philosophy. *Translated with an Introduction by Mario Domandi* TB/1097

ERNST CASSIRER: Rousseau, Kant and Goethe. *Introduction by Peter Gay* TB/1092

FREDERICK COPLESTON: Medieval Philosophy° TB/376

F. M. CORNFORD: From Religion to Philosophy: *A Study in the Origins of Western Speculation*§ TB/20

WILFRID DESAN: The Tragic Finale: *An Essay on the Philosophy of Jean-Paul Sartre* TB/1030

PAUL FRIEDLÄNDER: Plato: *An Introduction* TB/2017

ETIENNE GILSON: Dante and Philosophy TB/1089

WILLIAM CHASE GREENE: Moira: *Fate, Good, and Evil in Greek Thought* TB/1104

W. K. C. GUTHRIE: The Greek Philosophers: *From Thales to Aristotle*° TB/1008

F. H. HEINEMANN: Existentialism and the Modern Predicament TB/28

EDMUND HUSSERL: Phenomenology, and the Crisis of Philosophy. *Translated with an Introduction by Quentin Lauer* TB/1170

IMMANUEL KANT: The Doctrine of Virtue, *being Part II of The Metaphysic of Morals. Translated with Notes and Introduction by Mary J. Gregor. Foreword by H. J. Paton* TB/110

IMMANUEL KANT: Groundwork of the Metaphysic of Morals. *Translated and analyzed by H. J. Paton* TB/1159

IMMANUEL KANT: Lectures on Ethics.§ *Introduction by Lewis W. Beck* TB/105

QUENTIN LAUER: Phenomenology: *Its Genesis and Prospect* TB/1169

JOHN MACQUARRIE: An Existentialist Theology: *A Comparison of Heidegger and Bultmann.*° *Preface by Rudolf Bultmann* TB/125

MICHAEL POLANYI: Personal Knowledge: *Towards a Post-Critical Philosophy* TB/1158

WILLARD VAN ORMAN QUINE: From a Logical Point of View: *Logico-Philosophical Essays* TB/566

BERTRAND RUSSELL et al.: The Philosophy of Bertrand Russell. *Edited by Paul Arthur Schilpp* Vol. I TB/1095; Vol. II TB/1096

L. S. STEBBING: A Modern Introduction to Logic TB/538

ALFRED NORTH WHITEHEAD: Process and Reality: *An Essay in Cosmology* TB/1033

WILHELM WINDELBAND: A History of Philosophy Vol. I: *Greek, Roman, Medieval* TB/38
Vol. II: *Renaissance, Enlightenment, Modern* TB/39

Philosophy of History

NICOLAS BERDYAEV: The Beginning and the End§ TB/14

NICOLAS BERDYAEV: The Destiny of Man TB/61

WILHELM DILTHEY: Pattern and Meaning in History: *Thoughts on History and Society.*° *Edited with an Introduction by H. P. Rickman* TB/1075

RAYMOND KLIBANSKY & H. J. PATON, Eds.: Philosophy and History: *The Ernst Cassirer Festschrift. Illus.* TB/1115

JOSE ORTEGA Y GASSET: The Modern Theme. *Introduction by Jose Ferrater Mora* TB/1038

KARL R. POPPER: The Poverty of Historicism° TB/1126

W. H. WALSH: Philosophy of History: *An Introduction* TB/1020

Political Science & Government

JEREMY BENTHAM: The Handbook of Political Fallacies: *Introduction by Crane Brinton* TB/1069

KENNETH E. BOULDING: Conflict and Defense: *A General Theory* TB/3024

CRANE BRINTON: English Political Thought in the Nineteenth Century TB/1071

EDWARD S. CORWIN: American Constitutional History: *Essays edited by Alpheus T. Mason and Gerald Garvey* TB/1136

ROBERT DAHL & CHARLES E. LINDBLOM: Politics, Economics, and Welfare: *Planning and Politico-Economic Systems Resolved into Basic Social Processes* TB/3037

JOHN NEVILLE FIGGIS: Political Thought from Gerson to Grotius: 1414-1625: *Seven Studies. Introduction by Garrett Mattingly* TB/1032

F. L. GANSHOF: Feudalism TB/1058

G. P. GOOCH: English Democratic Ideas in the Seventeenth Century TB/1006

ROBERT H. JACKSON: The Supreme Court in the American System of Government TB/1106

DAN N. JACOBS, Ed.: The New Communist Manifesto and Related Documents TB/1078

DAN N. JACOBS & HANS BAERWALD, Eds.: Chinese Communism: *Selected Documents* TB/3031

KINGSLEY MARTIN: French Liberal Thought in the Eighteenth Century: *Political Ideas from Bayle to Condorcet* TB/1114

JOHN STUART MILL: On Bentham and Coleridge. *Introduction by F. R. Leavis* TB/1070

JOHN B. MORRALL: Political Thought in Medieval Times TB/1076

KARL R. POPPER: The Open Society and Its Enemies Vol. I: *The Spell of Plato* TB/1101
Vol. II: *The High Tide of Prophecy: Hegel, Marx, and the Aftermath* TB/1102

HENRI DE SAINT-SIMON: Social Organization, The Science of Man, and Other Writings. *Edited and Translated by Felix Markham* TB/1152

JOSEPH A. SCHUMPETER: Capitalism, Socialism and Democracy TB/3008

Psychology

ALFRED ADLER: Problems of Neurosis. *Introduction by Heinz L. Ansbacher* TB/1145

ALFRED ADLER: The Individual Psychology of Alfred Adler. *Edited by Heinz L. and Rowena R. Ansbacher* TB/1154

ANTON T. BOISEN: The Exploration of the Inner World: *A Study of Mental Disorder and Religious Experience* TB/87

LEON FESTINGER, HENRY W. RIECKEN, STANLEY SCHACHTER: When Prophecy Fails: *A Social and Psychological Study of a Modern Group that Predicted the Destruction of the World* TB/1132

SIGMUND FREUD: On Creativity and the Unconscious: *Papers on the Psychology of Art, Literature, Love, Religion.*§ *Intro. by Benjamin Nelson* TB/45

C. JUDSON HERRICK: The Evolution of Human Nature TB/545

7

Christianity: The Middle Ages and The Reformation

JOHANNES ECKHART: Meister Eckhart: A Modern Translation by R. B. Blakney   TB/8

DESIDERIUS ERASMUS: Christian Humanism and the Reformation: Selected Writings. Edited and translated by John C. Olin   TB/1166

G. P. FEDOTOV: The Russian Religious Mind: Kievan Christianity, the tenth to the thirteenth centuries   TB/70

ÉTIENNE GILSON: Dante and Philosophy   TB/1089

WILLIAM HALLER: The Rise of Puritanism   TB/22

JOHAN HUIZINGA: Erasmus and the Age of Reformation. Illus.   TB/19

DAVID KNOWLES: The English Mystical Tradition   TB/302

JOHN T. McNEILL: Makers of the Christian Tradition: From Alfred the Great to Schleiermacher   TB/121

A. C. McGIFFERT: Protestant Thought Before Kant. Preface by Jaroslav Pelikan   TB/93

GORDON RUPP: Luther's Progress to the Diet of Worms°   TB/120

Christianity: The Protestant Tradition

KARL BARTH: Church Dogmatics: A Selection.   TB/95

KARL BARTH: Dogmatics in Outline   TB/56

KARL BARTH: The Word of God and the Word of Man   TB/13

WINTHROP HUDSON: The Great Tradition of the American Churches   TB/98

SOREN KIERKEGAARD: Edifying Discourses. Edited with an Introduction by Paul Holmer   TB/32

SOREN KIERKEGAARD: The Journals of Kierkegaard.° Edited with an Introduction by Alexander Dru   TB/52

SOREN KIERKEGAARD: The Point of View for My Work as an Author: A Report to History.§ Preface by Benjamin Nelson   TB/88

SOREN KIERKEGAARD: The Present Age.§ Translated and edited by Alexander Dru. Introduction by Walter Kaufmann   TB/94

SOREN KIERKEGAARD: Purity of Heart   TB/4

SOREN KIERKEGAARD: Repetition: An Essay in Experimental Psychology. Translated with Introduction & Notes by Walter Lowrie   TB/117

SOREN KIERKEGAARD: Works of Love: Some Christian Reflections in the Form of Discourses   TB/122

WALTER LOWRIE: Kierkegaard: A Life   Vol. I   TB/89
    Vol. II   TB/90

PERRY MILLER: Errand into the Wilderness   TB/1139

PERRY MILLER & T. H. JOHNSON, Editors: The Puritans: A Sourcebook of Their Writings
    Vol. I   TB/1093
    Vol. II   TB/1094

KENNETH B. MURDOCK: Literature and Theology in Colonial New England   TB/99

F. SCHLEIERMACHER: The Christian Faith. Introduction by Richard R. Niebuhr   Volume I TB/108
    Volume II TB/109

F. SCHLEIERMACHER: On Religion: Speeches to Its Cultured Despisers. Intro. by Rudolf Otto   TB/36

PAUL TILLICH: Dynamics of Faith   TB/42

EVELYN UNDERHILL: Worship   TB/10

G. VAN DER LEEUW: Religion in Essence and Manifestation: A Study in Phenomenology. Appendices by Hans H. Penner   Vol. I TB/100; Vol. II TB/101

Christianity: The Roman and Eastern Traditions

THOMAS CORBISHLEY, s. J.: Roman Catholicism   TB/112

G. P. FEDOTOV: The Russian Religious Mind: Kievan Christianity, the tenth to the thirteenth centuries   TB/70

G. P. FEDOTOV, Ed.: A Treasury of Russian Spirituality   TB/303

DAVID KNOWLES: The English Mystical Tradition   TB/302

GABRIEL MARCEL: Homo Viator: Introduction to a Metaphysic of Hope   TB/397

GUSTAVE WEIGEL, s.J.: Catholic Theology in Dialogue   TB/301

Oriental Religions: Far Eastern, Near Eastern

TOR ANDRAE: Mohammed: The Man and His Faith   TB/62

EDWARD CONZE: Buddhism: Its Essence and Development.° Foreword by Arthur Waley   TB/58

EDWARD CONZE et al., Editors: Buddhist Texts Through the Ages   TB/113

ANANDA COOMARASWAMY: Buddha and the Gospel of Buddhism. Illus.   TB/119

H. G. CREEL: Confucius and the Chinese Way   TB/63

FRANKLIN EDGERTON, Trans. & Ed.: The Bhagavad Gita   TB/115

SWAMI NIKHILANANDA, Trans. & Ed.: The Upanishads: A One-Volume Abridgment   TB/114

HELLMUT WILHELM: Change: Eight Lectures on the I Ching   TB/2019

Philosophy of Religion

RUDOLF BULTMANN: History and Eschatology: The Presence of Eternity   TB/91

RUDOLF BULTMANN AND FIVE CRITICS: Kerygma and Myth: A Theological Debate   TB/80

RUDOLF BULTMANN and KARL KUNDSIN: Form Criticism: Two Essays on New Testament Research. Translated by Frederick C. Grant   TB/96

MIRCEA ELIADE: The Sacred and the Profane   TB/81

LUDWIG FEUERBACH: The Essence of Christianity.§ Introduction by Karl Barth. Foreword by H. Richard Niebuhr   TB/11

ADOLF HARNACK: What is Christianity?§ Introduction by Rudolf Bultmann   TB/17

FRIEDRICH HEGEL: On Christianity: Early Theological Writings. Edited by Richard Kroner and T. M. Knox   TB/79

9

Code to Torchbook Libraries:

TB/1+	: The Cloister Library
TB/301+	: The Cathedral Library
TB/501+	: The Science Library
TB/1001+	: The Academy Library
TB/2001+	: The Bollingen Library
TB/3001+	: The University Library

A LETTER TO THE READER

Overseas, there is considerable belief
that we are a country of extreme conservatism and
that we cannot accommodate to social change.

Books about America in the hands of
readers abroad can help change those ideas.

The U. S. Information Agency cannot,
by itself, meet the vast need for books about
the United States.

You can help.

Harper Torchbooks provides three packets
of books on American history, economics,
sociology, literature and politics to
help meet the need.

To send a packet of Torchbooks [*] overseas,
all you need do is send your check for $7 (which
includes cost of shipping) to Harper & Row.
The U. S. Information Agency will distrib-
ute the books to libraries, schools, and other
centers all over the world.

I ask every American to support this
program, part of a worldwide BOOKS USA campaign.

I ask you to share in the opportunity to
help tell others about America.

EDWARD R. MURROW
Director,
U. S. Information Agency

[*retailing at $10.85 to $12.00]

PACKET I: *Twentieth Century America*

Dulles/America's Rise to World Power, 1898-1954
Cochran/The American Business System, 1900-1955
Zabel, Editor/Literary Opinion in America (two volumes)
Drucker/The New Society: *The Anatomy of Industrial Order*
Fortune Editors/America in the Sixties: *The Economy and the Society*

PACKET II: *American History*

Billington/The Far Western Frontier, 1830-1860
Mowry/The Era of Theodore Roosevelt and the
 Birth of Modern America, 1900-1912
Faulkner/Politics, Reform, and Expansion, 1890-1900
Cochran & Miller/The Age of Enterprise: *A Social History of
 Industrial America*
Tyler/Freedom's Ferment: *American Social History from the
 Revolution to the Civil War*

PACKET III: *American History*

Hansen/The Atlantic Migration, 1607-1860
Degler/Out of Our Past: *The Forces that Shaped Modern America*
Probst, Editor/The Happy Republic: *A Reader in Tocqueville's America*
Alden/The American Revolution, 1775-1783
Wright/The Cultural Life of the American Colonies, 1607-1763

*Your gift will be acknowledged directly to you by the overseas recipient.
Simply fill out the coupon, detach and mail with your check or money order.*

HARPER & ROW, PUBLISHERS · BOOKS USA DEPT.
49 East 33rd Street, New York 16, N. Y.

Packet I ☐   Packet II ☐   Packet III ☐

Please send the BOOKS USA library packet(s) indicated above, in my
name, to the area checked below. Enclosed is my remittance in the
amount of _____ for _____ packet(s) at $7.00 each.

_____ Africa   _____ Latin America

_____ Far East   _____ Near East

Name_____

Address_____

_____

NOTE: *This offer expires December 31, 1966.*